‍W9-DDM-322   G-7706

Sunday's Word

Year A

GIA Publications, Inc.

Introduction

Sunday's Word is a publication prepared in response to an expressed pastoral need. It is for use in conjunction with a hymnal and service book or other music resource, and is intended for those who wish to preread the scriptures of the day as preparation for the celebration, or who have difficulty hearing or feel the need to read the text as it is proclaimed for full comprehension. Similarly, the eucharistic prayers are also included.

It contains the responsorial psalm for each Sunday and major feast in a musical setting taken from *Lectionary Psalms: Michel Guimont*. The cantor verses, guitar chords, and keyboard accompaniment are found in this one volume (G-4986). *Sunday's Word* also contains the Order of Mass, with music from Steven Janco's setting, *Mass of the Angels and Saints*. The full score (G-4442FS) and other editions are available from GIA.

Finally, the *Roman Missal* antiphons for entrance and communion are printed for each day for use in Masses at which there is no singing at those places.

GLORIA

The Gloria is omitted during Advent, Lent, and most weekdays.

Refrain

Glo-ry to God in the high-est, and peace to his peo-ple on earth.

Verses

1. Lord God, heavenly King, almighty God and Father,
   we worship you, we give you thanks, we praise you for your glory. *(To refrain)*

2. Lord Jesus Christ, only Son of the Father, Lord God, Lamb of God,
   you take away the sin of the world: have mercy on us;
   you are seated at the right hand of the Father: receive our prayer. *(To refrain)*

3. For you alone are the Holy One, you alone are the Lord,
   you alone are the Most High, Jesus Christ,
   with the Holy Spirit, in the glory of God the Father. *(To refrain)*

A - men.

Music: *Mass of the Angels and Saints*, Steven R. Janco, © 1996, GIA Publications, Inc.

OPENING PRAYER

LITURGY OF THE WORD

READING I
In conclusion:

      Reader: The word of the Lord.

      Assembly: **Thanks be to God.**

After a period of silence, the responsorial psalm is sung.

READING II
In conclusion:

      Reader: The word of the Lord.

      Assembly: **Thanks be to God.**

A time of silence follows the reading.

GOSPEL

Al - le - lu - ia, al - le-lu-ia, al - le - lu - ia.

Al - le - lu - ia, al - le - lu - ia, al - le - lu - ia.

Optional Verse Response

After first phrase: *After second phrase:*   **D.C.**

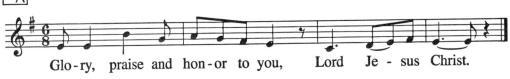

Al - le - lu - ia.   Al - le - lu - ia.

Music: *Mass of the Angels and Saints*, Steven R. Janco, © 1996, GIA Publications, Inc.

During Lent one of the following acclamations replaces the alleluia.

A

Glo - ry, praise and hon - or to you,   Lord   Je - sus   Christ.

Music: *Mass of the Angels and Saints*, Steven R. Janco, © 1996, GIA Publications, Inc.

Or:

B   **Praise and honor to you, Lord Jesus Christ, King of endless glory!**

C   **Praise and honor to you, Lord Jesus Christ!**

D   **Glory and praise to you, Lord Jesus Christ!**

E   **Glory to you, Word of God, Lord Jesus Christ!**

Deacon (or priest): The Lord be with you.
       Assembly: **And also with you.**
         Deacon: A reading from the holy gospel according to N.
       Assembly: **Glory to you, Lord.**

After the reading:
         Deacon: The gospel of the Lord.
       Assembly: **Praise to you, Lord Jesus Christ.**

HOMILY

PROFESSION OF FAITH

We believe in one God,
    the Father, the Almighty,
    maker of heaven and earth,
    of all that is seen and unseen.

We believe in one Lord, Jesus Christ,
    the only Son of God,
    eternally begotten of the Father,
    God from God, Light from Light,
    true God from true God,
    begotten, not made, one in Being with the Father.
    Through him all things were made.
    For us men and for our salvation he came down from heaven:
bow ⌐by the power of the Holy Spirit
    ⌐ he was born of the Virgin Mary, and became man.
    For our sake he was crucified under Pontius Pilate;
        he suffered, died, and was buried.
        On the third day he rose again
            in fulfillment of the Scriptures;
        he ascended into heaven
            and is seated at the right hand of the Father.
    He will come again in glory to judge the living and the dead,
        and his kingdom will have no end.

We believe in the Holy Spirit, the Lord, the giver of life,
    who proceeds from the Father and the Son.
    With the Father and the Son he is worshiped and glorified.
    He has spoken through the Prophets.
    We believe in one holy catholic and apostolic Church.
    We acknowledge one baptism for the forgiveness of sins.
    We look for the resurrection of the dead,
        and the life of the world to come. Amen.

GENERAL INTERCESSIONS

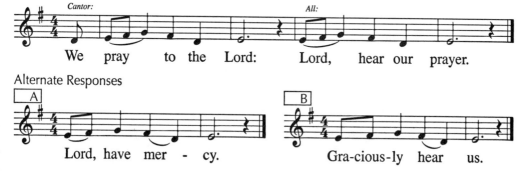

Cantor: We pray to the Lord: All: Lord, hear our prayer.

Alternate Responses

A: Lord, have mer - cy.

B: Gra-cious-ly hear us.

Music: *Mass of the Angels and Saints*, Steven R. Janco, © 1996, GIA Publications, Inc.

LITURGY OF THE EUCHARIST

PREPARATION OF THE ALTAR AND THE GIFTS

Bread and wine are brought to the table and the deacon or priest prepares these gifts.
The prayers may be said aloud, and all may respond:

Blessed be God for ever.

The priest then invites all to pray.

Assembly: **May the Lord accept the sacrifice at your hands**
for the praise and glory of his name,
for our good, and the good of all his Church.

The priest says the prayer over the gifts and all respond: **Amen.**

EUCHARISTIC PRAYER

Priest: The Lord be with you. All: And al - so with you.

Priest: Lift up your hearts. All: We lift them up to the Lord.

Priest: Let us give thanks to the Lord our God.

All: It is right to give him thanks and praise.

Music: *Mass of the Angels and Saints*, Steven R. Janco, © 1996, GIA Publications, Inc.

SANCTUS

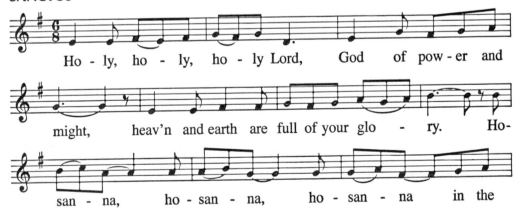

Ho - ly, ho - ly, ho - ly Lord, God of pow - er and might, heav'n and earth are full of your glo - ry. Ho-san - na, ho - san - na, ho - san - na in the

high - est. Ho - san - na, ho - san - na, ho -
san - na in the high-est. Bless - ed is he who comes in the
name of the Lord. Ho - san - na, ho -
san - na, ho - san - na in the high - est. Ho -
san - na, ho - san - na, ho - san - na in the high-est.

Music: *Mass of the Angels and Saints*, Steven R. Janco, © 1996, GIA Publications, Inc.

The various Eucharistic Prayers continue on page 13.

MEMORIAL ACCLAMATION

A

Christ has died, Christ is ris - en, Christ will come a - gain.

Christ has died, Christ is ris - en, Christ will come a - gain.

Text: ICEL, © 1973
Music: *Mass of the Angels and Saints*, Steven R. Janco, © 1996, GIA Publications, Inc.

B

Dy - ing you de - stroyed our death, ris - ing you re-stored our life.

Lord Je - sus, come in glo - ry. Lord Je - sus, come in glo - ry.

Text: ICEL, © 1973
Music: *Mass of the Angels and Saints*, Steven R. Janco, © 1996, GIA Publications, Inc.

C

When we eat this bread, when we drink this cup, we proclaim your death, Lord Je - sus, un - til you come in glo - ry.

Text: ICEL, © 1973
Music: *Mass of the Angels and Saints*, Steven R. Janco, © 1996, GIA Publications, Inc.

D

Lord, by your cross and res - ur - rec - tion you have set us free.
You are the Sav - ior of the world, the Sav - ior of the world.

Text: ICEL, © 1973
Music: *Mass of the Angels and Saints*, Steven R. Janco, © 1996, GIA Publications, Inc.

AMEN

Priest: Through him, with him, in him, in the unity of the Holy Spirit, all glory and honor is yours, almighty Father, for ever and ever.

A - men, a - men, a - men.

A - men, a - men, a - men.

Music: *Mass of the Angels and Saints*, Steven R. Janco, © 1996, GIA Publications, Inc.

COMMUNION RITE
THE LORD'S PRAYER

Assembly: **Our Father, who art in heaven,**
hallowed be thy name;
thy kingdom come;
thy will be done on earth as it is in heaven.
Give us this day our daily bread;
and forgive us our trespasses
as we forgive those who trespass against us;
and lead us not into temptation,
but deliver us from evil.

Priest: Deliver us, Lord. . . for the coming of our Savior, Jesus Christ.

Assembly: **For the kingdom, the power, and the glory are yours,**
now and for ever.

SIGN OF PEACE

Priest: The peace of the Lord be with you always.
Assembly: **And also with you.**

All exchange a sign of peace.

AGNUS DEI

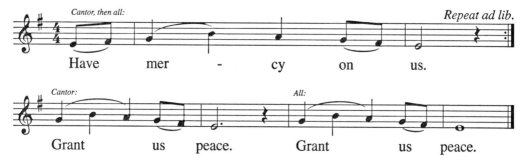

Music: *Mass of the Angels and Saints*, Steven R. Janco, © 1996, GIA Publications, Inc.

Priest: This is the Lamb of God...his supper.
Assembly: **Lord, I am not worthy to receive you,**
but only say the word and I shall be healed.

Minister of communion: The body (blood) of Christ.
Communicant: **Amen.**

CONCLUDING RITE

GREETING AND BLESSING

Priest: The Lord be with you.

Assembly: **And also with you.**

| Optional | *When the bishop blesses the people he adds the following:* |

Bishop: Blessed be the name of the Lord.

Assembly: **Now and for ever.**

Bishop: Our help is in the name of the Lord.

Assembly: **Who made heaven and earth.**

The blessing may be in a simple or solemn form. All respond to the blessing or to each part of the blessing: **Amen.**

DISMISSAL

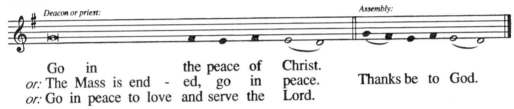

Go in the peace of Christ.
or: The Mass is end - ed, go in peace.
or: Go in peace to love and serve the Lord.

Thanks be to God.

EASTER DISMISSAL

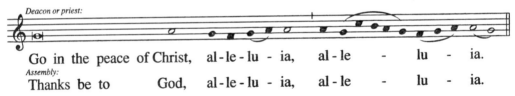

Go in the peace of Christ, al-le-lu - ia, al - le - lu - ia.

Assembly:

Thanks be to God, al-le-lu - ia, al - le - lu - ia.

Eucharistic Prayer I

We come to you, Father,
with praise and thanksgiving,
through Jesus Christ your Son.
Through him we ask you to accept and
bless
these gifts we offer you in sacrifice.
We offer them for your holy catholic
Church,
watch over it, Lord, and guide it;
grant it peace and unity throughout the
world.
We offer them for N. our Pope,
for N. our bishop,
and for all who hold and teach the catholic
faith
that comes to us from the apostles.

Remember, Lord, your people,
especially those for whom we now pray,
N. and N.
Remember all of us gathered here before
you.
You know how firmly we believe in you
and dedicate ourselves to you.
We offer you this sacrifice of praise
for ourselves and those who are dear to us.
We pray to you, our living and true God,
for our well-being and redemption.

In union with the whole Church
******

Christmas and during the Octave
we celebrate that day (night)
when Mary without loss of her
virginity
gave the world its savior.
******

Epiphany
we celebrate that day
when your only Son,
sharing your eternal glory,
showed himself in a human body.
******

Holy Thursday
we celebrate that day
when Jesus Christ, our Lord,
was betrayed for us.
******

Easter Octave and Second Sunday
we celebrate that day (night)
when Jesus Christ, our Lord,
rose from the dead in his human body.
******

Ascension
we celebrate that day
when your Son, our Lord,
took his place with you
and raised our frail human nature to glory.
******

Pentecost
we celebrate that day of Pentecost
when the Holy Spirit appeared to the
apostles
in the form of countless tongues.
******

we honor Mary,
the ever-virgin mother of Jesus Christ our
Lord and God.
We honor Joseph, her husband,
the apostles and martyrs
Peter and Paul, Andrew,
[James, John, Thomas,
James, Philip,
Bartholomew, Matthew, Simon and Jude;
we honor Linus, Cletus, Clement, Sixtus,
Cornelius, Cyprian, Lawrence,
Chrysogonus,
John and Paul, Cosmas and Damian]
and all the saints.
May their merits and prayers
gain us your constant help and
protection.
[Through Christ our Lord. Amen.]

Father, accept this offering
from your whole family.
******

Holy Thursday
in memory of the day when Jesus Christ,
our Lord,
gave the mysteries of his body and blood
for his disciples to celebrate.
******

Easter Octave and Second Sunday
and from those born into the new life

of water and the Holy Spirit,
with all their sins forgiven.
******

Grant us your peace in this life,
save us from final damnation,
and count us among those you have
chosen.
[Through Christ our Lord. Amen.]

Bless and approve our offering;
make it acceptable to you,
an offering in spirit and in truth.
Let it become for us
the body and blood of Jesus Christ,
your only Son, our Lord.
[Through Christ our Lord. Amen.]

The day before he suffered
******
Holy Thursday
to save us and all men,
that is today,
******
he took bread in his sacred hands
and looking up to heaven,
to you, his almighty Father,
he gave you thanks and praise.
He broke the bread,
gave it to his disciples, and said:
Take this, all of you, and eat it:
this is my body which will be given up for
you.

When supper was ended,
he took the cup.
Again he gave you thanks and praise,
gave the cup to his disciples, and said:
Take this, all of you, and drink from it:
this is the cup of my blood,
the blood of the new and everlasting
covenant.
It will be shed for you and for all
so that sins may be forgiven.
Do this in memory of me.

Let us proclaim the mystery of faith:
A Christ has died,
Christ is risen,
Christ will come again.

B Dying you destroyed our death,

rising you restored our life.
Lord Jesus, come in glory.

C When we eat this bread and drink
this cup,
we proclaim your death, Lord Jesus,
until you come in glory.

D Lord, by your cross and resurrection
you have set us free.
You are the Savior of the world.

Father, we celebrate the memory of Christ,
your Son.
We, your people and your ministers,
recall his passion,
his resurrection from the dead,
and his ascension into glory;
and from the many gifts you have given us
we offer to you, God of glory and majesty,
this holy and perfect sacrifice:
the bread of life
and the cup of eternal salvation.
Look with favor on these offerings
and accept them as once you accepted
the gifts of your servant Abel,
the sacrifice of Abraham, our father in
faith,
and the bread and wine offered by your
priest Melchisedech.

Almighty God,
we pray that your angel may take this
sacrifice
to your altar in heaven.
Then, as we receive from this altar
the sacred body and blood of your Son,
let us be filled with every grace and
blessing.
[Through Christ our Lord. Amen.]

Remember, Lord, those who have died
and have gone before us marked with the
sign of faith,
especially those for whom we now pray,
N. and N.
May these, and all who sleep in Christ,
find in your presence
light, happiness, and peace.
[Through Christ our Lord. Amen.]

For ourselves, too, we ask
some share in the fellowship of your apos-
   tles and martyrs,
with John the Baptist, Stephen, Matthias,
   Barnabas,
[Ignatius, Alexander, Marcellinus, Peter,
Felicity, Perpetua, Agatha, Lucy,
Agnes, Cecilia, Anastasia]
and all the saints.
Though we are sinners,
we trust in your mercy and love.
Do not consider what we truly deserve,
but grant us your forgiveness.
Through Christ our Lord.

Through him you give us all these gifts.
you fill them with life and goodness,
you bless them and make them holy.

Through him,
with him,
in him,
in the unity of the Holy Spirit,
all glory and honor is yours,
almighty Father,
for ever and ever.

Amen.

Eucharistic Prayer II

Father, it is our duty and our
   salvation,
always and everywhere
to give you thanks
through your beloved Son, Jesus Christ.

He is the Word through whom you made
   the universe,
the Savior you sent to redeem us.
By the power of the Holy Spirit
he took flesh and was born of the Virgin
   Mary.
For our sake he opened his arms on the
   cross;
he put an end to death
and revealed the resurrection.
In this he fulfilled your will
and won for you a holy people.

And so we join the angels and the saints
in proclaiming your glory
as we say:

Holy, holy, holy Lord, God of power
   and might,
heaven and earth are full of your
   glory.
   Hosanna in the highest.
Blessed is he who comes in the name
   of the Lord.
   Hosanna in the highest.

Lord, you are holy indeed,
the fountain of all holiness.
Let your Spirit come upon these gifts to
   make them holy,
so that they may become for us
the body and blood of our Lord, Jesus
   Christ.

Before he was given up to death,
a death he freely accepted,
he took bread and gave you thanks.
He broke the bread,
gave it to his disciples, and said:
Take this, all of you, and eat it:
this is my body which will be given up for
   you.

When supper was ended, he took the cup.
Again he gave you thanks and praise,
gave the cup to his disciples, and said:
Take this, all of you, and drink from it:
this is the cup of my blood,
the blood of the new and everlasting
   covenant.
It will be shed for you and for all
so that sins may be forgiven.
Do this in memory of me.

Let us proclaim the mystery of faith:
A Christ has died,
   Christ is risen,
   Christ will come again.

B Dying you destroyed our death,
  rising you restored our life.
  Lord Jesus, come in glory.

C When we eat this bread and drink
    this cup,
  we proclaim your death, Lord Jesus,
  until you come in glory.

D Lord, by your cross and resurrection
  you have set us free.
  You are the Savior of the world.

In memory of his death and
  resurrection,
we offer you, Father, this life-giving
  bread,
this saving cup.
We thank you for counting us worthy
to stand in your presence and serve you.
May all of us who share in the body and
  blood of Christ
be brought together in unity by the Holy
  Spirit.

Lord, remember your Church
  throughout the world;
make us grow in love,

together with N. our Pope,
N., our bishop, and all the clergy.

Remember our brothers and sisters
who have gone to their rest
in the hope of rising again;
bring them and all the departed
into the light of your presence.
Have mercy on us all;
make us worthy to share eternal life
with Mary, the virgin Mother of God,
with the apostles, and with all the saints
who have done your will throughout the
  ages.
May we praise you in union with them,
and give you glory
through your Son, Jesus Christ.

Through him,
with him,
in him,
in the unity of the Holy Spirit,
all glory and honor is yours,
almighty Father,
for ever and ever.

Amen.

Eucharistic Prayer III

Father, you are holy indeed,
and all creation rightly gives you praise.
All life, all holiness comes from you
through your Son, Jesus Christ our Lord,
by the working of the Holy Spirit.
From age to age you gather a people to
  yourself,
so that from east to west
a perfect offering may be made
to the glory of your name.

And so, Father, we bring you these gifts.
We ask you to make them holy by the
  power of your Spirit,
that they may become the body and blood
of your Son, our Lord Jesus Christ,
at whose command we celebrate this
  eucharist.

On the night he was betrayed,
he took bread and gave you thanks and
  praise.
He broke the bread, gave it to his
  disciples, and said:
Take this, all of you, and eat it:
this is my body which will be given up for
  you.

When supper was ended, he took the cup.
Again he gave you thanks and praise,
gave the cup to his disciples, and said:
Take this, all of you, and drink from it:
this is the cup of my blood,
the blood of the new and everlasting
  covenant.
It will be shed for you and for all
so that sins may be forgiven.
Do this in memory of me.

Let us proclaim the mystery of faith:
A Christ has died,
    Christ is risen,
    Christ will come again.

B Dying you destroyed our death,
    rising you restored our life.
    Lord Jesus, come in glory.

C When we eat this bread and drink
    this cup,
    we proclaim your death, Lord Jesus,
    until you come in glory.

D Lord, by your cross and resurrection
    you have set us free.
    You are the Savior of the world.

Father, calling to mind the death your Son
    endured for our salvation,
his glorious resurrection and ascension
    into heaven,
and ready to greet him when he comes
    again,
we offer you in thanksgiving this holy and
    living sacrifice.

Look with favor on your Church's offer-
    ing,
and see the Victim whose death has recon-
    ciled us to yourself.
Grant that we, who are nourished by his
    body and blood,
may be filled with his Holy Spirit,
and become one body, one spirit in Christ.

May he make us an everlasting gift to you
and enable us to share in the
    inheritance of your saints,
with Mary, the virgin Mother of God;

with the apostles, the martyrs,
[Saint N.—*the saint of the day or the
    patron saint*]
    and all your saints,
on whose constant intercession we rely for
    help.

Lord, may this sacrifice,
which has made our peace with you,
advance the peace and salvation of all the
    world.
Strengthen in faith and love your
    pilgrim Church on earth;
your servant, Pope N., our bishop N.,
and all the bishops,
with the clergy and the entire people your
    Son has gained for you.
Father, hear the prayers of the family you
    have gathered here before you.
In mercy and love unite all your
    children wherever they may be.

Welcome into your kingdom our departed
    brothers and sisters,
and all who have left this world in your
    friendship.
We hope to enjoy for ever the vision of
    your glory,
through Christ our Lord, from whom all
    good things come.

Through him,
with him,
in him,
in the unity of the Holy Spirit,
all glory and honor is yours,
almighty Father,
for ever and ever.

Amen.

Eucharistic Prayer IV

Father in heaven,
it is right that we should give you thanks
    and glory:
you are the one God, living and true.
Through all eternity you live in
    unapproachable light.

Source of life and goodness, you have
    created all things,
to fill your creatures with every
    blessing
and lead all men to the joyful vision of
    your light.

Countless hosts of angels stand before you
  to do your will;
they look upon your splendor
and praise you, night and day.
United with them,
and in the name of every creature under
  heaven,
we too praise your glory as we say:

Holy, holy, holy Lord, God of power
  and might,
heaven and earth are full of your glory.
  Hosanna in the highest.
Blessed is he who comes in the name
  of the Lord.
  Hosanna in the highest.

Father, we acknowledge your greatness:
all your actions show your wisdom and
  love.
You formed man in your own likeness
and set him over the whole world
to serve you, his creator,
and to rule over all creatures.
Even when he disobeyed you and lost
  your friendship
you did not abandon him to the power of
  death,
but helped all men to seek and find you.
Again and again you offered a covenant
  to man,
and through the prophets taught him to
  hope for salvation.
Father, you so loved the world
that in the fullness of time you sent your
  only Son to be our Savior.

He was conceived through the power of
  the Holy Spirit,
and born of the Virgin Mary,
a man like us in all things but sin.
To the poor he proclaimed the good news
  of salvation,
to prisoners, freedom,
and to those in sorrow, joy.
In fulfillment of your will
he gave himself up to death;
but by rising from the dead,
he destroyed death and restored life.
And that we might live no longer for ourselves but for him,

he sent the Holy Spirit from you, Father,
as his first gift to those who believe,
to complete his work on earth
and bring us the fullness of grace.

Father, may this Holy Spirit sanctify these
  offerings.
Let them become the body and blood of
  Jesus Christ our Lord
as we celebrate the great mystery
which he left us as an everlasting
  covenant.

He always loved those who were his own
  in the world.
When the time came for him to be
  glorified by you, his heavenly Father,
he showed the depth of his love.

While they were at supper,
he took bread, said the blessing, broke the
  bread,
and gave it to his disciples, saying:
Take this, all of you, and eat it:
this is my body which will be given up for
  you.

In the same way, he took the cup, filled
  with wine.
He gave you thanks, and giving the cup to
  his disciples, said:
Take this, all of you, and drink from it:
this is the cup of my blood,
the blood of the new and everlasting
  covenant.
It will be shed for you and for all
so that sins may be forgiven.
Do this in memory of me.

Let us proclaim the mystery of faith:
A Christ has died,
  Christ is risen,
  Christ will come again.

B Dying you destroyed our death,
  rising you restored our life.
  Lord Jesus, come in glory.

C When we eat this bread and drink
  this cup,

we proclaim your death, Lord Jesus,
until you come in glory.

D Lord, by your cross and resurrection
you have set us free.
You are the Savior of the world.

Father, we now celebrate this
memorial of our redemption.
We recall Christ's death, his descent
among the dead,
his resurrection, and his ascension to your
right hand;
and, looking forward to his coming in
glory,
we offer you his body and blood,
the acceptable sacrifice
which brings salvation to the whole world.

Lord, look upon this sacrifice which you
have given to your Church;
and by your Holy Spirit, gather all who
share this one bread and one cup
into the one body of Christ, a living
sacrifice of praise.

Lord, remember those for whom we offer
this sacrifice,
especially N. our Pope,
N. our bishop, and bishops and clergy
everywhere.

Remember those who take part in this
offering,
those here present and all your people,
and all who seek you with a sincere heart.
Remember those who have died in the
peace of Christ
and all the dead whose faith is known to
you alone.
Father, in your mercy grant also to us,
your children,
to enter into our heavenly inheritance
in the company of the Virgin Mary, the
Mother of God,
and your apostles and saints.
Then, in your kingdom, freed from the
corruption of sin and death,
we shall sing your glory with every
creature through Christ our Lord,
through whom you give us everything that
is good.

Through him,
with him,
in him,
in the unity of the Holy Spirit,
all glory and honor is yours,
almighty Father,
for ever and ever.
Amen.

Eucharistic Prayer—Reconciliation I

Father, all-powerful and ever-living God,
we do well always and everywhere to give
you thanks and praise.
You never cease to call us
to a new and more abundant life.

God of love and mercy,
you are always ready to forgive;
we are sinners,
and you invite us
to trust in your mercy.

Time and time again
we broke your covenant,
but you did not abandon us.

Instead, through your Son, Jesus our Lord,
you bound yourself even more closely to
the human family
by a bond that can never be broken.

Now is the time
for your people to turn back to you
and to be renewed in Christ your Son,
a time of grace and reconciliation.

You invite us
to serve the family of mankind
by opening our hearts
to the fullness of your Holy Spirit.

In wonder and gratitude,
we join our voices with the choirs of
    heaven
to proclaim the power of your love
and to sing of our salvation in Christ:

Holy, holy, holy Lord, God of power and
    might,
heaven and earth are full of your glory.
    Hosanna in the highest.
Blessed is he who comes in the name of
    the Lord.
Hosanna in the highest.

Father,
from the beginning of time
you have always done what is good for
    man
so that we may be holy as you are holy.

Look with kindness on your people
gathered here before you:
send forth the power of your Spirit
so that these gifts may become for us
the body and blood of your beloved Son,
    Jesus the Christ,
in whom we have become your sons and
    daughters.

When we were lost
and could not find the way to you,
you loved us more than ever:
Jesus, your Son, innocent and without sin,
gave himself into our hands
and was nailed to a cross.
Yet before he stretched out his arms
    between heaven and earth
in the everlasting sign of your covenant,
he desired to celebrate the Paschal feast
in the company of his disciples.

While they were at supper,
he took bread and gave you thanks and
    praise.
He broke the bread, gave it to his
    disciples, and said:
Take this, all of you, and eat it:
this is my body which will be given up for
    you.

At the end of the meal,
knowing that he was to reconcile all things
    in himself
by the blood of his cross,
he took the cup, filled with wine.
Again he gave you thanks, handed the cup
    to his friends,
    and said:
Take this, all of you, and drink from it:
this is the cup of my blood,
the blood of the new and everlasting
    covenant.
It will be shed for you and for all
so that sins may be forgiven.
Do this in memory of me.

Let us proclaim the mystery of faith:
A Christ has died,
    Christ is risen,
    Christ will come again.

B Dying you destroyed our death,
    rising you restored our life.
    Lord Jesus, come in glory.

C When we eat this bread and drink
    this cup,
    we proclaim your death, Lord Jesus,
    until you come in glory.

D Lord, by your cross and resurrection
    you have set us free.
    You are the Savior of the world.

We do this in memory of Jesus Christ,
our Passover and our lasting peace.
We celebrate his death and
    resurrection
and look for the coming of that day
when he will return to give us the
    fullness of joy.
Therefore we offer you, God ever faithful
    and true,
the sacrifice which restores man to your
    friendship.

Father,
look with love
on those you have called
to share in the one sacrifice of Christ.

By the power of your Holy Spirit
make them one body,
healed of all division.

Keep us all
in communion of mind and heart
with N., our pope, and N., our bishop.
Help us to work together
for the coming of your kingdom,
until at last we stand in your presence
to share the life of the saints,
in the company of the Virgin Mary and the
  apostles
and of our departed brothers and
  sisters
whom we commend to your mercy.

Then, freed from every shadow of death,
we shall take our place in the new
  creation
and give you thanks
with Christ, our risen Lord.

Through him,
with him,
in him,
in the unity of the Holy Spirit,
all glory and honor is yours,
almighty Father,
for ever and ever.

Amen.

Eucharistic Prayer—Reconciliation II

Father, all-powerful and ever-living God,
we praise and thank you through Jesus
  Christ our Lord
for your presence and action in the world.

In the midst of conflict and division,
we know it is you
who turn our minds to thoughts of peace.
Your Spirit changes our hearts:
enemies begin to speak to one another,
those who were estranged join hands in
  friendship,
and nations seek the way of peace
  together.

Your Spirit is at work
when understanding puts an end to strife,
when hatred is quenched by mercy,
and vengeance gives way to forgiveness.

For this we should never cease
to thank and praise you.
We join with all the choirs of heaven
as they sing for ever to your glory:

Holy, holy, holy Lord, God of power and
  might,
Heaven and earth are full of your glory.
  Hosanna in the highest.
Blessed is he who comes in the name of
  the Lord.

Hosanna in the highest.

God of power and might,
we praise you through your Son, Jesus
  Christ,
who comes in your name.
He is the Word that brings salvation.
He is the hand you stretch out to
  sinners.
He is the way that leads to your peace.

God our Father,
we had wandered far from you,
but through your Son you have brought us
  back.
You gave him up to death
so that we might turn again to you
and find our way to one another.

Therefore we celebrate the
  reconciliation
Christ has gained for us.

We ask you to sanctify these gifts
by the power of your Spirit,
as we now fulfill your Son's
  command.

While he was at supper
on the night before he died for us,
he took bread in his hands,

and gave you thanks and praise.
He broke the bread,
gave it to his disciples, and said:
Take this, all of you, and eat it:
this is my body which will be given up for
　　you.

At the end of the meal he took the cup.
Again he praised you for your
　　goodness,
gave the cup to his disciples, and said:
Take this, all of you, and drink from it:
this is the cup of my blood,
the blood of the new and everlasting
　　covenant.
It will be shed for you and for all
so that sins may be forgiven.
Do this in memory of me.

Let us proclaim the mystery of faith:
A Christ has died,
　　Christ is risen,
　　Christ will come again.

B Dying you destroyed our death,
　　rising you restored our life.
　　Lord Jesus, come in glory.

C When we eat this bread and drink
　　　this cup,
　　we proclaim your death, Lord Jesus,
　　until you come in glory.

D Lord, by your cross and resurrection
　　you have set us free.
　　You are the Savior of the world.

Lord our God,
your Son has entrusted to us
this pledge of his love.
We celebrate the memory of his death and
　　resurrection

and bring you the gift you have given us,
the sacrifice of reconciliation.
Therefore, we ask you, Father,
to accept us, together with your Son.

Fill us with his Spirit
through our sharing in this meal.
May he take away all that divides us.

May this Spirit keep us always in
　　communion
with N., our pope, N., our bishop,
with all the bishops and all your
　　people.
Father, make your Church throughout the
　　world
a sign of unity and an instrument of your
　　peace.

You have gathered us here
around the table of your Son,
in fellowship with the Virgin Mary,
　　　Mother of God, and all the saints.

In that new world where the fullness of
　　　your peace will be revealed,
gather people of every race, language, and
　　way of life
to share in the one eternal banquet
with Jesus Christ the Lord.

Through him,
with him,
in him,
in the unity of the Holy Spirit,
all glory and honor is yours,
almighty Father,
for ever and ever.

Amen.

November 28, 2010

FIRST SUNDAY OF ADVENT

ENTRANCE ANTIPHON *Psalm 24:1–3*

To you, my God, I lift my soul, I trust in you; let me never come to shame. Do not let my enemies laugh at me. No one who waits for you is ever put to shame.

READING I *Isaiah 2:1–5 / 1*

This is what Isaiah, son of Amoz, saw
concerning Judah and Jerusalem.
In days to come,
the mountain of the LORD's house
shall be established as the highest
mountain
and raised above the hills.
All nations shall stream toward it;
many peoples shall come and say:
"Come, let us climb the LORD's
mountain,
to the house of the God of Jacob,
that he may instruct us in his ways,
and we may walk in his paths."

For from Zion shall go forth instruction,
and the word of the LORD from
Jerusalem.
He shall judge between the nations,
and impose terms on many peoples.
They shall beat their swords into
plowshares
and their spears into pruning hooks;
one nation shall not raise the sword
against another,
nor shall they train for war again.
O house of Jacob, come,
let us walk in the light of the LORD!

RESPONSORIAL PSALM *Psalm 122:1–2, 3–4, 4–5, 6–7, 8–9*

Let us go rejoicing to the house of the Lord.

I rejoiced because they said to me,
"We will go up to the house of the
LORD."
And now we have set foot
within your gates, O Jerusalem. ℟.

Jerusalem, built as a city
with compact unity.
To it the tribes go up,
the tribes of the LORD. ℟.

According to the decree for Israel,
to give thanks to the name of the LORD.

In it are set up judgment seats,
seats for the house of David. ℟.

Pray for the peace of Jerusalem!
May those who love you prosper!
May peace be within your walls,
prosperity in your buildings. ℟.

Because of my brothers and friends
I will say, "Peace be within you!"
Because of the house of the LORD, our
God,
I will pray for your good. ℟.

READING II *Romans 13:11–14*

Brothers and sisters: You know the time; it is the hour now for you to awake from sleep. For our salvation is nearer now than when we first believed; the night is advanced, the day is at hand. Let us then throw off the works of darkness and put on the armor of light; let us conduct ourselves properly as in the day, not in orgies and drunkenness, not in promiscuity and lust, not in rivalry and jealousy. But put on the Lord Jesus Christ, and make no provision for the desires of the flesh.

Jesus said to his disciples: "As it was in the days of Noah, so it will be at the coming of the Son of Man. In those days before the flood, they were eating and drinking, marrying and giving in marriage, up to the day that Noah entered the ark. They did not know until the flood came and carried them all away. So will it be also at the coming of the Son of Man. Two men will be out in the field; one will be taken, and one will be left. Two women will be grinding at the mill; one will be taken, and one will be left. Therefore, stay awake! For you do not know on which day your Lord will come. Be sure of this: if the master of the house had known the hour of night when the thief was coming, he would have stayed awake and not let his house be broken into. So too, you also must be prepared, for at an hour you do not expect, the Son of Man will come."

COMMUNION ANTIPHON   *Psalm 85:13*
The Lord will shower his gifts, and our land will yield its fruit.

December 5, 2010

SECOND SUNDAY OF ADVENT

ENTRANCE ANTIPHON   *See Isaiah 30:19, 30*
People of Zion, the Lord will come to save all nations, and your hearts will exult to hear his majestic voice.

READING I   *Isaiah 11:1–10 / 4*

On that day, a shoot shall sprout from
    the stump of Jesse,
    and from his roots a bud shall
      blossom.
The spirit of the LORD shall rest upon him:
    a spirit of wisdom and of
      understanding,
a spirit of counsel and of strength,
    a spirit of knowledge and of fear
      of the LORD,
    and his delight shall be the fear
      of the LORD.
Not by appearance shall he judge,
    nor by hearsay shall he decide,
but he shall judge the poor with justice,
    and decide aright for the land's
      afflicted.
He shall strike the ruthless with the rod
    of his mouth,
    and with the breath of his lips he
      shall slay the wicked.
Justice shall be the band around his waist,
    and faithfulness a belt upon his hips.

Then the wolf shall be a guest of the
    lamb,
    and the leopard shall lie down with
      the kid;
the calf and the young lion shall browse
    together,
    with a little child to guide them.
The cow and the bear shall be neighbors,
    together their young shall rest;
    the lion shall eat hay like the ox.
The baby shall play by the cobra's den,
    and the child lay his hand on the
      adder's lair.
There shall be no harm or ruin on all my
    holy mountain;
    for the earth shall be filled with
      knowledge of the LORD,
    as water covers the sea.
On that day, the root of Jesse,
    set up as a signal for the nations,
the Gentiles shall seek out,
    for his dwelling shall be glorious.

RESPONSORIAL PSALM

Psalm 72:1–2, 7–8, 12–13, 17

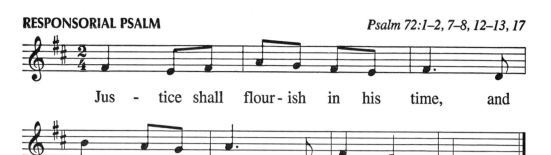

Jus - tice shall flour-ish in his time, and full - ness of peace for ev - er.

O God, with your judgment endow the king,
and with your justice, the king's son;
he shall govern your people with justice
and your afflicted ones with
judgment. ℟.

Justice shall flower in his days,
and profound peace, till the moon be
no more.
May he rule from sea to sea,
and from the River to the ends of the
earth. ℟.

For he shall rescue the poor when he
cries out,
and the afflicted when he has no
one to help him.
He shall have pity for the lowly and
the poor;
the lives of the poor he shall save. ℟.

May his name be blessed forever;
as long as the sun his name shall
remain.
In him shall all the tribes of the earth
be blessed;
all the nations shall proclaim his
happiness. ℟.

READING II
Romans 15:4–9

Brothers and sisters: Whatever was written previously was written for our instruction, that by endurance and by the encouragement of the Scriptures we might have hope. May the God of endurance and encouragement grant you to think in harmony with one another, in keeping with Christ Jesus, that with one accord you may with one voice glorify the God and Father of our Lord Jesus Christ.

Welcome one another, then, as Christ welcomed you, for the glory of God. For I say that Christ became a minister of the circumcised to show God's truthfulness, to confirm the promises to the patriarchs, but so that the Gentiles might glorify God for his mercy. As it is written:

Therefore, I will praise you among the Gentiles
and sing praises to your name.

GOSPEL
Matthew 3:1–12

John the Baptist appeared, preaching in the desert of Judea and saying, "Repent, for the kingdom of heaven is at hand!" It was of him that the prophet Isaiah had spoken when he said:

A voice of one crying out in the desert,
Prepare the way of the Lord,
make straight his paths.

John wore clothing made of camel's hair and had a leather belt around his waist. His food was locusts and wild honey. At that time Jerusalem, all Judea, and the whole region around the Jordan were going out to him and were being baptized by him in the Jordan

River as they acknowledged their sins.

When he saw many of the Pharisees and Sadducees coming to his baptism, he said to them, "You brood of vipers! Who warned you to flee from the coming wrath? Produce good fruit as evidence of your repentance. And do not presume to say to yourselves, 'We have Abraham as our father.' For I tell you, God can raise up children to Abraham from these stones. Even now the ax lies at the root of the trees. Therefore every tree that does not bear good fruit will be cut down and thrown into the fire. I am baptizing you with water, for repentance, but the one who is coming after me is mightier than I. I am not worthy to carry his sandals. He will baptize you with the Holy Spirit and fire. His winnowing fan is in his hand. He will clear his threshing floor and gather his wheat into his barn, but the chaff he will burn with unquenchable fire."

COMMUNION ANTIPHON *Baruch 5:5; 4:36*
Rise up, Jerusalem, stand on the heights, and see the joy that is coming to you from God.

December 8, 2010

THE IMMACULATE CONCEPTION OF THE BLESSED VIRGIN MARY

ENTRANCE ANTIPHON *Isaiah 61:10*
I exult for joy in the Lord, my soul rejoices in my God; for he has clothed me in the garment of salvation and robed me in the cloak of justice, like a bride adorned with her jewels.

READING I *Genesis 3:9–15, 20 / 689*
After the man, Adam, had eaten of the tree, the LORD God called to the man and asked him, "Where are you?" He answered, "I heard you in the garden; but I was afraid, because I was naked, so I hid myself." Then he asked, "Who told you that you were naked? You have eaten, then, from the tree of which I had forbidden you to eat!" The man replied, "The woman whom you put here with me— she gave me fruit from the tree, and so I ate it." The LORD God then asked the woman, "Why did you do such a thing?" The woman answered, "The serpent tricked me into it, so I ate it."

Then the LORD God said to the serpent:
"Because you have done this, you shall be banned
    from all the animals
    and from all the wild creatures;
on your belly shall you crawl,
    and dirt shall you eat
    all the days of your life.
I will put enmity between you and the woman,
    and between your offspring and hers;
he will strike at your head,
    while you strike at his heel."
The man called his wife Eve, because she became the mother of all the living.

RESPONSORIAL PSALM

Psalm 98:1, 2–3, 3–4

Sing to the Lord a new song, for he has done mar-vel-ous deeds.

Sing to the LORD a new song,
 for he has done wondrous deeds;
His right hand has won victory for him,
 his holy arm. ℟.

The LORD has made his salvation known:
 in the sight of the nations he has
 revealed his justice.

He has remembered his kindness and
 his faithfulness
 toward the house of Israel. ℟.

All the ends of the earth have seen
 the salvation by our God.
Sing joyfully to the LORD, all you lands;
 break into song; sing praise. ℟.

READING II

Ephesians 1:3–6, 11–12

Brothers and sisters: Blessed be the God and Father of our Lord Jesus Christ, who has blessed us in Christ with every spiritual blessing in the heavens, as he chose us in him, before the foundation of the world, to be holy and without blemish before him. In love he destined us for adoption to himself through Jesus Christ, in accord with the favor of his will, for the praise of the glory of his grace that he granted us in the beloved.

In him we were also chosen, destined in accord with the purpose of the One who accomplishes all things according to the intention of his will, so that we might exist for the praise of his glory, we who first hoped in Christ.

GOSPEL

Luke 1:26–38

The angel Gabriel was sent from God to a town of Galilee called Nazareth, to a virgin betrothed to a man named Joseph, of the house of David, and the virgin's name was Mary. And coming to her, he said, "Hail, full of grace! The Lord is with you." But she was greatly troubled at what was said and pondered what sort of greeting this might be. Then the angel said to her, "Do not be afraid, Mary, for you have found favor with God. Behold, you will conceive in your womb and bear a son, and you shall name him Jesus. He will be great and will be called Son of the Most High, and the Lord God will give him the throne of David his father, and he will rule over the house of Jacob forever, and of his Kingdom there will be no end." But Mary said to the angel, "How can this be, since I have no relations with a man?" And the angel said to her in reply, "The Holy Spirit will come upon you, and the power of the Most High will overshadow you. Therefore the child to be born will be called holy, the Son of God. And behold, Elizabeth, your relative, has also conceived a son in her old age, and this is the sixth month for her who was called barren; for nothing will be impossible for God." Mary said, "Behold, I am the handmaid of the Lord. May it be done to me according to your word." Then the angel departed from her.

COMMUNION ANTIPHON

All honor to you, Mary! From you arose the sun of justice, Christ our God.

THIRD SUNDAY OF ADVENT

ENTRANCE ANTIPHON *Philippians 4:4, 5*

Rejoice in the Lord always; again I say, rejoice! The Lord is near.

READING I *Isaiah 35:1–6a, 10 / 7*

The desert and the parched land will
 exult;
  the steppe will rejoice and bloom.
They will bloom with abundant flowers,
  and rejoice with joyful song.
The glory of Lebanon will be given to
  them,
  the splendor of Carmel and Sharon;
they will see the glory of the LORD,
  the splendor of our God.
Strengthen the hands that are feeble,
  make firm the knees that are weak,
say to those whose hearts are frightened:
  Be strong, fear not!
Here is your God,

he comes with vindication;
with divine recompense
he comes to save you.
Then will the eyes of the blind be
  opened,
  the ears of the deaf be cleared;
then will the lame leap like a stag,
  then the tongue of the mute will sing.

Those whom the LORD has ransomed
  will return
  and enter Zion singing,
  crowned with everlasting joy;
they will meet with joy and gladness,
  sorrow and mourning will flee.

RESPONSORIAL PSALM *Psalm 146:6–7, 8–9, 9–10*

Or: Alleluia.

Lord, come and save us.

The LORD God keeps faith forever,
  secures justice for the oppressed,
  gives food to the hungry.
The LORD sets captives free. ℟.

The LORD gives sight to the blind;
  the LORD raises up those who were
  bowed down.
The LORD loves the just;

the LORD protects strangers. ℟.

The fatherless and the widow he
  sustains,
  but the way of the wicked he thwarts.
The LORD shall reign forever;
  your God, O Zion, through all
  generations. ℟.

READING II *James 5:7–10*

Be patient, brothers and sisters, until the coming of the Lord. See how the farmer waits
for the precious fruit of the earth, being patient with it until it receives the early and the
late rains. You too must be patient. Make your hearts firm, because the coming of the
Lord is at hand. Do not complain, brothers and sisters, about one another, that you may
not be judged. Behold, the Judge is standing before the gates. Take as an example of
hardship and patience, brothers and sisters, the prophets who spoke in the name of the
Lord.

GOSPEL   *Matthew 11:2–11*

When John the Baptist heard in prison of the works of the Christ, he sent his disciples to Jesus with this question, "Are you the one who is to come, or should we look for another?" Jesus said to them in reply, "Go and tell John what you hear and see: the blind regain their sight, the lame walk, lepers are cleansed, the deaf hear, the dead are raised, and the poor have the good news proclaimed to them. And blessed is the one who takes no offense at me."

As they were going off, Jesus began to speak to the crowds about John, "What did you go out to the desert to see? A reed swayed by the wind? Then what did you go out to see? Someone dressed in fine clothing? Those who wear fine clothing are in royal palaces. Then why did you go out? To see a prophet? Yes, I tell you, and more than a prophet. This is the one about whom it is written:

> Behold, I am sending my messenger ahead of you;
> > he will prepare your way before you.

Amen, I say to you, among those born of women there has been none greater than John the Baptist; yet the least in the kingdom of heaven is greater than he."

COMMUNION ANTIPHON   *See Isaiah 35:4*
Say to the anxious: be strong and fear not, our God will come to save us.

December 19, 2010

FOURTH SUNDAY OF ADVENT

ENTRANCE ANTIPHON   *Isaiah 45:8*
Let the clouds rain down the Just One, and the earth bring forth a Savior.

READING I   *Isaiah 7:10–14 / 10*
The LORD spoke to Ahaz, saying: Ask for a sign from the LORD, your God; let it be deep as the netherworld, or high as the sky! But Ahaz answered, "I will not ask! I will not tempt the LORD!" Then Isaiah said: Listen, O house of David! Is it not enough for you to weary people, must you also weary my God? Therefore the Lord himself will give you this sign: the virgin shall conceive, and bear a son, and shall name him Emmanuel.

RESPONSORIAL PSALM   *Psalm 24:1–2, 3–4, 5–6*

Let the Lord en-ter; he is king of glo-ry.

The LORD's are the earth and its fullness;
  the world and those who dwell in it.
For he founded it upon the seas
  and established it upon the rivers. ℟.

Who can ascend the mountain of the
    LORD?
  or who may stand in his holy place?
One whose hands are sinless,

  whose heart is clean,
  who desires not what is vain. ℟.

He shall receive a blessing from the
    LORD,
  a reward from God his savior.
Such is the race that seeks for him,
  that seeks the face of the God of
    Jacob. ℟.

READING II

Romans 1:1–7

Paul, a slave of Christ Jesus, called to be an apostle and set apart for the gospel of God, which he promised previously through his prophets in the holy Scriptures, the gospel about his Son, descended from David according to the flesh, but established as Son of God in power according to the Spirit of holiness through resurrection from the dead, Jesus Christ our Lord. Through him we have received the grace of apostleship, to bring about the obedience of faith, for the sake of his name, among all the Gentiles, among whom are you also, who are called to belong to Jesus Christ; to all the beloved of God in Rome, called to be holy. Grace to you and peace from God our Father and the Lord Jesus Christ.

GOSPEL

Matthew 1:18–24

This is how the birth of Jesus Christ came about. When his mother Mary was betrothed to Joseph, but before they lived together, she was found with child through the Holy Spirit. Joseph her husband, since he was a righteous man, yet unwilling to expose her to shame, decided to divorce her quietly. Such was his intention when, behold, the angel of the Lord appeared to him in a dream and said, "Joseph, son of David, do not be afraid to take Mary your wife into your home. For it is through the Holy Spirit that this child has been conceived in her. She will bear a son and you are to name him Jesus, because he will save his people from their sins." All this took place to fulfill what the Lord had said through the prophet:

> Behold, the virgin shall conceive and bear a son,
> and they shall name him Emmanuel,

which means "God is with us." When Joseph awoke, he did as the angel of the Lord had commanded him and took his wife into his home.

COMMUNION ANTIPHON

Isaiah 7:14

The Virgin is with child and shall bear a son, and she will call him Emmanuel.

December 24, 2010

THE NATIVITY OF THE LORD (CHRISTMAS): VIGIL MASS

ENTRANCE ANTIPHON

Exodus 16:6–7

Today you will know that the Lord is coming to save us, and in the morning you will see his glory.

READING I

Isaiah 62:1–5 / 13

For Zion's sake I will not be silent,
for Jerusalem's sake I will not be quiet,
until her vindication shines forth like the dawn
and her victory like a burning torch.

Nations shall behold your vindication,
and all the kings your glory;
you shall be called by a new name
pronounced by the mouth of the LORD.
You shall be a glorious crown in the hand of the LORD,
a royal diadem held by your God.
No more shall people call you "Forsaken,"
or your land "Desolate,"
but you shall be called "My Delight,"
and your land "Espoused."
For the LORD delights in you
and makes your land his spouse.
As a young man marries a virgin,
your Builder shall marry you;
and as a bridegroom rejoices in his bride
so shall your God rejoice in you.

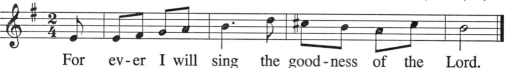

For ev-er I will sing the good-ness of the Lord.

I have made a covenant with my chosen
    one,
  I have sworn to David my servant:
forever will I confirm your posterity
    and establish your throne for all
    generations. ℟.

Blessed the people who know the joyful
    shout;
  in the light of your countenance, O
  Lord, they walk.

At your name they rejoice all the day,
  and through your justice they are
  exalted. ℟.

He shall say of me, "You are my father,
  my God, the rock, my savior."
Forever I will maintain my kindness
    toward him,
  and my covenant with him stands
  firm. ℟.

READING II   *Acts 13:16–17, 22–25*

When Paul reached Antioch in Pisidia and entered the synagogue, he stood up, motioned with his hand, and said, "Fellow Israelites and you others who are God-fearing, listen. The God of this people Israel chose our ancestors and exalted the people during their sojourn in the land of Egypt. With uplifted arm he led them out of it. Then he removed Saul and raised up David as king; of him he testified, 'I have found David, son of Jesse, a man after my own heart; he will carry out my every wish.' From this man's descendants God, according to his promise, has brought to Israel a savior, Jesus. John heralded his coming by proclaiming a baptism of repentance to all the people of Israel; and as John was completing his course, he would say, 'What do you suppose that I am? I am not he. Behold, one is coming after me; I am not worthy to unfasten the sandals of his feet.'"

GOSPEL   *Matthew 1:1–25 or 1:18–25*
For short form read only the part in brackets.

The book of the genealogy of Jesus Christ, the son of David, the son of Abraham.
    Abraham became the father of Isaac, Isaac the father of Jacob, Jacob the father of Judah and his brothers. Judah became the father of Perez and Zerah, whose mother was Tamar. Perez became the father of Hezron, Hezron the father of Ram, Ram the father of Amminadab. Amminadab became the father of Nahshon, Nahshon the father of Salmon, Salmon the father of Boaz, whose mother was Rahab. Boaz became the father of Obed, whose mother was Ruth. Obed became the father of Jesse, Jesse the father of David the king.
    David became the father of Solomon, whose mother had been the wife of Uriah. Solomon became the father of Rehoboam, Rehoboam the father of Abijah, Abijah the father of Asaph. Asaph became the father of Jehoshaphat, Jehoshaphat the father of Joram, Joram the father of Uzziah. Uzziah became the father of Jotham, Jotham the father of Ahaz, Ahaz the father of Hezekiah. Hezekiah became the father of Manasseh, Manasseh the father of Amos, Amos the father of Josiah. Josiah became the father of Jechoniah and his brothers at the time of the Babylonian exile.
    After the Babylonian exile, Jechoniah became the father of Shealtiel, Shealtiel the father of Zerubbabel, Zerubbabel the father of Abiud. Abiud became the father of

Eliakim, Eliakim the father of Azor, Azor the father of Zadok. Zadok became the father of Achim, Achim the father of Eliud, Eliud the father of Eleazar. Eleazar became the father of Matthan, Matthan the father of Jacob, Jacob the father of Joseph, the husband of Mary. Of her was born Jesus who is called the Christ.

Thus the total number of generations from Abraham to David is fourteen generations; from David to the Babylonian exile, fourteen generations; from the Babylonian exile to the Christ, fourteen generations.

Now [this is how the birth of Jesus Christ came about. When his mother Mary was betrothed to Joseph, but before they lived together, she was found with child through the Holy Spirit. Joseph her husband, since he was a righteous man, yet unwilling to expose her to shame, decided to divorce her quietly. Such was his intention when, behold, the angel of the Lord appeared to him in a dream and said, "Joseph, son of David, do not be afraid to take Mary your wife into your home. For it is through the Holy Spirit that this child has been conceived in her. She will bear a son and you are to name him Jesus, because he will save his people from their sins." All this took place to fulfill what the Lord had said through the prophet:

Behold, the virgin shall conceive and bear a son,
    and they shall name him Emmanuel,

which means "God is with us." When Joseph awoke, he did as the angel of the Lord had commanded him and took his wife into his home. He had no relations with her until she bore a son, and he named him Jesus.]

COMMUNION ANTIPHON   *See Isaiah 40:5*
The glory of the Lord will be revealed, and all mankind will see the saving power of God.

December 25, 2010

THE NATIVITY OF THE LORD (CHRISTMAS): MASS AT MIDNIGHT

ENTRANCE ANTIPHON   *Psalm 2:7*
The Lord said to me: You are my Son; this day have I begotten you.

READING I   *Isaiah 9:1–6 / 14*

The people who walked in darkness
    have seen a great light;
upon those who dwelt in the land of
    gloom
    a light has shone.
You have brought them abundant joy
    and great rejoicing,
as they rejoice before you as at the
    harvest,
    as people make merry when
        dividing spoils.
For the yoke that burdened them,
    the pole on their shoulder,
and the rod of their taskmaster

you have smashed, as on the day
    of Midian.
For every boot that tramped in battle,
    every cloak rolled in blood,
    will be burned as fuel for flames.
For a child is born to us, a son is given
    us;
    upon his shoulder dominion rests.
They name him Wonder-Counselor,
        God-Hero,
    Father-Forever, Prince of Peace.
His dominion is vast
    and forever peaceful,

from David's throne, and over his
kingdom,
which he confirms and sustains
by judgment and justice,

both now and forever.
The zeal of the LORD of hosts will do
this!

RESPONSORIAL PSALM

Psalm 96:1–2, 2–3, 11–12, 13

To-day, to-day, to-day is born our Sav-ior, Christ the Lord.

Sing to the LORD a new song;
sing to the LORD, all you lands.
Sing to the LORD; bless his name. ℟.

Announce his salvation, day after day.
Tell his glory among the nations;
among all peoples, his wondrous
deeds. ℟.

Let the heavens be glad and the earth
rejoice;
let the sea and what fills it resound;

let the plains be joyful and all that is
in them!
Then shall all the trees of the forest
exult. ℟.

They shall exult before the LORD, for he
comes;
for he comes to rule the earth.
He shall rule the world with justice
and the peoples with his
constancy. ℟.

READING II

Titus 2:11–14

Beloved: The grace of God has appeared, saving all and training us to reject godless ways and worldly desires and to live temperately, justly, and devoutly in this age, as we await the blessed hope, the appearance of the glory of our great God and savior Jesus Christ, who gave himself for us to deliver us from all lawlessness and to cleanse for himself a people as his own, eager to do what is good.

GOSPEL

Luke 2:1–14

In those days a decree went out from Caesar Augustus that the whole world should be enrolled. This was the first enrollment, when Quirinius was governor of Syria. So all went to be enrolled, each to his own town. And Joseph too went up from Galilee from the town of Nazareth to Judea, to the city of David that is called Bethlehem, because he was of the house and family of David, to be enrolled with Mary, his betrothed, who was with child. While they were there, the time came for her to have her child, and she gave birth to her firstborn son. She wrapped him in swaddling clothes and laid him in a manger, because there was no room for them in the inn.

Now there were shepherds in that region living in the fields and keeping the night watch over their flock. The angel of the Lord appeared to them and the glory of the Lord shone around them, and they were struck with great fear. The angel said to them, "Do not be afraid; for behold, I proclaim to you good news of great joy that will be for all the people. For today in the city of David a savior has been born for you who is Christ and Lord. And this will be a sign for you: you will find an infant wrapped in swaddling clothes and lying in a manger." And suddenly there was a multitude of the heavenly host with the angel, praising God and saying:

> "Glory to God in the highest
> and on earth peace to those on whom his favor rests."

COMMUNION ANTIPHON   *John 1:14*
The Word of God became man; we have seen his glory.

December 25, 2010

THE NATIVITY OF THE LORD (CHRISTMAS): MASS AT DAWN

ENTRANCE ANTIPHON   *See Isaiah 9:2, 6; Luke 1:33*
A light will shine on us this day, the Lord is born for us: he shall be called Wonderful God, Prince of peace, Father of the world to come; and his kingship will never end.

READING I   *Isaiah 62:11–12 / 15*

See, the LORD proclaims
   to the ends of the earth:
say to daughter Zion,
   your savior comes!
Here is his reward with him,
his recompense before him.
They shall be called the holy people,
   the redeemed of the LORD,
and you shall be called "Frequented,"
   a city that is not forsaken.

RESPONSORIAL PSALM   *Psalm 97:1, 6, 11–12*

A light will shine on us this day: the Lord is born for us.

The LORD is king; let the earth rejoice;
   let the many isles be glad.
The heavens proclaim his justice,
   and all peoples see his glory. ℟.

Light dawns for the just;
   and gladness, for the upright of heart.
Be glad in the LORD, you just,
   and give thanks to his holy name. ℟.

READING II   *Titus 3:4–7*
Beloved:
   When the kindness and generous love
      of God our savior appeared,
   not because of any righteous deeds
      we had done
   but because of his mercy,
he saved us through the bath of
   rebirth
and renewal by the Holy Spirit,
whom he richly poured out on us
   through Jesus Christ our savior,
so that we might be justified by his
   grace
and become heirs in hope of
   eternal life.

GOSPEL   *Luke 2:15–20*
When the angels went away from them to heaven, the shepherds said to one another, "Let us go, then, to Bethlehem to see this thing that has taken place, which the Lord has made known to us." So they went in haste and found Mary and Joseph, and the infant

lying in the manger. When they saw this, they made known the message that had been told them about this child. All who heard it were amazed by what had been told them by the shepherds. And Mary kept all these things, reflecting on them in her heart. Then the shepherds returned, glorifying and praising God for all they had heard and seen, just as it had been told to them.

COMMUNION ANTIPHON *See Zechariah 9:9*
Daughter of Zion, exult; shout aloud, daughter of Jerusalem! Your King is coming, the Holy One, the Savior of the world.

December 25, 2010
THE NATIVITY OF THE LORD (CHRISTMAS): MASS DURING THE DAY

ENTRANCE ANTIPHON *Isaiah 9:6*
A child is born for us, a son given to us; dominion is laid on his shoulder, and he shall be called Wonderful-Counsellor.

READING I *Isaiah 52:7–10 / 16*

How beautiful upon the mountains
    are the feet of him who brings glad
        tidings,
announcing peace, bearing good news,
    announcing salvation, and saying to
        Zion,
"Your God is King!"

Hark! Your sentinels raise a cry,
    together they shout for joy,

for they see directly, before their eyes,
    the LORD restoring Zion.
Break out together in song,
    O ruins of Jerusalem!
For the LORD comforts his people,
    he redeems Jerusalem.
The LORD has bared his holy arm
    in the sight of all the nations;
all the ends of the earth will behold
    the salvation of our God.

RESPONSORIAL PSALM *Psalm 98:1, 2–3, 3–4, 5–6*

All the ends of the earth have seen the sav - ing pow'r of God.

Sing to the LORD a new song,
    for he has done wondrous deeds;
his right hand has won victory for him,
    his holy arm. ℟.

The LORD has made his salvation known:
    in the sight of the nations he has
        revealed his justice.
He has remembered his kindness and his
    faithfulness
toward the house of Israel. ℟.

All the ends of the earth have seen
    the salvation by our God.
Sing joyfully to the LORD, all you lands;
    break into song; sing praise. ℟.

Sing praise to the LORD with the harp,
    with the harp and melodious song.
With trumpets and the sound of the horn
    sing joyfully before the King, the
    LORD. ℟.

Brothers and sisters: In times past, God spoke in partial and various ways to our ancestors through the prophets; in these last days, he has spoken to us through the Son, whom he made heir of all things and through whom he created the universe,

who is the refulgence of his glory, the very imprint of his being,
and who sustains all things by his mighty word.
When he had accomplished purification from sins,
he took his seat at the right hand of the Majesty on high,
as far superior to the angels
as the name he has inherited is more excellent than theirs.

For to which of the angels did God ever say:
You are my son; this day I have begotten you?
Or again:
I will be a father to him, and he shall be a son to me?
And again, when he leads the firstborn into the world, he says:
Let all the angels of God worship him.

GOSPEL *John 1:1–18 or 1:1–5, 9–14*

For short form read only the parts in brackets.

[In the beginning was the Word,
and the Word was with God,
and the Word was God.
He was in the beginning with God.
All things came to be through him,
and without him nothing came to be.
What came to be through him was life,
and this life was the light of the human race;
the light shines in the darkness,
and the darkness has not overcome it.]

A man named John was sent from God. He came for testimony, to testify to the light, so that all might believe through him. He was not the light, but came to testify to the light. [The true light, which enlightens everyone, was coming into the world.

He was in the world,
and the world came to be through him,
but the world did not know him.
He came to what was his own,
but his own people did not accept him.

But to those who did accept him he gave power to become children of God, to those who believe in his name, who were born not by natural generation nor by human choice nor by a man's decision but of God.

And the Word became flesh
and made his dwelling among us,
and we saw his glory,
the glory as of the Father's only Son,
full of grace and truth.]

John testified to him and cried out, saying, "This was he of whom I said, 'The one who is coming after me ranks ahead of me because he existed before me.'" From his fullness we have all received, grace in place of grace, because while the law was given through Moses, grace and truth came through Jesus Christ. No one has ever seen God. The only Son, God, who is at the Father's side, has revealed him.

December 26, 2010

THE HOLY FAMILY OF JESUS, MARY, AND JOSEPH

ENTRANCE ANTIPHON *Luke 2:16*
The shepherds hastened to Bethlehem, where they found Mary and Joseph, and the baby lying in a manger.

READING I *Sirach 3:2–7, 12–14 / 17*

God sets a father in honor over his
  children;
  a mother's authority he confirms
  over her sons.
Whoever honors his father atones
  for sins,
  and preserves himself from them.
When he prays, he is heard;
  he stores up riches who reveres
  his mother.
Whoever honors his father is
  gladdened by children,
  and, when he prays, is heard.
Whoever reveres his father will live a

long life;
he who obeys his father brings
  comfort to his mother.

My son, take care of your father when
  he is old;
grieve him not as long as he lives.
Even if his mind fail, be considerate of
  him;
  revile him not all the days of his life;
kindness to a father will not be forgotten,
  firmly planted against the debt of
  your sins
—a house raised in justice to you.

RESPONSORIAL PSALM *Psalm 128:1–2, 3, 4–5*

Bless-ed are those who fear the Lord and walk in his ways.

Blessed is everyone who fears the LORD,
  who walks in his ways!
For you shall eat the fruit of your
  handiwork;
  blessed shall you be, and favored. ℟.

Your wife shall be like a fruitful vine
  in the recesses of your home;
your children like olive plants
  around your table. ℟.

Behold, thus is the man blessed
  who fears the LORD.
The LORD bless you from Zion:
  may you see the prosperity of
  Jerusalem
  all the days of your life. ℟.

READING II *Colossians 3:12–21 or 3:12–17*
For short form read only the part in brackets.

[Brothers and sisters: Put on, as God's chosen ones, holy and beloved, heartfelt compassion, kindness, humility, gentleness, and patience, bearing with one another and forgiving one another, if one has a grievance against another; as the Lord has forgiven you, so must you also do. And over all these put on love, that is, the bond of perfection. And let the peace of Christ control your hearts, the peace into which you were also called in one body. And be thankful. Let the word of Christ dwell in you richly, as in all wisdom you teach and admonish one another, singing psalms, hymns, and spiritual songs with gratitude in your hearts to God. And whatever you do, in word or in deed, do everything in the name of the Lord Jesus, giving thanks to God the Father through him.]

Wives, be subordinate to your husbands, as is proper in the Lord. Husbands, love your wives, and avoid any bitterness toward them. Children, obey your parents in everything, for this is pleasing to the Lord. Fathers, do not provoke your children, so they may not become discouraged.

GOSPEL   *Matthew 2:13–15, 19–23*

When the magi had departed, behold, the angel of the Lord appeared to Joseph in a dream and said, "Rise, take the child and his mother, flee to Egypt, and stay there until I tell you. Herod is going to search for the child to destroy him." Joseph rose and took the child and his mother by night and departed for Egypt. He stayed there until the death of Herod, that what the Lord had said through the prophet might be fulfilled, *Out of Egypt I called my son.*

When Herod had died, behold, the angel of the Lord appeared in a dream to Joseph in Egypt and said, "Rise, take the child and his mother and go to the land of Israel, for those who sought the child's life are dead." He rose, took the child and his mother, and went to the land of Israel. But when he heard that Archelaus was ruling over Judea in place of his father Herod, he was afraid to go back there. And because he had been warned in a dream, he departed for the region of Galilee. He went and dwelt in a town called Nazareth, so that what had been spoken through the prophets might be fulfilled, *He shall be called a Nazorean.*

COMMUNION ANTIPHON   *Baruch 3:38*
Our God has appeared on earth, and lived among men.

January 2, 2011
THE EPIPHANY OF THE LORD

ENTRANCE ANTIPHON   *See Malachi 3:1; 1 Chronicles 19:12*
The Lord and ruler is coming; kingship is his, and government and power.

READING I   *Isaiah 60:1–6 / 20*

Rise up in splendor, Jerusalem! Your
    light has come,
    the glory of the Lord shines upon
      you.
See, darkness covers the earth,
    and thick clouds cover the peoples;
but upon you the LORD shines,
    and over you appears his glory.
Nations shall walk by your light,
    and kings by your shining radiance.
Raise your eyes and look about;

they all gather and come to you:
your sons come from afar,
    and your daughters in the arms of
      their nurses.

Then you shall be radiant at what you see,
    your heart shall throb and overflow,
for the riches of the sea shall be emptied
    out before you,
    the wealth of nations shall be
      brought to you.

Caravans of camels shall fill you,
dromedaries from Midian and Ephah;
all from Sheba shall come
bearing gold and frankincense,
and proclaiming the praises of the
LORD.

RESPONSORIAL PSALM

Psalm 72:1–2, 7–8, 10–11, 12–13

Lord, ev-'ry na-tion on earth will a-dore you.

O God, with your judgment endow the
king,
and with your justice, the king's son;
he shall govern your people with justice
and your afflicted ones with
judgment. ℟.

Justice shall flower in his days,
and profound peace, till the moon be
no more.
May he rule from sea to sea,
and from the River to the ends of the
earth. ℟.

The kings of Tarshish and the Isles shall
offer gifts;
the kings of Arabia and Seba shall
bring tribute.
All kings shall pay him homage,
all nations shall serve him. ℟.

For he shall rescue the poor when he
cries out,
and the afflicted when he has no one
to help him.
He shall have pity for the lowly and the
poor;
the lives of the poor he shall save. ℟.

READING II

Ephesians 3:2–3a, 5–6

Brothers and sisters: You have heard of the stewardship of God's grace that was given
to me for your benefit, namely, that the mystery was made known to me by revelation.
It was not made known to people in other generations as it has now been revealed to his
holy apostles and prophets by the Spirit: that the Gentiles are coheirs, members of the
same body, and copartners in the promise in Christ Jesus through the gospel.

GOSPEL

Matthew 2:1–12

When Jesus was born in Bethlehem of Judea, in the days of King Herod, behold, magi
from the east arrived in Jerusalem, saying, "Where is the newborn king of the Jews? We
saw his star at its rising and have come to do him homage." When King Herod heard
this, he was greatly troubled, and all Jerusalem with him. Assembling all the chief priests
and the scribes of the people, he inquired of them where the Christ was to be born. They
said to him, "In Bethlehem of Judea, for thus it has been written through the prophet:
And you, Bethlehem, land of Judah,
are by no means least among the rulers of Judah;
since from you shall come a ruler,
who is to shepherd my people Israel."
Then Herod called the magi secretly and ascertained from them the time of the star's
appearance. He sent them to Bethlehem and said, "Go and search diligently for the
child. When you have found him, bring me word, that I too may go and do him homage." After their audience with the king they set out. And behold, the star that they had
seen at its rising preceded them, until it came and stopped over the place where the
child was. They were overjoyed at seeing the star, and on entering the house they saw
the child with Mary his mother. They prostrated themselves and did him homage. Then

they opened their treasures and offered him gifts of gold, frankincense, and myrrh. And having been warned in a dream not to return to Herod, they departed for their country by another way.

COMMUNION ANTIPHON *See Matthew 2:2*
We have seen his star in the east, and have come with gifts to adore the Lord.

January 9, 2011

THE BAPTISM OF THE LORD

ENTRANCE ANTIPHON *See Matthew 3:16–17*
When the Lord had been baptized, the heavens opened, and the Spirit came down like a dove to rest on him. Then the voice of the Father thundered: This is my beloved Son, with him I am well pleased.

READING I *Isaiah 42:1–4, 6–7 / 21*

Thus says the LORD:
Here is my servant whom I uphold,
    my chosen one with whom I am
      pleased,
upon whom I have put my spirit;
    he shall bring forth justice to the
      nations,
not crying out, not shouting,
    not making his voice heard in the
      street.
A bruised reed he shall not break,
    and a smoldering wick he shall not
      quench,
until he establishes justice on the earth;

the coastlands will wait for his
    teaching.

I, the LORD, have called you for the
    victory of justice,
    I have grasped you by the hand;
I formed you, and set you
    as a covenant of the people,
    a light for the nations,
to open the eyes of the blind,
    to bring out prisoners from
      confinement,
    and from the dungeon, those who
      live in darkness.

RESPONSORIAL PSALM *Psalm 29:1–2, 3–4, 3, 9–10*

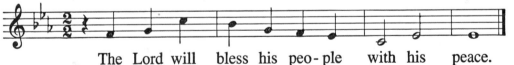

The Lord will bless his peo-ple with his peace.

Give to the LORD, you sons of God,
    give to the LORD glory and praise,
Give to the LORD the glory due his name;
    adore the LORD in holy attire. ℟.

The voice of the LORD is over the waters,
    the LORD, over vast waters.
The voice of the LORD is mighty;

the voice of the LORD is majestic. ℟.

The God of glory thunders,
    and in his temple all say, "Glory!"
The LORD is enthroned above the flood;
    the LORD is enthroned as king
      forever. ℟.

READING II *Acts 10:34–38*
Peter proceeded to speak to those gathered in the house of Cornelius, saying: "In truth, I see that God shows no partiality. Rather, in every nation whoever fears him and acts

uprightly is acceptable to him. You know the word that he sent to the Israelites as he proclaimed peace through Jesus Christ, who is Lord of all, what has happened all over Judea, beginning in Galilee after the baptism that John preached, how God anointed Jesus of Nazareth with the Holy Spirit and power. He went about doing good and healing all those oppressed by the devil, for God was with him."

GOSPEL *Matthew 3:13–17*
Jesus came from Galilee to John at the Jordan to be baptized by him. John tried to prevent him, saying, "I need to be baptized by you, and yet you are coming to me?" Jesus said to him in reply, "Allow it now, for thus it is fitting for us to fulfill all righteousness." Then he allowed him. After Jesus was baptized, he came up from the water and behold, the heavens were opened for him, and he saw the Spirit of God descending like a dove and coming upon him. And a voice came from the heavens, saying, "This is my beloved Son, with whom I am well pleased."

COMMUNION ANTIPHON *John 1:32, 34*
This is he of whom John said: I have seen and have given witness that this is the Son of God.

January 16, 2011
SECOND SUNDAY IN ORDINARY TIME

ENTRANCE ANTIPHON *Psalm 65:4*
May all the earth give you worship and praise, and break into song to your name, O God, Most High.

READING I *Isaiah 49:3, 5–6 / 64*

The LORD said to me: You are my servant,
Israel, through whom I show my glory.
Now the LORD has spoken
who formed me as his servant from the womb,
that Jacob may be brought back to him
and Israel gathered to him;
and I am made glorious in the sight of the LORD,
and my God is now my strength!
It is too little, the LORD says, for you to be my servant,
to raise up the tribes of Jacob,
and restore the survivors of Israel;
I will make you a light to the nations,
that my salvation may reach to the ends of the earth.

RESPONSORIAL PSALM *Psalm 40:2, 4, 7–8, 8–9, 10*

Here am I, Lord; here am I, Lord;   I come to do your will.

I have waited, waited for the LORD,
and he stooped toward me and heard my cry.

And he put a new song into my mouth,
a hymn to our God. ℟.

Sacrifice or offering you wished not,
but ears open to obedience you gave
me.
Holocausts or sin-offerings you sought
not;
then said I, "Behold I come." ℟.

"In the written scroll it is prescribed for
me,

to do your will, O my God, is my
delight,
and your law is within my heart!" ℟.

I announced your justice in the vast
assembly;
I did not restrain my lips, as you,
O LORD, know. ℟.

READING II
1 Corinthians 1:1–3

Paul, called to be an apostle of Christ Jesus by the will of God, and Sosthenes our brother, to the church of God that is in Corinth, to you who have been sanctified in Christ Jesus, called to be holy, with all those everywhere who call upon the name of our Lord Jesus Christ, their Lord and ours. Grace to you and peace from God our Father and the Lord Jesus Christ.

GOSPEL
John 1:29–34

John the Baptist saw Jesus coming toward him and said, "Behold, the Lamb of God, who takes away the sin of the world. He is the one of whom I said, 'A man is coming after me who ranks ahead of me because he existed before me.' I did not know him, but the reason why I came baptizing with water was that he might be made known to Israel." John testified further, saying, "I saw the Spirit come down like a dove from heaven and remain upon him. I did not know him, but the one who sent me to baptize with water told me, 'On whomever you see the Spirit come down and remain, he is the one who will baptize with the Holy Spirit.' Now I have seen and testified that he is the Son of God."

COMMUNION ANTIPHON
1 John 4:16

We know and believe in God's love for us.

January 23, 2011
THIRD SUNDAY IN ORDINARY TIME

ENTRANCE ANTIPHON
Psalm 95:1, 6

Sing a new song to the Lord! Sing to the Lord, all the earth. Truth and beauty surround him, he lives in holiness and glory.

READING I
Isaiah 8:23—9:3 / 67

First the LORD degraded the land of Zebulun and the land of Naphtali; but in the end he has glorified the seaward road, the land west of the Jordan, the District of the Gentiles.

Anguish has taken wing, dispelled is darkness:
for there is no gloom where but now there was distress.
The people who walked in darkness
have seen a great light;
upon those who dwelt in the land of gloom
a light has shone.
You have brought them abundant joy

and great rejoicing,
as they rejoice before you as at the harvest,
   as people make merry when dividing spoils.
For the yoke that burdened them,
   the pole on their shoulder,
and the rod of their taskmaster
   you have smashed, as on the day of Midian.

RESPONSORIAL PSALM
Psalm 27:1, 4, 13–14

The Lord is my light and my sal - va - tion.

The Lᴏʀᴅ is my light and my salvation;
   whom should I fear?
The Lᴏʀᴅ is my life's refuge;
   of whom should I be afraid? ℟.

One thing I ask of the Lᴏʀᴅ;
   this I seek:
to dwell in the house of the Lᴏʀᴅ
   all the days of my life,

that I may gaze on the loveliness of the
   Lᴏʀᴅ
and contemplate his temple. ℟.

I believe that I shall see the bounty of the
   Lᴏʀᴅ
in the land of the living.
Wait for the Lᴏʀᴅ with courage;
   be stouthearted, and wait for the
   Lᴏʀᴅ. ℟.

READING II
1 Corinthians 1:10–13, 17

I urge you, brothers and sisters, in the name of our Lord Jesus Christ, that all of you
agree in what you say, and that there be no divisions among you, but that you be united
in the same mind and in the same purpose. For it has been reported to me about you,
my brothers and sisters, by Chloe's people, that there are rivalries among you. I mean
that each of you is saying, "I belong to Paul," or "I belong to Apollos," or "I belong to
Cephas," or "I belong to Christ." Is Christ divided? Was Paul crucified for you? Or were
you baptized in the name of Paul? For Christ did not send me to baptize but to preach the
gospel, and not with the wisdom of human eloquence, so that the cross of Christ might
not be emptied of its meaning.

GOSPEL
Matthew 4:12–23 or 4:12–17

For short form read only the part in brackets.

[When Jesus heard that John had been arrested, he withdrew to Galilee. He left Nazareth
and went to live in Capernaum by the sea, in the region of Zebulun and Naphtali, that
what had been said through Isaiah the prophet might be fulfilled:
   Land of Zebulun and land of Naphtali,
      the way to the sea, beyond the Jordan,
      Galilee of the Gentiles,
   the people who sit in darkness have seen a great light,
   on those dwelling in a land overshadowed by death
      light has arisen.
From that time on, Jesus began to preach and say, "Repent, for the kingdom of heaven
is at hand."]

As he was walking by the Sea of Galilee, he saw two brothers, Simon who is called Peter, and his brother Andrew, casting a net into the sea; they were fishermen. He said to them, "Come after me, and I will make you fishers of men." At once they left their nets and followed him. He walked along from there and saw two other brothers, James, the son of Zebedee, and his brother John. They were in a boat, with their father Zebedee, mending their nets. He called them, and immediately they left their boat and their father and followed him. He went around all of Galilee, teaching in their synagogues, proclaiming the gospel of the kingdom, and curing every disease and illness among the people.

COMMUNION ANTIPHON *John 8:12*
I am the light of the world, says the Lord; the man who follows me will have the light of life.

January 30, 2011
FOURTH SUNDAY IN ORDINARY TIME

ENTRANCE ANTIPHON *Psalm 105:47*
Save us, Lord our God, and gather us together from the nations, that we may proclaim your holy name and glory in your praise.

READING I *Zephaniah 2:3; 3:12–13 / 70*

Seek the LORD, all you humble of the
　　earth,
　who have observed his law;
seek justice, seek humility;
　　perhaps you may be sheltered
　　on the day of the LORD's anger.

But I will leave as a remnant in your
　　midst
　a people humble and lowly,

who shall take refuge in the name of the
　　LORD:
　the remnant of Israel.
They shall do no wrong
　and speak no lies;
nor shall there be found in their mouths
　a deceitful tongue;
they shall pasture and couch their flocks
　with none to disturb them.

RESPONSORIAL PSALM *Psalm 146:6–7, 8–9, 9–10*
Or: Alleluia.

Bless-ed the poor in spir-it; the king-dom of heav-en is theirs!

The LORD keeps faith forever,
  secures justice for the oppressed,
  gives food to the hungry.
The LORD sets captives free. ℟.

The LORD gives sight to the blind;
  the LORD raises up those who were
  bowed down.
The LORD loves the just;

the LORD protects strangers. ℟.

The fatherless and the widow the LORD
  sustains,
  but the way of the wicked he thwarts.
The LORD shall reign forever;
  your God, O Zion, through all
  generations. Alleluia. ℟.

READING II
1 Corinthians 1:26–31

Consider your own calling, brothers and sisters. Not many of you were wise by human standards, not many were powerful, not many were of noble birth. Rather, God chose the foolish of the world to shame the wise, and God chose the weak of the world to shame the strong, and God chose the lowly and despised of the world, those who count for nothing, to reduce to nothing those who are something, so that no human being might boast before God. It is due to him that you are in Christ Jesus, who became for us wisdom from God, as well as righteousness, sanctification, and redemption, so that, as it is written, "Whoever boasts, should boast in the Lord."

GOSPEL
Matthew 5:1–12a

When Jesus saw the crowds, he went up the mountain, and after he had sat down, his disciples came to him. He began to teach them, saying:
  "Blessed are the poor in spirit,
    for theirs is the kingdom of heaven.
  Blessed are they who mourn,
    for they will be comforted.
  Blessed are the meek,
    for they will inherit the land.
  Blessed are they who hunger and thirst for righteousness,
    for they will be satisfied.
  Blessed are the merciful,
    for they will be shown mercy.
  Blessed are the clean of heart,
    for they will see God.
  Blessed are the peacemakers,
    for they will be called children of God.
  Blessed are they who are persecuted for the sake of righteousness,
    for theirs is the kingdom of heaven.
Blessed are you when they insult you and persecute you and utter every kind of evil against you falsely because of me. Rejoice and be glad, for your reward will be great in heaven."

COMMUNION ANTIPHON
Matthew 5:3–4

Happy are the poor in spirit; the kingdom of heaven is theirs! Happy are the lowly; they shall inherit the land.

February 6, 2011

FIFTH SUNDAY IN ORDINARY TIME

ENTRANCE ANTIPHON *Psalm 94:6–7*
Come, let us worship the Lord. Let us bow down in the presence of our maker, for he is the Lord our God.

READING I *Isaiah 58:7–10 / 73*
Thus says the LORD:
   Share your bread with the hungry,
      shelter the oppressed and the homeless;
   clothe the naked when you see them,
      and do not turn your back on your own.
   Then your light shall break forth like the dawn,
      and your wound shall quickly be healed;
   your vindication shall go before you,
      and the glory of the LORD shall be your rear guard.
   Then you shall call, and the LORD will answer,
      you shall cry for help, and he will say: Here I am!
   If you remove from your midst
      oppression, false accusation and malicious speech;
   if you bestow your bread on the hungry
      and satisfy the afflicted;
   then light shall rise for you in the darkness,
      and the gloom shall become for you like midday.

RESPONSORIAL PSALM *Psalm 112:4–5, 6–7, 8–9*
Or: Alleluia.

The just man is a light in dark-ness to the up-right.

Light shines through the darkness for the
      upright;
   he is gracious and merciful and just.
Well for the man who is gracious and
      lends,
   who conducts his affairs with
      justice. ℟.

He shall never be moved;
   the just one shall be in everlasting
      remembrance.

An evil report he shall not fear;
   his heart is firm, trusting in the
      LORD. ℟.

His heart is steadfast; he shall not fear.
   Lavishly he gives to the poor;
his justice shall endure forever;
   his horn shall be exalted in
      glory. ℟.

READING II *1 Corinthians 2:1–5*
When I came to you, brothers and sisters, proclaiming the mystery of God, I did not come with sublimity of words or of wisdom. For I resolved to know nothing while I was

with you except Jesus Christ, and him crucified. I came to you in weakness and fear and much trembling, and my message and my proclamation were not with persuasive words of wisdom, but with a demonstration of Spirit and power, so that your faith might rest not on human wisdom but on the power of God.

GOSPEL
Matthew 5:13–16

Jesus said to his disciples: "You are the salt of the earth. But if salt loses its taste, with what can it be seasoned? It is no longer good for anything but to be thrown out and trampled underfoot. You are the light of the world. A city set on a mountain cannot be hidden. Nor do they light a lamp and then put it under a bushel basket; it is set on a lamp stand, where it gives light to all in the house. Just so, your light must shine before others, that they may see your good deeds and glorify your heavenly Father."

COMMUNION ANTIPHON
Matthew 5:5–6

Happy are the sorrowing; they shall be consoled. Happy those who hunger and thirst for what is right; they shall be satisfied.

February 13, 2011
SIXTH SUNDAY IN ORDINARY TIME

ENTRANCE ANTIPHON
Psalm 30:3–4

Lord, be my rock of safety, the stronghold that saves me. For the honor of your name, lead me and guide me.

READING I
Sirach 15:15–20 / 76

If you choose you can keep the
    commandments, they will save
      you;
  if you trust in God, you too shall live;
he has set before you fire and water;
  to whichever you choose, stretch
    forth your hand.
Before man are life and death, good
  and evil,
whichever he chooses shall be given
  him.
Immense is the wisdom of the Lord;
  he is mighty in power, and all-seeing.
The eyes of God are on those who fear
  him;
  he understands man's every deed.
No one does he command to act unjustly,
  to none does he give license to sin.

RESPONSORIAL PSALM
Psalm 119:1–2, 4–5, 17–18, 33–34

Bless - ed are they who fol - low the law of the Lord!

Blessed are they whose way is
  blameless,
  who walk in the law of the LORD.
Blessed are they who observe his
  decrees,
  who seek him with all their heart. ℟.

You have commanded that your precepts
  be diligently kept.
Oh, that I might be firm in the ways
  of keeping your statutes! ℟.

Be good to your servant, that I may live
and keep your words.
Open my eyes, that I may consider
the wonders of your law. ℟.

Instruct me, O LORD, in the way of

your statutes,
that I may exactly observe them.
Give me discernment, that I may observe
your law
and keep it with all my heart. ℟.

READING II 1 Corinthians 2:6–10

Brothers and sisters: We speak a wisdom to those who are mature, not a wisdom of this age, nor of the rulers of this age who are passing away. Rather, we speak God's wisdom, mysterious, hidden, which God predetermined before the ages for our glory, and which none of the rulers of this age knew; for, if they had known it, they would not have crucified the Lord of glory. But as it is written:

What eye has not seen, and ear has not heard,
and what has not entered the human heart,
what God has prepared for those who love him,

this God has revealed to us through the Spirit.

For the Spirit scrutinizes everything, even the depths of God.

GOSPEL Matthew 5:17–37 or 5:20–22a, 27–28, 33–34a, 37

For short form read only the parts in brackets.

[Jesus said to his disciples:] "Do not think that I have come to abolish the law or the prophets. I have come not to abolish but to fulfill. Amen, I say to you, until heaven and earth pass away, not the smallest letter or the smallest part of a letter will pass from the law, until all things have taken place. Therefore, whoever breaks one of the least of these commandments and teaches others to do so will be called least in the kingdom of heaven. But whoever obeys and teaches these commandments will be called greatest in the kingdom of heaven. [I tell you, unless your righteousness surpasses that of the scribes and Pharisees, you will not enter the kingdom of heaven.

"You have heard that it was said to your ancestors *You shall not kill; and whoever kills will be liable to judgment.* But I say to you, whoever is angry with his brother will be liable to judgment;] and whoever says to his brother, 'Raqa,' will be answerable to the Sanhedrin; and whoever says, 'You fool,' will be liable to fiery Gehenna. Therefore, if you bring your gift to the altar, and there recall that your brother has anything against you, leave your gift there at the altar, go first and be reconciled with your brother, and then come and offer your gift. Settle with your opponent quickly while on the way to court. Otherwise your opponent will hand you over to the judge, and the judge will hand you over to the guard, and you will be thrown into prison. Amen, I say to you, you will not be released until you have paid the last penny.

["You have heard that it was said, *You shall not commit adultery.* But I say to you, everyone who looks at a woman with lust has already committed adultery with her in his heart.] If your right eye causes you to sin, tear it out and throw it away. It is better for you to lose one of your members than to have your whole body thrown into Gehenna. And if your right hand causes you to sin, cut it off and throw it away. It is better for you to lose one of your members than to have your whole body go into Gehenna.

"It was also said, *Whoever divorces his wife must give her a bill of divorce.* But I say to you, whoever divorces his wife —unless the marriage is unlawful— causes her to commit adultery, and whoever marries a divorced woman commits adultery.

["Again you have heard that it was said to your ancestors, *Do not take a false oath, but make good to the Lord all that you vow.* But I say to you, do not swear at all;] not by heaven, for it is God's throne; nor by the earth, for it is his footstool; nor by Jerusalem, for it is the city of the great King. Do not swear by your head, for you cannot make a single hair white or black. [Let your 'Yes' mean 'Yes,' and your 'No' mean 'No.' Anything more is from the evil one."]

COMMUNION ANTIPHON　　　　　　　　　　　　　　　　　　　　　*John 3:16*
God loved the world so much, he gave his only Son, that all who believe in him might not perish, but might have eternal life.

February 20, 2011
SEVENTH SUNDAY IN ORDINARY TIME

ENTRANCE ANTIPHON　　　　　　　　　　　　　　　　　　　　　*Psalm 12:6*
Lord, your mercy is my hope, my heart rejoices in your saving power. I will sing to the Lord for his goodness to me.

READING I　　　　　　　　　　　　　　　　　　　*Leviticus 19:1–2, 17–18 / 79*
The LORD said to Moses, "Speak to the whole Israelite community and tell them: Be holy, for I, the LORD, your God, am holy.

"You shall not bear hatred for your brother or sister in your heart. Though you may have to reprove your fellow citizen, do not incur sin because of him. Take no revenge and cherish no grudge against any of your people. You shall love your neighbor as your-self. I am the LORD."

RESPONSORIAL PSALM　　　　　　　　　　　　*Psalm 103:1–2, 3–4, 8, 10, 12–13*

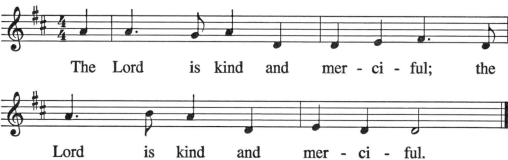

The Lord is kind and mer - ci - ful; the
Lord is kind and mer - ci - ful.

Bless the LORD, O my soul;
　and all my being, bless his holy name.
Bless the LORD, O my soul,
　and forget not all his benefits. ℟.

He pardons all your iniquities,
　heals all your ills.
He redeems your life from destruction,
　crowns you with kindness and
　　compassion. ℟.

Merciful and gracious is the LORD,
　slow to anger and abounding in

kindness.
Not according to our sins does he deal
　with us,
nor does he requite us according to
　our crimes. ℟.

As far as the east is from the west,
　so far has he put our transgressions
　from us.
As a father has compassion on his
　children,
so the LORD has compassion on
　those who fear him. ℟.

READING II   *1 Corinthians 3:16–23*

Brothers and sisters: Do you not know that you are the temple of God, and that the Spirit of God dwells in you? If anyone destroys God's temple, God will destroy that person; for the temple of God, which you are, is holy.

Let no one deceive himself. If any one among you considers himself wise in this age, let him become a fool, so as to become wise. For the wisdom of this world is foolishness in the eyes of God, for it is written:

God catches the wise in their own ruses,

and again:

The Lord knows the thoughts of the wise,
*   that they are vain.*

So let no one boast about human beings, for everything belongs to you, Paul or Apollos or Cephas, or the world or life or death, or the present or the future: all belong to you, and you to Christ, and Christ to God.

GOSPEL   *Matthew 5:38–48*

Jesus said to his disciples: "You have heard that it was said, *An eye for an eye and a tooth for a tooth*. But I say to you, offer no resistance to one who is evil. When someone strikes you on your right cheek, turn the other one as well. If anyone wants to go to law with you over your tunic, hand over your cloak as well. Should anyone press you into service for one mile, go for two miles. Give to the one who asks of you, and do not turn your back on one who wants to borrow.

"You have heard that it was said, *You shall love your neighbor and hate your enemy*. But I say to you, love your enemies and pray for those who persecute you, that you may be children of your heavenly Father, for he makes his sun rise on the bad and the good, and causes rain to fall on the just and the unjust. For if you love those who love you, what recompense will you have? Do not the tax collectors do the same? And if you greet your brothers only, what is unusual about that? Do not the pagans do the same? So be perfect, just as your heavenly Father is perfect."

COMMUNION ANTIPHON   *Psalm 9:2–3*

I will tell all your marvelous works. I will rejoice and be glad in you, and sing to your name, Most High.

February 27, 2011

EIGHTH SUNDAY IN ORDINARY TIME

ENTRANCE ANTIPHON   *Psalm 17:19–20*

The Lord has been my strength; he has led me into freedom. He saved me because he loves me.

READING I   *Isaiah 49:14–15 / 82*

Zion said, "The LORD has forsaken me;
    my Lord has forgotten me."
Can a mother forget her infant,
    be without tenderness for the child

of her womb?
Even should she forget,
    I will never forget you.

RESPONSORIAL PSALM

Psalm 62:2–3, 6–7, 8–9

Rest in God a-lone, rest in God a-lone, my soul.

Only in God is my soul at rest;
    from him comes my salvation.
He only is my rock and my salvation,
    my stronghold; I shall not be
        disturbed at all. ℟.

Only in God be at rest, my soul,
    for from him comes my hope.
He only is my rock and my salvation,

my stronghold; I shall not be
    disturbed. ℟.

With God is my safety and my glory,
    he is the rock of my strength; my
        refuge is in God.
Trust in him at all times, O my people!
    Pour out your hearts before him. ℟.

READING II

1 Corinthians 4:1–5

Brothers and sisters: Thus should one regard us: as servants of Christ and stewards of the mysteries of God. Now it is of course required of stewards that they be found trustworthy. It does not concern me in the least that I be judged by you or any human tribunal; I do not even pass judgment on myself; I am not conscious of anything against me, but I do not thereby stand acquitted; the one who judges me is the Lord. Therefore do not make any judgment before the appointed time, until the Lord comes, for he will bring to light what is hidden in darkness and will manifest the motives of our hearts, and then everyone will receive praise from God.

GOSPEL

Matthew 6:24–34

Jesus said to his disciples: "No one can serve two masters. He will either hate one and love the other, or be devoted to one and despise the other. You cannot serve God and mammon.

"Therefore I tell you, do not worry about your life, what you will eat or drink, or about your body, what you will wear. Is not life more than food and the body more than clothing? Look at the birds in the sky; they do not sow or reap, they gather nothing into barns, yet your heavenly Father feeds them. Are not you more important than they? Can any of you by worrying add a single moment to your life-span? Why are you anxious about clothes? Learn from the way the wild flowers grow. They do not work or spin. But I tell you that not even Solomon in all his splendor was clothed like one of them. If God so clothes the grass of the field, which grows today and is thrown into the oven tomorrow, will he not much more provide for you, O you of little faith? So do not worry and say, 'What are we to eat?' or 'What are we to drink?' or 'What are we to wear?' All these things the pagans seek. Your heavenly Father knows that you need them all. But seek first the kingdom of God and his righteousness, and all these things will be given you besides. Do not worry about tomorrow; tomorrow will take care of itself. Sufficient for a day is its own evil."

COMMUNION ANTIPHON

Matthew 28:20

I, the Lord, am with you always, until the end of the world.

NINTH SUNDAY IN ORDINARY TIME

ENTRANCE ANTIPHON *Psalm 24:16, 18*

O look at me and be merciful, for I am wretched and alone. See my hardship and my poverty, and pardon all my sins.

READING I *Deuteronomy 11:18, 26–28, 32 / 85*

Moses told the people, "Take these words of mine into your heart and soul. Bind them at your wrist as a sign, and let them be a pendant on your forehead.

"I set before you here, this day, a blessing and a curse: a blessing for obeying the commandments of the LORD, your God, which I enjoin on you today; a curse if you do not obey the commandments of the LORD, your God, but turn aside from the way I ordain for you today, to follow other gods, whom you have not known. Be careful to observe all the statutes and decrees that I set before you today."

RESPONSORIAL PSALM *Psalm 31:2–3, 3–4, 17, 25*

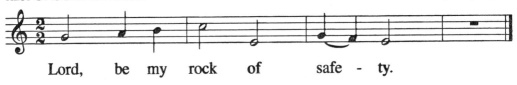

Lord, be my rock of safe - ty.

In you, O LORD, I take refuge;
   let me never be put to shame.
In your justice rescue me,
    incline your ear to me,
    make haste to deliver me! ℟.

Be my rock of refuge,
   a stronghold to give me safety.

You are my rock and my fortress;
   for your name's sake you will lead
   and guide me. ℟.

Let your face shine upon your servant;
   save me in your kindness.
Take courage and be stouthearted,
   all you who hope in the LORD. ℟.

READING II *Romans 3:21–25, 28*

Brothers and sisters: Now the righteousness of God has been manifested apart from the law, though testified to by the law and the prophets, the righteousness of God through faith in Jesus Christ for all who believe. For there is no distinction; all have sinned and are deprived of the glory of God. They are justified freely by his grace through the redemption in Christ Jesus, whom God set forth as an expiation, through faith, by his blood. For we consider that a person is justified by faith apart from works of the law.

GOSPEL *Matthew 7:21–27*

Jesus said to his disciples: "Not everyone who says to me, 'Lord, Lord,' will enter the kingdom of heaven, but only the one who does the will of my Father in heaven. Many will say to me on that day, 'Lord, Lord, did we not prophesy in your name? Did we not drive out demons in your name? Did we not do mighty deeds in your name?' Then I will declare to them solemnly, 'I never knew you. Depart from me, you evildoers.'

"Everyone who listens to these words of mine and acts on them will be like a wise man who built his house on rock. The rain fell, the floods came, and the winds blew and buffeted the house. But it did not collapse; it had been set solidly on rock. And everyone who listens to these words of mine but does not act on them will be like a fool who built his house on sand. The rain fell, the floods came, and the winds blew and buffeted the house. And it collapsed and was completely ruined."

COMMUNION ANTIPHON *Psalm 16:6*
I call upon you, God, for you will answer me; bend your ear and hear my prayer.

March 9, 2011
ASH WEDNESDAY

ENTRANCE ANTIPHON *See Wisdom 11:24–25, 27*
Lord, you are merciful to all, and hate nothing you have created. You overlook the sins of men to bring them to repentance. You are the Lord our God.

READING I *Joel 2:12–18 / 219*

Even now, says the LORD,
   return to me with your whole heart,
   with fasting, and weeping, and
      mourning;
Rend your hearts, not your garments,
   and return to the LORD, your God.
For gracious and merciful is he,
   slow to anger, rich in kindness,
   and relenting in punishment.
Perhaps he will again relent
   and leave behind him a blessing,
Offerings and libations,
   for the LORD, your God.

Blow the trumpet in Zion!
   proclaim a fast,
   call an assembly;
Gather the people,
   notify the congregation;

Assemble the elders,
   gather the children
   and the infants at the breast;
Let the bridegroom quit his room,
   and the bride her chamber.
Between the porch and the altar
   let the priests, the ministers of the
   LORD, weep,
And say, "Spare, O LORD, your people,
   and make not your heritage a
      reproach,
   with the nations ruling over them!
Why should they say among the peoples,
   'Where is their God?'"

Then the LORD was stirred to concern for
   his land
   and took pity on his people.

RESPONSORIAL PSALM *Psalm 51:3–4, 5–6ab, 12–13, 14 and 17*

Be mer-ci-ful, O Lord, for we have sinned.

Have mercy on me, O God, in your
   goodness;
   in the greatness of your compassion
   wipe out my offense.
Thoroughly wash me from my guilt
   and of my sin cleanse me. ℞.

For I acknowledge my offense,
   and my sin is before me always:
"Against you only have I sinned,
   and done what is evil in your
   sight." ℞.

A clean heart create for me, O God,
and a steadfast spirit renew within
me.
Cast me not out from your presence,
and your Holy Spirit take not from
me. ℟.

Give me back the joy of your salvation,
and a willing spirit sustain in me.
O Lord, open my lips,
and my mouth shall proclaim your
praise. ℟.

READING II
2 Corinthians 5:20—6:2

Brothers and sisters: We are ambassadors for Christ, as if God were appealing through us. We implore you on behalf of Christ, be reconciled to God. For our sake he made him to be sin who did not know sin, so that we might become the righteousness of God in him.

Working together, then, we appeal to you not to receive the grace of God in vain. For he says: *In an acceptable time I heard you, and on the day of salvation I helped you.* Behold, now is a very acceptable time; behold, now is the day of salvation.

GOSPEL
Matthew 6:1–6, 16–18

Jesus said to his disciples: "Take care not to perform righteous deeds in order that people may see them; otherwise, you will have no recompense from your heavenly Father. When you give alms, do not blow a trumpet before you, as the hypocrites do in the synagogues and in the streets to win the praise of others. Amen, I say to you, they have received their reward. But when you give alms, do not let your left hand know what your right is doing, so that your almsgiving may be secret. And your Father who sees in secret will repay you.

"When you pray, do not be like the hypocrites, who love to stand and pray in the synagogues and on street corners so that others may see them. Amen, I say to you, they have received their reward. But when you pray, go to your inner room, close the door, and pray to your Father in secret. And your Father who sees in secret will repay you.

"When you fast, do not look gloomy like the hypocrites. They neglect their appearance, so that they may appear to others to be fasting. Amen, I say to you, they have received their reward. But when you fast, anoint your head and wash your face, so that you may not appear to be fasting, except to your Father who is hidden. And your Father who sees what is hidden will repay you."

COMMUNION ANTIPHON
Psalm 1:2–3

The man who meditates day and night on the law of the Lord will yield fruit in due season.

March 13, 2011

FIRST SUNDAY OF LENT

ENTRANCE ANTIPHON
Psalm 90:15–16

When he calls to me, I will answer; I will rescue him and give him honor. Long life and contentment will be his.

READING I
Genesis 2:7–9; 3:1–7 / 22

The LORD God formed man out of the clay of the ground and blew into his nostrils the breath of life, and so man became a living being.

Then the LORD God planted a garden in Eden, in the east, and placed there the man whom he had formed. Out of the ground the LORD God made various trees grow that were delightful to look at and good for food, with the tree of life in the middle of the garden and the tree of the knowledge of good and evil.

Now the serpent was the most cunning of all the animals that the LORD God had made. The serpent asked the woman, "Did God really tell you not to eat from any of the trees in the garden?" The woman answered the serpent: "We may eat of the fruit of the trees in the garden; it is only about the fruit of the tree in the middle of the garden that God said, 'You shall not eat it or even touch it, lest you die.'" But the serpent said to the woman: "You certainly will not die! No, God knows well that the moment you eat of it your eyes will be opened and you will be like gods who know what is good and what is evil." The woman saw that the tree was good for food, pleasing to the eyes, and desirable for gaining wisdom. So she took some of its fruit and ate it; and she also gave some to her husband, who was with her, and he ate it. Then the eyes of both of them were opened, and they realized that they were naked; so they sewed fig leaves together and made loincloths for themselves.

RESPONSORIAL PSALM *Psalm 51:3–4, 5–6, 12–13, 14, 17*

Be mer-ci-ful, O Lord, for we have sinned.

Have mercy on me, O God, in your
goodness;
in the greatness of your compassion
wipe out my offense.
Thoroughly wash me from my guilt
and of my sin cleanse me. ℟.

For I acknowledge my offense,
and my sin is before me always:
"Against you only have I sinned,
and done what is evil in your
sight." ℟.

A clean heart create for me, O God,
and a steadfast spirit renew within
me.
Cast me not out from your presence,
and your Holy Spirit take not from
me. ℟.

Give me back the joy of your salvation,
and a willing spirit sustain in me.
O Lord, open my lips,
and my mouth shall proclaim your
praise. ℟.

READING II *Romans 5:12–19 or 5:12, 17–19*
For short form read only the parts in brackets.

[Brothers and sisters: Through one man sin entered the world, and through sin, death, and thus death came to all men, inasmuch as all sinned—] for up to the time of the law, sin was in the world, though sin is not accounted when there is no law. But death reigned from Adam to Moses, even over those who did not sin after the pattern of the trespass of Adam, who is the type of the one who was to come.

But the gift is not like the transgression. For if by the transgression of the one, the many died, how much more did the grace of God and the gracious gift of the one man Jesus Christ overflow for the many. And the gift is not like the result of the one who sinned. For after one sin there was the judgment that brought condemnation; but the gift, after many transgressions, brought acquittal. [For if, by the transgression of the one, death came to reign through that one, how much more will those who receive the abundance of grace and of the gift of justification come to reign in life through the one Jesus Christ. In conclusion, just as through one transgression condemnation came upon all, so, through one righteous act, acquittal and life came to all. For just as through the disobedience of the one man the many were made sinners, so, through the obedience of the one, the many will be made righteous.]

GOSPEL *Matthew 4:1–11*

At that time Jesus was led by the Spirit into the desert to be tempted by the devil. He fasted for forty days and forty nights, and afterwards he was hungry. The tempter approached and said to him, "If you are the Son of God, command that these stones become loaves of bread."
He said in reply, "It is written:
> One does not live on bread alone,
>> but on every word that comes forth
> from the mouth of God."

Then the devil took him to the holy city, and made him stand on the parapet of the temple, and said to him, "If you are the Son of God, throw yourself down. For it is written:
> He will command his angels concerning you
>> and with their hands they will support you,
> lest you dash your foot against a stone."

Jesus answered him, "Again it is written, *You shall not put the Lord, your God, to the test.*" Then the devil took him up to a very high mountain, and showed him all the kingdoms of the world in their magnificence, and he said to him, "All these I shall give to you, if you will prostrate yourself and worship me." At this, Jesus said to him, "Get away, Satan! It is written:
> The Lord, your God, shall you worship
>> and him alone shall you serve."

Then the devil left him and, behold, angels came and ministered to him.

COMMUNION ANTIPHON *Matthew 4:4*

Man does not live on bread alone, but on every word that comes from the mouth of God.

March 20, 2011

SECOND SUNDAY OF LENT

ENTRANCE ANTIPHON *Psalm 24:6, 3, 22*

Remember your mercies, Lord, your tenderness from ages past. Do not let our enemies triumph over us; O God, deliver Israel from all her distress.

READING I *Genesis 12:1–4a / 25*

The Lord said to Abram: "Go forth from the land of your kinsfolk and from your father's house to a land that I will show you.

> "I will make of you a great nation,
>> and I will bless you;

I will make your name great,
 so that you will be a blessing.
I will bless those who bless you
 and curse those who curse you.
All the communities of the earth
 shall find blessing in you."

Abram went as the Lord directed him.

RESPONSORIAL PSALM
Psalm 33:4–5, 18–19, 20, 22

Lord, let your mer-cy be on us, as we place our trust in you.

Upright is the word of the Lord,
 and all his works are trustworthy.
He loves justice and right;
 of the kindness of the Lord the earth
  is full. ℟.

See, the eyes of the Lord are upon those
 who fear him,
 upon those who hope for his
  kindness,

to deliver them from death
 and preserve them in spite of
  famine. ℟.

Our soul waits for the Lord,
 who is our help and our shield.
May your kindness, O Lord, be
 upon us
 who have put our hope in you. ℟.

READING II
2 Timothy 1:8b–10
Beloved: Bear your share of hardship for the gospel with the strength that comes from God.

He saved us and called us to a holy life, not according to our works but according to his own design and the grace bestowed on us in Christ Jesus before time began, but now made manifest through the appearance of our savior Christ Jesus, who destroyed death and brought life and immortality to light through the gospel.

GOSPEL
Matthew 17:1–9
Jesus took Peter, James, and John his brother, and led them up a high mountain by themselves. And he was transfigured before them; his face shone like the sun and his clothes became white as light. And behold, Moses and Elijah appeared to them, conversing with him. Then Peter said to Jesus in reply, "Lord, it is good that we are here. If you wish, I will make three tents here, one for you, one for Moses, and one for Elijah." While he was still speaking, behold, a bright cloud cast a shadow over them, then from the cloud came a voice that said, "This is my beloved Son, with whom I am well pleased; listen to him." When the disciples heard this, they fell prostrate and were very much afraid. But Jesus came and touched them, saying, "Rise, and do not be afraid." And when the disciples raised their eyes, they saw no one else but Jesus alone.

As they were coming down from the mountain, Jesus charged them, "Do not tell the vision to anyone until the Son of Man has been raised from the dead."

COMMUNION ANTIPHON
Matthew 17:5
This is my Son, my beloved, in whom is all my delight: listen to him.

March 27, 2011
THIRD SUNDAY OF LENT

ENTRANCE ANTIPHON *Psalm 24:15–16*

My eyes are ever fixed on the Lord, for he releases my feet from the snare. O look at me and be merciful, for I am wretched and alone.

If the first scrutiny takes place today: *Ezekiel 36:23–26*

I will prove my holiness through you. I will gather you from the ends of the earth: I will pour clean water on you and wash away all your sins. I will give you a new spirit within you, says the Lord.

READING I *Exodus 17:3–7 / 28*

In those days, in their thirst for water, the people grumbled against Moses, saying, "Why did you ever make us leave Egypt? Was it just to have us die here of thirst with our children and our livestock?" So Moses cried out to the LORD, "What shall I do with this people? A little more and they will stone me!" The LORD answered Moses, "Go over there in front of the people, along with some of the elders of Israel, holding in your hand, as you go, the staff with which you struck the river. I will be standing there in front of you on the rock in Horeb. Strike the rock, and the water will flow from it for the people to drink." This Moses did, in the presence of the elders of Israel. The place was called Massah and Meribah, because the Israelites quarreled there and tested the LORD, saying, "Is the LORD in our midst or not?"

RESPONSORIAL PSALM *Psalm 95:1–2, 6–7, 8–9*

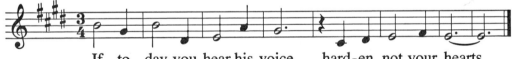

If to-day you hear his voice, hard-en not your hearts.

Come, let us sing joyfully to the LORD;
    let us acclaim the Rock of our
      salvation.
Let us come into his presence with
    thanksgiving;
    let us joyfully sing psalms to him. ℟.

Come, let us bow down in worship;
    let us kneel before the LORD who
      made us.
For he is our God,

and we are the people he shepherds,
    the flock he guides. ℟.

Oh, that today you would hear his voice:
    "Harden not your hearts as at
      Meribah,
    as in the day of Massah in the desert,
where your fathers tempted me;
    they tested me though they had seen
      my works." ℟.

READING II *Romans 5:1–2, 5–8*

Brothers and sisters: Since we have been justified by faith, we have peace with God through our Lord Jesus Christ, through whom we have gained access by faith to this grace in which we stand, and we boast in hope of the glory of God.

And hope does not disappoint, because the love of God has been poured out into our hearts through the Holy Spirit who has been given to us. For Christ, while we were still helpless, died at the appointed time for the ungodly. Indeed, only with difficulty does one die for a just person, though perhaps for a good person one might even find courage to die. But God proves his love for us in that while we were still sinners Christ died for us.

GOSPEL
John 4:5–42 or 4:5–15, 19b–26, 39a, 40–42

For short form read only the parts in brackets.

[Jesus came to a town of Samaria called Sychar, near the plot of land that Jacob had given to his son Joseph. Jacob's well was there. Jesus, tired from his journey, sat down there at the well. It was about noon.

A woman of Samaria came to draw water. Jesus said to her, "Give me a drink." His disciples had gone into the town to buy food. The Samaritan woman said to him, "How can you, a Jew, ask me, a Samaritan woman, for a drink?" —For Jews use nothing in common with Samaritans—. Jesus answered and said to her, "If you knew the gift of God and who is saying to you, 'Give me a drink,' you would have asked him and he would have given you living water." The woman said to him, "Sir, you do not even have a bucket and the cistern is deep; where then can you get this living water? Are you greater than our father Jacob, who gave us this cistern and drank from it himself with his children and his flocks?" Jesus answered and said to her, "Everyone who drinks this water will be thirsty again; but whoever drinks the water I shall give will never thirst; the water I shall give will become in him a spring of water welling up to eternal life." The woman said to him, "Sir, give me this water, so that I may not be thirsty or have to keep coming here to draw water."]

Jesus said to her, "Go call your husband and come back." The woman answered and said to him, "I do not have a husband." Jesus answered her, "You are right in saying, 'I do not have a husband.' For you have had five husbands, and the one you have now is not your husband. What you have said is true." The woman said to him, "Sir, [I can see that you are a prophet. Our ancestors worshiped on this mountain; but you people say that the place to worship is in Jerusalem." Jesus said to her, "Believe me, woman, the hour is coming when you will worship the Father neither on this mountain nor in Jerusalem. You people worship what you do not understand; we worship what we understand, because salvation is from the Jews. But the hour is coming, and is now here, when true worshipers will worship the Father in Spirit and truth; and indeed the Father seeks such people to worship him. God is Spirit, and those who worship him must worship in Spirit and truth." The woman said to him, "I know that the Messiah is coming, the one called the Christ; when he comes, he will tell us everything." Jesus said to her, "I am he, the one speaking with you."]

At that moment his disciples returned, and were amazed that he was talking with a woman, but still no one said, "What are you looking for?" or "Why are you talking with her?" The woman left her water jar and went into the town and said to the people, "Come see a man who told me everything I have done. Could he possibly be the Christ?" They went out of the town and came to him. Meanwhile, the disciples urged him, "Rabbi, eat." But he said to them, "I have food to eat of which you do not know." So the disciples said to one another, "Could someone have brought him something to eat?" Jesus said to them, "My food is to do the will of the one who sent me and to finish his work. Do you not say, 'In four months the harvest will be here'? I tell you, look up and see the fields ripe for the harvest. The reaper is already receiving payment and gathering crops for eternal life, so that the sower and reaper can rejoice together. For here the saying is verified that 'One sows and another reaps.' I sent you to reap what you have not worked for; others have done the work, and you are sharing the fruits of their work."

[Many of the Samaritans of that town began to believe in him] because of the word of the woman who testified, "He told me everything I have done." [When the Samaritans came to him, they invited him to stay with them; and he stayed there two days. Many more began to believe in him because of his word, and they said to the woman, "We no longer believe because of your word; for we have heard for ourselves, and we know that this is truly the savior of the world."]

COMMUNION ANTIPHON *John 4:13–14*
Whoever drinks the water that I shall give him, says the Lord, will have a spring inside him, welling up for eternal life.

April 3, 2011
FOURTH SUNDAY OF LENT

ENTRANCE ANTIPHON *Isaiah 66:10–11*
Rejoice, Jerusalem! Be glad for her, you who love her; rejoice with her, you who mourned for her, and you will find contentment at her consoling breasts.

If the second scrutiny takes place today: *Ezekiel 36:23–26*
I will prove my holiness through you. I will gather you from the ends of the earth: I will pour clean water on you and wash away all your sins. I will give you a new spirit within you, says the Lord.

READING I *1 Samuel 16:1b, 6–7, 10–13a / 31*
The LORD said to Samuel: "Fill your horn with oil, and be on your way. I am sending you to Jesse of Bethlehem, for I have chosen my king from among his sons."

As Jesse and his sons came to the sacrifice, Samuel looked at Eliab and thought, "Surely the LORD's anointed is here before him." But the LORD said to Samuel: "Do not judge from his appearance or from his lofty stature, because I have rejected him. Not as man sees does God see, because man sees the appearance but the LORD looks into the heart." In the same way Jesse presented seven sons before Samuel, but Samuel said to Jesse, "The LORD has not chosen any one of these." Then Samuel asked Jesse, "Are these all the sons you have?" Jesse replied, "There is still the youngest, who is tending the sheep." Samuel said to Jesse, "Send for him; we will not begin the sacrificial banquet until he arrives here." Jesse sent and had the young man brought to them. He was ruddy, a youth handsome to behold and making a splendid appearance. The LORD said, "There—anoint him, for this is the one!" Then Samuel, with the horn of oil in hand, anointed David in the presence of his brothers; and from that day on, the spirit of the LORD rushed upon David.

RESPONSORIAL PSALM *Psalm 23:1–3a, 3b–4, 5, 6*

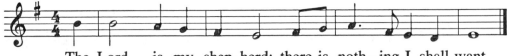

The Lord   is my shep-herd; there is noth-ing I shall want.

The LORD is my shepherd; I shall not
    want.
In verdant pastures he gives me

repose;
beside restful waters he leads me;
    he refreshes my soul. ℟.

He guides me in right paths
for his name's sake.
Even though I walk in the dark valley
I fear no evil; for you are at my side
with your rod and your staff
that give me courage. ℟.

You spread the table before me
in the sight of my foes;

you anoint my head with oil;
my cup overflows. ℟.

Only goodness and kindness follow me
all the days of my life;
and I shall dwell in the house of the
LORD
for years to come. ℟.

READING II
Ephesians 5:8–14

Brothers and sisters: You were once darkness, but now you are light in the Lord. Live as children of light, for light produces every kind of goodness and righteousness and truth. Try to learn what is pleasing to the Lord. Take no part in the fruitless works of darkness; rather expose them, for it is shameful even to mention the things done by them in secret; but everything exposed by the light becomes visible, for everything that becomes visible is light. Therefore, it says:
"Awake, O sleeper,
and arise from the dead,
and Christ will give you light."

GOSPEL
John 9:1–41 or 9:1, 6–9, 13–17, 34–38

For short form read only the parts in brackets.

[As Jesus passed by he saw a man blind from birth.] His disciples asked him, "Rabbi, who sinned, this man or his parents, that he was born blind?" Jesus answered, "Neither he nor his parents sinned; it is so that the works of God might be made visible through him. We have to do the works of the one who sent me while it is day. Night is coming when no one can work. While I am in the world, I am the light of the world." When he had said this, [he spat on the ground and made clay with the saliva, and smeared the clay on his eyes, and said to him, "Go wash in the Pool of Siloam" —which means Sent—. So he went and washed, and came back able to see.

His neighbors and those who had seen him earlier as a beggar said, "Isn't this the one who used to sit and beg?" Some said, "It is," but others said, "No, he just looks like him." He said, "I am."] So they said to him, "How were your eyes opened?" He replied, "The man called Jesus made clay and anointed my eyes and told me, 'Go to Siloam and wash.' So I went there and washed and was able to see." And they said to him, "Where is he?" He said, "I don't know."

[They brought the one who was once blind to the Pharisees. Now Jesus had made clay and opened his eyes on a sabbath. So then the Pharisees also asked him how he was able to see. He said to them, "He put clay on my eyes, and I washed, and now I can see." So some of the Pharisees said, "This man is not from God, because he does not keep the sabbath." But others said, "How can a sinful man do such signs?" And there was a division among them. So they said to the blind man again, "What do you have to say about him, since he opened your eyes?" He said, "He is a prophet."]

Now the Jews did not believe that he had been blind and gained his sight until they summoned the parents of the one who had gained his sight. They asked them, "Is this your son, who you say was born blind? How does he now see?" His parents answered and said, "We know that this is our son and that he was born blind. We do not know how he sees now, nor do we know who opened his eyes. Ask him, he is of age; he can speak for himself." His parents said this because they were afraid of the Jews, for the Jews had already agreed that if anyone acknowledged him as the Christ, he would be expelled from the synagogue. For this reason his parents said, "He is of age; question him."

So a second time they called the man who had been blind and said to him, "Give God the praise! We know that this man is a sinner." He replied, "If he is a sinner, I do not know. One thing I do know is that I was blind and now I see." So they said to him, "What did he do to you? How did he open your eyes?" He answered them, "I told you already and you did not listen. Why do you want to hear it again? Do you want to become his disciples, too?" They ridiculed him and said, "You are that man's disciple; we are disciples of Moses! We know that God spoke to Moses, but we do not know where this one is from." The man answered and said to them, "This is what is so amazing, that you do not know where he is from, yet he opened my eyes. We know that God does not listen to sinners, but if one is devout and does his will, he listens to him. It is unheard of that anyone ever opened the eyes of a person born blind. If this man were not from God, he would not be able to do anything." [They answered and said to him, "You were born totally in sin, and are you trying to teach us?" Then they threw him out.

When Jesus heard that they had thrown him out, he found him and said, "Do you believe in the Son of Man?" He answered and said, "Who is he, sir, that I may believe in him?" Jesus said to him, "You have seen him, the one speaking with you is he." He said, "I do believe, Lord," and he worshiped him.] Then Jesus said, "I came into this world for judgment, so that those who do not see might see, and those who do see might become blind."

Some of the Pharisees who were with him heard this and said to him, "Surely we are not also blind, are we?" Jesus said to them, "If you were blind, you would have no sin; but now you are saying, 'We see,' so your sin remains."

COMMUNION ANTIPHON *See John 9:11*
The Lord rubbed my eyes; I went away and washed; then I could see, and I believed in God.

April 10, 2011

FIFTH SUNDAY OF LENT

ENTRANCE ANTIPHON *Psalm 42:1–2*
Give me justice, O God, and defend my cause against the wicked; rescue me from deceitful and unjust men. You, O God, are my refuge.

If the third scrutiny takes place today: *Ezekiel 36:23–26*
I will prove my holiness through you. I will gather you from the ends of the earth: I will pour clean water on you and wash away all your sins. I will give you a new spirit within you, says the Lord.

READING I *Ezekiel 37:12–14 / 34*
Thus says the Lord GOD: O my people, I will open your graves and have you rise from them, and bring you back to the land of Israel. Then you shall know that I am the LORD, when I open your graves and have you rise from them, O my people! I will put my spirit in you that you may live, and I will settle you upon your land; thus you shall know that I am the LORD. I have promised, and I will do it, says the LORD.

RESPONSORIAL PSALM

Psalm 130:1–2, 3–4, 5–6, 7–8

With the Lord there is mer-cy, and full-ness of re-demp-tion.

Out of the depths I cry to you, O LORD;
    LORD, hear my voice!
Let your ears be attentive
    to my voice in supplication. ℟.

I trust in the LORD;
    my soul trusts in his word.
More than sentinels wait for the dawn,
    let Israel wait for the LORD. ℟.

If you, O LORD, mark iniquities,
    LORD, who can stand?
But with you is forgiveness,
    that you may be revered. ℟.

For with the LORD is kindness
    and with him is plenteous
      redemption;
and he will redeem Israel
    from all their iniquities. ℟.

READING II

Romans 8:8–11

Brothers and sisters: Those who are in the flesh cannot please God. But you are not in the flesh; on the contrary, you are in the spirit, if only the Spirit of God dwells in you. Whoever does not have the Spirit of Christ does not belong to him. But if Christ is in you, although the body is dead because of sin, the spirit is alive because of righteousness. If the Spirit of the one who raised Jesus from the dead dwells in you, the one who raised Christ from the dead will give life to your mortal bodies also, through his Spirit dwelling in you.

GOSPEL

John 11:1–45 or 11:3–7, 17, 20–27, 33b–45

For short form read only the parts in brackets.

Now a man was ill, Lazarus from Bethany, the village of Mary and her sister Martha. Mary was the one who had anointed the Lord with perfumed oil and dried his feet with her hair; it was her brother Lazarus who was ill. So [the sisters (of Lazarus) sent word to Jesus saying, "Master, the one you love is ill." When Jesus heard this he said, "This illness is not to end in death, but is for the glory of God, that the Son of God may be glorified through it." Now Jesus loved Martha and her sister and Lazarus. So when he heard that he was ill, he remained for two days in the place where he was. Then after this he said to his disciples, "Let us go back to Judea."] The disciples said to him, "Rabbi, the Jews were just trying to stone you, and you want to go back there?" Jesus answered, "Are there not twelve hours in a day? If one walks during the day, he does not stumble, because he sees the light of this world. But if one walks at night, he stumbles, because the light is not in him." He said this, and then told them, "Our friend Lazarus is asleep, but I am going to awaken him." So the disciples said to him, "Master, if he is asleep, he will be saved." But Jesus was talking about his death, while they thought that he meant ordinary sleep. So then Jesus said to them clearly, "Lazarus has died. And I am glad for you that I was not there, that you may believe. Let us go to him." So Thomas, called Didymus, said to his fellow disciples, "Let us also go to die with him."

[When Jesus arrived, he found that Lazarus had already been in the tomb for four days.] Now Bethany was near Jerusalem, only about two miles away. And many of the Jews had come to Martha and Mary to comfort them about their brother. [When Martha heard that Jesus was coming, she went to meet him; but Mary sat at home. Martha said to Jesus, "Lord, if you had been here, my brother would not have died. But even now I know that whatever you ask of God, God will give you." Jesus said to her, "Your brother will rise." Martha said to him, "I know he will rise, in the resurrection on the last day." Jesus told her, "I am the resurrection and the life; whoever believes in me, even if he dies, will live, and everyone who lives and believes in me will never die. Do you believe this?" She said to him, "Yes, Lord. I have come to believe that you are the Christ, the Son of God, the one who is coming into the world."]

When she had said this, she went and called her sister Mary secretly, saying, "The teacher is here and is asking for you." As soon as she heard this, she rose quickly and went to him. For Jesus had not yet come into the village, but was still where Martha had met him. So when the Jews who were with her in the house comforting her saw Mary get up quickly and go out, they followed her, presuming that she was going to the tomb to weep there. When Mary came to where Jesus was and saw him, she fell at his feet and said to him, "Lord, if you had been here, my brother would not have died." When Jesus saw her weeping and the Jews who had come with her weeping, [he became perturbed and deeply troubled, and said, "Where have you laid him?" They said to him, "Sir, come and see." And Jesus wept. So the Jews said, "See how he loved him." But some of them said, "Could not the one who opened the eyes of the blind man have done something so that this man would not have died?"

So Jesus, perturbed again, came to the tomb. It was a cave, and a stone lay across it. Jesus said, "Take away the stone." Martha, the dead man's sister, said to him, "Lord, by now there will be a stench; he has been dead for four days." Jesus said to her, "Did I not tell you that if you believe you will see the glory of God?" So they took away the stone. And Jesus raised his eyes and said, "Father, I thank you for hearing me. I know that you always hear me; but because of the crowd here I have said this, that they may believe that you sent me." And when he had said this, he cried out in a loud voice, "Lazarus, come out!" The dead man came out, tied hand and foot with burial bands, and his face was wrapped in a cloth. So Jesus said to them, "Untie him and let him go."

Now many of the Jews who had come to Mary and seen what he had done began to believe in him.]

COMMUNION ANTIPHON *John 11:26*
He who lives and believes in me will not die for ever, said the Lord.

April 17, 2011

PALM SUNDAY OF THE LORD'S PASSION

GOSPEL *Matthew 21:1–11 / 37*
When Jesus and the disciples drew near Jerusalem and came to Bethphage on the Mount of Olives, Jesus sent two disciples, saying to them, "Go into the village opposite you, and immediately you will find an ass tethered, and a colt with her. Untie them and bring them here to me. And if anyone should say anything to you, reply, 'The master has need of them.' Then he will send them at once." This happened so that what had been spoken through the prophet might be fulfilled:
Say to daughter Zion,
"Behold, your king comes to you,
meek and riding on an ass,
and on a colt, the foal of a beast of burden."
The disicples went and did as Jesus had ordered them. They brought the ass and the colt and laid their cloaks over them, and he sat upon them. The very large crowd spread their

cloaks on the road, while others cut branches from the trees and strewed them on the road. The crowds preceding him and those following kept crying out and saying:
"Hosanna to the Son of David;
blessed is he who comes in the name of the Lord;
hosanna in the highest."
And when he entered Jerusalem the whole city was shaken and asked, "Who is this?" And the crowds replied, "This is Jesus the prophet, from Nazareth in Galilee."

The Simple Entrance:
ENTRANCE ANTIPHON
Six days before the solemn passover the Lord came to Jerusalem, and children waving palm branches ran out to welcome him. They loudly praised the Lord: Blessed are you who have come to us so rich in love and mercy.

Psalm 23:9–10
Open wide the doors and gates.
Lift high the ancient portals.
The King of glory enters.

Who is this King of glory?
He is God the mighty Lord.
Hosanna in the highest.

Blessed are you who have come to us
so rich in love and mercy.
Hosanna in the highest.

READING I
Isaiah 50:4–7 / 38

The Lord GOD has given me
a well-trained tongue,
that I might know how to speak to the weary
a word that will rouse them.
Morning after morning
he opens my ear that I may hear;
and I have not rebelled,
have not turned back.
I gave my back to those who beat me,
my cheeks to those who plucked my beard;
my face I did not shield
from buffets and spitting.

The Lord GOD is my help,
therefore I am not disgraced;
I have set my face like flint,
knowing that I shall not be put to shame.

RESPONSORIAL PSALM
Psalm 22:8–9, 17–18, 19–20, 23–24

My God, my God, why have you a - ban - doned me?

All who see me scoff at me;
they mock me with parted lips, they wag their heads:
"He relied on the LORD; let him deliver him,
let him rescue him, if he loves him." ℟.

Indeed, many dogs surround me,
a pack of evildoers closes in upon me;
They have pierced my hands and my feet;
I can count all my bones. ℟.

They divide my garments among them,
  and for my vesture they cast lots.
But you, O LORD, be not far from me;
  O my help, hasten to aid me. ℟.

I will proclaim your name to my brethren;
  in the midst of the assembly I will

praise you:
"You who fear the LORD, praise him;
  all you descendants of Jacob, give
    glory to him;
  revere him, all you descendants of
    Israel!" ℟.

READING II

Philippians 2:6–11

Christ Jesus, though he was in the form
    of God,
  did not regard equality with God
  something to be grasped.
Rather, he emptied himself,
  taking the form of a slave,
  coming in human likeness;
  and found human in appearance,
  he humbled himself,
  becoming obedient to the point of
    death,

even death on a cross.
Because of this, God greatly exalted him
  and bestowed on him the name
  which is above every name,
  that at the name of Jesus
  every knee should bend,
  of those in heaven and on earth and
    under the earth,
  and every tongue confess that
Jesus Christ is Lord,
  to the glory of God the Father.

GOSPEL

Matthew 26:14—27:66 or 27:11–54

The symbols of the following passion narrative represent:
  + Christ;   N narrator;   V voice;   C crowd.

N The Passion of our Lord Jesus Christ according to Matthew.
For short form read only the part in brackets.

N One of the Twelve, who was called Judas Iscariot, went to the chief priests and said,
V "What are you willing to give me if I hand him over to you?"
N They paid him thirty pieces of silver, and from that time on he looked for an opportunity to hand him over.

On the first day of the Feast of Unleavened Bread, the disciples approached Jesus and said,
V "Where do you want us to prepare for you to eat the Passover?"
N He said,
+ "Go into the city to a certain man and tell him, 'The teacher says, "My appointed time draws near; in your house I shall celebrate the Passover with my disciples."'"
N The disciples then did as Jesus had ordered, and prepared the Passover.

When it was evening, he reclined at table with the Twelve. And while they were eating, he said,
+ "Amen, I say to you, one of you will betray me."
N Deeply distressed at this, they began to say to him one after another,
V "Surely it is not I, Lord?"
N He said in reply,
+ "He who has dipped his hand into the dish with me is the one who will betray me. The Son of Man indeed goes, as it is written of him, but woe to that man by whom the Son of Man is betrayed. It would be better for that man if he had never been born."
N Then Judas, his betrayer, said in reply,
V "Surely it is not I, Rabbi?"
N He answered,
+ "You have said so."

N While they were eating, Jesus took bread, said the blessing, broke it, and giving it to his disciples said,

+ "Take and eat; this is my body."

N Then he took a cup, gave thanks, and gave it to them, saying,

+ "Drink from it, all of you, for this is my blood of the covenant, which will be shed on behalf of many for the forgiveness of sins. I tell you, from now on I shall not drink this fruit of the vine until the day when I drink it with you new in the kingdom of my Father."

N Then, after singing a hymn, they went out to the Mount of Olives.

Then Jesus said to them,

+ "This night all of you will have your faith in me shaken, for it is written:
   I will strike the shepherd,
      and the sheep of the flock will be
      dispersed;
but after I have been raised up, I shall go before you to Galilee."

N Peter said to him in reply,

V "Though all may have their faith in you shaken, mine will never be."

N Jesus said to him,

+ "Amen, I say to you, this very night before the cock crows, you will deny me three times."

N Peter said to him,

V "Even though I should have to die with you, I will not deny you."

N And all the disciples spoke likewise.

Then Jesus came with them to a place called Gethsemane, and he said to his disciples,

+ "Sit here while I go over there and pray."

N He took along Peter and the two sons of Zebedee, and began to feel sorrow and distress. Then he said to them,

+ "My soul is sorrowful even to death. Remain here and keep watch with me."

N He advanced a little and fell prostrate in prayer, saying,

+ "My Father, if it is possible, let this cup pass from me; yet, not as I will, but as you will."

N When he returned to his disciples he found them asleep. He said to Peter,

+ "So you could not keep watch with me for one hour? Watch and pray that you may not undergo the test. The spirit is willing, but the flesh is weak."

N Withdrawing a second time, he prayed again,

+ "My Father, if it is not possible that this cup pass without my drinking it, your will be done!"

N Then he returned once more and found them asleep, for they could not keep their eyes open. He left them and withdrew again and prayed a third time, saying the same thing again. Then he returned to his disciples and said to them,

+ "Are you still sleeping and taking your rest? Behold, the hour is at hand when the Son of Man is to be handed over to sinners. Get up, let us go. Look, my betrayer is at hand."

N While he was still speaking, Judas, one of the Twelve, arrived, accompanied by a large crowd, with swords and clubs, who had come from the chief priests and the elders of the people. His betrayer had arranged a sign with them, saying,

V "The man I shall kiss is the one; arrest him."

N Immediately he went over to Jesus and said,

V "Hail, Rabbi!"

N and he kissed him. Jesus answered him,

+ "Friend, do what you have come for."

N Then stepping forward they laid hands on Jesus and arrested him. And behold, one of those who accompanied Jesus put his hand to his sword, drew it, and struck the high priest's servant, cutting off his ear. Then Jesus said to him,

+ "Put your sword back into its sheath, for all who take the sword will perish by the sword. Do you think that I cannot call upon my Father and he will not provide me at this moment with more than twelve legions of angels? But then how would the Scriptures be fulfilled which say that it must come to pass in this way?"

N At that hour Jesus said to the crowds,

+ "Have you come out as against a robber, with swords and clubs to seize me? Day after day I sat teaching in the temple area, yet you did not arrest me. But all this has come to pass that the writings of the prophets may be fulfilled."

N Then all the disciples left him and fled.

Those who had arrested Jesus led him away to Caiaphas the high priest, where the scribes and the elders were assembled. Peter was following him at a distance as far as the high priest's courtyard, and going inside he sat down with the servants to see the outcome.

The chief priests and the entire Sanhedrin kept trying to obtain false testimony against Jesus in order to put him to death, but they found none, though many false witnesses came forward. Finally two came forward who stated,

C "This man said, 'I can destroy the temple of God and within three days rebuild it.'"

N The high priest rose and addressed him,

V "Have you no answer? What are these men testifying against you?"

N But Jesus was silent. Then the high priest said to him,

V "I order you to tell us under oath before the living God whether you are the Christ, the Son of God."

N Jesus said to him in reply,

+ "You have said so. But I tell you:
From now on you will see 'the Son of Man
    seated at the right hand of the Power'
    and 'coming on the clouds of
    heaven.'"

N Then the high priest tore his robes and said,

V "He has blasphemed! What further need have we of witnesses? You have now heard the blasphemy; what is your opinion?"

N They said in reply,

C "He deserves to die!"

N Then they spat in his face and struck him, while some slapped him, saying,

C "Prophesy for us, Christ: who is it that struck you?"

N Now Peter was sitting outside in the courtyard. One of the maids came over to him and said,

C "You too were with Jesus the Galilean."

N But he denied it in front of everyone, saying,

V "I do not know what you are talking about!"

N As he went out to the gate, another girl saw him and said to those who were there,

C "This man was with Jesus the Nazorean."

N Again he denied it with an oath,

V "I do not know the man!"

N A little later the bystanders came over and said to Peter,

C "Surely you too are one of them; even your speech gives you away."

N At that he began to curse and to swear,

V "I do not know the man."

N And immediately a cock crowed. Then Peter remembered the word that Jesus had spoken: "Before the cock crows you will deny me three times." He went out and began to weep bitterly.

When it was morning, all the chief priests and the elders of the people took counsel against Jesus to put him to death. They bound him, led him away, and handed him over to Pilate, the governor.

Then Judas, his betrayer, seeing that Jesus had been condemned, deeply regretted what he had done. He returned the thirty pieces of silver to the chief priests and elders, saying,

V "I have sinned in betraying innocent blood."

N They said,

C "What is that to us? Look to it yourself."

N Flinging the money into the temple, he

departed and went off and hanged himself. The chief priests gathered up the money, but said,

C "It is not lawful to deposit this in the temple treasury, for it is the price of blood."

N After consultation, they used it to buy the potter's field as a burial place for foreigners. That is why that field even today is called the Field of Blood. Then was fulfilled what had been said through Jeremiah the prophet, *And they took the thirty pieces of silver, the value of a man with a price on his head, a price set by some of the Israelites, and they paid it out for the potter's field just as the Lord had commanded me.*

Now [Jesus stood before the governor, and he questioned him,

V "Are you the king of the Jews?"

N Jesus said,

+ "You say so."

N And when he was accused by the chief priests and elders, he made no answer. Then Pilate said to him,

V "Do you not hear how many things they are testifying against you?"

N But he did not answer him one word, so that the governor was greatly amazed.

Now on the occasion of the feast the governor was accustomed to release to the crowd one prisoner whom they wished. And at that time they had a notorious prisoner called Barabbas. So when they had assembled, Pilate said to them,

V "Which one do you want me to release to you, Barabbas, or Jesus called Christ?"

N For he knew that it was out of envy that they had handed him over. While he was still seated on the bench, his wife sent him a message, "Have nothing to do with that righteous man. I suffered much in a dream today because of him."

The chief priests and the elders persuaded the crowds to ask for Barabbas but to destroy Jesus. The governor said to them in reply,

V "Which of the two do you want me to release to you?"

N They answered,

C "Barabbas!"

N Pilate said to them,

V "Then what shall I do with Jesus called Christ?"

N They all said,

C "Let him be crucified!"

N But he said,

V "Why? What evil has he done?"

N They only shouted the louder,

C "Let him be crucified!"

N When Pilate saw that he was not succeeding at all, but that a riot was breaking out instead, he took water and washed his hands in the sight of the crowd, saying,

V "I am innocent of this man's blood. Look to it yourselves."

N And the whole people said in reply,

C "His blood be upon us and upon our children."

N Then he released Barabbas to them, but after he had Jesus scourged, he handed him over to be crucified.

Then the soldiers of the governor took Jesus inside the praetorium and gathered the whole cohort around him. They stripped off his clothes and threw a scarlet military cloak about him. Weaving a crown out of thorns, they placed it on his head, and a reed in his right hand. And kneeling before him, they mocked him, saying,

C "Hail, King of the Jews!"

N They spat upon him and took the reed and kept striking him on the head. And when they had mocked him, they stripped him of the cloak, dressed him in his own clothes, and led him off to crucify him.

As they were going out, they met a Cyrenian named Simon; this man they pressed into service to carry his cross.

And when they came to a place called Golgotha —which means Place of the Skull—, they gave Jesus wine to drink mixed with gall. But when he had tasted it, he refused to drink. After they had crucified him, they divided his garments by casting lots; then they sat down and kept watch over him there. And they placed over his head the written charge against him: This is Jesus, the King of the Jews. Two revolutionaries were crucified with him, one on his right and the other on his left. Those passing by reviled him, shaking their heads and saying,

C "You who would destroy the temple and rebuild it in three days, save yourself, if you are the Son of God, and come down from the cross!"

N Likewise the chief priests with the scribes and elders mocked him and said,

C "He saved others; he cannot save himself. So he is the king of Israel! Let him come down from the cross now, and we will believe in him. He trusted in God; let him deliver him now if he wants him. For he said, 'I am the Son of God.'"

N The revolutionaries who were crucified with him also kept abusing him in the same way.

From noon onward, darkness came over the whole land until three in the afternoon. And about three o'clock Jesus cried out in a loud voice,

+ "Eli, Eli, lema sabachthani?"

N which means,

+ "My God, my God, why have you forsaken me?"

N Some of the bystanders who heard it said,

C "This one is calling for Elijah."

N Immediately one of them ran to get a sponge; he soaked it in wine, and putting it on a reed, gave it to him to drink. But the rest said,

C "Wait, let us see if Elijah comes to save him."

N But Jesus cried out again in a loud voice, and gave up his spirit.

Here all kneel and pause for a short time.

N And behold, the veil of the sanctuary was torn in two from top to bottom. The earth quaked, rocks were split, tombs were opened, and the bodies of many saints who had fallen asleep were raised. And coming forth from their tombs after his resurrection, they entered the holy city and appeared to many. The centurion and the men with him who were keeping watch over Jesus feared greatly when they saw the earthquake and all that was happening, and they said,

C "Truly, this was the Son of God!"]

N There were many women there, looking on from a distance, who had followed Jesus from Galilee, ministering to him. Among them were Mary Magdalene and Mary the mother of James and Joseph, and the mother of the sons of Zebedee.

When it was evening, there came a rich man from Arimathea named Joseph, who was himself a disciple of Jesus. He went to Pilate and asked for the body of Jesus; then Pilate ordered it to be handed over. Taking the body, Joseph wrapped it in clean linen and laid it in his new tomb that he had hewn in the rock. Then he rolled a huge stone across the entrance to the tomb and departed. But Mary Magdalene and the other Mary remained sitting there, facing the tomb.

The next day, the one following the day of preparation, the chief priests and the Pharisees gathered before Pilate and said,

C "Sir, we remember that this impostor while still alive said, 'After three days I will be raised up.' Give orders, then, that the grave be secured until the third day, lest his disciples come and steal him and say to the people, 'He has been raised from the dead.' This last imposture would be worse than the first."

N Pilate said to them,

V "The guard is yours; go, secure it as best you can."

N So they went and secured the tomb by fixing a seal to the stone and setting the guard.

April 21, 2011

HOLY THURSDAY

ENTRANCE ANTIPHON   *See Galatians 6:14*
We should glory in the cross of our Lord Jesus Christ, for he is our salvation, our life and our resurrection; through him we are saved and made free.

READING I   *Exodus 12:1–8, 11–14 / 39*

The LORD said to Moses and Aaron in the land of Egypt, "This month shall stand at the head of your calendar; you shall reckon it the first month of the year. Tell the whole community of Israel: On the tenth of this month every one of your families must procure for itself a lamb, one apiece for each household. If a family is too small for a whole lamb, it shall join the nearest household in procuring one and shall share in the lamb in proportion to the number of persons who partake of it. The lamb must be a year-old male and without blemish. You may take it from either the sheep or the goats. You shall keep it until the fourteenth day of this month, and then, with the whole assembly of Israel present, it shall be slaughtered during the evening twilight. They shall take some of its blood and apply it to the two doorposts and the lintel of every house in which they partake of the lamb. That same night they shall eat its roasted flesh with unleavened bread and bitter herbs.

"This is how you are to eat it: with your loins girt, sandals on your feet and your staff in hand, you shall eat like those who are in flight. It is the Passover of the LORD. For on this same night I will go through Egypt, striking down every firstborn of the land, both man and beast, and executing judgment on all the gods of Egypt—I, the LORD! But the blood will mark the houses where you are. Seeing the blood, I will pass over you; thus, when I strike the land of Egypt, no destructive blow will come upon you.

"This day shall be a memorial feast for you, which all your generations shall celebrate with pilgrimage to the LORD, as a perpetual institution."

RESPONSORIAL PSALM   *Psalm 116:12–13, 15–16bc, 17–18*

Our bless-ing-cup   is a com-mun-ion with the Blood of Christ.

How shall I make a return to the LORD
    for all the good he has done for me?
The cup of salvation I will take up,
    and I will call upon the name of the
      LORD. ℟.

Precious in the eyes of the LORD
    is the death of his faithful ones.
I am your servant, the son of your
handmaid;
you have loosed my bonds. ℟.

To you will I offer sacrifice of
    thanksgiving,
    and I will call upon the name of the
      LORD.
My vows to the LORD I will pay
    in the presence of all his people. ℟.

READING II

I Corinthians 11:23–26

Brothers and sisters: I received from the Lord what I also handed on to you, that the Lord Jesus, on the night he was handed over, took bread, and, after he had given thanks, broke it and said, "This is my body that is for you. Do this in remembrance of me." In the same way also the cup, after supper, saying, "This cup is the new covenant in my blood. Do this, as often as you drink it, in remembrance of me." For as often as you eat this bread and drink the cup, you proclaim the death of the Lord until he comes.

GOSPEL

John 13:1–15

Before the feast of Passover, Jesus knew that his hour had come to pass from this world to the Father. He loved his own in the world and he loved them to the end. The devil had already induced Judas, son of Simon the Iscariot, to hand him over. So, during supper, fully aware that the Father had put everything into his power and that he had come from God and was returning to God, he rose from supper and took off his outer garments. He took a towel and tied it around his waist. Then he poured water into a basin and began to wash the disciples' feet and dry them with the towel around his waist. He came to Simon Peter, who said to him, "Master, are you going to wash my feet?" Jesus answered and said to him, "What I am doing, you do not understand now, but you will understand later." Peter said to him, "You will never wash my feet." Jesus answered him, "Unless I wash you, you will have no inheritance with me." Simon Peter said to him, "Master, then not only my feet, but my hands and head as well." Jesus said to him, "Whoever has bathed has no need except to have his feet washed, for he is clean all over; so you are clean, but not all." For he knew who would betray him; for this reason, he said, "Not all of you are clean."

So when he had washed their feet and put his garments back on and reclined at table again, he said to them, "Do you realize what I have done for you? You call me 'teacher' and 'master,' and rightly so, for indeed I am. If I, therefore, the master and teacher, have washed your feet, you ought to wash one another's feet. I have given you a model to follow, so that as I have done for you, you should also do."

COMMUNION ANTIPHON

1 Corinthians 11:24–25

This body will be given for you. This is the cup of the new covenant in my blood; whenever you receive them, do so in remembrance of me.

April 22, 2011

GOOD FRIDAY OF THE LORD'S PASSION

READING I

Isaiah 52:13—53:12 / 40

See, my servant shall prosper,
    he shall be raised high and greatly
      exalted.
Even as many were amazed at him—
    so marred was his look beyond
      human semblance
and his appearance beyond that of
      the sons of man—
so shall he startle many nations,
    because of him kings shall stand
      speechless;

for those who have not been told shall see,
    those who have not heard shall
      ponder it.

Who would believe what we have heard?
    To whom has the arm of the LORD
      been revealed?
He grew up like a sapling before him,
    like a shoot from the parched earth;
there was in him no stately bearing to
    make us look at him,

nor appearance that would attract us to him.
He was spurned and avoided by people, a man of suffering, accustomed to infirmity,
one of those from whom people hide their faces,
spurned, and we held him in no esteem.

Yet it was our infirmities that he bore, our sufferings that he endured,
while we thought of him as stricken, as one smitten by God and afflicted.
But he was pierced for our offenses, crushed for our sins;
upon him was the chastisement that makes us whole,
by his stripes we were healed.
We had all gone astray like sheep, each following his own way;
but the LORD laid upon him the guilt of us all.

Though he was harshly treated, he submitted
and opened not his mouth;
like a lamb led to the slaughter or a sheep before the shearers,
he was silent and opened not his mouth.
Oppressed and condemned, he was taken away,

and who would have thought any more of his destiny?
When he was cut off from the land of the living,
and smitten for the sin of his people,
a grave was assigned him among the wicked
and a burial place with evildoers,
though he had done no wrong nor spoken any falsehood.
But the LORD was pleased to crush him in infirmity.

If he gives his life as an offering for sin, he shall see his descendants in a long life,
and the will of the LORD shall be accomplished through him.

Because of his affliction he shall see the light in fullness of days;
through his suffering, my servant shall justify many,
and their guilt he shall bear.
Therefore I will give him his portion among the great,
and he shall divide the spoils with the mighty,
because he surrendered himself to death and was counted among the wicked;
and he shall take away the sins of many, and win pardon for their offenses.

RESPONSORIAL PSALM *Psalm 31:2, 6, 12–13, 15–16, 17, 25*

Fa - ther, in - to your hands I com - mend my spir - it.

In you, O LORD, I take refuge;
let me never be put to shame.
In your justice rescue me.
Into your hands I commend my spirit;
you will redeem me, O LORD, O faithful God. ℟.

For all my foes I am an object of reproach,
a laughingstock to my neighbors, and a dread to my friends;

they who see me abroad flee from me.
I am forgotten like the unremembered dead;
I am like a dish that is broken. ℟.

But my trust is in you, O LORD;
I say, "You are my God.
In your hands is my destiny; rescue me from the clutches of my enemies and my persecutors." ℟.

Let your face shine upon your servant;
save me in your kindness.

Take courage and be stouthearted,
all you who hope in the LORD. ℟.

READING II

Hebrews 4:14–16; 5:7–9

Brothers and sisters: Since we have a great high priest who has passed through the heavens, Jesus, the Son of God, let us hold fast to our confession. For we do not have a high priest who is unable to sympathize with our weaknesses, but one who has similarly been tested in every way, yet without sin. So let us confidently approach the throne of grace to receive mercy and to find grace for timely help.

In the days when Christ was in the flesh, he offered prayers and supplications with loud cries and tears to the one who was able to save him from death, and he was heard because of his reverence. Son though he was, he learned obedience from what he suffered; and when he was made perfect, he became the source of eternal salvation for all who obey him.

GOSPEL

John 18:1—19:42

The symbols of the following passion narrative represent:

+ Christ;   N narrator;   V voice;   C crowd.

N The Passion of our Lord Jesus Christ according to John.

N Jesus went out with his disciples across the Kidron valley to where there was a garden, into which he and his disciples entered. Judas his betrayer also knew the place, because Jesus had often met there with his disciples. So Judas got a band of soldiers and guards from the chief priests and the Pharisees and went there with lanterns, torches, and weapons. Jesus, knowing everything that was going to happen to him, went out and said to them,

+ "Whom are you looking for?"

N They answered him,

C "Jesus the Nazorean."

N He said to them,

+ "I AM."

N Judas his betrayer was also with them. When he said to them, "I AM," they turned away and fell to the ground. So he again asked them,

+ "Whom are you looking for?"

N They said,

C "Jesus the Nazorean."

N Jesus answered,

+ "I told you that I AM. So if you are looking for me, let these men go."

N This was to fulfill what he had said, "I have not lost any of those you gave me." Then Simon Peter, who had a sword, drew it, struck the high priest's slave, and cut off his right ear. The slave's name was Malchus. Jesus said to Peter,

+ "Put your sword into its scabbard. Shall I not drink the cup that the Father gave me?"

N So the band of soldiers, the tribune, and the Jewish guards seized Jesus, bound him, and brought him to Annas first. He was the father-in-law of Caiaphas, who was high priest that year. It was Caiaphas who had counseled the Jews that it was better that one man should die rather than the people.

Simon Peter and another disciple followed Jesus. Now the other disciple was known to the high priest, and he entered the courtyard of the high priest with Jesus. But Peter stood at the gate outside. So the other disciple, the acquaintance of the high priest, went out and spoke to the gatekeeper and brought Peter in. Then the maid who was the gatekeeper said to Peter,

C "You are not one of this man's disciples, are you?"

N He said,

V "I am not."

N Now the slaves and the guards were standing around a charcoal fire that they had made, because it was cold, and were warming themselves. Peter was also standing there keeping warm.

The high priest questioned Jesus about his disciples and about his doctrine. Jesus answered him,

+ "I have spoken publicly to the world. I have always taught in a synagogue or in the temple area where all the Jews gather, and in secret I have said nothing. Why ask me? Ask those who heard me what I said to them. They know what I said."

N When he had said this, one of the temple guards standing there struck Jesus and said,

V "Is this the way you answer the high priest?"

N Jesus answered him,

+ "If I have spoken wrongly, testify to the wrong; but if I have spoken rightly, why do you strike me?"

N Then Annas sent him bound to Caiaphas the high priest.

Now Simon Peter was standing there keeping warm. And they said to him,

C "You are not one of his disciples, are you?"

N He denied it and said,

V "I am not."

N One of the slaves of the high priest, a relative of the one whose ear Peter had cut off, said,

C "Didn't I see you in the garden with him?"

N Again Peter denied it. And immediately the cock crowed.

Then they brought Jesus from Caiaphas to the praetorium. It was morning. And they themselves did not enter the praetorium, in order not to be defiled so that they could eat the Passover. So Pilate came out to them and said,

V "What charge do you bring against this man?"

N They answered and said to him,

C "If he were not a criminal, we would not have handed him over to you."

N At this, Pilate said to them,

V "Take him yourselves, and judge him according to your law."

N The Jews answered him,

C "We do not have the right to execute anyone,"

N in order that the word of Jesus might be fulfilled that he said indicating the kind of death he would die. So Pilate went back into the praetorium and summoned Jesus and said to him,

V "Are you the King of the Jews?"

N Jesus answered,

+ "Do you say this on your own or have others told you about me?"

N Pilate answered,

V "I am not a Jew, am I? Your own nation and the chief priests handed you over to me. What have you done?"

N Jesus answered,

+ "My kingdom does not belong to this world. If my kingdom did belong to this world, my attendants would be fighting to keep me from being handed over to the Jews. But as it is, my kingdom is not here."

N So Pilate said to him,

V "Then you are a king?"

N Jesus answered,

+ "You say I am a king. For this I was born and for this I came into the world, to testify to the truth. Everyone who belongs to the truth listens to my voice."

N Pilate said to him,

V "What is truth?"

N When he had said this, he again went out to the Jews and said to them,

V "I find no guilt in him. But you have a custom that I release one prisoner to you at Passover. Do you want me to release to you the King of the Jews?"

N They cried out again,

C "Not this one but Barabbas!"

N Now Barabbas was a revolutionary.

Then Pilate took Jesus and had him scourged. And the soldiers wove a crown out of thorns and placed it on his head, and clothed him in a purple cloak, and they came to him and said,

C "Hail, King of the Jews!"

N And they struck him repeatedly. Once more Pilate went out and said to them,

V "Look, I am bringing him out to you, so that you may know that I find no guilt in him."

N So Jesus came out, wearing the crown of thorns and the purple cloak. And Pilate said to them,

V "Behold, the man!"

N When the chief priests and the guards saw him they cried out,

C "Crucify him, crucify him!"

N Pilate said to them,

V "Take him yourselves and crucify him. I find no guilt in him."

N The Jews answered,

C "We have a law, and according to that law he ought to die, because he made himself the Son of God."

N Now when Pilate heard this statement, he became even more afraid, and went back into the praetorium and said to Jesus,

V "Where are you from?"

N Jesus did not answer him. So Pilate said to him,

V "Do you not speak to me? Do you not know that I have power to release you and I have power to crucify you?"

N Jesus answered him,

+ "You would have no power over me if it had not been given to you from above. For this reason the one who handed me over to you has the greater sin."

N Consequently, Pilate tried to release him; but the Jews cried out,

C "If you release him, you are not a Friend of Caesar. Everyone who makes himself a king opposes Caesar."

N When Pilate heard these words he brought Jesus out and seated him on the judge's bench in the place called Stone Pavement, in Hebrew, Gabbatha. It was preparation day for Passover, and it was about noon. And he said to the Jews,

V "Behold, your king!"

N They cried out,

C "Take him away, take him away! Crucify him!"

N Pilate said to them,

V "Shall I crucify your king?"

N The chief priests answered,

C "We have no king but Caesar."

N Then he handed him over to them to be crucified.

So they took Jesus, and, carrying the cross himself, he went out to what is called the Place of the Skull, in Hebrew, Golgotha. There they crucified him, and with him two others, one on either side, with Jesus in the middle. Pilate also had an inscription written and put on the cross. It read, "Jesus the Nazorean, the King of the Jews." Now many of the Jews read this inscription, because the place where Jesus was crucified was near the city; and it was written in Hebrew, Latin, and Greek. So the chief priests of the Jews said to Pilate,

C "Do not write 'The King of the Jews,' but that he said, 'I am the King of the Jews'."

N Pilate answered,

V "What I have written, I have written."

N When the soldiers had crucified Jesus, they took his clothes and divided them into four shares, a share for each soldier. They also took his tunic, but the tunic was seamless, woven in one piece from the top down. So they said to one another,

C "Let's not tear it, but cast lots for it to see whose it will be,"

N in order that the passage of Scripture might be fulfilled that says:

They divided my garments among them,
and for my vesture they cast lots.

This is what the soldiers did. Standing by the cross of Jesus were his mother and his mother's sister, Mary the wife of Clopas, and Mary of Magdala. When Jesus saw his mother and the disciple there whom he loved he said to his mother,

+ "Woman, behold, your son."

N Then he said to the disciple,

+ "Behold, your mother."

N And from that hour the disciple took her into his home.

After this, aware that everything was now finished, in order that the Scripture might be fulfilled, Jesus said,

+ "I thirst."

N There was a vessel filled with common wine. So they put a sponge soaked in wine on a sprig of hyssop and put it up to his mouth. When Jesus had taken the wine, he said,

+ "It is finished."

N And bowing his head, he handed over the spirit.

Here all kneel and pause for a short time.

N Now since it was preparation day, in order that the bodies might not remain on the cross on the sabbath, for the sabbath day of that week was a solemn one, the Jews asked Pilate that their legs be broken and that they be taken down. So the soldiers came and broke the legs of the first and then of the other one who was crucified with Jesus. But when they came to Jesus and saw that he was already dead, they did not break his legs, but one soldier thrust his lance into his side, and immediately blood and water flowed out. An eyewitness has testified, and his testimony is true; he knows that he is speaking the truth, so that you also may come to believe. For this happened so that the Scripture passage might be fulfilled:
Not a bone of it will be broken. And again another passage says:
They will look upon him whom they have pierced.

After this, Joseph of Arimathea, secretly a disciple of Jesus for fear of the Jews, asked Pilate if he could remove the body of Jesus. And Pilate permitted it. So he came and took his body. Nicodemus, the one who had first come to him at night, also came bringing a mixture of myrrh and aloes weighing about one hundred pounds. They took the body of Jesus and bound it with burial cloths along with the spices, according to the Jewish burial custom. Now in the place where he had been crucified there was a garden, and in the garden a new tomb, in which no one had yet been buried. So they laid Jesus there because of the Jewish preparation day; for the tomb was close by.

April 23, 2011
EASTER VIGIL

READING I *Genesis 1:1—2:2 or 1:1, 26–31a / 41*
For short form read only the parts in brackets.

[In the beginning, when God created the heavens and the earth,] the earth was a formless wasteland, and darkness covered the abyss, while a mighty wind swept over the waters.

Then God said, "Let there be light," and there was light. God saw how good the light was. God then separated the light from the darkness. God called the light "day," and the darkness he called "night." Thus evening came, and morning followed—the first day.

Then God said, "Let there be a dome in the middle of the waters, to separate one body of water from the other." And so it happened: God made the dome, and it separated the water above the dome from the water below it. God called the dome "the sky." Evening came, and morning followed—the second day.

Then God said, "Let the water under the sky be gathered into a single basin, so that the dry land may appear." And so it happened: the water under the sky was gathered into its basin, and the dry land appeared. God called the dry land "the earth," and the basin of the water he called "the sea." God saw how good it was. Then God said, "Let the earth bring forth vegetation: every kind of plant that bears seed and every kind of fruit tree on earth that bears fruit with its seed in it." And so it happened: the earth brought forth every kind of plant that bears seed and every kind of fruit tree on earth that bears fruit with its seed in it. God saw how good it was. Evening came, and morning followed—the third day.

Then God said: "Let there be lights in the dome of the sky, to separate day from night. Let them mark the fixed times, the days and the years, and serve as luminaries in the dome of the sky, to shed light upon the earth." And so it happened: God made the two great lights, the greater one to govern the day, and the lesser one to govern the night; and he made the stars. God set them in the dome of the sky, to shed light upon the earth, to govern the day and the night, and to separate the light from the darkness. God saw how good it was. Evening came, and morning followed—the fourth day.

Then God said, "Let the water teem with an abundance of living creatures, and on the earth let birds fly beneath the dome of the sky." And so it happened: God created the great sea monsters and all kinds of swimming creatures with which the water teems, and all kinds of winged birds. God saw how good it was, and God blessed them, saying, "Be fertile, multiply, and fill the water of the seas; and let the birds multiply on the earth." Evening came, and morning followed—the fifth day.

Then God said, "Let the earth bring forth all kinds of living creatures: cattle, creeping things, and wild animals of all kinds." And so it happened: God made all kinds of wild animals, all kinds of cattle, and all kinds of creeping things of the earth. God saw how good it was. Then [God said: "Let us make man in our image, after our likeness. Let them have dominion over the fish of the sea, the birds of the air, and the cattle, and over all the wild animals and all the creatures that crawl on the ground."

God created man in his image;
in the image of God he created him;
male and female he created them.

God blessed them, saying: "Be fertile and multiply; fill the earth and subdue it. Have dominion over the fish of the sea, the birds of the air, and all the living things that move on the earth." God also said: "See, I give you every seed-bearing plant all over the earth and every tree that has seed-bearing fruit on it to be your food; and to all the animals of the land, all the birds of the air, and all the living creatures that crawl on the ground, I give all the green plants for food." And so it happened. God looked at everything he had made, and he found it very good.] Evening came, and morning followed—the sixth day.

Thus the heavens and the earth and all their array were completed. Since on the seventh day God was finished with the work he had been doing, he rested on the seventh day from all the work he had undertaken.

RESPONSORIAL PSALM 1. *Psalm 104:1–2, 5–6, 10, 12, 13–14, 24, 35*

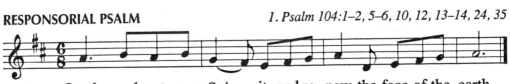

Lord, send out your Spir - it, and re - new the face of the earth.

Bless the LORD, O my soul!
   O LORD, my God, you are great
     indeed!
You are clothed with majesty and glory,
   robed in light as with a cloak. ℟.

You fixed the earth upon its foundation,
   not to be moved forever;
with the ocean, as with a garment, you
   covered it;
     above the mountains the waters
     stood. ℟.

You send forth springs into the
   watercourses
   that wind among the mountains.
Beside them the birds of heaven dwell;

from among the branches they send
   forth their song. ℟.

You water the mountains from your
     palace;
   the earth is replete with the fruit of
     your works.
You raise grass for the cattle,
   and vegetation for man's use,
producing bread from the earth. ℟.

How manifold are your works, O LORD!
   In wisdom you have wrought them
     all —
   the earth is full of your creatures.
Bless the LORD, O my soul! ℟.

Or:

RESPONSORIAL PSALM   *2. Psalm 33:4–5, 6–7, 12–13, 20 and 22*

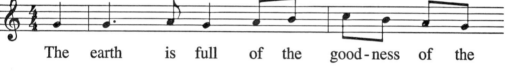

The earth is full of the good-ness of the

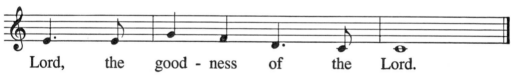

Lord, the good-ness of the Lord.

Upright is the word of the LORD,
   and all his works are trustworthy.
He loves justice and right;
   of the kindness of the LORD the earth
     is full. ℟.

By the word of the LORD the heavens
   were made;
   by the breath of his mouth all their host.
He gathers the waters of the sea as in a
   flask;
   in cellars he confines the deep. ℟.

Blessed the nation whose God is the
     LORD,
   the people he has chosen for his
     own inheritance.
From heaven the LORD looks down;
   he sees all mankind. ℟.

Our soul waits for the LORD,
   who is our help and our shield.
May your kindness, O LORD, be upon us
   who have put our hope in you. ℟.

READING II   *Genesis 22:1–18 or 22:1–2, 9a, 10–13, 15–18*
For short form read only the parts in brackets.

[God put Abraham to the test. He called to him, "Abraham!" "Here I am," he replied.
Then God said: "Take your son Isaac, your only one, whom you love, and go to the land
of Moriah. There you shall offer him up as a holocaust on a height that I will point out to

you."] Early the next morning Abraham saddled his donkey, took with him his son Isaac and two of his servants as well, and with the wood that he had cut for the holocaust, set out for the place of which God had told him.

On the third day Abraham got sight of the place from afar. Then he said to his servants: "Both of you stay here with the donkey, while the boy and I go on over yonder. We will worship and then come back to you." Thereupon Abraham took the wood for the holocaust and laid it on his son Isaac's shoulders, while he himself carried the fire and the knife. As the two walked on together, Isaac spoke to his father Abraham: "Father!" Isaac said. "Yes, son," he replied. Isaac continued, "Here are the fire and the wood, but where is the sheep for the holocaust?" "Son," Abraham answered, "God himself will provide the sheep for the holocaust." Then the two continued going forward.

[When they came to the place of which God had told him, Abraham built an altar there and arranged the wood on it.] Next he tied up his son Isaac, and put him on top of the wood on the altar. [Then he reached out and took the knife to slaughter his son. But the LORD's messenger called to him from heaven, "Abraham, Abraham!" "Here I am," he answered. "Do not lay your hand on the boy," said the messenger. "Do not do the least thing to him. I know now how devoted you are to God, since you did not withhold from me your own beloved son." As Abraham looked about, he spied a ram caught by its horns in the thicket. So he went and took the ram and offered it up as a holocaust in place of his son.] Abraham named the site Yahweh-yireh; hence people now say, "On the mountain the LORD will see."

[Again the LORD's messenger called to Abraham from heaven and said: "I swear by myself, declares the LORD, that because you acted as you did in not withholding from me your beloved son, I will bless you abundantly and make your descendants as countless as the stars of the sky and the sands of the seashore; your descendants shall take possession of the gates of their enemies, and in your descendants all the nations of the earth shall find blessing—all this because you obeyed my command."]

RESPONSORIAL PSALM   *Psalm 16:5, 8, 9–10, 11*

You   are my in - her - i - tance,   O   Lord.

O LORD, my allotted portion and my cup,
  you it is who hold fast my lot.
I set the LORD ever before me;
  with him at my right hand I shall
    not be disturbed. ℟.

because you will not abandon my soul to
    the netherworld,
  nor will you suffer your faithful one
    to undergo corruption. ℟.

Therefore my heart is glad and my soul
    rejoices,
  my body, too, abides in confidence;

You will show me the path to life,
  fullness of joys in your presence,
  the delights at your right hand
    forever. ℟.

READING III   *Exodus 14:15—15:1*
The LORD said to Moses, "Why are you crying out to me? Tell the Israelites to go forward. And you, lift up your staff and, with hand outstretched over the sea, split the sea in two, that the Israelites may pass through it on dry land. But I will make the Egyptians so obstinate that they will go in after them. Then I will receive glory through Pharaoh and all his army, his chariots and charioteers. The Egyptians shall know that I am the

LORD, when I receive glory through Pharaoh and his chariots and charioteers."

The angel of God, who had been leading Israel's camp, now moved and went around behind them. The column of cloud also, leaving the front, took up its place behind them, so that it came between the camp of the Egyptians and that of Israel. But the cloud now became dark, and thus the night passed without the rival camps coming any closer together all night long. Then Moses stretched out his hand over the sea, and the LORD swept the sea with a strong east wind throughout the night and so turned it into dry land. When the water was thus divided, the Israelites marched into the midst of the sea on dry land, with the water like a wall to their right and to their left.

The Egyptians followed in pursuit; all Pharaoh's horses and chariots and charioteers went after them right into the midst of the sea. In the night watch just before dawn the LORD cast through the column of the fiery cloud upon the Egyptian force a glance that threw it into a panic; and he so clogged their chariot wheels that they could hardly drive. With that the Egyptians sounded the retreat before Israel, because the LORD was fighting for them against the Egyptians.

Then the LORD told Moses, "Stretch out your hand over the sea, that the water may flow back upon the Egyptians, upon their chariots and their charioteers." So Moses stretched out his hand over the sea, and at dawn the sea flowed back to its normal depth. The Egyptians were fleeing head on toward the sea, when the LORD hurled them into its midst. As the water flowed back, it covered the chariots and the charioteers of Pharaoh's whole army which had followed the Israelites into the sea. Not a single one of them escaped. But the Israelites had marched on dry land through the midst of the sea, with the water like a wall to their right and to their left. Thus the LORD saved Israel on that day from the power of the Egyptians. When Israel saw the Egyptians lying dead on the seashore and beheld the great power that the LORD had shown against the Egyptians, they feared the LORD and believed in him and in his servant Moses.

Then Moses and the Israelites sang this song to the LORD:

I will sing to the LORD, for he is gloriously triumphant;
horse and chariot he has cast into the sea.

RESPONSORIAL PSALM

Exodus 15:1–2, 3–4, 5–6, 17–18

Let us sing to the Lord; he has cov-ered him-self in glo-ry.

I will sing to the LORD, for he is
gloriously triumphant;
horse and chariot he has cast into
the sea.
My strength and my courage is the LORD,
and he has been my savior.
He is my God, I praise him;
the God of my father, I extol him. ℟.

The LORD is a warrior,
LORD is his name!
Pharaoh's chariots and army he hurled
into the sea;
the elite of his officers were
submerged in the Red Sea. ℟.

The flood waters covered them,
they sank into the depths like a stone.
Your right hand, O LORD, magnificent
in power,
your right hand, O LORD, has
shattered the enemy. ℟.

You brought in the people you redeemed
and planted them on the mountain
of your inheritance—
the place where you made your seat, O
LORD,
the sanctuary, LORD, which your
hands established.
The LORD shall reign forever and ever. ℟.

READING IV

Isaiah 54:5–14

The One who has become your
    husband is your Maker;
    his name is the LORD of hosts;
your redeemer is the Holy One of
    Israel,
    called God of all the earth.
The LORD calls you back,
    like a wife forsaken and grieved in
    spirit,
    a wife married in youth and then
    cast off,
    says your God.
For a brief moment I abandoned you,
    but with great tenderness I will take
    you back.
In an outburst of wrath, for a moment
    I hid my face from you;
but with enduring love I take pity on you,
    says the LORD, your redeemer.
This is for me like the days of Noah,
    when I swore that the waters of Noah
    should never again deluge the earth;
so I have sworn not to be angry with you,
or to rebuke you.
Though the mountains leave their place
    and the hills be shaken,
my love shall never leave you
    nor my covenant of peace be
    shaken,
    says the LORD, who has mercy
    on you.
O afflicted one, storm-battered and
    unconsoled,
    I lay your pavements in carnelians,
    and your foundations in sapphires;
I will make your battlements of rubies,
    your gates of carbuncles,
    and all your walls of precious stones.
All your children shall be taught by the
    LORD,
    and great shall be the peace of your
    children.
In justice shall you be established,
    far from the fear of oppression,
    where destruction cannot come near
    you.

RESPONSORIAL PSALM

Psalm 30:2, 4, 5–6, 11–12, 13

I will praise you, Lord, for you have res-cued me.

I will extol you, O LORD, for you drew me
    clear
    and did not let my enemies rejoice
    over me.
O LORD, you brought me up from the
    netherworld;
    you preserved me from among those
    going down into the pit. ℟.

Sing praise to the LORD, you his
    faithful ones,
and give thanks to his holy name.
For his anger lasts but a moment;
    a lifetime, his good will.
At nightfall, weeping enters in,
    but with the dawn, rejoicing. ℟.

Hear, O LORD, and have pity on me;
    O LORD, be my helper.
You changed my mourning into dancing;
    O LORD, my God, forever will I
    give you thanks. ℟.

READING V

Isaiah 55:1–11

Thus says the LORD:
All you who are thirsty,
    come to the water!
You who have no money,
    come, receive grain and eat;
come, without paying and without cost,
    drink wine and milk!
Why spend your money for what is not
    bread,
    your wages for what fails to satisfy?
Heed me, and you shall eat well,
    you shall delight in rich fare.
Come to me heedfully,
    listen, that you may have life.

I will renew with you the everlasting
covenant,
the benefits assured to David.
As I made him a witness to the peoples,
a leader and commander of nations,
so shall you summon a nation you
knew not,
and nations that knew you not shall
run to you,
because of the LORD, your God,
the Holy One of Israel, who has
glorified you.

Seek the LORD while he may be found,
call him while he is near.
Let the scoundrel forsake his way,
and the wicked man his thoughts;
let him turn to the LORD for mercy;
to our God, who is generous in
forgiving.

For my thoughts are not your thoughts,
nor are your ways my ways, says
the LORD.
As high as the heavens are above the
earth,
so high are my ways above your ways
and my thoughts above your thoughts.

For just as from the heavens
the rain and snow come down
and do not return there
till they have watered the earth,
making it fertile and fruitful,
giving seed to the one who sows
and bread to the one who eats,
so shall my word be
that goes forth from my mouth;
my word shall not return to me void,
but shall do my will,
achieving the end for which I sent it.

RESPONSORIAL PSALM   *Isaiah 12:2–3, 4bcd, 5–6*

You will draw wa-ter joy-ful-ly from the springs of sal - va-tion.

God indeed is my savior;
I am confident and unafraid.
My strength and my courage is the LORD,
and he has been my savior.
With joy you will draw water
at the fountain of salvation. ℟.

Give thanks to the LORD, acclaim his
name;
among the nations make known his

deeds,
proclaim how exalted is his name. ℟.

Sing praise to the LORD for his glorious
achievement;
let this be known throughout all the
earth.
Shout with exultation, O city of Zion,
for great in your midst
is the Holy One of Israel! ℟.

READING VI   *Baruch 3:9–15, 32—4:4*
Hear, O Israel, the commandments of
life:
listen, and know prudence!
How is it, Israel,
that you are in the land of your foes,
grown old in a foreign land,
defiled with the dead,
accounted with those destined for
the netherworld?
You have forsaken the fountain of
wisdom!
Had you walked in the way of God,

you would have dwelt in enduring
peace.
Learn where prudence is,
where strength, where understanding;
that you may know also
where are length of days, and life,
where light of the eyes, and peace.
Who has found the place of wisdom,
who has entered into her treasuries?

The One who knows all things knows
her;

he has probed her by his knowledge—
the One who established the earth for all time,
and filled it with four-footed beasts;
he who dismisses the light, and it departs,
calls it, and it obeys him trembling;
before whom the stars at their posts shine and rejoice;
when he calls them, they answer, "Here we are!"
shining with joy for their Maker.
Such is our God;
no other is to be compared to him:
he has traced out the whole way of understanding,
and has given her to Jacob, his servant,
to Israel, his beloved son.

Since then she has appeared on earth, and moved among people.
She is the book of the precepts of God, the law that endures forever;
all who cling to her will live, but those will die who forsake her.
Turn, O Jacob, and receive her: walk by her light toward splendor.
Give not your glory to another, your privileges to an alien race.
Blessed are we, O Israel;
for what pleases God is known to us!

RESPONSORIAL PSALM

Psalm 19:8, 9, 10, 11

Lord, you have the words of ev - er-last-ing life.

The law of the LORD is perfect, refreshing the soul;
the decree of the LORD is trustworthy, giving wisdom to the simple. ℟.

The precepts of the LORD are right, rejoicing the heart;
the command of the LORD is clear, enlightening the eye. ℟.

The fear of the LORD is pure, enduring forever;
the ordinances of the LORD are true, all of them just. ℟.

They are more precious than gold, than a heap of purest gold;
sweeter also than syrup or honey from the comb. ℟.

READING VII

Ezekiel 36:16–17a, 18–28

The word of the LORD came to me, saying: Son of man, when the house of Israel lived in their land, they defiled it by their conduct and deeds. Therefore I poured out my fury upon them because of the blood that they poured out on the ground, and because they defiled it with idols. I scattered them among the nations, dispersing them over foreign lands; according to their conduct and deeds I judged them. But when they came among the nations wherever they came, they served to profane my holy name, because it was said of them: "These are the people of the LORD, yet they had to leave their land." So I have relented because of my holy name which the house of Israel profaned among the nations where they came. Therefore say to the house of Israel: Thus says the Lord GOD: Not for your sakes do I act, house of Israel, but for the sake of my holy name, which you profaned among the nations to which you came. I will prove the holiness of my great name, profaned among the nations, in whose midst you have profaned it. Thus the nations shall know that I am the LORD, says the Lord GOD, when in their sight I prove my holiness through you. For I will take you away from among the nations, gather you from all the foreign lands, and bring you back to your own land. I will sprinkle clean water upon you to cleanse you from all your impurities, and from all your idols I will cleanse you. I will give you a new heart and place a new spirit within you, taking from your bodies your stony hearts and giving you natural hearts. I will put my spirit within you and make you live by my statutes, careful to observe my decrees. You shall live in the land I gave your fathers; you shall be my people, and I will be your God.

RESPONSORIAL PSALM

1. When baptism is celebrated — Psalm 42:3, 5; 43:3, 4

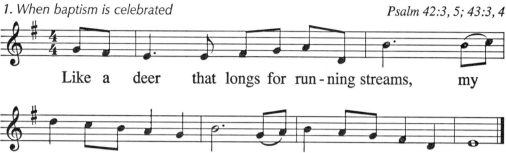

Like a deer that longs for run-ning streams, my soul longs for you, my God; my soul longs for you, my God.

Athirst is my soul for God, the living God.
When shall I go and behold the
face of God? ℟.

I went with the throng
and led them in procession to the
house of God,
amid loud cries of joy and thanksgiving,
with the multitude keeping
festival. ℟.

Send forth your light and your fidelity;
they shall lead me on
and bring me to your holy mountain,
to your dwelling-place. ℟.

Then will I go in to the altar of God,
the God of my gladness and joy;
then will I give you thanks upon the
harp,
O God, my God! ℟.

2. When baptism is not celebrated — Isaiah 12:2–3, 4bcd, 5–6

You will draw wa-ter joy-ful-ly from the springs of sal-va-tion.

God indeed is my savior;
I am confident and unafraid.
My strength and my courage is the LORD,
and he has been my savior.
With joy you will draw water
at the fountain of salvation. ℟.

Give thanks to the LORD, acclaim his
name;
among the nations make known his

deeds,
proclaim how exalted is his name. ℟.

Sing praise to the LORD for his glorious
achievement;
let this be known throughout all the
earth.
Shout with exultation, O city of Zion,
for great in your midst
is the Holy One of Israel! ℟.

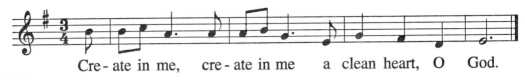

Cre - ate in me,   cre - ate in me   a clean heart, O   God.

A clean heart create for me, O God,
  and a steadfast spirit renew within
  me.
Cast me not out from your presence,
  and your Holy Spirit take not from
  me. ℟.

Give me back the joy of your salvation,
  and a willing spirit sustain in me.

I will teach transgressors your ways,
  and sinners shall return to you. ℟.

For you are not pleased with sacrifices;
  should I offer a holocaust, you
  would not accept it.
My sacrifice, O God, is a contrite spirit;
  a heart contrite and humbled, O God,
  you will not spurn. ℟.

EPISTLE   *Romans 6:3–11*
Brothers and sisters: Are you unaware that we who were baptized into Christ Jesus were
baptized into his death? We were indeed buried with him through baptism into death,
so that, just as Christ was raised from the dead by the glory of the Father, we too might
live in newness of life.

For if we have grown into union with him through a death like his, we shall also be
united with him in the resurrection. We know that our old self was crucified with him, so
that our sinful body might be done away with, that we might no longer be in slavery to
sin. For a dead person has been absolved from sin. If, then, we have died with Christ, we
believe that we shall also live with him. We know that Christ, raised from the dead, dies
no more; death no longer has power over him. As to his death, he died to sin once and
for all; as to his life, he lives for God. Consequently, you too must think of yourselves
as being dead to sin and living for God in Christ Jesus.

RESPONSORIAL PSALM   *Psalm 118:1–2, 16–17, 22–23*

Al - le - lu - ia, al - le - lu - ia, al - le - lu - ia!

Give thanks to the LORD, for he is good,
  for his mercy endures forever.
Let the house of Israel say,
  "His mercy endures forever." ℟.

"The right hand of the LORD has struck
  with power;
  the right hand of the LORD is exalted.

I shall not die, but live,
  and declare the works of the LORD." ℟.

The stone which the builders rejected
  has become the cornerstone.
By the LORD has this been done;
  it is wonderful in our eyes. ℟.

GOSPEL   *Matthew 28:1–10*
After the sabbath, as the first day of the week was dawning, Mary Magdalene and the
other Mary came to see the tomb. And behold, there was a great earthquake; for an angel
of the Lord descended from heaven, approached, rolled back the stone, and sat upon it.

His appearance was like lightning and his clothing was white as snow. The guards were shaken with fear of him and became like dead men. Then the angel said to the women in reply, "Do not be afraid! I know that you are seeking Jesus the crucified. He is not here, for he has been raised just as he said. Come and see the place where he lay. Then go quickly and tell his disciples, 'He has been raised from the dead, and he is going before you to Galilee; there you will see him.' Behold, I have told you." Then they went away quickly from the tomb, fearful yet overjoyed, and ran to announce this to his disciples. And behold, Jesus met them on their way and greeted them. They approached, embraced his feet, and did him homage. Then Jesus said to them, "Do not be afraid. Go tell my brothers to go to Galilee, and there they will see me."

COMMUNION ANTIPHON   *1 Corinthians 5:7–8*
Christ has become our paschal sacrifice; let us feast with the unleavened bread of sincerity and truth, alleluia.

April 24, 2011

EASTER SUNDAY:
THE RESURRECTION OF THE LORD

ENTRANCE ANTIPHON   *Psalm 138:18, 5–6*
I have risen: I am with you once more; you placed your hand on me to keep me safe. How great is the depth of your wisdom, alleluia!

READING I   *Acts 10:34a, 37–43 / 42*
Peter proceeded to speak and said: "You know what has happened all over Judea, beginning in Galilee after the baptism that John preached, how God anointed Jesus of Nazareth with the Holy Spirit and power. He went about doing good and healing all those oppressed by the devil, for God was with him. We are witnesses of all that he did both in the country of the Jews and in Jerusalem. They put him to death by hanging him on a tree. This man God raised on the third day and granted that he be visible, not to all the people, but to us, the witnesses chosen by God in advance, who ate and drank with him after he rose from the dead. He commissioned us to preach to the people and testify that he is the one appointed by God as judge of the living and the dead. To him all the prophets bear witness, that everyone who believes in him will receive forgiveness of sins through his name."

RESPONSORIAL PSALM

Or: Alleluia.

This is the day the Lord has made; let us re - joice and be glad.

Give thanks to the LORD, for he is good,
   for his mercy endures forever.
Let the house of Israel say,
   "His mercy endures forever." ℟.

"The right hand of the LORD has struck
      with power;
   the right hand of the LORD is exalted."

I shall not die, but live,
   and declare the works of the LORD. ℟.

The stone which the builders rejected
   has become the cornerstone.
By the LORD has this been done;
   it is wonderful in our eyes. ℟.

READING II
Colossians 3:1–4

Brothers and sisters: If then you were raised with Christ, seek what is above, where Christ is seated at the right hand of God. Think of what is above, not of what is on earth. For you have died, and your life is hidden with Christ in God. When Christ your life appears, then you too will appear with him in glory.

Or:

READING II
1 Corinthians 5:6b–8

Brothers and sisters: Do you not know that a little yeast leavens all the dough? Clear out the old yeast, so that you may become a fresh batch of dough, inasmuch as you are unleavened. For our paschal lamb, Christ, has been sacrificed. Therefore, let us celebrate the feast, not with the old yeast, the yeast of malice and wickedness, but with the unleavened bread of sincerity and truth.

SEQUENCE

Christians, to the Paschal Victim
   Offer your thankful praises!
A Lamb the sheep redeems;
   Christ, who only is sinless,
   Reconciles sinners to the Father.
Death and life have contended in that
      combat stupendous:
   The Prince of life, who died, reigns
      immortal.
Speak, Mary, declaring
   What you saw, wayfaring.

"The tomb of Christ, who is living,
   The glory of Jesus' resurrection;
Bright angels attesting,
   The shroud and napkin resting.
Yes, Christ my hope is arisen;
   To Galilee he goes before you."
Christ indeed from death is risen,
   our new life obtaining.
Have mercy, victor King, ever
   reigning!
Amen. Alleluia.

The Gospel from the Easter Vigil, (see page 86) may be read in place of the following Gospel at any time of the day.

GOSPEL

John 20:1–9

On the first day of the week, Mary of Magdala came to the tomb early in the morning, while it was still dark, and saw the stone removed from the tomb. So she ran and went to Simon Peter and to the other disciple whom Jesus loved, and told them, "They have taken the Lord from the tomb, and we don't know where they put him." So Peter and the other disciple went out and came to the tomb. They both ran, but the other disciple ran faster than Peter and arrived at the tomb first; he bent down and saw the burial cloths there, but did not go in. When Simon Peter arrived after him, he went into the tomb and saw the burial cloths there, and the cloth that had covered his head, not with the burial cloths but rolled up in a separate place. Then the other disciple also went in, the one who had arrived at the tomb first, and he saw and believed. For they did not yet understand the Scripture that he had to rise from the dead.

Or:

GOSPEL (FOR AFTERNOON OR EVENING MASS)

Luke 24:13–35 / 46

That very day, the first day of the week, two of Jesus' disciples were going to a village seven miles from Jerusalem called Emmaus, and they were conversing about all the things that had occurred. And it happened that while they were conversing and debating, Jesus himself drew near and walked with them, but their eyes were prevented from recognizing him. He asked them, "What are you discussing as you walk along?" They stopped, looking downcast. One of them, named Cleopas, said to him in reply, "Are you the only visitor to Jerusalem who does not know of the things that have taken place there in these days?" And he replied to them, "What sort of things?" They said to him, "The things that happened to Jesus the Nazarene, who was a prophet mighty in deed and word before God and all the people, how our chief priests and rulers both handed him over to a sentence of death and crucified him. But we were hoping that he would be the one to redeem Israel; and besides all this, it is now the third day since this took place. Some women from our group, however, have astounded us: they were at the tomb early in the morning and did not find his body; they came back and reported that they had indeed seen a vision of angels who announced that he was alive. Then some of those with us went to the tomb and found things just as the women had described, but him they did not see." And he said to them, "Oh, how foolish you are! How slow of heart to believe all that the prophets spoke! Was it not necessary that the Christ should suffer these things and enter into his glory?" Then beginning with Moses and all the prophets, he interpreted to them what referred to him in all the Scriptures. As they approached the village to which they were going, he gave the impression that he was going on farther. But they urged him, "Stay with us, for it is nearly evening and the day is almost over." So he went in to stay with them. And it happened that, while he was with them at table, he took bread, said the blessing, broke it, and gave it to them. With that their eyes were opened and they recognized him, but he vanished from their sight. Then they said to each other, "Were not our hearts burning within us while he spoke to us on the way and opened the Scriptures to us?" So they set out at once and returned to Jerusalem where they found gathered together the eleven and those with them who were saying, "The Lord has truly been raised and has appeared to Simon!" Then the two recounted what had taken place on the way and how he was made known to them in the breaking of bread.

COMMUNION ANTIPHON

1 Corinthians 5:7–8

Christ has become our paschal sacrifice; let us feast with the unleavened bread of sincerity and truth, alleluia.

SECOND SUNDAY OF EASTER
DIVINE MERCY SUNDAY

ENTRANCE ANTIPHON *1 Peter 2:2*

Like newborn children you should thirst for milk, on which your spirit can grow to strength, alleluia.

READING I *Acts 2:42–47 / 43*

They devoted themselves to the teaching of the apostles and to the communal life, to the breaking of bread and to the prayers. Awe came upon everyone, and many wonders and signs were done through the apostles. All who believed were together and had all things in common; they would sell their property and possessions and divide them among all according to each one's need. Every day they devoted themselves to meeting together in the temple area and to breaking bread in their homes. They ate their meals with exultation and sincerity of heart, praising God and enjoying favor with all the people. And every day the Lord added to their number those who were being saved.

RESPONSORIAL PSALM *Psalm 118:2–4, 13–15, 22–24*

Or: Alleluia.

Give thanks to the Lord for he is good,

his love is ev - er - last - ing.

Let the house of Israel say,
  "His mercy endures forever."
Let the house of Aaron say,
  "His mercy endures forever."
Let those who fear the LORD say,
  "His mercy endures forever." ℟.

I was hard pressed and was falling,
  but the LORD helped me.
My strength and my courage is the LORD,

and he has been my savior.
The joyful shout of victory
  in the tents of the just. ℟.

The stone which the builders rejected
  has become the cornerstone.
By the LORD has this been done;
  it is wonderful in our eyes.
This is the day the LORD has made;
  let us be glad and rejoice in it. ℟.

READING II *1 Peter 1:3–9*

Blessed be the God and Father of our Lord Jesus Christ, who in his great mercy gave us a new birth to a living hope through the resurrection of Jesus Christ from the dead, to an inheritance that is imperishable, undefiled, and unfading, kept in heaven for you who by the power of God are safeguarded through faith, to a salvation that is ready to be revealed in the final time. In this you rejoice, although now for a little while you may have to suffer through various trials, so that the genuineness of your faith, more precious than gold that is perishable even though tested by fire, may prove to be for praise, glory, and honor at the revelation of Jesus Christ. Although you have not seen him you love him; even though you do not see him now yet believe in him, you rejoice with an indescribable and glorious joy, as you attain the goal of your faith, the salvation of your souls.

GOSPEL
John 20:19–31

On the evening of that first day of the week, when the doors were locked, where the disciples were, for fear of the Jews, Jesus came and stood in their midst and said to them, "Peace be with you." When he had said this, he showed them his hands and his side. The disciples rejoiced when they saw the Lord. Jesus said to them again, "Peace be with you. As the Father has sent me, so I send you." And when he had said this, he breathed on them and said to them, "Receive the Holy Spirit. Whose sins you forgive are forgiven them, and whose sins you retain are retained."

Thomas, called Didymus, one of the Twelve, was not with them when Jesus came. So the other disciples said to him, "We have seen the Lord." But he said to them, "Unless I see the mark of the nails in his hands and put my finger into the nailmarks and put my hand into his side, I will not believe."

Now a week later his disciples were again inside and Thomas was with them. Jesus came, although the doors were locked, and stood in their midst and said, "Peace be with you." Then he said to Thomas, "Put your finger here and see my hands, and bring your hand and put it into my side, and do not be unbelieving, but believe." Thomas answered and said to him, "My Lord and my God!" Jesus said to him, "Have you come to believe because you have seen me? Blessed are those who have not seen and have believed."

Now, Jesus did many other signs in the presence of his disciples that are not written in this book. But these are written that you may come to believe that Jesus is the Christ, the Son of God, and that through this belief you may have life in his name.

COMMUNION ANTIPHON
See John 20:27

Jesus spoke to Thomas: Put your hand here, and see the place of the nails. Doubt no longer, but believe, alleluia.

May 8, 2011

THIRD SUNDAY OF EASTER

ENTRANCE ANTIPHON
Psalm 65:1–2

Let all the earth cry out to God with joy; praise the glory of his name; proclaim his glorious praise, alleluia.

READING I
Acts 2:14, 22–33 / 46

Then Peter stood up with the Eleven, raised his voice, and proclaimed: "You who are Jews, indeed all of you staying in Jerusalem. Let this be known to you, and listen to my words. You who are Israelites, hear these words. Jesus the Nazarene was a man commended to you by God with mighty deeds, wonders, and signs, which God worked through him in your midst, as you yourselves know. This man, delivered up by the set plan and foreknowledge of God, you killed, using lawless men to crucify him. But God raised him up, releasing him from the throes of death, because it was impossible for him to be held by it. For David says of him:

I saw the Lord ever before me,
with him at my right hand I shall not be disturbed.

Therefore my heart has been glad and my tongue has exulted;
   my flesh, too, will dwell in hope,
because you will not abandon my soul to the netherworld,
   nor will you suffer your holy one to see corruption.
You have made known to me the paths of life;
   you will fill me with joy in your presence.

"My brothers, one can confidently say to you about the patriarch David that he died and was buried, and his tomb is in our midst to this day. But since he was a prophet and knew that God had sworn an oath to him that he would set one of his descendants upon his throne, he foresaw and spoke of the resurrection of the Christ, that neither was he abandoned to the netherworld nor did his flesh see corruption. God raised this Jesus; of this we are all witnesses. Exalted at the right hand of God, he received the promise of the Holy Spirit from the Father and poured him forth, as you see and hear."

RESPONSORIAL PSALM   *Psalm 16:1–2, 5, 7–8, 9–10, 11*
Or: Alleluia.

Lord, you will show us the path of life.

Keep me, O God, for in you I take refuge;
   I say to the LORD, "My Lord are
      you."
O LORD, my allotted portion and my cup,
   you it is who hold fast my lot. ℞.

I bless the LORD who counsels me;
   even in the night my heart exhorts
      me.
I set the LORD ever before me;
   with him at my right hand I shall
      not be disturbed. ℞.

Therefore my heart is glad and my soul
      rejoices,
   my body, too, abides in confidence;
because you will not abandon my soul
      to the netherworld,
   nor will you suffer your faithful one
      to undergo corruption. ℞.

You will show me the path to life,
   abounding joy in your presence,
   the delights at your right hand
      forever. ℞.

READING II   *1 Peter 1:17–21*
Beloved: If you invoke as Father him who judges impartially according to each one's works, conduct yourselves with reverence during the time of your sojourning, realizing that you were ransomed from your futile conduct, handed on by your ancestors, not with perishable things like silver or gold but with the precious blood of Christ as of a spotless unblemished lamb.

He was known before the foundation of the world but revealed in the final time for you, who through him believe in God who raised him from the dead and gave him glory, so that your faith and hope are in God.

GOSPEL   *Luke 24:13–35*
That very day, the first day of the week, two of Jesus' disciples were going to a village seven miles from Jerusalem called Emmaus, and they were conversing about all the things that had occurred. And it happened that while they were conversing and debating, Jesus himself drew near and walked with them, but their eyes were prevented from

recognizing him. He asked them, "What are you discussing as you walk along?" They stopped, looking downcast. One of them, named Cleopas, said to him in reply, "Are you the only visitor to Jerusalem who does not know of the things that have taken place there in these days?" And he replied to them, "What sort of things?" They said to him, "The things that happened to Jesus the Nazarene, who was a prophet mighty in deed and word before God and all the people, how our chief priests and rulers both handed him over to a sentence of death and crucified him. But we were hoping that he would be the one to redeem Israel; and besides all this, it is now the third day since this took place. Some women from our group, however, have astounded us: they were at the tomb early in the morning and did not find his body; they came back and reported that they had indeed seen a vision of angels who announced that he was alive. Then some of those with us went to the tomb and found things just as the women had described, but him they did not see." And he said to them, "Oh, how foolish you are! How slow of heart to believe all that the prophets spoke! Was it not necessary that the Christ should suffer these things and enter into his glory?" Then beginning with Moses and all the prophets, he interpreted to them what referred to him in all the Scriptures. As they approached the village to which they were going, he gave the impression that he was going on farther. But they urged him, "Stay with us, for it is nearly evening and the day is almost over." So he went in to stay with them. And it happened that, while he was with them at table, he took bread, said the blessing, broke it, and gave it to them. With that their eyes were opened and they recognized him, but he vanished from their sight. Then they said to each other, "Were not our hearts burning within us while he spoke to us on the way and opened the Scriptures to us?" So they set out at once and returned to Jerusalem where they found gathered together the eleven and those with them who were saying, "The Lord has truly been raised and has appeared to Simon!" Then the two recounted what had taken place on the way and how he was made known to them in the breaking of bread.

COMMUNION ANTIPHON *Luke 24:35*
The disciples recognized the Lord Jesus in the breaking of bread, alleluia.

May 15, 2011

FOURTH SUNDAY OF EASTER

ENTRANCE ANTIPHON *Psalm 32:5–6*
The earth is full of the goodness of the Lord; by the word of the Lord the heavens were made, alleluia.

READING I *Acts 2:14a, 36–41 / 49*
Then Peter stood up with the Eleven, raised his voice, and proclaimed: "Let the whole house of Israel know for certain that God has made both Lord and Christ, this Jesus whom you crucified."

Now when they heard this, they were cut to the heart, and they asked Peter and the other apostles, "What are we to do, my brothers?" Peter said to them, "Repent and be baptized, every one of you, in the name of Jesus Christ for the forgiveness of your sins; and you will receive the gift of the Holy Spirit. For the promise is made to you and to your children and to all those far off, whomever the Lord our God will call." He testified with many other arguments, and was exhorting them, "Save yourselves from this corrupt generation." Those who accepted his message were baptized, and about three thousand persons were added that day.

RESPONSORIAL PSALM

Psalm 23:1–3a, 3b–4, 5, 6

Or: Alleluia.

The Lord is my shep-herd; there is noth - ing I shall want.

The LORD is my shepherd; I shall not
    want.
  In verdant pastures he gives me
    repose;
beside restful waters he leads me;
  he refreshes my soul. ℟.

He guides me in right paths
  for his name's sake.
Even though I walk in the dark valley
  I fear no evil; for you are at my side
with your rod and your staff

that give me courage. ℟.

You spread the table before me
  in the sight of my foes;
you anoint my head with oil;
  my cup overflows. ℟.

Only goodness and kindness follow me
  all the days of my life;
and I shall dwell in the house of the
    LORD
  for years to come. ℟.

READING II

1 Peter 2:20b–25

Beloved: If you are patient when you suffer for doing what is good, this is a grace before God. For to this you have been called, because Christ also suffered for you, leaving you an example that you should follow in his footsteps.
    He committed no sin, and no deceit was found in his mouth.

When he was insulted, he returned no insult; when he suffered, he did not threaten; instead, he handed himself over to the one who judges justly. He himself bore our sins in his body upon the cross, so that, free from sin, we might live for righteousness. By his wounds you have been healed. For you had gone astray like sheep, but you have now returned to the shepherd and guardian of your souls.

GOSPEL

John 10:1–10

Jesus said: "Amen, amen, I say to you, whoever does not enter a sheepfold through the gate but climbs over elsewhere is a thief and a robber. But whoever enters through the gate is the shepherd of the sheep. The gatekeeper opens it for him, and the sheep hear his voice, as the shepherd calls his own sheep by name and leads them out. When he has driven out all his own, he walks ahead of them, and the sheep follow him, because they recognize his voice. But they will not follow a stranger; they will run away from him, because they do not recognize the voice of strangers." Although Jesus used this figure of speech, the Pharisees did not realize what he was trying to tell them.

    So Jesus said again, "Amen, amen, I say to you, I am the gate for the sheep. All who came before me are thieves and robbers, but the sheep did not listen to them. I am the gate. Whoever enters through me will be saved, and will come in and go out and find pasture. A thief comes only to steal and slaughter and destroy; I came so that they might have life and have it more abundantly."

COMMUNION ANTIPHON

The Good Shepherd is risen! He who laid down his life for his sheep, who died for his flock, he is risen, alleluia.

May 22, 2011
FIFTH SUNDAY OF EASTER

ENTRANCE ANTIPHON *Psalm 97:1–2*
Sing to the Lord a new song, for he has done marvelous deeds; he has revealed to the nations his saving power, alleluia.

READING I *Acts 6:1–7 / 52*
As the number of disciples continued to grow, the Hellenists complained against the Hebrews because their widows were being neglected in the daily distribution. So the Twelve called together the community of the disciples and said, "It is not right for us to neglect the word of God to serve at table. Brothers, select from among you seven reputable men, filled with the Spirit and wisdom, whom we shall appoint to this task, whereas we shall devote ourselves to prayer and to the ministry of the word." The proposal was acceptable to the whole community, so they chose Stephen, a man filled with faith and the Holy Spirit, also Philip, Prochorus, Nicanor, Timon, Parmenas, and Nicholas of Antioch, a convert to Judaism. They presented these men to the apostles who prayed and laid hands on them. The word of God continued to spread, and the number of the disciples in Jerusalem increased greatly; even a large group of priests were becoming obedient to the faith.

RESPONSORIAL PSALM *Psalm 33:1–2, 4–5, 18–19*
Or: Alleluia.

Lord, let your mer-cy be on us, as we place our trust in you.

Exult, you just, in the LORD;
   praise from the upright is fitting.
Give thanks to the LORD on the harp;
   with the ten-stringed lyre chant his
     praises. ℟.

Upright is the word of the LORD,
   and all his works are trustworthy.
He loves justice and right;

of the kindness of the LORD the earth
   is full. ℟.

See, the eyes of the LORD are upon those
   who fear him,
   upon those who hope for his kindness,
to deliver them from death
   and preserve them in spite of
     famine. ℟.

READING II *1 Peter 2:4–9*
Beloved: Come to him, a living stone, rejected by human beings but chosen and precious in the sight of God, and, like living stones, let yourselves be built into a spiritual house to be a holy priesthood to offer spiritual sacrifices acceptable to God through Jesus Christ. For it says in Scripture:
   Behold, I am laying a stone in Zion,
   a cornerstone, chosen and precious,
   and whoever believes in it shall not be put to shame.
Therefore, its value is for you who have faith, but for those without faith:
   The stone that the builders rejected
   has become the cornerstone,

and

A stone that will make people stumble,
and a rock that will make them fall.

They stumble by disobeying the word, as is their destiny.

You are "a chosen race, a royal priesthood, a holy nation, a people of his own, so that you may announce the praises" of him who called you out of darkness into his wonderful light.

GOSPEL
John 14:1–12

Jesus said to his disciples: "Do not let your hearts be troubled. You have faith in God; have faith also in me. In my Father's house there are many dwelling places. If there were not, would I have told you that I am going to prepare a place for you? And if I go and prepare a place for you, I will come back again and take you to myself, so that where I am you also may be. Where I am going you know the way." Thomas said to him, "Master, we do not know where you are going; how can we know the way?" Jesus said to him, "I am the way and the truth and the life. No one comes to the Father except through me. If you know me, then you will also know my Father. From now on you do know him and have seen him." Philip said to him, "Master, show us the Father, and that will be enough for us." Jesus said to him, "Have I been with you for so long a time and you still do not know me, Philip? Whoever has seen me has seen the Father. How can you say, 'Show us the Father'? Do you not believe that I am in the Father and the Father is in me? The words that I speak to you I do not speak on my own. The Father who dwells in me is doing his works. Believe me that I am in the Father and the Father is in me, or else, believe because of the works themselves. Amen, amen, I say to you, whoever believes in me will do the works that I do, and will do greater ones than these, because I am going to the Father."

COMMUNION ANTIPHON
John 15:5

I am the vine and you are the branches, says the Lord; he who lives in me, and I in him, will bear much fruit, alleluia.

May 29, 2011
SIXTH SUNDAY OF EASTER

(When the Lord's Ascension is celebrated on the following Sunday, the second reading and gospel given for the Seventh Sunday of Easter may be read on the Sixth Sunday.)

ENTRANCE ANTIPHON
See Isaiah 48:20

Speak out with a voice of joy; let it be heard to the ends of the earth: The Lord has set his people free, alleluia.

READING I
Acts 8:5–8, 14–17 / 55

Philip went down to the city of Samaria and proclaimed the Christ to them. With one accord, the crowds paid attention to what was said by Philip when they heard it and saw the signs he was doing. For unclean spirits, crying out in a loud voice, came out of many possessed people, and many paralyzed or crippled people were cured. There was great joy in that city.

Now when the apostles in Jerusalem heard that Samaria had accepted the word of God, they sent them Peter and John, who went down and prayed for them, that they might receive the Holy Spirit, for it had not yet fallen upon any of them; they had only been baptized in the name of the Lord Jesus. Then they laid hands on them and they received the Holy Spirit.

RESPONSORIAL PSALM
Or: Alleluia.

Psalm 66:1–3, 4–5, 6–7, 16, 20

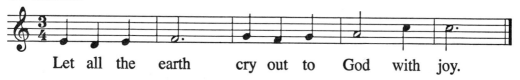

Let all the earth cry out to God with joy.

Shout joyfully to God, all the earth,
  sing praise to the glory of his name;
  proclaim his glorious praise.
Say to God, "How tremendous are
    your deeds!" ℟.

"Let all on earth worship and sing praise
    to you,
  sing praise to your name!"
Come and see the works of God,
  his tremendous deeds among the
    children of Adam. ℟.

He has changed the sea into dry land;
  through the river they passed on foot;
  therefore let us rejoice in him.
He rules by his might forever. ℟.

Hear now, all you who fear God, while
    I declare
  what he has done for me.
Blessed be God who refused me not
  my prayer or his kindness! ℟.

READING II
1 Peter 3:15–18

Beloved: Sanctify Christ as Lord in your hearts. Always be ready to give an explanation to anyone who asks you for a reason for your hope, but do it with gentleness and reverence, keeping your conscience clear, so that, when you are maligned, those who defame your good conduct in Christ may themselves be put to shame. For it is better to suffer for doing good, if that be the will of God, than for doing evil.

For Christ also suffered for sins once, the righteous for the sake of the unrighteous, that he might lead you to God. Put to death in the flesh, he was brought to life in the Spirit.

GOSPEL
John 14:15–21

Jesus said to his disciples: "If you love me, you will keep my commandments. And I will ask the Father, and he will give you another Advocate to be with you always, the Spirit of truth, whom the world cannot accept, because it neither sees nor knows him. But you know him, because he remains with you, and will be in you. I will not leave you orphans; I will come to you. In a little while the world will no longer see me, but you will see me, because I live and you will live. On that day you will realize that I am in my Father and you are in me and I in you. Whoever has my commandments and observes them is the one who loves me. And whoever loves me will be loved by my Father, and I will love him and reveal myself to him."

COMMUNION ANTIPHON
John 14:15–16

If you love me, keep my commandments, says the Lord. The Father will send you the Holy Spirit, to be with you for ever, alleluia.

ASCENSION OF THE LORD

ENTRANCE ANTIPHON *Acts 1:11*

Men of Galilee, why do you stand looking in the sky? The Lord will return, just as you have seen him ascend, alleluia.

READING I *Acts 1:1–11 / 58*

In the first book, Theophilus, I dealt with all that Jesus did and taught until the day he was taken up, after giving instructions through the Holy Spirit to the apostles whom he had chosen. He presented himself alive to them by many proofs after he had suffered, appearing to them during forty days and speaking about the kingdom of God. While meeting with them, he enjoined them not to depart from Jerusalem, but to wait for "the promise of the Father about which you have heard me speak; for John baptized with water, but in a few days you will be baptized with the Holy Spirit."

When they had gathered together they asked him, "Lord, are you at this time going to restore the kingdom to Israel?" He answered them, "It is not for you to know the times or seasons that the Father has established by his own authority. But you will receive power when the Holy Spirit comes upon you, and you will be my witnesses in Jerusalem, throughout Judea and Samaria, and to the ends of the earth." When he had said this, as they were looking on, he was lifted up, and a cloud took him from their sight. While they were looking intently at the sky as he was going, suddenly two men dressed in white garments stood beside them. They said, "Men of Galilee, why are you standing there looking at the sky? This Jesus who has been taken up from you into heaven will return in the same way as you have seen him going into heaven."

RESPONSORIAL PSALM *Psalm 47:2–3, 6–7, 8–9*

Or: Alleluia.

God mounts his throne to shouts of joy: a blare of trum-pets for the Lord.

All you peoples, clap your hands,
    shout to God with cries of gladness,
For the Lord, the Most High, the
        awesome,
    is the great king over all the earth. ℟.

God mounts his throne amid shouts of
        joy;
    the Lord, amid trumpet blasts.

Sing praise to God, sing praise;
    sing praise to our king, sing praise. ℟.

For king of all the earth is God;
    sing hymns of praise.
God reigns over the nations,
    God sits upon his holy throne. ℟.

READING II *Ephesians 1:17–23*

Brothers and sisters: May the God of our Lord Jesus Christ, the Father of glory, give you a Spirit of wisdom and revelation resulting in knowledge of him. May the eyes of your hearts be enlightened, that you may know what is the hope that belongs to his call, what are the riches of glory in his inheritance among the holy ones, and what is the surpassing greatness of his power for us who believe, in accord with the exercise of his great might, which he worked in Christ, raising him from the dead and seating him at his right hand in the heavens, far above every principality, authority, power, and dominion, and every name that is named not only in this age but also in the one to come. And he put all things beneath his feet and gave him as head over all things to the church, which is his body, the fullness of the one who fills all things in every way.

GOSPEL *Matthew 28:16–20*

The eleven disciples went to Galilee, to the mountain to which Jesus had ordered them. When they saw him, they worshiped, but they doubted. Then Jesus approached and said to them, "All power in heaven and on earth has been given to me. Go, therefore, and make disciples of all nations, baptizing them in the name of the Father, and of the Son, and of the Holy Spirit, teaching them to observe all that I have commanded you. And behold, I am with you always, until the end of the age."

COMMUNION ANTIPHON *Matthew 28:20*

I, the Lord, am with you always, until the end of the world, alleluia.

June 5, 2011

SEVENTH SUNDAY OF EASTER

(In those places where the solemnity of the Ascension of the Lord has been transferred to the Seventh Sunday of Easter, the Mass and readings of the Ascension are used.)

ENTRANCE ANTIPHON *Psalm 26:7–9*

Lord, hear my voice when I call to you. My heart has prompted me to seek your face; I seek it, Lord; do not hide from me, alleluia.

READING I *Acts 1:12–14 / 59*

After Jesus had been taken up to heaven the apostles returned to Jerusalem from the mount called Olivet, which is near Jerusalem, a sabbath day's journey away.

When they entered the city they went to the upper room where they were staying, Peter and John and James and Andrew, Philip and Thomas, Bartholomew and Matthew, James son of Alphaeus, Simon the Zealot, and Judas son of James. All these devoted themselves with one accord to prayer, together with some women, and Mary the mother of Jesus, and his brothers.

RESPONSORIAL PSALM

Or: Alleluia.

Psalm 27:1, 4, 7–8

I be - lieve that I shall see the good things of the

Lord in the land of the liv - ing.

The LORD is my light and my salvation;
    whom should I fear?
The LORD is my life's refuge;
    of whom should I be afraid? ℟.

One thing I ask of the LORD;
    this I seek:
To dwell in the house of the LORD
    all the days of my life,

That I may gaze on the loveliness of
    the LORD
    and contemplate his temple. ℟.

Hear, O LORD, the sound of my call;
    have pity on me, and answer me.
Of you my heart speaks; you my glance
    seeks. ℟.

READING II

1 Peter 4:13–16

Beloved: Rejoice to the extent that you share in the sufferings of Christ, so that when his glory is revealed you may also rejoice exultantly. If you are insulted for the name of Christ, blessed are you, for the Spirit of glory and of God rests upon you. But let no one among you be made to suffer as a murderer, a thief, an evildoer, or as an intriguer. But whoever is made to suffer as a Christian should not be ashamed but glorify God because of the name.

GOSPEL

John 17:1–11a

Jesus raised his eyes to heaven and said, "Father, the hour has come. Give glory to your son, so that your son may glorify you, just as you gave him authority over all people, so that your son may give eternal life to all you gave him. Now this is eternal life, that they should know you, the only true God, and the one whom you sent, Jesus Christ. I glorified you on earth by accomplishing the work that you gave me to do. Now glorify me, Father, with you, with the glory that I had with you before the world began.

"I revealed your name to those whom you gave me out of the world. They belonged to you, and you gave them to me, and they have kept your word. Now they know that everything you gave me is from you, because the words you gave to me I have given to them, and they accepted them and truly understood that I came from you, and they have believed that you sent me. I pray for them. I do not pray for the world but for the ones you have given me, because they are yours, and everything of mine is yours and everything of yours is mine, and I have been glorified in them. And now I will no longer be in the world, but they are in the world, while I am coming to you."

COMMUNION ANTIPHON

John 17:22

This is the prayer of Jesus: that his believers may become one as he is one with the Father, alleluia.

VIGIL OF PENTECOST

ENTRANCE ANTIPHON *See Romans 5:5; 8:11*
The love of God has been poured into our hearts by his Spirit living in us, alleluia.

READING I *Genesis 11:1–9 / 62*
The whole world spoke the same language, using the same words. While the people were migrating in the east, they came upon a valley in the land of Shinar and settled there. They said to one another, "Come, let us mold bricks and harden them with fire." They used bricks for stone, and bitumen for mortar. Then they said, "Come, let us build ourselves a city and a tower with its top in the sky, and so make a name for ourselves; otherwise we shall be scattered all over the earth."

The LORD came down to see the city and the tower that the people had built. Then the LORD said: "If now, while they are one people, all speaking the same language, they have started to do this, nothing will later stop them from doing whatever they presume to do. Let us then go down there and confuse their language, so that one will not understand what another says." Thus the LORD scattered them from there all over the earth, and they stopped building the city. That is why it was called Babel, because there the LORD confused the speech of all the world. It was from that place that he scattered them all over the earth.

Or:

READING I *Exodus 19:3–8a, 16–20b*
Moses went up the mountain to God. Then the LORD called to him and said, "Thus shall you say to the house of Jacob; tell the Israelites: You have seen for yourselves how I treated the Egyptians and how I bore you up on eagle wings and brought you here to myself. Therefore, if you hearken to my voice and keep my covenant, you shall be my special possession, dearer to me than all other people, though all the earth is mine. You shall be to me a kingdom of priests, a holy nation. That is what you must tell the Israelites." So Moses went and summoned the elders of the people. When he set before them all that the LORD had ordered him to tell them, the people all answered together, "Everything the LORD has said, we will do."

On the morning of the third day there were peals of thunder and lightning, and a heavy cloud over the mountain, and a very loud trumpet blast, so that all the people in the camp trembled. But Moses led the people out of the camp to meet God, and they stationed themselves at the foot of the mountain. Mount Sinai was all wrapped in smoke, for the LORD came down upon it in fire. The smoke rose from it as though from a furnace, and the whole mountain trembled violently. The trumpet blast grew louder and louder, while Moses was speaking, and God answering him with thunder.

When the LORD came down to the top of Mount Sinai, he summoned Moses to the top of the mountain.

Or:

READING I *Ezekiel 37:1–14*
The hand of the LORD came upon me, and he led me out in the spirit of the LORD and set me in the center of the plain, which was now filled with bones. He made me walk among the bones in every direction so that I saw how many they were on the surface of

the plain. How dry they were! He asked me: Son of man, can these bones come to life? I answered, "Lord God, you alone know that." Then he said to me: Prophesy over these bones, and say to them: Dry bones, hear the word of the Lord! Thus says the Lord God to these bones: See! I will bring spirit into you, that you may come to life. I will put sinews upon you, make flesh grow over you, cover you with skin, and put spirit in you so that you may come to life and know that I am the Lord. I, Ezekiel, prophesied as I had been told, and even as I was prophesying I heard a noise; it was a rattling as the bones came together, bone joining bone. I saw the sinews and the flesh come upon them, and the skin cover them, but there was no spirit in them. Then the Lord said to me: Prophesy to the spirit, prophesy, son of man, and say to the spirit: Thus says the Lord God: From the four winds come, O spirit, and breathe into these slain that they may come to life. I prophesied as he told me, and the spirit came into them; they came alive and stood upright, a vast army. Then he said to me: Son of man, these bones are the whole house of Israel. They have been saying, "Our bones are dried up, our hope is lost, and we are cut off." Therefore, prophesy and say to them: Thus says the Lord God: O my people, I will open your graves and have you rise from them, and bring you back to the land of Israel. Then you shall know that I am the Lord, when I open your graves and have you rise from them, O my people! I will put my spirit in you that you may live, and I will settle you upon your land; thus you shall know that I am the Lord. I have promised, and I will do it, says the Lord.

Or:

READING I   *Joel 3:1–5*

Thus says the Lord:
I will pour out my spirit upon all flesh.
Your sons and daughters shall prophesy,
   your old men shall dream dreams,
   your young men shall see visions;
even upon the servants and the handmaids,
   in those days, I will pour out my spirit.
And I will work wonders in the heavens
      and on the earth,
   blood, fire, and columns of smoke;
the sun will be turned to darkness,
and the moon to blood,
at the coming of the day of the Lord,
   the great and terrible day.
Then everyone shall be rescued
   who calls on the name of the Lord;
for on Mount Zion there shall be a
      remnant,
   as the Lord has said,
and in Jerusalem survivors
   whom the Lord shall call.

RESPONSORIAL PSALM   *Psalm 104:1–2, 24, 35, 27–28, 29, 30*
Or: Alleluia.

Lord, send out your Spir - it, and re - new the face of the earth.

Bless the Lord, O my soul!
   O Lord, my God, you are great
      indeed!
You are clothed with majesty and glory,
   robed in light as with a cloak. ℟.

How manifold are your works, O Lord!
   In wisdom you have wrought them
      all—

the earth is full of your creatures;
   bless the Lord, O my soul!
   Alleluia. ℟.

Creatures all look to you
   to give them food in due time.
When you give it to them, they gather it;
   when you open your hand, they are
      filled with good things. ℟.

If you take away their breath, they perish
    and return to their dust.
When you send forth your spirit, they are created,
    and you renew the face of the earth. ℟.

READING II
Romans 8:22–27
Brothers and sisters: We know that all creation is groaning in labor pains even until now; and not only that, but we ourselves, who have the firstfruits of the Spirit, we also groan within ourselves as we wait for adoption, the redemption of our bodies. For in hope we were saved. Now hope that sees is not hope. For who hopes for what one sees? But if we hope for what we do not see, we wait with endurance.

In the same way, the Spirit too comes to the aid of our weakness; for we do not know how to pray as we ought, but the Spirit himself intercedes with inexpressible groanings. And the one who searches hearts knows what is the intention of the Spirit, because he intercedes for the holy ones according to God's will.

GOSPEL
John 7:37–39
On the last and greatest day of the feast, Jesus stood up and exclaimed, "Let anyone who thirsts come to me and drink. As Scripture says:
Rivers of living water will flow from within him who believes in me."

He said this in reference to the Spirit that those who came to believe in him were to receive. There was, of course, no Spirit yet, because Jesus had not yet been glorified.

COMMUNION ANTIPHON
John 7:37
On the last day of the festival, Jesus stood and cried aloud: If anyone is thirsty, let him come to me and drink, alleluia.

June 12, 2011
PENTECOST SUNDAY

ENTRANCE ANTIPHON
See Romans 5:5, 8:11
The love of God has been poured into our hearts by his Spirit living in us, alleluia.

READING I
Acts 2:1–11 / 63
When the time for Pentecost was fulfilled, they were all in one place together. And suddenly there came from the sky a noise like a strong driving wind, and it filled the entire house in which they were. Then there appeared to them tongues as of fire, which parted and came to rest on each one of them. And they were all filled with the Holy Spirit and began to speak in different tongues, as the Spirit enabled them to proclaim.

Now there were devout Jews from every nation under heaven staying in Jerusalem. At this sound, they gathered in a large crowd, but they were confused because each one heard them speaking in his own language. They were astounded, and in amazement they asked, "Are not all these people who are speaking Galileans? Then how does each of us hear them in his native language? We are Parthians, Medes, and Elamites, inhabitants of Mesopotamia, Judea and Cappadocia, Pontus and Asia, Phrygia and Pamphylia, Egypt and the districts of Libya near Cyrene, as well as travelers from Rome, both Jews and converts to Judaism, Cretans and Arabs, yet we hear them speaking in our own tongues of the mighty acts of God."

RESPONSORIAL PSALM

Or: Alleluia.

Psalm 104:1, 24, 29–30, 31, 34

Lord, send out your Spir - it, and re - new the face of the earth.

Bless the LORD, O my soul!
O LORD, my God, you are great
indeed!
How manifold are your works, O LORD!
the earth is full of your creatures. ℟.

May the glory of the LORD endure
forever;
may the LORD be glad in his works!

Pleasing to him be my theme;
I will be glad in the LORD. ℟.

If you take away their breath, they perish
and return to their dust.
When you send forth your spirit, they are
created,
and you renew the face of the
earth. ℟.

READING II

1 Corinthians 12:3b–7, 12–13

Brothers and sisters: No one can say, "Jesus is Lord," except by the Holy Spirit.

There are different kinds of spiritual gifts but the same Spirit; there are different forms of service but the same Lord; there are different workings but the same God who produces all of them in everyone. To each individual the manifestation of the Spirit is given for some benefit.

As a body is one though it has many parts, and all the parts of the body, though many, are one body, so also Christ. For in one Spirit we were all baptized into one body, whether Jews or Greeks, slaves or free persons, and we were all given to drink of one Spirit.

SEQUENCE

Come, Holy Spirit, come!
And from your celestial home
Shed a ray of light divine!
Come, Father of the poor!
Come, source of all our store!
Come, within our bosoms shine.
You, of comforters the best;
You, the soul's most welcome guest;
Sweet refreshment here below;
In our labor, rest most sweet;
Grateful coolness in the heat;
Solace in the midst of woe.
O most blessed Light divine,
Shine within these hearts of yours,
And our inmost being fill!
Where you are not, we have naught,

Nothing good in deed or thought,
Nothing free from taint of ill.
Heal our wounds, our strength renew;
On our dryness pour your dew;
Wash the stains of guilt away:
Bend the stubborn heart and will;
Melt the frozen, warm the chill;
Guide the steps that go astray.
On the faithful, who adore
And confess you, evermore
In your sevenfold gift descend;
Give them virtue's sure reward;
Give them your salvation, Lord;
Give them joys that never end.
Amen. Alleluia.

GOSPEL

John 20:19–23

On the evening of that first day of the week, when the doors were locked, where the disciples were, for fear of the Jews, Jesus came and stood in their midst and said to them, "Peace be with you." When he had said this, he showed them his hands and his side. The disciples rejoiced when they saw the Lord. Jesus said to them again, "Peace be with you. As the Father has sent me, so I send you." And when he had said this, he breathed on them and said to them, "Receive the Holy Spirit. Whose sins you forgive are forgiven them, and whose sins you retain are retained."

COMMUNION ANTIPHON

Acts 2:4, 11

They were all filled with the Holy Spirit, and they spoke of the great things God had done, alleluia.

June 19, 2011

THE MOST HOLY TRINITY

ENTRANCE ANTIPHON

Blessed be God the Father and his only-begotten Son and the Holy Spirit: for he has shown that he loves us.

READING I

Exodus 34:4b–6, 8–9 / 164

Early in the morning Moses went up Mount Sinai as the LORD had commanded him, taking along the two stone tablets.

Having come down in a cloud, the LORD stood with Moses there and proclaimed his name, "LORD." Thus the LORD passed before him and cried out, "The LORD, the LORD, a merciful and gracious God, slow to anger and rich in kindness and fidelity." Moses at once bowed down to the ground in worship. Then he said, "If I find favor with you, O LORD, do come along in our company. This is indeed a stiff-necked people; yet pardon our wickedness and sins, and receive us as your own."

RESPONSORIAL PSALM

Daniel 3:52, 53, 54, 55

Glo - ry and praise for ev - er- more.

Blessed are you, O Lord, the God of our fathers,
praiseworthy and exalted above all forever;
and blessed is your holy and glorious name,
praiseworthy and exalted above all for all ages. ℟.

Blessed are you in the temple of your holy glory,
praiseworthy and glorious above all forever. ℟.

Blessed are you on the throne of your kingdom,
praiseworthy and exalted above all forever. ℟.

Blessed are you who look into the depths from your throne upon the cherubim,
praiseworthy and exalted above all forever. ℟.

READING II   *2 Corinthians 13:11–13*

Brothers and sisters, rejoice. Mend your ways, encourage one another, agree with one another, live in peace, and the God of love and peace will be with you. Greet one another with a holy kiss. All the holy ones greet you.

The grace of the Lord Jesus Christ and the love of God and the fellowship of the Holy Spirit be with all of you.

GOSPEL   *John 3:16–18*

God so loved the world that he gave his only Son, so that everyone who believes in him might not perish but might have eternal life. For God did not send his Son into the world to condemn the world, but that the world might be saved through him. Whoever believes in him will not be condemned, but whoever does not believe has already been condemned, because he has not believed in the name of the only Son of God.

COMMUNION ANTIPHON   *Galatians 4:6*

You are the sons of God, so God has given you the Spirit of his Son to form your hearts and make you cry out: Abba, Father.

June 26, 2011

THE MOST HOLY BODY AND BLOOD OF CHRIST

ENTRANCE ANTIPHON   *Psalm 80:17*

The Lord fed his people with the finest wheat and honey; their hunger was satisfied.

READING I   *Deuteronomy 8:2–3, 14b–16a / 167*

Moses said to the people: "Remember how for forty years now the Lᴏʀᴅ, your God, has directed all your journeying in the desert, so as to test you by affliction and find out whether or not it was your intention to keep his commandments. He therefore let you be afflicted with hunger, and then fed you with manna, a food unknown to you and your fathers, in order to show you that not by bread alone does one live, but by every word that comes forth from the mouth of the Lᴏʀᴅ.

"Do not forget the Lᴏʀᴅ, your God, who brought you out of the land of Egypt, that place of slavery; who guided you through the vast and terrible desert with its saraph serpents and scorpions, its parched and waterless ground; who brought forth water for you from the flinty rock and fed you in the desert with manna, a food unknown to your fathers."

RESPONSORIAL PSALM   *Psalm 147:12–13, 14–15, 19–20*
Or: Alleluia.

O   praise   the   Lord,   Je - ru - sa - lem.

Glorify the Lord, O Jerusalem;
praise your God, O Zion.
For he has strengthened the bars of your
gates;
he has blessed your children within
you. ℟.

He has granted peace in your borders;
with the best of wheat he fills you.
He sends forth his command to the earth;
swiftly runs his word! ℟.

He has proclaimed his word to Jacob,
his statutes and his ordinances to
Israel.
He has not done thus for any other
nation;
his ordinances he has not made
known to them. Alleluia. ℟.

READING II *1 Corinthians 10:16–17*

Brothers and sisters: The cup of blessing that we bless, is it not a participation in the blood of Christ? The bread that we break, is it not a participation in the body of Christ? Because the loaf of bread is one, we, though many, are one body, for we all partake of the one loaf.

The sequence Laud, O Zion *(Lauda Sion), or the shorter form beginning with the verse* Lo! the angel's food is given, *may be sung before the Alleluia.*

GOSPEL *John 6:51–58*

Jesus said to the Jewish crowds: "I am the living bread that came down from heaven; whoever eats this bread will live forever; and the bread that I will give is my flesh for the life of the world."

The Jews quarreled among themselves, saying, "How can this man give us his flesh to eat?" Jesus said to them, "Amen, amen, I say to you, unless you eat the flesh of the Son of Man and drink his blood, you do not have life within you. Whoever eats my flesh and drinks my blood has eternal life, and I will raise him on the last day. For my flesh is true food, and my blood is true drink. Whoever eats my flesh and drinks my blood remains in me and I in him. Just as the living Father sent me and I have life because of the Father, so also the one who feeds on me will have life because of me. This is the bread that came down from heaven. Unlike your ancestors who ate and still died, whoever eats this bread will live forever."

COMMUNION ANTIPHON *John 6:57*

Whoever eats my flesh and drinks my blood will live in me and I in him, says the Lord.

July 3, 2011

FOURTEENTH SUNDAY IN ORDINARY TIME

ENTRANCE ANTIPHON *Psalm 47:10–11*

Within your temple, we ponder your loving kindness, O God. As your name, so also your praise reaches to the ends of the earth; your right hand is filled with justice.

READING I

Zechariah 9:9–10 / 100

Thus says the LORD:
Rejoice heartily, O daughter Zion,
  shout for joy, O daughter Jerusalem!
See, your king shall come to you;
  a just savior is he,
meek, and riding on an ass,
  on a colt, the foal of an ass.
He shall banish the chariot from
  Ephraim,
and the horse from Jerusalem;
the warrior's bow shall be banished,
  and he shall proclaim peace to the
  nations.
His dominion shall be from sea to sea,
  and from the River to the ends of
  the earth.

RESPONSORIAL PSALM

Psalm 145:1–2, 8–9, 10–11, 13–14

Or: Alleluia.

I will praise your name for ev-er, my king and my God.

I will extol you, O my God and King,
  and I will bless your name forever
  and ever.
Every day will I bless you,
  and I will praise your name forever
  and ever. ℟.

The LORD is gracious and merciful,
  slow to anger and of great kindness.
The LORD is good to all
  and compassionate toward all his
  works. ℟.

Let all your works give you thanks, O
  LORD,
  and let your faithful ones bless you.
Let them discourse of the glory of your
  kingdom
  and speak of your might. ℟.

The LORD is faithful in all his words
  and holy in all his works.
The LORD lifts up all who are falling
  and raises up all who are bowed
  down. ℟.

READING II

Romans 8:9, 11–13

Brothers and sisters: You are not in the flesh; on the contrary, you are in the spirit, if only the Spirit of God dwells in you. Whoever does not have the Spirit of Christ does not belong to him. If the Spirit of the one who raised Jesus from the dead dwells in you, the one who raised Christ from the dead will give life to your mortal bodies also, through his Spirit that dwells in you. Consequently, brothers and sisters, we are not debtors to the flesh, to live according to the flesh. For if you live according to the flesh, you will die, but if by the Spirit you put to death the deeds of the body, you will live.

GOSPEL

Matthew 11:25–30

At that time Jesus exclaimed: "I give praise to you, Father, Lord of heaven and earth, for although you have hidden these things from the wise and the learned you have revealed them to little ones. Yes, Father, such has been your gracious will. All things have been handed over to me by my Father. No one knows the Son except the Father, and no one knows the Father except the Son and anyone to whom the Son wishes to reveal him.

"Come to me, all you who labor and are burdened, and I will give you rest. Take my yoke upon you and learn from me, for I am meek and humble of heart; and you will find rest for yourselves. For my yoke is easy, and my burden light."

Come to me, all you that labor and are burdened, and I will give you rest, says the Lord.

July 10, 2011

FIFTEENTH SUNDAY IN ORDINARY TIME

ENTRANCE ANTIPHON *Psalm 16:15*
In my justice I shall see your face, O Lord; when your glory appears, my joy will be full.

READING I *Isaiah 55:10–11 / 103*

Thus says the LORD:
Just as from the heavens
  the rain and snow come down
and do not return there
  till they have watered the earth,
  making it fertile and fruitful,
giving seed to the one who sows

and bread to the one who eats,
so shall my word be
  that goes forth from my mouth;
my word shall not return to me void,
  but shall do my will,
  achieving the end for which I sent it.

RESPONSORIAL PSALM *Psalm 65:10, 11, 12–13, 14*

The seed that falls on good ground will yield a fruit - ful har - vest.

You have visited the land and watered it;
  greatly have you enriched it.
God's watercourses are filled;
  you have prepared the grain. ℟.

Thus have you prepared the land:
  drenching its furrows,
  breaking up its clods,
softening it with showers,
  blessing its yield. ℟.

You have crowned the year with your
  bounty,
  and your paths overflow with a rich
  harvest;
the untilled meadows overflow with it,
  and rejoicing clothes the hills. ℟.

The fields are garmented with flocks
  and the valleys blanketed with grain.
They shout and sing for joy. ℟.

READING II *Romans 8:18–23*
Brothers and sisters: I consider that the sufferings of this present time are as nothing compared with the glory to be revealed for us. For creation awaits with eager expectation the revelation of the children of God; for creation was made subject to futility, not of its own accord but because of the one who subjected it, in hope that creation itself would be set free from slavery to corruption and share in the glorious freedom of the children

of God. We know that all creation is groaning in labor pains even until now; and not only that, but we ourselves, who have the firstfruits of the Spirit, we also groan within ourselves as we wait for adoption, the redemption of our bodies.

GOSPEL

Matthew 13:1–23 or 13:1–9

For short form read only the part in brackets.

[On that day, Jesus went out of the house and sat down by the sea. Such large crowds gathered around him that he got into a boat and sat down, and the whole crowd stood along the shore. And he spoke to them at length in parables, saying: "A sower went out to sow. And as he sowed, some seed fell on the path, and birds came and ate it up. Some fell on rocky ground, where it had little soil. It sprang up at once because the soil was not deep, and when the sun rose it was scorched, and it withered for lack of roots. Some seed fell among thorns, and the thorns grew up and choked it. But some seed fell on rich soil, and produced fruit, a hundred or sixty or thirtyfold. Whoever has ears ought to hear."]

The disciples approached him and said, "Why do you speak to them in parables?" He said to them in reply, "Because knowledge of the mysteries of the kingdom of heaven has been granted to you, but to them it has not been granted. To anyone who has, more will be given and he will grow rich; from anyone who has not, even what he has will be taken away. This is why I speak to them in parables, because *they look but do not see and hear but do not listen or understand.* Isaiah's prophecy is fulfilled in them, which says:

You shall indeed hear but not understand,
you shall indeed look but never see.
Gross is the heart of this people,
they will hardly hear with their ears,
they have closed their eyes,
lest they see with their eyes
and hear with their ears
and understand with their hearts and be converted,
and I heal them.

"But blessed are your eyes, because they see, and your ears, because they hear. Amen, I say to you, many prophets and righteous people longed to see what you see but did not see it, and to hear what you hear but did not hear it.

"Hear then the parable of the sower. The seed sown on the path is the one who hears the word of the kingdom without understanding it, and the evil one comes and steals away what was sown in his heart. The seed sown on rocky ground is the one who hears the word and receives it at once with joy. But he has no root and lasts only for a time. When some tribulation or persecution comes because of the word, he immediately falls away. The seed sown among thorns is the one who hears the word, but then worldly anxiety and the lure of riches choke the word and it bears no fruit. But the seed sown on rich soil is the one who hears the word and understands it, who indeed bears fruit and yields a hundred or sixty or thirtyfold."

COMMUNION ANTIPHON

John 6:57

Whoever eats my flesh and drinks my blood will live in me and I in him, says the Lord.

SIXTEENTH SUNDAY IN ORDINARY TIME

ENTRANCE ANTIPHON *Psalm 53:6, 8*

God himself is my help. The Lord upholds my life. I will offer you a willing sacrifice; I will praise your name, O Lord, for its goodness.

READING I *Wisdom 12:13, 16–19 / 106*

There is no god besides you who have the care of all,
　that you need show you have not unjustly condemned.
For your might is the source of justice;
　your mastery over all things makes you lenient to all.
For you show your might when the perfection of your power is disbelieved;
　and in those who know you, you rebuke temerity.
But though you are master of might, you judge with clemency,
　and with much lenience you govern us;
　for power, whenever you will, attends you.
And you taught your people, by these deeds,
　that those who are just must be kind;
and you gave your children good ground for hope
　that you would permit repentance for their sins.

RESPONSORIAL PSALM *Psalm 86:5–6, 9–10, 15–16*

Lord, you are good and for - giv - ing.

You, O LORD, are good and forgiving,
　abounding in kindness to all who
　　call upon you.
Hearken, O LORD, to my prayer
　and attend to the sound of my
　　pleading. ℟.

All the nations you have made shall come
　and worship you, O LORD,
　and glorify your name.

For you are great, and you do wondrous
　deeds;
　you alone are God. ℟.

You, O LORD, are a God merciful and
　gracious,
　slow to anger, abounding in kindness
　　and fidelity.
Turn toward me, and have pity on me;
　give your strength to your servant. ℟.

READING II *Romans 8:26–27*

Brothers and sisters: The Spirit comes to the aid of our weakness; for we do not know how to pray as we ought, but the Spirit himself intercedes with inexpressible groanings. And the one who searches hearts knows what is the intention of the Spirit, because he intercedes for the holy ones according to God's will.

GOSPEL

Matthew 13:24–43 or 13:24–30

For short form read only the part in brackets.

[Jesus proposed another parable to the crowds, saying: "The kingdom of heaven may be likened to a man who sowed good seed in his field. While everyone was asleep his enemy came and sowed weeds all through the wheat, and then went off. When the crop grew and bore fruit, the weeds appeared as well. The slaves of the householder came to him and said, 'Master, did you not sow good seed in your field? Where have the weeds come from?' He answered, 'An enemy has done this.' His slaves said to him, 'Do you want us to go and pull them up?' He replied, 'No, if you pull up the weeds you might uproot the wheat along with them. Let them grow together until harvest; then at harvest time I will say to the harvesters, "First collect the weeds and tie them in bundles for burning; but gather the wheat into my barn."'"]

He proposed another parable to them. "The kingdom of heaven is like a mustard seed that a person took and sowed in a field. It is the smallest of all the seeds, yet when full-grown it is the largest of plants. It becomes a large bush, and the 'birds of the sky come and dwell in its branches.'"

He spoke to them another parable. "The kingdom of heaven is like yeast that a woman took and mixed with three measures of wheat flour until the whole batch was leavened."

All these things Jesus spoke to the crowds in parables. He spoke to them only in parables, to fulfill what had been said through the prophet:

I will open my mouth in parables,
I will announce what has lain hidden from the foundation of the world.

Then, dismissing the crowds, he went into the house. His disciples approached him and said, "Explain to us the parable of the weeds in the field." He said in reply, "He who sows good seed is the Son of Man, the field is the world, the good seed the children of the kingdom. The weeds are the children of the evil one, and the enemy who sows them is the devil. The harvest is the end of the age, and the harvesters are angels. Just as weeds are collected and burned up with fire, so will it be at the end of the age. The Son of Man will send his angels, and they will collect out of his kingdom all who cause others to sin and all evildoers. They will throw them into the fiery furnace, where there will be wailing and grinding of teeth. Then the righteous will shine like the sun in the kingdom of their Father. Whoever has ears ought to hear."

COMMUNION ANTIPHON

Revelation 3:20

I stand at the door and knock, says the Lord. If anyone hears my voice and opens the door, I will come in and sit down to supper with him, and he with me.

July 24, 2011

SEVENTEENTH SUNDAY IN ORDINARY TIME

ENTRANCE ANTIPHON

Psalm 67:6–7, 36

God is in his holy dwelling; he will give a home to the lonely, he gives power and strength to his people.

READING I
1 Kings 3:5, 7–12 / 109

The LORD appeared to Solomon in a dream at night. God said, "Ask something of me and I will give it to you." Solomon answered: "O LORD, my God, you have made me, your servant, king to succeed my father David; but I am a mere youth, not knowing at all how to act. I serve you in the midst of the people whom you have chosen, a people so vast that it cannot be numbered or counted. Give your servant, therefore, an understanding heart to judge your people and to distinguish right from wrong. For who is able to govern this vast people of yours?"

The LORD was pleased that Solomon made this request. So God said to him: "Because you have asked for this— not for a long life for yourself, nor for riches, nor for the life of your enemies, but for understanding so that you may know what is right— I do as you requested. I give you a heart so wise and understanding that there has never been anyone like you up to now, and after you there will come no one to equal you."

RESPONSORIAL PSALM
Psalm 119:57, 72, 76–77, 127–128, 129–130

Lord, I love your com - mands.

I have said, O LORD, that my part
　is to keep your words.
The law of your mouth is to me more
　　precious
　　than thousands of gold and silver
　　pieces. R̀.

Let your kindness comfort me
　according to your promise to your
　　servants.
Let your compassion come to me that I
　may live,

for your law is my delight. R̀.

For I love your commands
　more than gold, however fine.
For in all your precepts I go forward;
　every false way I hate. R̀.

Wonderful are your decrees;
　therefore I observe them.
The revelation of your words sheds light,
　giving understanding to the simple. R̀.

READING II
Romans 8:28–30

Brothers and sisters: We know that all things work for good for those who love God, who are called according to his purpose. For those he foreknew he also predestined to be conformed to the image of his Son, so that he might be the firstborn among many brothers and sisters. And those he predestined he also called; and those he called he also justified; and those he justified he also glorified.

GOSPEL
Matthew 13:44–52 or 13:44–46
For short form read only the part in brackets.

[Jesus said to his disciples: "The kingdom of heaven is like a treasure buried in a field, which a person finds and hides again, and out of joy goes and sells all that he has and buys that field. Again, the kingdom of heaven is like a merchant searching for fine pearls. When he finds a pearl of great price, he goes and sells all that he has and buys it.] Again, the kingdom of heaven is like a net thrown into the sea, which collects fish of every kind. When it is full they haul it ashore and sit down to put what is good into buckets. What is bad they throw away. Thus it will be at the end of the age. The angels will go out and separate the wicked from the righteous and throw them into the fiery furnace, where there will be wailing and grinding of teeth.

"Do you understand all these things?" They answered, "Yes." And he replied, "Then every scribe who has been instructed in the kingdom of heaven is like the head of a household who brings from his storeroom both the new and the old."

COMMUNION ANTIPHON *Matthew 5:7–8*

Happy are those who show mercy; mercy shall be theirs. Happy are the poor of heart, for they shall see God.

July 31, 2011

EIGHTEENTH SUNDAY IN ORDINARY TIME

ENTRANCE ANTIPHON *Psalm 69:2, 6*

God, come to my help. Lord, quickly give me assistance. You are the one who helps me and sets me free: Lord, do not be long in coming.

READING I *Isaiah 55:1–3 / 112*

Thus says the LORD:
All you who are thirsty,
   come to the water!
You who have no money,
   come, receive grain and eat;
Come, without paying and without cost,
   drink wine and milk!
Why spend your money for what is
     not bread;
your wages for what fails to satisfy?
Heed me, and you shall eat well,
   you shall delight in rich fare.
Come to me heedfully,
   listen, that you may have life.
I will renew with you the everlasting
     covenant,
   the benefits assured to David.

RESPONSORIAL PSALM *Psalm 145:8–9, 15–16, 17–18*

The hand of the Lord feeds us; he an-swers all our needs.

The LORD is gracious and merciful,
   slow to anger and of great kindness.
The LORD is good to all
   and compassionate toward all his
     works. ℟.

The eyes of all look hopefully to you,
   and you give them their food in due
     season;
you open your hand
   and satisfy the desire of every
     living thing. ℟.

The LORD is just in all his ways
   and holy in all his works.
The LORD is near to all who call upon
     him,
   to all who call upon him in truth. ℟.

READING II *Romans 8:35, 37–39*

Brothers and sisters: What will separate us from the love of Christ? Will anguish, or distress, or persecution, or famine, or nakedness, or peril, or the sword? No, in all these things we conquer overwhelmingly through him who loved us. For I am convinced that neither death, nor life, nor angels, nor principalities, nor present things, nor future things, nor powers, nor height, nor depth, nor any other creature will be able to separate us from the love of God in Christ Jesus our Lord.

GOSPEL

Matthew 14:13–21

When Jesus heard of the death of John the Baptist, he withdrew in a boat to a deserted place by himself. The crowds heard of this and followed him on foot from their towns. When he disembarked and saw the vast crowd, his heart was moved with pity for them, and he cured their sick. When it was evening, the disciples approached him and said, "This is a deserted place and it is already late; dismiss the crowds so that they can go to the villages and buy food for themselves." Jesus said to them, "There is no need for them to go away; give them some food yourselves." But they said to him, "Five loaves and two fish are all we have here." Then he said, "Bring them here to me," and he ordered the crowds to sit down on the grass. Taking the five loaves and the two fish, and looking up to heaven, he said the blessing, broke the loaves, and gave them to the disciples, who in turn gave them to the crowds. They all ate and were satisfied, and they picked up the fragments left over— twelve wicker baskets full. Those who ate were about five thousand men, not counting women and children.

COMMUNION ANTIPHON

Wisdom 16:20

You gave us bread from heaven, Lord: a sweet-tasting bread that was very good to eat.

August 7, 2011

NINETEENTH SUNDAY IN ORDINARY TIME

ENTRANCE ANTIPHON

Psalm 73:20, 19, 22, 23

Lord, be true to your covenant, forget not the life of your poor ones for ever. Rise up, O God, and defend your cause; do not ignore the shouts of your enemies.

READING I

1 Kings 19:9a, 11–13a / 115

At the mountain of God, Horeb, Elijah came to a cave where he took shelter. Then the LORD said to him, "Go outside and stand on the mountain before the LORD; the LORD will be passing by." A strong and heavy wind was rending the mountains and crushing rocks before the LORD— but the LORD was not in the wind. After the wind there was an earthquake— but the LORD was not in the earthquake. After the earthquake there was fire— but the LORD was not in the fire. After the fire there was a tiny whispering sound. When he heard this, Elijah hid his face in his cloak and went and stood at the entrance of the cave.

RESPONSORIAL PSALM

Psalm 85:9, 10, 11–12, 13–14

Lord, let us see your kind-ness, and grant us your sal-va-tion.

I will hear what God proclaims;
    the LORD— for he proclaims peace.
Near indeed is his salvation to those who

fear him,
glory dwelling in our land. ℟.

Kindness and truth shall meet;
    justice and peace shall kiss.
Truth shall spring out of the earth,
    and justice shall look down from
        heaven. ℟.

The LORD himself will give his benefits;
    our land shall yield its increase.
Justice shall walk before him,
    and prepare the way of his steps. ℟.

READING II
Romans 9:1–5

Brothers and sisters: I speak the truth in Christ, I do not lie; my conscience joins with the Holy Spirit in bearing me witness that I have great sorrow and constant anguish in my heart. For I could wish that I myself were accursed and cut off from Christ for the sake of my own people, my kindred according to the flesh. They are Israelites; theirs the adoption, the glory, the covenants, the giving of the law, the worship, and the promises; theirs the patriarchs, and from them, according to the flesh, is the Christ, who is over all, God blessed forever. Amen.

GOSPEL
Matthew 14:22–33

After he had fed the people, Jesus made the disciples get into a boat and precede him to the other side, while he dismissed the crowds. After doing so, he went up on the mountain by himself to pray. When it was evening he was there alone. Meanwhile the boat, already a few miles offshore, was being tossed about by the waves, for the wind was against it. During the fourth watch of the night, he came toward them walking on the sea. When the disciples saw him walking on the sea they were terrified. "It is a ghost," they said, and they cried out in fear. At once Jesus spoke to them, "Take courage, it is I; do not be afraid." Peter said to him in reply, "Lord, if it is you, command me to come to you on the water." He said, "Come." Peter got out of the boat and began to walk on the water toward Jesus. But when he saw how strong the wind was he became frightened; and, beginning to sink, he cried out, "Lord, save me!" Immediately Jesus stretched out his hand and caught Peter, and said to him, "O you of little faith, why did you doubt?" After they got into the boat, the wind died down. Those who were in the boat did him homage, saying, "Truly, you are the Son of God."

COMMUNION ANTIPHON
John 6:52

The bread I shall give is my flesh for the life of the world, says the Lord.

August 14, 2011

TWENTIETH SUNDAY IN ORDINARY TIME

ENTRANCE ANTIPHON
Psalm 83:10–11

God, our protector, keep us in mind; always give strength to your people. For if we can be with you even one day, it is better than a thousand without you.

READING I
Isaiah 56:1, 6–7 / 118

Thus says the LORD:
Observe what is right, do what is just;
    for my salvation is about to come,
    my justice, about to be revealed.

The foreigners who join themselves to
    the LORD,

ministering to him,
loving the name of the LORD,
    and becoming his servants—
all who keep the sabbath free from
        profanation
    and hold to my covenant,
them I will bring to my holy mountain

and make joyful in my house of
prayer;
their burnt offerings and sacrifices
will be acceptable on my altar,
for my house shall be called
a house of prayer for all peoples.

RESPONSORIAL PSALM
Psalm 67:2–3, 5, 6, 8

O God, O God, let all the na-tions praise you!

May God have pity on us and bless us;
may he let his face shine upon us.
So may your way be known upon earth;
among all nations, your salvation. ℟.

May the nations be glad and exult
because you rule the peoples in equity;

the nations on the earth you guide. ℟.

May the peoples praise you, O God;
may all the peoples praise you!
May God bless us,
and may all the ends of the earth
fear him! ℟.

READING II
Romans 11:13–15, 29–32

Brothers and sisters: I am speaking to you Gentiles. Inasmuch as I am the apostle to the Gentiles, I glory in my ministry in order to make my race jealous and thus save some of them. For if their rejection is the reconciliation of the world, what will their acceptance be but life from the dead?

For the gifts and the call of God are irrevocable. Just as you once disobeyed God but have now received mercy because of their disobedience, so they have now disobeyed in order that, by virtue of the mercy shown to you, they too may now receive mercy. For God delivered all to disobedience, that he might have mercy upon all.

GOSPEL
Matthew 15:21–28

At that time, Jesus withdrew to the region of Tyre and Sidon. And behold, a Canaanite woman of that district came and called out, "Have pity on me, Lord, Son of David! My daughter is tormented by a demon." But Jesus did not say a word in answer to her. Jesus' disciples came and asked him, "Send her away, for she keeps calling out after us." He said in reply, "I was sent only to the lost sheep of the house of Israel." But the woman came and did Jesus homage, saying, "Lord, help me." He said in reply, "It is not right to take the food of the children and throw it to the dogs." She said, "Please, Lord, for even the dogs eat the scraps that fall from the table of their masters." Then Jesus said to her in reply, "O woman, great is your faith! Let it be done for you as you wish." And the woman's daughter was healed from that hour.

COMMUNION ANTIPHON
Psalm 129:7

With the Lord there is mercy, and fullness of redemption.

TWENTY-FIRST SUNDAY IN ORDINARY TIME

ENTRANCE ANTIPHON *Psalm 85:1–3*
Listen, Lord, and answer me. Save your servant who trusts in you. I call to you all day long, have mercy on me, O Lord.

READING I *Isaiah 22:19–23 / 121*
Thus says the LORD to Shebna, master of the palace:
"I will thrust you from your office
  and pull you down from your station.
On that day I will summon my servant Eliakim, son of Hilkiah;
I will clothe him with your robe,
  and gird him with your sash,
  and give over to him your authority.

He shall be a father to the inhabitants of Jerusalem,
  and to the house of Judah.
I will place the key of the House of David on Eliakim's shoulder;
  when he opens, no one shall shut,
  when he shuts, no one shall open.
I will fix him like a peg in a sure spot,
  to be a place of honor for his family."

RESPONSORIAL PSALM *Psalm 138:1–2, 2–3, 6, 8*

Lord, your love is e-ter-nal; do not for-sake the work of your hands.

I will give thanks to you, O LORD, with all my heart,
  for you have heard the words of my mouth;
in the presence of the angels I will sing your praise;
  I will worship at your holy temple. R̶.

I will give thanks to your name,
  because of your kindness and your truth:
when I called, you answered me;
  you built up strength within me. R̶.

The LORD is exalted, yet the lowly he sees,
  and the proud he knows from afar.
Your kindness, O LORD, endures forever;
  forsake not the work of your hands. R̶.

READING II *Romans 11:33–36*
Oh, the depth of the riches and wisdom and knowledge of God! How inscrutable are his judgments and how unsearchable his ways!
For who has known the mind of the Lord
  or who has been his counselor?
Or who has given the Lord anything
  that he may be repaid?
For from him and through him and for him are all things. To him be glory forever. Amen.

GOSPEL *Matthew 16:13–20*
Jesus went into the region of Caesarea Philippi and he asked his disciples, "Who do people say that the Son of Man is?" They replied, "Some say John the Baptist, others Elijah, still others Jeremiah or one of the prophets." He said to them, "But who do you say that I am?" Simon Peter said in reply, "You are the Christ, the Son of the living God."

Jesus said to him in reply, "Blessed are you, Simon son of Jonah. For flesh and blood has not revealed this to you, but my heavenly Father. And so I say to you, you are Peter, and upon this rock I will build my church, and the gates of the netherworld shall not prevail against it. I will give you the keys to the kingdom of heaven. Whatever you bind on earth shall be bound in heaven; and whatever you loose on earth shall be loosed in heaven." Then he strictly ordered his disciples to tell no one that he was the Christ.

COMMUNION ANTIPHON *John 6:55*
The Lord says: The man who eats my flesh and drinks my blood will live for ever; I shall raise him to life on the last day.

August 28, 2011

TWENTY-SECOND SUNDAY IN ORDINARY TIME

ENTRANCE ANTIPHON *Psalm 85:3, 5*
I call to you all day long, have mercy on me, O Lord. You are good and forgiving, full of love for all who call to you.

READING I *Jeremiah 20:7–9 / 124*

You duped me, O LORD, and I let
    myself be duped;
you were too strong for me, and you
    triumphed.
All the day I am an object of laughter;
    everyone mocks me.

Whenever I speak, I must cry out,
    violence and outrage is my message;
the word of the LORD has brought me

derision and reproach all the day.

I say to myself, I will not mention him,
    I will speak in his name no more.
But then it becomes like fire burning in
    my heart,
    imprisoned in my bones;
I grow weary holding it in, I cannot
    endure it.

RESPONSORIAL PSALM *Psalm 63:2, 3–4, 5–6, 8–9*

My soul is thirst-ing for you, O Lord, thirst-ing for you my God.

O God, you are my God whom I seek;
    for you my flesh pines and my soul
    thirsts
    like the earth, parched, lifeless and
    without water. ℟.

Thus have I gazed toward you in the
    sanctuary
    to see your power and your glory,
for your kindness is a greater good than
    life;
    my lips shall glorify you. ℟.

Thus will I bless you while I live;
    lifting up my hands, I will call upon
    your name.
As with the riches of a banquet shall my
    soul be satisfied,
    and with exultant lips my mouth
    shall praise you. ℟.

You are my help,
    and in the shadow of your wings I
    shout for joy.
My soul clings fast to you;
    your right hand upholds me. ℟.

READING II *Romans 12:1–2*

I urge you, brothers and sisters, by the mercies of God, to offer your bodies as a living sacrifice, holy and pleasing to God, your spiritual worship. Do not conform yourselves to this age but be transformed by the renewal of your mind, that you may discern what is the will of God, what is good and pleasing and perfect.

GOSPEL *Matthew 16:21–27*

Jesus began to show his disciples that he must go to Jerusalem and suffer greatly from the elders, the chief priests, and the scribes, and be killed and on the third day be raised. Then Peter took Jesus aside and began to rebuke him, "God forbid, Lord! No such thing shall ever happen to you." He turned and said to Peter, "Get behind me, Satan! You are an obstacle to me. You are thinking not as God does, but as human beings do."

Then Jesus said to his disciples, "Whoever wishes to come after me must deny himself, take up his cross, and follow me. For whoever wishes to save his life will lose it, but whoever loses his life for my sake will find it. What profit would there be for one to gain the whole world and forfeit his life? Or what can one give in exchange for his life? For the Son of Man will come with his angels in his Father's glory, and then he will repay all according to his conduct."

COMMUNION ANTIPHON *Matthew 5:9–10*

Happy are the peacemakers; they shall be called sons of God. Happy are they who suffer persecution for justice' sake; the kingdom of heaven is theirs.

September 4, 2011

TWENTY-THIRD SUNDAY IN ORDINARY TIME

ENTRANCE ANTIPHON *Psalm 118:137, 124*

Lord, you are just, and the judgments you make are right. Show mercy when you judge me, your servant.

READING I *Ezekiel 33:7–9 / 127*

Thus says the LORD: You, son of man, I have appointed watchman for the house of Israel; when you hear me say anything, you shall warn them for me. If I tell the wicked, "O wicked one, you shall surely die," and you do not speak out to dissuade the wicked from his way, the wicked shall die for his guilt, but I will hold you responsible for his death. But if you warn the wicked, trying to turn him from his way, and he refuses to turn from his way, he shall die for his guilt, but you shall save yourself.

RESPONSORIAL PSALM *Psalm 95:1–2, 6–7, 8–9*

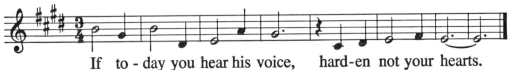

If to-day you hear his voice, hard-en not your hearts.

Come, let us sing joyfully to the LORD; let us acclaim the rock of our salvation.

Let us come into his presence with thanksgiving; let us joyfully sing psalms to him. ℟.

Come, let us bow down in worship;
let us kneel before the LORD who
made us.
For he is our God,
and we are the people he shepherds,
the flock he guides. ℟.

Oh, that today you would hear his voice:
"Harden not your hearts as at
Meribah,
as in the day of Massah in the desert,
where your fathers tempted me;
they tested me though they had seen
my works." ℟.

READING II
Romans 13:8–10

Brothers and sisters: Owe nothing to anyone, except to love one another; for the one who loves another has fulfilled the law. The commandments, "You shall not commit adultery; you shall not kill; you shall not steal; you shall not covet," and whatever other commandment there may be, are summed up in this saying, namely, "You shall love your neighbor as yourself." Love does no evil to the neighbor; hence, love is the fulfillment of the law.

GOSPEL
Matthew 18:15–20

Jesus said to his disciples: "If your brother sins against you, go and tell him his fault between you and him alone. If he listens to you, you have won over your brother. If he does not listen, take one or two others along with you, so that 'every fact may be established on the testimony of two or three witnesses.' If he refuses to listen to them, tell the church. If he refuses to listen even to the church, then treat him as you would a Gentile or a tax collector. Amen, I say to you, whatever you bind on earth shall be bound in heaven, and whatever you loose on earth shall be loosed in heaven. Again, amen, I say to you, if two of you agree on earth about anything for which they are to pray, it shall be granted to them by my heavenly Father. For where two or three are gathered together in my name, there am I in the midst of them."

COMMUNION ANTIPHON
Psalm 41:2–3

Like a deer that longs for running streams, my soul longs for you, my God. My soul is thirsting for the living God.

September 11, 2011
TWENTY-FOURTH SUNDAY IN ORDINARY TIME

ENTRANCE ANTIPHON
See Sirach 36:18

Give peace, Lord, to those who wait for you and your prophets will proclaim you as you deserve. Hear the prayers of your servant and of your people Israel.

READING I
Sirach 27:30—28:7 / 130

Wrath and anger are hateful things,
yet the sinner hugs them tight.
The vengeful will suffer the LORD's
vengeance,
for he remembers their sins in detail.
Forgive your neighbor's injustice;
then when you pray, your own sins
will be forgiven.
Could anyone nourish anger against

another
and expect healing from the LORD?
Could anyone refuse mercy to another
like himself,
can he seek pardon for his own sins?
If one who is but flesh cherishes wrath,
who will forgive his sins?
Remember your last days, set enmity
aside;

remember death and decay, and cease
from sin!
Think of the commandments, hate not
your neighbor;
remember the Most High's covenant,
and overlook faults.

RESPONSORIAL PSALM

Psalm 103:1–2, 3–4, 9–10, 11–12

The Lord is kind and mer - ci - ful,
slow to an - ger, and rich in com - pas - sion.

Bless the LORD, O my soul;
and all my being, bless his holy name.
Bless the LORD, O my soul,
and forget not all his benefits. ℟.

He pardons all your iniquities,
heals all your ills.
He redeems your life from destruction,
crowns you with kindness and
compassion. ℟.

He will not always chide,
nor does he keep his wrath forever.

Not according to our sins does he deal
with us,
nor does he requite us according to
our crimes. ℟.

For as the heavens are high above the
earth,
so surpassing is his kindness toward
those who fear him.
As far as the east is from the west,
so far has he put our transgressions
from us. ℟.

READING II
Romans 14:7–9

Brothers and sisters: None of us lives for oneself, and no one dies for oneself. For if we live, we live for the Lord, and if we die, we die for the Lord; so then, whether we live or die, we are the Lord's. For this is why Christ died and came to life, that he might be Lord of both the dead and the living.

GOSPEL
Matthew 18:21–35

Peter approached Jesus and asked him, "Lord, if my brother sins against me, how often must I forgive? As many as seven times?" Jesus answered, "I say to you, not seven times but seventy-seven times. That is why the kingdom of heaven may be likened to a king who decided to settle accounts with his servants. When he began the accounting, a debtor was brought before him who owed him a huge amount. Since he had no way of paying it back, his master ordered him to be sold, along with his wife, his children, and all his property, in payment of the debt. At that, the servant fell down, did him homage, and said, 'Be patient with me, and I will pay you back in full.' Moved with compassion the master of that servant let him go and forgave him the loan. When that servant had left, he found one of his fellow servants who owed him a much smaller amount. He seized him and started to choke him, demanding, 'Pay back what you owe.' Falling to his knees, his fellow servant begged him, 'Be patient with me, and I will pay you back.' But he refused. Instead, he had the fellow servant put in prison until he paid back the debt. Now when his fellow servants saw what had happened, they were deeply disturbed, and went to their master and reported the whole affair. His master summoned him and said to him, 'You wicked servant! I forgave you your entire debt because you begged me to. Should you not have had pity on your fellow servant, as I had pity on you?' Then in anger his master handed him over to the torturers until he should pay back the whole debt. So will my heavenly Father do to you, unless each of you forgives your brother from your heart."

COMMUNION ANTIPHON *See 1 Corinthians 10:16*
The cup that we bless is a communion with the blood of Christ; and the bread that we break is a communion with the body of the Lord.

September 18, 2011

TWENTY-FIFTH SUNDAY IN ORDINARY TIME

ENTRANCE ANTIPHON
I am the Savior of all people, says the Lord. Whatever their troubles, I will answer their cry, and I will always be their Lord.

READING I *Isaiah 55:6–9 / 133*
Seek the LORD while he may be found,
　call him while he is near.
Let the scoundrel forsake his way,
　and the wicked his thoughts;
let him turn to the LORD for mercy;
　to our God, who is generous in
　　forgiving.
For my thoughts are not your thoughts,
nor are your ways my ways, says the
　LORD.
As high as the heavens are above the
　earth,
so high are my ways above your ways
and my thoughts above your
　thoughts.

RESPONSORIAL PSALM *Psalm 145:2–3, 8–9, 17–18*

The Lord is near to all who call on him.

Every day will I bless you,
　and I will praise your name forever
　and ever.
Great is the LORD and highly to be
　praised;
　his greatness is unsearchable. ℟.

The LORD is gracious and merciful,
　slow to anger and of great kindness.

The LORD is good to all
　and compassionate toward all his
　works. ℟.

The LORD is just in all his ways
　and holy in all his works.
The LORD is near to all who call upon
　him,
　to all who call upon him in truth. ℟.

READING II *Philippians 1:20c–24, 27a*
Brothers and sisters: Christ will be magnified in my body, whether by life or by death. For to me life is Christ, and death is gain. If I go on living in the flesh, that means fruitful labor for me. And I do not know which I shall choose. I am caught between the two. I long to depart this life and be with Christ, for that is far better. Yet that I remain in the

flesh is more necessary for your benefit.

Only, conduct yourselves in a way worthy of the gospel of Christ.

GOSPEL *Matthew 20:1–16a*

Jesus told his disciples this parable: "The kingdom of heaven is like a landowner who went out at dawn to hire laborers for his vineyard. After agreeing with them for the usual daily wage, he sent them into his vineyard. Going out about nine o'clock, the landowner saw others standing idle in the marketplace, and he said to them, 'You too go into my vineyard, and I will give you what is just.' So they went off. And he went out again around noon, and around three o'clock, and did likewise. Going out about five o'clock, the landowner found others standing around, and said to them, 'Why do you stand here idle all day?' They answered, 'Because no one has hired us.' He said to them, 'You too go into my vineyard.' When it was evening the owner of the vineyard said to his foreman, 'Summon the laborers and give them their pay, beginning with the last and ending with the first.' When those who had started about five o'clock came, each received the usual daily wage. So when the first came, they thought that they would receive more, but each of them also got the usual wage. And on receiving it they grumbled against the landowner, saying, 'These last ones worked only one hour, and you have made them equal to us, who bore the day's burden and the heat.' He said to one of them in reply, 'My friend, I am not cheating you. Did you not agree with me for the usual daily wage? Take what is yours and go. What if I wish to give this last one the same as you? Or am I not free to do as I wish with my own money? Are you envious because I am generous?' Thus, the last will be first, and the first will be last."

COMMUNION ANTIPHON *John 10:14*

I am the Good Shepherd, says the Lord; I know my sheep, and mine know me.

September 25, 2011

TWENTY-SIXTH SUNDAY IN ORDINARY TIME

ENTRANCE ANTIPHON *Daniel 3:31, 29, 30, 43, 42*

O Lord, you had just cause to judge men as you did: because we sinned against you and disobeyed your will. But now show us your greatness of heart, and treat us with your unbounded kindness.

READING I *Ezekiel 18:25–28 / 136*

Thus says the Lord: You say, "The Lord's way is not fair!" Hear now, house of Israel: Is it my way that is unfair, or rather, are not your ways unfair? When someone virtuous turns away from virtue to commit iniquity, and dies, it is because of the iniquity he committed that he must die. But if he turns from the wickedness he has committed, and does what is right and just, he shall preserve his life; since he has turned away from all the sins that he has committed, he shall surely live, he shall not die.

RESPONSORIAL PSALM *Psalm 25:4–5, 6–7, 8–9*

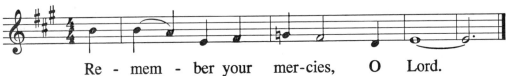

Re - mem - ber your mer-cies, O Lord.

Your ways, O Lord, make known to me;
  teach me your paths,
guide me in your truth and teach me,
  for you are God my savior. ℟.

Remember that your compassion, O
  Lord,
  and your love are from of old.
The sins of my youth and my frailties
  remember not;

in your kindness remember me,
  because of your goodness, O
  Lord. ℟.

Good and upright is the Lord;
  thus he shows sinners the way.
He guides the humble to justice,
  and teaches the humble his way. ℟.

READING II   *Philippians 2:1–11 or 2:1–5*
For short form read only the part in brackets.

[Brothers and sisters: If there is any encouragement in Christ, any solace in love, any participation in the Spirit, any compassion and mercy, complete my joy by being of the same mind, with the same love, united in heart, thinking one thing. Do nothing out of selfishness or out of vainglory; rather, humbly regard others as more important than yourselves, each looking out not for his own interests, but also for those of others. Have in you the same attitude that is also in Christ Jesus,]
  Who, though he was in the form of God,
    did not regard equality with God
    something to be grasped.
  Rather, he emptied himself,
    taking the form of a slave,
    coming in human likeness;
    and found human in appearance,
    he humbled himself,
    becoming obedient to the point of death,
    even death on a cross.
  Because of this, God greatly exalted him
    and bestowed on him the name
    which is above every name,
    that at the name of Jesus
    every knee should bend,
    of those in heaven and on earth and under the earth,
    and every tongue confess that
    Jesus Christ is Lord,
    to the glory of God the Father.

GOSPEL   *Matthew 21:28–32*
Jesus said to the chief priests and elders of the people: "What is your opinion? A man had two sons. He came to the first and said, 'Son, go out and work in the vineyard today.' He said in reply, 'I will not,' but afterwards changed his mind and went. The man came to the other son and gave the same order. He said in reply, 'Yes, sir,' but did not go. Which of the two did his father's will?" They answered, "The first." Jesus said to them, "Amen, I say to you, tax collectors and prostitutes are entering the kingdom of God before you. When John came to you in the way of righteousness, you did not believe him; but tax collectors and prostitutes did. Yet even when you saw that, you did not later change your minds and believe him."

1 John 3:16

This is how we know what love is: Christ gave up his life for us; and we too must give up our lives for our brothers.

October 2, 2011

TWENTY-SEVENTH SUNDAY IN ORDINARY TIME

ENTRANCE ANTIPHON
Esther 13:9, 10–11

O Lord, you have given everything its place in the world, and no one can make it otherwise. For it is your creation, the heavens and the earth and the stars: you are the Lord of all.

READING I
Isaiah 5:1–7 / 139

Let me now sing of my friend,
    my friend's song concerning his
        vineyard.
My friend had a vineyard
    on a fertile hillside;
he spaded it, cleared it of stones,
    and planted the choicest vines;
within it he built a watchtower,
    and hewed out a wine press.
Then he looked for the crop of grapes,
    but what it yielded was wild grapes.

Now, inhabitants of Jerusalem and
        people of Judah,
    judge between me and my vineyard:
What more was there to do for my
        vineyard
    that I had not done?
Why, when I looked for the crop of grapes,

did it bring forth wild grapes?
Now, I will let you know
    what I mean to do with my vineyard:
take away its hedge, give it to grazing,
    break through its wall, let it be
        trampled!
Yes, I will make it a ruin:
    it shall not be pruned or hoed,
    but overgrown with thorns and
        briers;
I will command the clouds
    not to send rain upon it.
The vineyard of the LORD of hosts is the
        house of Israel,
    and the people of Judah are his
        cherished plant;
he looked for judgment, but see,
        bloodshed!
for justice, but hark, the outcry!

RESPONSORIAL PSALM
Psalm 80:9, 12, 13–14, 15–16, 19–20

The vine-yard of the Lord is the house of Is-ra-el.

A vine from Egypt you transplanted;
    you drove away the nations and
        planted it.
It put forth its foliage to the Sea,
    its shoots as far as the River. ℟.

Why have you broken down its walls,
    so that every passer-by plucks its fruit,
The boar from the forest lays it waste,

and the beasts of the field feed upon
    it? ℟.

Once again, O LORD of hosts,
    look down from heaven, and see;
take care of this vine,
    and protect what your right hand has
        planted,
    the son of man whom you yourself
        made strong. ℟.

Then we will no more withdraw from you; give us new life, and we will call upon your name.

O Lord, God of hosts, restore us; if your face shine upon us, then we shall be saved. ℟.

READING II
Philippians 4:6–9

Brothers and sisters: Have no anxiety at all, but in everything, by prayer and petition, with thanksgiving, make your requests known to God. Then the peace of God that surpasses all understanding will guard your hearts and minds in Christ Jesus.

Finally, brothers and sisters, whatever is true, whatever is honorable, whatever is just, whatever is pure, whatever is lovely, whatever is gracious, if there is any excellence and if there is anything worthy of praise, think about these things. Keep on doing what you have learned and received and heard and seen in me. Then the God of peace will be with you.

GOSPEL
Matthew 21:33–43

Jesus said to the chief priests and the elders of the people: "Hear another parable. There was a landowner who planted a vineyard, put a hedge around it, dug a wine press in it, and built a tower. Then he leased it to tenants and went on a journey. When vintage time drew near, he sent his servants to the tenants to obtain his produce. But the tenants seized the servants and one they beat, another they killed, and a third they stoned. Again he sent other servants, more numerous than the first ones, but they treated them in the same way. Finally, he sent his son to them, thinking, 'They will respect my son.' But when the tenants saw the son, they said to one another, 'This is the heir. Come, let us kill him and acquire his inheritance.' They seized him, threw him out of the vineyard, and killed him. What will the owner of the vineyard do to those tenants when he comes?" They answered him, "He will put those wretched men to a wretched death and lease his vineyard to other tenants who will give him the produce at the proper times." Jesus said to them, "Did you never read in the Scriptures:

The stone that the builders rejected
* has become the cornerstone;*
by the Lord has this been done,
* and it is wonderful in our eyes?*

Therefore, I say to you, the kingdom of God will be taken away from you and given to a people that will produce its fruit."

COMMUNION ANTIPHON
Lamentations 3:25

The Lord is good to those who hope in him, to those who are searching for his love.

October 9, 2011
TWENTY-EIGHTH SUNDAY IN ORDINARY TIME

ENTRANCE ANTIPHON
Psalm 129:3–4

If you, O Lord, laid bare our guilt, who could endure it? But you are forgiving, God of Israel.

READING I
Isaiah 25:6–10a / 142

On this mountain the Lord of hosts
  will provide for all peoples
a feast of rich food and choice wines,

juicy, rich food and pure, choice wines.
On this mountain he will destroy

the veil that veils all peoples,
the web that is woven over all nations;
he will destroy death forever.
The Lord GOD will wipe away
the tears from every face;
the reproach of his people he will remove
from the whole earth; for the LORD
has spoken.

On that day it will be said:
"Behold our God, to whom we looked
to save us!
This is the LORD for whom we looked;
let us rejoice and be glad that he has saved us!"
For the hand of the LORD will rest on
this mountain.

RESPONSORIAL PSALM

Psalm 23:1–3a, 3b–4, 5, 6

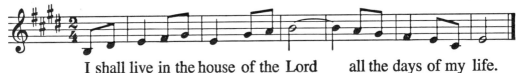

I shall live in the house of the Lord   all the days of my life.

The LORD is my shepherd; I shall not want.
In verdant pastures he gives me repose;
beside restful waters he leads me;
he refreshes my soul. ℟.

You spread the table before me
in the sight of my foes;
you anoint my head with oil;
my cup overflows. ℟.

He guides me in right paths
for his name's sake.
Even though I walk in the dark valley
I fear no evil; for you are at my side
with your rod and your staff
that give me courage. ℟.

Only goodness and kindness follow me
all the days of my life;
and I shall dwell in the house of the LORD
for years to come. ℟.

READING II

Philippians 4:12–14, 19–20

Brothers and sisters: I know how to live in humble circumstances; I know also how to live with abundance. In every circumstance and in all things I have learned the secret of being well fed and of going hungry, of living in abundance and of being in need. I can do all things in him who strengthens me. Still, it was kind of you to share in my distress.

My God will fully supply whatever you need, in accord with his glorious riches in Christ Jesus. To our God and Father, glory forever and ever. Amen.

GOSPEL

Matthew 22:1–14 or 22:1–10

For short form read only the part in brackets.

[Jesus again in reply spoke to the chief priests and elders of the people in parables, saying, "The kingdom of heaven may be likened to a king who gave a wedding feast for his son. He dispatched his servants to summon the invited guests to the feast, but they refused to come. A second time he sent other servants, saying, 'Tell those invited: "Behold, I have prepared my banquet, my calves and fattened cattle are killed, and everything is ready; come to the feast.'" Some ignored the invitation and went away, one to his farm, another to his business. The rest laid hold of his servants, mistreated them, and killed them. The king was enraged and sent his troops, destroyed those murderers, and burned their city. Then he said to his servants, 'The feast is ready, but those who were invited were not worthy to come. Go out, therefore, into the main roads and invite to the feast whomever you find.' The servants went out into the streets and gathered all they found, bad and good alike, and the hall was filled with guests.] But when the king came in to meet the guests, he saw a man there not dressed in a wedding garment. The king said to him, 'My friend, how is it that you came in here without a wedding garment?' But he was reduced to silence. Then the king said to his attendants, 'Bind his hands and feet, and cast him into the darkness outside, where there will be wailing and grinding of teeth.' Many are invited, but few are chosen."

COMMUNION ANTIPHON *1 John 3:2*
When the Lord is revealed we shall be like him, for we shall see him as he is.

October 16, 2011

TWENTY-NINTH SUNDAY IN ORDINARY TIME

ENTRANCE ANTIPHON *Psalm 16:6, 8*
I call upon you, God, for you will answer me; bend your ear and hear my prayer. Guard me as the pupil of your eye; hide me in the shade of your wings.

READING I *Isaiah 45:1, 4–6 / 145*

Thus says the LORD to his anointed,
  Cyrus,
  whose right hand I grasp,
subduing nations before him,
  and making kings run in his service,
opening doors before him
  and leaving the gates unbarred:
For the sake of Jacob, my servant,
  of Israel, my chosen one,
I have called you by your name,
  giving you a title, though you knew

me not.
I am the LORD and there is no other,
  there is no God besides me.
It is I who arm you, though you know
  me not,
so that toward the rising and the
  setting of the sun
people may know that there is none
  besides me.
I am the LORD, there is no other.

RESPONSORIAL PSALM *Psalm 96:1, 3, 4–5, 7–8, 9–10*

Give the Lord glo - ry and hon - or.

Sing to the LORD a new song;
  sing to the LORD, all you lands.
Tell his glory among the nations;
  among all peoples, his wondrous
  deeds. ℟.

For great is the LORD and highly to be
  praised;
  awesome is he, beyond all gods.
For all the gods of the nations are things
  of nought,
  but the LORD made the heavens. ℟.

Give to the LORD, you families of
  nations,
  give to the LORD glory and praise;
  give to the LORD the glory due his
  name!
Bring gifts, and enter his courts. ℟.

Worship the LORD, in holy attire;
  tremble before him, all the earth;
say among the nations: The LORD is king,
  he governs the peoples with
  equity. ℟.

READING II   *1 Thessalonians 1:1–5b*

Paul, Silvanus, and Timothy to the church of the Thessalonians in God the Father and the Lord Jesus Christ: grace to you and peace. We give thanks to God always for all of you, remembering you in our prayers, unceasingly calling to mind your work of faith and labor of love and endurance in hope of our Lord Jesus Christ, before our God and Father, knowing, brothers and sisters loved by God, how you were chosen. For our gospel did not come to you in word alone, but also in power and in the Holy Spirit and with much conviction.

GOSPEL   *Matthew 22:15–21*

The Pharisees went off and plotted how they might entrap Jesus in speech. They sent their disciples to him, with the Herodians, saying, "Teacher, we know that you are a truthful man and that you teach the way of God in accordance with the truth. And you are not concerned with anyone's opinion, for you do not regard a person's status. Tell us, then, what is your opinion: Is it lawful to pay the census tax to Caesar or not?" Knowing their malice, Jesus said, "Why are you testing me, you hypocrites? Show me the coin that pays the census tax." Then they handed him the Roman coin. He said to them, "Whose image is this and whose inscription?" They replied, "Caesar's." At that he said to them, "Then repay to Caesar what belongs to Caesar and to God what belongs to God."

COMMUNION ANTIPHON   *Mark 10:45*

The Son of Man came to give his life as a ransom for many.

October 23, 2011

THIRTIETH SUNDAY IN ORDINARY TIME

ENTRANCE ANTIPHON   *Psalm 104:3–4*

Let hearts rejoice who search for the Lord. Seek the Lord and his strength, seek always the face of the Lord.

READING I   *Exodus 22:20–26 / 148*

Thus says the LORD: "You shall not molest or oppress an alien, for you were once aliens yourselves in the land of Egypt. You shall not wrong any widow or orphan. If ever you wrong them and they cry out to me, I will surely hear their cry. My wrath will flare up, and I will kill you with the sword; then your own wives will be widows, and your children orphans.

"If you lend money to one of your poor neighbors among my people, you shall not act like an extortioner toward him by demanding interest from him. If you take your neighbor's cloak as a pledge, you shall return it to him before sunset; for this cloak of his is the only covering he has for his body. What else has he to sleep in? If he cries out to me, I will hear him; for I am compassionate."

RESPONSORIAL PSALM   *Psalm 18:2–3, 3–4, 47, 51*

I love you, Lord,   my strength,   my strength.

I love you, O Lord, my strength,
O Lord, my rock, my fortress, my
deliverer. ℟.

My God, my rock of refuge,
my shield, the horn of my salvation,
my stronghold!
Praised be the Lord, I exclaim,

and I am safe from my enemies. ℟.

The Lord lives and blessed be my rock!
Extolled be God my savior.
You who gave great victories to your
king
and showed kindness to your
anointed. ℟.

READING II   *1 Thessalonians 1:5c–10*

Brothers and sisters: You know what sort of people we were among you for your sake. And you became imitators of us and of the Lord, receiving the word in great affliction, with joy from the Holy Spirit, so that you became a model for all the believers in Macedonia and in Achaia. For from you the word of the Lord has sounded forth not only in Macedonia and in Achaia, but in every place your faith in God has gone forth, so that we have no need to say anything. For they themselves openly declare about us what sort of reception we had among you, and how you turned to God from idols to serve the living and true God and to await his Son from heaven, whom he raised from the dead, Jesus, who delivers us from the coming wrath.

GOSPEL   *Matthew 22:34–40*

When the Pharisees heard that Jesus had silenced the Sadducees, they gathered together, and one of them, a scholar of the law, tested him by asking, "Teacher, which commandment in the law is the greatest?" He said to him, "You shall love the Lord, your God, with all your heart, with all your soul, and with all your mind. This is the greatest and the first commandment. The second is like it: You shall love your neighbor as yourself. The whole law and the prophets depend on these two commandments."

COMMUNION ANTIPHON   *Psalm 19:6*

We will rejoice at the victory of God and make our boast in his great name.

October 30, 2011
THIRTY-FIRST SUNDAY IN ORDINARY TIME

ENTRANCE ANTIPHON   *Psalm 37:22–23*

Do not abandon me, Lord. My God, do not go away from me! Hurry to help me, Lord, my Savior.

READING I   *Malachi 1:14b–2:2b, 8–10 / 151*

A great King am I, says the Lord of
hosts,
and my name will be feared among
the nations.
And now, O priests, this commandment
is for you:
If you do not listen,
if you do not lay it to heart,

to give glory to my name, says the
Lord of hosts,
I will send a curse upon you
and of your blessing I will make a
curse.
You have turned aside from the way,
and have caused many to falter by
your instruction;

you have made void the covenant of
Levi,
says the LORD of hosts.
I, therefore, have made you contemptible
and base before all the people,
since you do not keep my ways,

but show partiality in your decisions.
Have we not all the one father?
Has not the one God created us?
Why then do we break faith with one
another,
violating the covenant of our fathers?

RESPONSORIAL PSALM

Psalm 131:1, 2, 3

In you, O Lord, I have found my peace.

O LORD, my heart is not proud,
nor are my eyes haughty;
I busy not myself with great things,
nor with things too sublime for me. ℟.

Nay rather, I have stilled and quieted

my soul like a weaned child.
Like a weaned child on its mother's lap,
so is my soul within me. ℟.

O Israel, hope in the LORD,
both now and forever. ℟.

READING II

1 Thessalonians 2:7b-9, 13

Brothers and sisters: We were gentle among you, as a nursing mother cares for her children. With such affection for you, we were determined to share with you not only the gospel of God, but our very selves as well, so dearly beloved had you become to us. You recall, brothers and sisters, our toil and drudgery. Working night and day in order not to burden any of you, we proclaimed to you the gospel of God.

And for this reason we too give thanks to God unceasingly, that, in receiving the word of God from hearing us, you received not a human word but, as it truly is, the word of God, which is now at work in you who believe.

GOSPEL

Matthew 23:1–12

Jesus spoke to the crowds and to his disciples, saying, "The scribes and the Pharisees have taken their seat on the chair of Moses. Therefore, do and observe all things whatsoever they tell you, but do not follow their example. For they preach but they do not practice. They tie up heavy burdens hard to carry and lay them on people's shoulders, but they will not lift a finger to move them. All their works are performed to be seen. They widen their phylacteries and lengthen their tassels. They love places of honor at banquets, seats of honor in synagogues, greetings in marketplaces, and the salutation 'Rabbi.' As for you, do not be called 'Rabbi.' You have but one teacher, and you are all brothers. Call no one on earth your father; you have but one Father in heaven. Do not be called 'Master'; you have but one master, the Christ. The greatest among you must be your servant. Whoever exalts himself will be humbled; but whoever humbles himself will be exalted."

COMMUNION ANTIPHON

Psalm 15:11

Lord, you will show me the path of life and fill me with joy in your presence.

ALL SAINTS

ENTRANCE ANTIPHON
Let us all rejoice in the Lord and keep a festival in honor of all the saints. Let us join with the angels in joyful praise to the Son of God.

READING I *Revelation 7:2–4, 9–14 / 667*

I, John, saw another angel come up from the East, holding the seal of the living God. He cried out in a loud voice to the four angels who were given power to damage the land and the sea, "Do not damage the land or the sea or the trees until we put the seal on the foreheads of the servants of our God." I heard the number of those who had been marked with the seal, one hundred and forty-four thousand marked from every tribe of the children of Israel.

After this I had a vision of a great multitude, which no one could count, from every nation, race, people, and tongue. They stood before the throne and before the Lamb, wearing white robes and holding palm branches in their hands. They cried out in a loud voice:

"Salvation comes from our God,
    who is seated on the throne,
and from the Lamb."

All the angels stood around the throne and around the elders and the four living creatures. They prostrated themselves before the throne, worshiped God, and exclaimed:

"Amen. Blessing and glory, wisdom and thanksgiving,
    honor, power, and might
    be to our God forever and ever. Amen."

Then one of the elders spoke up and said to me, "Who are these wearing white robes, and where did they come from?" I said to him, "My lord, you are the one who knows." He said to me, "These are the ones who have survived the time of great distress; they have washed their robes and made them white in the Blood of the Lamb."

RESPONSORIAL PSALM *Psalm 24:1bc–2, 3–4ab, 5–6*

Lord, this is the peo - ple that longs to see your face.

The LORD's are the earth and its fullness;
    the world and those who dwell in it.
For he founded it upon the seas
    and established it upon the rivers. R̸.

Who can ascend the mountain of the
        LORD?
    or who may stand in his holy place?
One whose hands are sinless, whose

heart is clean,
    who desires not what is vain. R̸.

He shall receive a blessing from the
        LORD,
    a reward from God his savior.
Such is the race that seeks for him,
    that seeks the face of the God of
        Jacob. R̸.

READING II *1 John 3:1–3*

Beloved: See what love the Father has bestowed on us that we may be called the children of God. Yet so we are. The reason the world does not know us is that it did not know him. Beloved, we are God's children now; what we shall be has not yet been revealed. We do know that when it is revealed we shall be like him, for we shall see him as he is. Everyone who has this hope based on him makes himself pure, as he is pure.

GOSPEL
Matthew 5:1–12a

When Jesus saw the crowds, he went up the mountain, and after he had sat down, his disciples came to him. He began to teach them, saying:
"Blessed are the poor in spirit,
> for theirs is the Kingdom of heaven.
Blessed are they who mourn,
> for they will be comforted.
Blessed are the meek,
> for they will inherit the land.
Blessed are they who hunger and thirst for righteousness,
> for they will be satisfied.
Blessed are the merciful,
> for they will be shown mercy.
Blessed are the clean of heart,
> for they will see God.
Blessed are the peacemakers,
> for they will be called children of God.
Blessed are they who are persecuted for the sake of righteousness,
> for theirs is the Kingdom of heaven.
Blessed are you when they insult you and persecute you and utter every kind of evil against you falsely because of me. Rejoice and be glad, for your reward will be great in heaven."

COMMUNION ANTIPHON
Matthew 5:8–10

Happy are the pure of heart for they shall see God. Happy the peacemakers; they shall be called sons of God. Happy are they who suffer persecution for justice' sake; the kingdom of heaven is theirs.

November 2, 2011

COMMEMORATION OF ALL THE FAITHFUL DEPARTED (ALL SOULS)

While several options exist from the Masses for the Dead, the Committee on Divine Worship has noted especially the readings given here.

ENTRANCE ANTIPHONS
I: Just as Jesus died and rose again, so will the Father bring with him those who have died in Jesus. Just as in Adam all men die, so in Christ all will be made alive.
(1 Thes 4:14; 1 Cor 15:22)

II: Give them eternal rest, O Lord, and may your light shine on them for ever.
(See 4 Ez 2:34–35)

III: God, who raised Jesus from the dead, will give new life to our own mortal bodies through his Spirit living in us. *(Rom 8:11)*

READING I

Wisdom 3:1–9 / 668

The souls of the just are in the hand of God,
    and no torment shall touch them.
They seemed, in the view of the foolish, to be dead;
    and their passing away was thought an affliction
    and their going forth from us, utter destruction.
But they are in peace.
For if before men, indeed, they be punished,
    yet is their hope full of immortality;
chastised a little, they shall be greatly blessed,
    because God tried them
    and found them worthy of himself.
As gold in the furnace, he proved them,
    and as sacrificial offerings he took them to himself.
In the time of their visitation they shall shine,
    and shall dart about as sparks through stubble;
they shall judge nations and rule over peoples,
    and the LORD shall be their King forever.
Those who trust in him shall understand truth,
    and the faithful shall abide with him in love:
because grace and mercy are with his holy ones,
    and his care is with his elect.

RESPONSORIAL PSALM

Psalm 23:1–3a, 3b–4, 5, 6

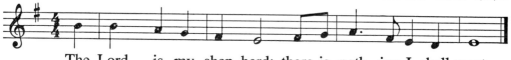

The Lord is my shep-herd; there is noth-ing I shall want.

Or:

Though I walk in the val - ley of dark - ness,

I fear no e - vil, for you are with me.

The LORD is my shepherd; I shall not
    want.
    In verdant pastures he gives me repose;
Beside restful waters he leads me;
    he refreshes my soul. ℟.

He guides me in right paths
    for his name's sake.
Even though I walk in the dark valley
    I fear no evil; for you are at my side
With your rod and your staff
    that give me courage. ℟.

You spread the table before me
in the sight of my foes;
You anoint my head with oil;
my cup overflows. ℟.

Only goodness and kindness follow me
all the days of my life;
And I shall dwell in the house of the
LORD
for years to come. ℟.

READING II   Romans 5:5–11

Brothers and sisters: Hope does not disappoint, because the love of God has been poured out into our hearts through the Holy Spirit that has been given to us. For Christ, while we were still helpless, died at the appointed time for the ungodly. Indeed, only with difficulty does one die for a just person, though perhaps for a good person one might even find courage to die. But God proves his love for us in that while we were still sinners Christ died for us. How much more then, since we are now justified by his Blood, will we be saved through him from the wrath. Indeed, if, while we were enemies, we were reconciled to God through the death of his Son, how much more, once reconciled, will we be saved by his life. Not only that, but we also boast of God through our Lord Jesus Christ, through whom we have now received reconciliation.

Or:

READING II   Romans 6:3–9

Brothers and sisters: Are you unaware that we who were baptized into Christ Jesus were baptized into his death? We were indeed buried with him through baptism into death, so that, just as Christ was raised from the dead by the glory of the Father, we too might live in newness of life.

For if we have grown into union with him through a death like his, we shall also be united with him in the resurrection. We know that our old self was crucified with him, so that our sinful body might be done away with, that we might no longer be in slavery to sin. For a dead person has been absolved from sin. If, then, we have died with Christ, we believe that we shall also live with him. We know that Christ, raised from the dead, dies no more; death no longer has power over him.

GOSPEL   John 6:37–40

Jesus said to the crowds: "Everything that the Father gives me will come to me, and I will not reject anyone who comes to me, because I came down from heaven not to do my own will but the will of the one who sent me. And this is the will of the one who sent me, that I should not lose anything of what he gave me, but that I should raise it on the last day. For this is the will of my Father, that everyone who sees the Son and believes in him may have eternal life, and I shall raise him on the last day."

COMMUNION ANTIPHONS
I: I am the resurrection and the life, says the Lord. If anyone believes in me, even though he dies, he will live. Anyone who lives and believes in me, will not die. *(Jn 11:25–26)*

II: May eternal light shine on them, O Lord, with all your saints for ever, for you are rich in mercy. Give them eternal rest, O Lord, and may perpetual light shine on them for ever, for you are rich in mercy. *(See 4 Ez 2:35, 34)*

III: We are waiting for our Savior, the Lord Jesus Christ; he will transfigure our lowly bodies into copies of his own glorious body. *(Phil 3:20–21)*

THIRTY-SECOND SUNDAY IN ORDINARY TIME

ENTRANCE ANTIPHON *Psalm 87:3*
Let my prayer come before you, Lord; listen, and answer me.

READING I

Wisdom 6:12–16 / 154

Resplendent and unfading is wisdom,
and she is readily perceived by
those who love her,
and found by those who seek her.
She hastens to make herself known in
anticipation of their desire;
whoever watches for her at dawn
shall not be disappointed,
for he shall find her sitting by his
gate.

For taking thought of wisdom is the
perfection of prudence,
and whoever for her sake keeps vigil
shall quickly be free from care;
because she makes her own rounds,
seeking those worthy of her,
and graciously appears to them in
the ways,
and meets them with all solicitude.

RESPONSORIAL PSALM

Psalm 63:2, 3–4, 5–6, 7–8

My soul is thirst-ing for you, O Lord,

thirst-ing for you my God.

O God, you are my God whom I seek;
for you my flesh pines and my soul
thirsts
like the earth, parched, lifeless and
without water. ℟.

Thus have I gazed toward you in the
sanctuary
to see your power and your glory,
for your kindness is a greater good than
life;
my lips shall glorify you. ℟.

Thus will I bless you while I live;
lifting up my hands, I will call upon
your name.
As with the riches of a banquet shall my
soul be satisfied,
and with exultant lips my mouth
shall praise you. ℟.

I will remember you upon my couch,
and through the night-watches I will
meditate on you:
you are my help,
and in the shadow of your wings I
shout for joy. ℟.

READING II

1 Thessalonians 4:13–18 or 4:13–14
For short form read only the part in brackets.

[We do not want you to be unaware, brothers and sisters, about those who have fallen asleep, so that you may not grieve like the rest, who have no hope. For if we believe that Jesus died and rose, so too will God, through Jesus, bring with him those who have fallen asleep.] Indeed, we tell you this, on the word of the Lord, that we who are alive, who are left until the coming of the Lord, will surely not precede those who have fallen asleep. For the Lord himself, with a word of command, with the voice of an archangel and with the trumpet of God, will come down from heaven, and the dead in Christ will rise first. Then we who are alive, who are left, will be caught up together with them in the clouds to meet the Lord in the air. Thus we shall always be with the Lord. Therefore, console one another with these words.

GOSPEL *Matthew 25:1–13*

Jesus told his disciples this parable: "The kingdom of heaven will be like ten virgins who took their lamps and went out to meet the bridegroom. Five of them were foolish and five were wise. The foolish ones, when taking their lamps, brought no oil with them, but the wise brought flasks of oil with their lamps. Since the bridegroom was long delayed, they all became drowsy and fell asleep. At midnight, there was a cry, 'Behold, the bridegroom! Come out to meet him!' Then all those virgins got up and trimmed their lamps. The foolish ones said to the wise, 'Give us some of your oil, for our lamps are going out.' But the wise ones replied, 'No, for there may not be enough for us and you. Go instead to the merchants and buy some for yourselves.' While they went off to buy it, the bridegroom came and those who were ready went into the wedding feast with him. Then the door was locked. Afterwards the other virgins came and said, 'Lord, Lord, open the door for us!' But he said in reply, 'Amen, I say to you, I do not know you.' Therefore, stay awake, for you know neither the day nor the hour."

COMMUNION ANTIPHON *Luke 24:35*

The disciples recognized the Lord Jesus in the breaking of the bread.

November 13, 2011
THIRTY-THIRD SUNDAY IN ORDINARY TIME

ENTRANCE ANTIPHON *Jeremiah 29:11, 12, 14*

The Lord says: my plans for you are peace and not disaster; when you call to me, I will listen to you, and I will bring you back to the place from which I exiled you.

READING I *Proverbs 31:10–13, 19–20, 30–31 / 157*

When one finds a worthy wife,
   her value is far beyond pearls.
Her husband, entrusting his heart to her,
   has an unfailing prize.
She brings him good, and not evil,
   all the days of her life.
She obtains wool and flax
   and works with loving hands.
She puts her hands to the distaff,
and her fingers ply the spindle.
She reaches out her hands to the poor,
   and extends her arms to the needy.
Charm is deceptive and beauty fleeting;
   the woman who fears the LORD is to
   be praised.
Give her a reward for her labors,
   and let her works praise her at the
   city gates.

RESPONSORIAL PSALM

Psalm 128:1–2, 3, 4–5

Bless - ed are those who fear the Lord.

Blessed are you who fear the LORD,
who walk in his ways!
For you shall eat the fruit of your
handiwork;
blessed shall you be, and favored. ℟.

Your wife shall be like a fruitful vine
in the recesses of your home;
your children like olive plants

around your table. ℟.

Behold, thus is the man blessed
who fears the LORD.
The LORD bless you from Zion:
may you see the prosperity of
Jerusalem
all the days of your life. ℟.

READING II

1 Thessalonians 5:1–6

Concerning times and seasons, brothers and sisters, you have no need for anything to be written to you. For you yourselves know very well that the day of the Lord will come like a thief at night. When people are saying, "Peace and security," then sudden disaster comes upon them, like labor pains upon a pregnant woman, and they will not escape.

But you, brothers and sisters, are not in darkness, for that day to overtake you like a thief. For all of you are children of the light and children of the day. We are not of the night or of darkness. Therefore, let us not sleep as the rest do, but let us stay alert and sober.

GOSPEL

Matthew 25:14–30 or 25:14–15, 19–21

For short form read only the parts in brackets.

[Jesus told his disciples this parable: "A man going on a journey called in his servants and entrusted his possessions to them. To one he gave five talents; to another, two; to a third, one—to each according to his ability. Then he went away.] Immediately the one who received five talents went and traded with them, and made another five. Likewise, the one who received two made another two. But the man who received one went off and dug a hole in the ground and buried his master's money.

["After a long time the master of those servants came back and settled accounts with them. The one who had received five talents came forward bringing the additional five. He said, 'Master, you gave me five talents. See, I have made five more.' His master said to him, 'Well done, my good and faithful servant. Since you were faithful in small matters, I will give you great responsibilities. Come, share your master's joy.'] Then the one who had received two talents also came forward and said, 'Master, you gave me two talents. See, I have made two more.' His master said to him, 'Well done, my good and faithful servant. Since you were faithful in small matters, I will give you great responsibilities. Come, share your master's joy.' Then the one who had received the one talent came forward and said, 'Master, I knew you were a demanding person, harvesting where you did not plant and gathering where you did not scatter; so out of fear I went off and buried your talent in the ground. Here it is back.' His master said to him in reply, 'You wicked, lazy servant! So you knew that I harvest where I did not plant and gather where I did not scatter? Should you not then have put my money in the bank so that I could have got it back with interest on my return? Now then! Take the talent from him and give it to the one with ten. For to everyone who has, more will be given and he will grow rich; but from the one who has not, even what he has will be taken away. And throw this useless servant into the darkness outside, where there will be wailing and grinding of teeth.'"

COMMUNION ANTIPHON
Mark 11:23, 24

I tell you solemnly, whatever you ask for in prayer, believe that you have received it, and it will be yours, says the Lord.

November 20, 2011

OUR LORD JESUS CHRIST THE KING

ENTRANCE ANTIPHON
Revelation 5:12; 1:6

The Lamb who was slain is worthy to receive strength and divinity, wisdom and power and honor: to him be glory and power for ever.

READING I
Ezekiel 34:11–12, 15–17 / 160

Thus says the Lord God: I myself will look after and tend my sheep. As a shepherd tends his flock when he finds himself among his scattered sheep, so will I tend my sheep. I will rescue them from every place where they were scattered when it was cloudy and dark. I myself will pasture my sheep; I myself will give them rest, says the Lord God. The lost I will seek out, the strayed I will bring back, the injured I will bind up, the sick I will heal, but the sleek and the strong I will destroy, shepherding them rightly.

As for you, my sheep, says the Lord God, I will judge between one sheep and another, between rams and goats.

RESPONSORIAL PSALM
Psalm 23:1–2, 2–3, 5–6

The Lord   is my shep-herd; there is noth-ing I shall want.

The LORD is my shepherd; I shall not
   want.
  In verdant pastures he gives me
    repose. ℟.

Beside restful waters he leads me;
  he refreshes my soul.
He guides me in right paths
  for his name's sake. ℟.

You spread the table before me
  in the sight of my foes;
you anoint my head with oil;
  my cup overflows. ℟.

Only goodness and kindness follow me
  all the days of my life;
and I shall dwell in the house of the
    LORD
  for years to come. ℟.

READING II
1 Corinthians 15:20–26, 28

Brothers and sisters: Christ has been raised from the dead, the firstfruits of those who have fallen asleep. For since death came through man, the resurrection of the dead came also through man. For just as in Adam all die, so too in Christ shall all be brought to life, but each one in proper order: Christ the firstfruits; then, at his coming, those who belong to Christ; then comes the end, when he hands over the kingdom to his God and Father, when he has destroyed every sovereignty and every authority and power. For he must reign until he has put all his enemies under his feet. The last enemy to be destroyed is death. When everything is subjected to him, then the Son himself will also be subjected to the one who subjected everything to him, so that God may be all in all.

GOSPEL
Matthew 25:31–46

Jesus said to his disciples: "When the Son of Man comes in his glory, and all the angels with him, he will sit upon his glorious throne, and all the nations will be assembled before him. And he will separate them one from another, as a shepherd separates the sheep from the goats. He will place the sheep on his right and the goats on his left. Then the king will say to those on his right, 'Come, you who are blessed by my Father. Inherit the kingdom prepared for you from the foundation of the world. For I was hungry and you gave me food, I was thirsty and you gave me drink, a stranger and you welcomed me, naked and you clothed me, ill and you cared for me, in prison and you visited me.' Then the righteous will answer him and say, 'Lord, when did we see you hungry and feed you, or thirsty and give you drink? When did we see you a stranger and welcome you, or naked and clothe you? When did we see you ill or in prison, and visit you?' And the king will say to them in reply, 'Amen, I say to you, whatever you did for one of the least brothers of mine, you did for me.' Then he will say to those on his left, 'Depart from me, you accursed, into the eternal fire prepared for the devil and his angels. For I was hungry and you gave me no food, I was thirsty and you gave me no drink, a stranger and you gave me no welcome, naked and you gave me no clothing, ill and in prison, and you did not care for me.' Then they will answer and say, 'Lord, when did we see you hungry or thirsty or a stranger or naked or ill or in prison, and not minister to your needs?' He will answer them, 'Amen, I say to you, what you did not do for one of these least ones, you did not do for me.' And these will go off to eternal punishment, but the righteous to eternal life."

COMMUNION ANTIPHON
Psalm 28:10–11

The Lord will reign for ever and will give his people the gift of peace.

November 24, 2011

THANKSGIVING DAY

While several options exist from the Mass "In Thanksgiving to God," the Committee on Divine Worship has noted especially the readings given here.

ENTRANCE ANTIPHON
See Psalm 136

Give thanks to the Lord for he is good; his love is everlasting. Give thanks to the Lord of lords, for his love is everlasting.

READING I
Sirach 50:22–24

And now, bless the God of all,
who has done wondrous things on earth;
Who fosters people's growth from their mother's womb,
and fashions them according to his will!
May he grant you joy of heart
and may peace abide among you;
May his goodness toward us endure in Israel
to deliver us in our days.

RESPONSORIAL PSALM I

1 Chronicles 29:10bc, 11, 12

℟. **We praise your glorious name, O mighty God.**

"Blessed may you be, O LORD,
 God of Israel our father,
 from eternity to eternity." ℟.

"Yours, O LORD, are grandeur and power,
 majesty, splendor, and glory.
For all in heaven and on earth is yours;
 yours, O LORD, is the sovereignty;

you are exalted as head over all." ℟.

"Riches and honor are from you,
 and you have dominion over all.
In your hand are power and might;
 it is yours to give grandeur and
 strength to all." ℟.

Or:

RESPONSORIAL PSALM II

Psalm 138:1–2a, 2bc–3, 4–5

℟. **Lord, I thank you for your faithfulness and love.**

I will give thanks to you, O LORD, with
 all of my heart,
 for you have heard the words of my
 mouth;
 in the presence of the angels I will
 sing your praise;
I will worship at your holy temple. ℟.

I will give thanks to your name,
Because of your kindness and your truth.

When I called, you answered me;
 you built up strength within me. ℟.

All the kings of the earth shall give
 thanks to you, O LORD,
 when they hear the words of your
 mouth;
And they shall sing of the ways of the
 LORD:
 "Great is the glory of the LORD." ℟.

Psalm 113:1–2, 3–4, 5–6, 7–8 or Psalm 145:2–3, 4–5, 6–7, 8–9, 10–11 may also be used.

READING II

1 Corinthians 1:3–9

Brothers and sisters: Grace to you and peace from God our Father and the Lord Jesus Christ.
   I give thanks to my God always on your account for the grace of God bestowed on you in Christ Jesus, that in him you were enriched in every way, with all discourse and all knowledge, as the testimony to Christ was confirmed among you, so that you are not lacking in any spiritual gift as you wait for the revelation of our Lord Jesus Christ. He will keep you firm to the end, irreproachable on the day of our Lord Jesus Christ. God is faithful, and by him you were called to fellowship with his Son, Jesus Christ our Lord.

GOSPEL

Luke 17:11–19

As Jesus continued his journey to Jerusalem, he traveled through Samaria and Galilee. As he was entering a village, ten persons with leprosy met him. They stood at a distance from him and raised their voices, saying, "Jesus, Master! Have pity on us!" And when he saw them, he said, "Go show yourselves to the priests." As they were going they were cleansed. And one of them, realizing he had been healed, returned, glorifying God in a loud voice; and he fell at the feet of Jesus and thanked him. He was a Samaritan. Jesus said in reply, "Ten were cleansed, were they not? Where are the other nine? Has none but this foreigner returned to give thanks to God?" Then he said to him, "Stand up and go; your faith has saved you."

COMMUNION ANTIPHON
O give thanks to the Lord, for he is good, for his great love is without end.

The Weekdays

Monday, November 29, 2010: First Week of Advent / 175 [Is 4:2–6/Mt 8:5–11]

ENTRANCE ANTIPHON: Nations, hear the message of the Lord, and make it known to the ends of the earth: Our Savior is coming. Have no more fear. *(See Jer 31:10; Is 35:4)*

RESPONSE: Let us go rejoicing to the house of the Lord.

GOSPEL VERSE: R/. Alleluia. Come and save us, Lord our God; let your face shine upon us, that we may be saved. R/. Alleluia. *(See Ps 80:4)*

COMMUNION ANTIPHON: Come to us, Lord, and bring us peace. We will rejoice in your presence and serve you with all our heart. *(See Ps 105:4–5; Is 38:3)*

Tuesday, November 30, 2010: Andrew—apostle / 684 [Rom 10:9–18/Mt 4:18–22]

ENTRANCE ANTIPHON: By the Sea of Galilee the Lord saw two brothers, Peter and Andrew. He called to them: come and follow me, and I will make you fishers of men. *(See Mt 4:18–19)*

RESPONSE: The judgments of the Lord are true, and all of them are just. *(Ps 19:10)*

Or: Your words, Lord, are Spirit and life. *(Jn 6:63)*

GOSPEL VERSE: R/. Alleluia. Come after me, says the Lord, and I will make you fishers of men. R/. Alleluia. *(Mt 4:19)*

COMMUNION ANTIPHON: Andrew told his brother Simon: We have found the Messiah, the Christ; and he brought him to Jesus. *(Jn 1:41–42)*

Wednesday, December 1, 2010: First Week of Advent / 177 [Is 25:6–10a/Mt 15:29–37]

ENTRANCE ANTIPHON: The Lord is coming and will not delay; he will bring every hidden thing to light and reveal himself to every nation. *(See Hb 2:3; 1 Cor 4:5)*

RESPONSE: I shall live in the house of the Lord all the days of my life. *(Ps 23:6cd)*

GOSPEL VERSE: R/. Alleluia. Behold, the Lord comes to save his people; blessed are those prepared to meet him. R/. Alleluia.

COMMUNION ANTIPHON: The Lord our God comes in strength and will fill his servants with joy. *(Is 40:10; see 34:5)*

Thursday, December 2, 2010: First Week of Advent / 178 [Is 26:1–6/Mt 7:21, 24–27]

ENTRANCE ANTIPHON: Lord, you are near, and all your commandments are just; long have I known that you decreed them for ever. *(See Ps 118:151–152)*

RESPONSE: Blessed is he who comes in the name of the Lord. *(Ps 118:26a) Or:* Alleluia.

GOSPEL VERSE: R/. Alleluia. Seek the LORD while he may be found; call him while he is near R/. Alleluia. *(Is 55:6)*

COMMUNION ANTIPHON: Let our lives be honest and holy in this present age, as we wait for the happiness to come when our great God reveals himself in glory. *(Ti 2:12–13)*

Friday, December 3, 2010: Francis Xavier—priest / 685 [1 Cor 9:16–19, 22–23/Mk 16:15–20]

ENTRANCE ANTIPHON: Proclaim his glory among the nations, his marvelous deeds to all the peoples; great is the Lord and worthy of all praise *(Ps 95:3–4)*

RESPONSE: Go out to all the world and tell the Good News. *(Mk 16:15)*

GOSPEL VERSE: R/. Alleluia. Go and teach all nations, says the Lord: I am with you always, until the end of the world. R/. Alleluia. *(Mt 28:19a–20b)*

COMMUNION ANTIPHON: The Lord sent disciples to proclaim to all the towns: the kingdom of God is very near to you. *(See Lk 10:1, 9)*

OR: First Week of Advent / 179 [Is 29:17–24/Mt 9:27–31]

ENTRANCE ANTIPHON: The Lord is coming from heaven in splendor to visit his people, and bring them peace and eternal life.

RESPONSE: The Lord is my light and my salvation. *(Ps 27:1a)*

GOSPEL VERSE: R/. Alleluia. Behold, our Lord shall come with power; he will enlighten the eyes of his servants. R/. Alleluia.

COMMUNION ANTIPHON: We are waiting for our Savior, the Lord Jesus Christ; he will transfigure our lowly bodies into copies of his own glorious body. *(Phil 3:20–21)*

Saturday, December 4, 2010: First Week of Advent / 180 [Is 30:19–21, 23–26/Mt 9:35–10:1, 5a, 6–8]

ENTRANCE ANTIPHON: Come, Lord, from your cherubim throne; let us see your face, and we shall be saved. *(Ps 79:4, 2)*

RESPONSE: Blessed are all who wait for the Lord. *(See Is 30:18d)*

GOSPEL VERSE: R/. Alleluia. The LORD is our Judge, our Lawgiver, our King; he it is who will save us. R/. Alleluia. *(Is 33:22)*

COMMUNION ANTIPHON: I am coming quickly, says the Lord, and will repay each man according to his deeds. *(Rv 22:12)*

OR: **John of Damascus**—*priest, doctor of the Church / 686 [2 Tm 1:13–14, 2:1–3/Mt 25:14–30 or Mt 25:14–23]*

ENTRANCE ANTIPHON: I will give you shepherds after my own heart, and they shall feed you on knowledge and sound teaching. *(Jer 3:15)*

RESPONSE: The judgments of the Lord are true, and all of them are just. *(Ps 19:10)*

Or: Your words, Lord, are spirit and life. *(Jn 6:63)*

GOSPEL VERSE: R/. Alleluia: All who love me will keep my words, and my Father will love them, and we will come to them. R/. Alleluia. *(Jn 14:23)*

COMMUNION ANTIPHON: The Son of Man did not come to be served, but to serve, and to give his life as a ransom for many. *(Mt 20:28)*

Monday, December 6, 2010: Second Week of Advent / 181 [Is 35:1–10/Lk 5:17–26]

ENTRANCE ANTIPHON: Nations, hear the message of the Lord, and make it known to the ends of the earth: Our Savior is coming. Have no more fear. *(See Jer 31:10; Is 35:4)*

RESPONSE: Our God will come to save us! *(Is 35:4f)*

GOSPEL VERSE: R/. Alleluia. Behold the king will come, the Lord of the earth, and he himself will lift the yoke of our captivity. R/. Alleluia.

COMMUNION ANTIPHON: Come to us, Lord, and bring us peace. We will rejoice in your presence and serve you with all our heart. *(See Ps 105:4–5; Is 38:3)*

OR: **Nicholas**—*bishop / 687 [Is 6:1–8/Lk 10:1–9]*

ENTRANCE ANTIPHON: I will raise up for myself a faithful priest; he will do what is in my heart and in my mind, says the Lord. *(1 Sm 2:35)*

RESPONSE: Here I am, Lord; I come to do your will. *(Ps 40:8a, 9a)*

GOSPEL VERSE: R/. Alleluia. The Lord sent me to bring glad tidings to the poor and to proclaim liberty to captives. R/. Alleluia. *(Lk 4:18)*

COMMUNION ANTIPHON: I came that men may have life, and have it to the full, says the Lord. *(Jn 10:10)*

Tuesday, December 7, 2010: Ambrose—bishop, doctor of the Church / 688 [Eph 3:8–12/Jn 10:11–16]

ENTRANCE ANTIPHON: The mouth of the just man utters wisdom, and his tongue speaks what is right; the law of his God is in his heart. *(Ps 36:30–31)*

RESPONSE: For ever I will sing the goodness of the Lord.

GOSPEL VERSE: R/. Alleluia. I am the good shepherd, says the Lord; I know my sheep, and mine know me. R/. Alleluia. *(Jn 10:14)*

COMMUNION ANTIPHON: The Lord has put his faithful servant in charge of his household, to give them their share of bread at the proper time. *(Lk 12:42)*

OR: **Second Week of Advent** / 182 [Is 40:1–11/Mt 18:12–14]

ENTRANCE ANTIPHON: See, the Lord is come and with him all his saints. Then there will be endless day. *(See Zech 14:5,7)*

RESPONSE: The Lord our God comes with power *(See Is 40:10ab)*

GOSPEL VERSE: R/. Alleluia. The day of the Lord is near: Behold, he comes to save us. R/. Alleluia.

COMMUNION ANTIPHON: The Lord is just; he will award the crown of justice to all who have longed for his coming. *(2 Tm 4:8)*

Wednesday, December 8, 2010: Immaculate Conception of the Blessed Virgin Mary

(See Sunday section)

Thursday, December 9, 2010: Second Week of Advent / 184 [Is 41:13–20/Mt 11:11–15]

ENTRANCE ANTIPHON: Lord, you are near, and all your commandments are just; long have I known that you decreed them for ever. *(See Ps 118:151–152)*

RESPONSE: The Lord is gracious and merciful; slow to anger and of great kindness. *(Ps 145:8)*

GOSPEL VERSE: R/. Alleluia. Let the clouds rain down the Just One, and the earth bring forth a Savior. R/. Alleluia. *(See Is 45:8)*

COMMUNION ANTIPHON: Let our lives be honest and holy in this present age, as we wait for the happiness to come when our great God reveals himself in glory. *(Ti 2:12–13)*

OR: ***Juan Diego Cuauhtlatoatzin—hermit / 689A, 737–742***

ENTRANCE ANTIPHON: The just man will rejoice in the Lord and hope in him, and all the upright of heart will be praised. *(Ps 63:11)*

RESPONSE: Blessed the man who fears the Lord. *(Ps 112:1) Or:* Alleluia.

GOSPEL VERSE: Remain in me, as I remain in you, says the Lord; whoever remains in me will bear much fruit. *(Jn 15:4a, 5b)*

COMMUNION ANTIPHON: He who serves me, follows me, says the Lord; and where I am, my servant will also be. *(Jn 12:26)*

Friday, December 10, 2010: Second Week of Advent / 185 [Is 48:17–19/Mt 11:16–19]

ENTRANCE ANTIPHON: The Lord is coming from heaven in splendor to visit his people, and bring them peace and eternal life.

RESPONSE: Those who follow you, Lord, will have the light of life. *(See Jn 8:12)*

GOSPEL VERSE: R/. Alleluia. The Lord will come; go out to meet him! He is the prince of peace. R/. Alleluia.

COMMUNION ANTIPHON: We are waiting for our Savior, the Lord Jesus Christ; he will transfigure our lowly bodies into copies of his own glorious body. *(Phil 3:20–21)*

Saturday, December 11, 2010: Second Week of Advent / 186 [Sir 48:1–4, 9–11//Mt 17:9a, 10–13]

ENTRANCE ANTIPHON: Come, Lord, from your cherubim throne; let us see your face, and we shall be saved. *(Ps 79:4, 2)*

RESPONSE: Lord, make us turn to you; let us see your face and we shall be saved. *(Ps 80:4)*

GOSPEL VERSE: R/. Alleluia. Prepare the way of the Lord, make straight his paths: All flesh shall see the salvation of God. R/. Alleluia. *(Lk 3:4, 6)*

COMMUNION ANTIPHON: I am coming quickly, says the Lord, and will repay each man according to his deeds. *(Rv 22:12)*

OR: ***Damasus I—pope / 690 [Acts 20:17–18a, 28–32, 36/Jn 15:9–17]***

ENTRANCE ANTIPHON: The Lord chose him to be his high priest; he opened his treasures and made him rich in all goodness.

RESPONSE: You are a priest for ever, in the line of Melchizedek. *(Ps 110:4b)*

GOSPEL VERSE: R/. Alleluia. I call you my friends, says the Lord, for I have made known to you all that the Father has told me. R/. Alleluia. *(Jn 15:15b)*

COMMUNION ANTIPHON: The good shepherd gives his life for his sheep. *(See Jn 10:11)*

Saturday, December 11 / Monday, December 13, 2010

(The following texts are used in locales where the celebration of Our Lady of Guadalupe is trasferred to December 11 or December 13 for 2010.)

690A [Zec 2:14–17 or Rv 11:19a, 12:1–6a, 10ab/Lk 1:26–38 or Lk 1:39–47; or any from 707–712]

ENTRANCE ANTIPHON: A great sign appeared in the sky, a woman clothed with the sun, with the moon under her feet, and on her head a crwon of twelve stars. *(Rv 12:1)*

RESPONSE: You are the highest honor of our race. *(Jdt 15:9d)*

GOSPEL VERSE: R/. Allelluia. Blessed are you, holy Virgin Mary, deserving of all praise; from you rose the sun of justice, Christ our God. R/. Aleluia.

COMMUNION ANTIPHON: God has not acted thus for any other nation; to no other people has he shown his love so clearly. (See Ps 147:20)

Monday, December 13, 2010: Lucy— virgin, martyr / 692 [2 Cor 10:17– 11:2/Mt 25:1–13]

ENTRANCE ANTIPHON: Here is a wise and faithful virgin who went with lighted lamp to meet her Lord.

RESPONSE: Into your hands, O Lord, I commend my spirit. (Ps 31:6)

GOSPEL VERSE: R/. Alleluia. This is the wise virgin, whom the Lord found waiting; at his coming, she went in with him to the wedding feast. R/. Alleluia.

COMMUNION ANTIPHON: The bridegroom is here; let us go out to meet Christ the Lord. (Mt 25:6)

OR: **Third Week of Advent** / 187 [Nm 24:2–7, 15–17a/Mt 21:23–27]

ENTRANCE ANTIPHON: Nations, hear the message of the Lord, and make it known to the ends of the earth: Our Savior is coming. Have no more fear. (See Jer 31:10; Is 35:4)

RESPONSE: Teach me your ways, O Lord, (Ps 25:4)

GOSPEL VERSE: R/. Alleluia. Show us, LORD, your love, and grant us your salvation. R/. Alleluia. (Ps 85:8)

COMMUNION ANTIPHON: Come to us, Lord, and bring us peace. We will rejoice in your presence and serve you with all our heart. (See Ps 105:4–5; Is 38:3)

Tuesday, December 14, 2010: John of the Cross—priest, doctor of the Church / 693 [1 Cor 2:1–10a/Lk 14:25–33]

ENTRANCE ANTIPHON: I should boast of nothing but the cross of our Lord Jesus Christ; through him the world is crucified to me and I to the world. (Gal 6:14)

RESPONSE: The mouth of the just murmurs wisdom. (Ps 37:30a)

GOSPEL VERSE: R/. Alleluia. Blessed are the poor in spirit; the Kingdom of heaven is theirs. R/. Alleluia. (Mt 5:3)

COMMUNION ANTIPHON: If anyone wishes to come after me, he must renounce himself, take up his cross, and follow me, says the Lord. (Mt 16:24)

OR: **Third Week of Advent** / 188 [Zep 3:1–2, 9–13/Mt 21:28–32]

ENTRANCE ANTIPHON: See, the Lord is coming and with him all his saints. Then there will be endless day. (See Zech 14:5, 7)

RESPONSE: The Lord hears the cry of the poor. (Ps 34:7a)

GOSPEL VERSE: R/. Alleluia. Come, O Lord, do not delay; forgive the sins of your peeople. R/. Alleluia.

COMMUNION ANTIPHON: The Lord is just; he will award the crown of justice to all who have longed for his coming. (2 Tm 4:8)

Wednesday, December 15, 2010: Third Week of Advent / 189 [Is 45:6b–8, 18, 21b–25/Lk 7:18b–23]

ENTRANCE ANTIPHON: The Lord is coming and will not delay; he will bring every hidden thing to light and reveal himself to every nation. (See Hb 2:3; 1 Cor 4:5)

RESPONSE: Let the clouds rain down the Just One, and the earth bring forth a Savior. (Is 45:8)

GOSPEL VERSE: R/. Alleluia. Raise your voice and tell the Good News: Behold, the Lord GOD comes with power. R/. Alleluia. (See Is 40:9–10)

COMMUNION ANTIPHON: The Lord our God comes in strength and will fill his servants with joy. (Is 40:10; see 34:5)

Thursday, December 16, 2010: Third Week of Advent / 190 [Is 54:1–10/ Lk 7:24–30]

ENTRANCE ANTIPHON: Lord, you are near, and all your commandments are just; long have I known that you decreed them for ever. (See Ps 118:151– 152)

RESPONSE: I will praise you, Lord, for you have rescued me. (Ps 30:2a)

GOSPEL VERSE: R/. Alleluia. Prepare the way of the Lord, make straight his paths: All flesh shall see the salvation of God. R/. Alleluia. (Lk 3:4, 6)

COMMUNION ANTIPHON: Let our lives be honest and holy in this present age, as we wait for the happiness to come when our great God reveals himself in glory. (Ti 2:12–13)

Friday, December 17, 2010: Third Week of Advent / 193 [Gn 49:2, 8–10/Mt 1:1–17]

ENTRANCE ANTIPHON: You heavens, sing for joy, and earth exult! Our Lord is coming; he will take pity on those in distress. *(See Is 49:13)*

RESPONSE: Justice shall flourish in his time, and fullness of peace for ever. *(See Ps 72:7)*

GOSPEL VERSE: R/. Alleluia. O Wisdom of our God Most High, guiding creation with power and love: come to teach us the path of knowledge!. R/. Alleluia.

COMMUNION ANTIPHON: The Desired of all nations is coming, and the house of the Lord will be filled with his glory. *(See Hg 2:8)*

Saturday, December 18, 2010: Third Week of Advent / 194 [Jer 23:5–8/ Mt 1:18–25]

ENTRANCE ANTIPHON: Christ our King is coming, the Lamb whom John proclaimed.

RESPONSE: Justice shall flourish in his time, and fullness of peace for ever. *(See Ps 72:7)*

GOSPEL VERSE: R/. Alleluia. O Leader of the House of Israel, giver of the Law to Moses on Sinai: come to rescue us with your mighty power! R/. Alleluia.

COMMUNION ANTIPHON: His name will be called Emmanuel, which means God is with us. *(Mt 1:23)*

Monday, December 20, 2010: Fourth Week of Advent / 196 [Is 7:10–14/ Lk 1:26–38]

ENTRANCE ANTIPHON: A shoot will spring from Jesse's stock, and all mankind will see the saving power of God. *(See Is 11:1; 40:5; Lk 3:6)*

RESPONSE: Let the Lord enter; he is the king of glory. *(See Ps 24:7c, 10b)*

GOSPEL VERSE: R/. Alleluia. O Key of David, opening the gates of God's eternal Kingdom: come and free the prisoners of darkness! R/. Alleluia.

COMMUNION ANTIPHON: The angel said to Mary: you shall conceive and bear a son, and you shall call him Jesus. *(Lk 1:31)*

Tuesday, December 21, 2010: Fourth Week of Advent / 197 [Sg 2:8–14 or Zep 3:14–18a/Lk 1:39–45]

ENTRANCE ANTIPHON: Soon the Lord God will come, and you will call him Emmanuel, for God is with us. *(See Is 7:14; 8:10)*

RESPONSE: Exult, you just, in the Lord! Sing to him a new song. *(Ps 33:1a, 3a)*

GOSPEL VERSE: R/. Alleluia. O Emmanuel, our King and Giver of Law: come to save us, Lord our God! R/. Alleluia.

COMMUNION ANTIPHON: Blessed are you for your firm believing, that the promises of the Lord would be fulfilled. *(Lk 1:45)*

OR: *Peter Canisius—priest, doctor of the Church / 694 [2 Tm 4:1–5/Mt 5:13–19]*

ENTRANCE ANTIPHON: Priests of God, bless the Lord; praise God, all you that are holy and humble of heart. *(Dn 3:84, 87)*

RESPONSE: Here I am, Lord; I come to do your will. *(Ps 40:8a, 9a)*

GOSPEL VERSE: R/. Alleluia. Let your light shine before others, that they may see your good deeds and glorify your heavenly Father. *(Mt 5:16)*

COMMUNION ANTIPHON: The Son of Man did not come to be served, but to serve, and to give his life as a ransom for many. *(Mt 20:28)*

Wednesday, December 22, 2010: Fourth Week of Advent / 198 [1 Sm 1:24–28/Lk 1:46–56]

ENTRANCE ANTIPHON: Gates, lift up your heads! Stand erect, ancient doors, and let in the King of glory. *(Ps 23:7)*

RESPONSE: My heart exults in the Lord, my Savior. *(See 1 Sm 2:1a)*

GOSPEL VERSE: R/. Alleluia. O King of all nations and keystone of the Church: come and save man, whom you formed from the dust! R/. Alleluia.

COMMUNION ANTIPHON: My soul proclaims the greatness of the Lord, for the Almighty has done great things for me. *(Lk 1:46, 49)*

Thursday, December 23, 2010: Fourth Week of Advent / 199 [Mal 3:1–4, 23–24/Lk 1:57–66]

ENTRANCE ANTIPHON: A little child is born for us, and he shall be called the mighty God; every race on earth shall be blessed in him. *(See Is 9:6; Ps 71:17)*

RESPONSE: Lift up your heads and see; your redemption is near at hand. *(See Lk 21:28)*

GOSPEL VERSE: R/. Alleluia. O King of all nations and keystone of the Church: come and save man, whom you formed from the dust! R/. Alleluia.

COMMUNION ANTIPHON: I stand at the door and knock, says the Lord. If anyone hears my voice and opens the door, I will come in and sit down to supper with him and he with me. *(Rv 3:20)*

OR: *John of Kanty—priest / 695 [Jm 2:14–17/Lk 6:27–38]*

ENTRANCE ANTIPHON: Come, you whom my Father has blessed, says the Lord: I was ill and you comforted me. I tell you, anything you did for one of my brothers, you did for me. *(Mt 25:34, 36, 40)*

RESPONSE: Blessed the man who fears the Lord. *(Ps 112:1) Or:* Alleluia

GOSPEL VERSE: R/. Alleluia. I give you a new commandment: love one another as I have loved you. R/. Alleluia *(Jn 13:34)*

COMMUNION ANTIPHON: By the love you have for one another, says the Lord, everyone will know that you are my disciples. *(Jn 13:35)*

Friday, December 24, 2010: Fourth Week of Advent / 200 [2 Sm 7:1–5, 8b–12, 14a, 16/Lk 1:67–79]

(Morning Mass)

ENTRANCE ANTIPHON: The appointed time has come; God has sent his Son into the world. *(See Gal 4:4)*

RESPONSE: For ever I will sing the goodness of the Lord. *(Ps 89:2)*

GOSPEL VERSE: R/. Alleluia. O Radiant Dawn, splendor of eternal light, sun of justice: come and shine on those who dwell in darkness and in the shadow of death. R/. Alleluia.

COMMUNION ANTIPHON: Blessed be the Lord God of Israel, for he has visited and redeemed his people. *(Lk 1:68)*

Saturday, December 25, 2010: Nativity of the Lord (Christmas)

(See Sunday section)

Monday, December 27, 2010: John— apostle, evangelist / 697 [1 Jn 1:1–4/Jn 20:1a, 2–8]

ENTRANCE ANTIPHON: At the last supper, John reclined close to the Lord. Blessed apostle, to you were revealed the heavenly secrets! Your lifegiving words have spread all over the earth!

RESPONSE: Rejoice in the Lord, you just! *(Ps 97:12)*

GOSPEL VERSE: R/. Alleluia. We praise you, God, we acclaim you as Lord; the glorious company of Apostles praise you. R/. Alleluia. *(See Te Deum)*

COMMUNION ANTIPHON: The Word of God became man, and lived among us. Of his riches we have all received. *(Jn 1:14, 16)*

Tuesday, December 28, 2010: Holy Innocents—martyrs / 698 [1 Jn 1: 5–2:2/Mt 2:13–18]

ENTRANCE ANTIPHON: These innocent children were slain for Christ. They follow the spotless Lamb, and proclaim for ever: Glory to you, Lord.

RESPONSE: Our soul has been rescued like a bird from the fowler's snare. *(Ps 124:7)*

GOSPEL VERSE: R/. Alleluia. We praise you, O God, we acclaim you as Lord; the white-robed army of martyrs praise you. R/. Alleluia. *(See Te Deum)*

COMMUNION ANTIPHON: These have been ransomed for God and the Lamb as the firstfruits of mankind; they follow the Lamb wherever he goes. *(Rv 14:4)*

Wednesday, December 29, 2010: Fifth Day in the Octave of Christmas / 202 [1 Jn 2:3–11/Lk 2:22–35]

ENTRANCE ANTIPHON: God loved the world so much, he gave his only Son, that all who believe in him might not perish, but might have eternal life. *(Jn 3:16)*

RESPONSE: Let the heavens be glad and the earth rejoice! *(Ps 96:11a)*

GOSPEL VERSE: R/. Alleluia. A light of revelation to the Gentiles and glory for your people Israel. R/. Alleluia. *(Lk 2:32)*

COMMUNION ANTIPHON: Through the tender compassion of our God, the dawn from on high shall break upon us. *(Lk 1:78)*

OR: ***Thomas Becket***—*bishop, martyr / 699 [2 Tm 2:8–13; 3:10–12/Mt 16:24–27]*

ENTRANCE ANTIPHON: I will look after my sheep, says the Lord, and I will raise up one shepherd who will pasture them. I, the Lord, will be their God. *(Ez 34:11, 23–24)*

RESPONSE: The Lord delivered me from all my fears. *(Ps 34:5)*

GOSPEL VERSE: R/. Alleluia. Blessed are those who hunger and thirst for righteousness; for they will be satisfied. R/. Alleluia. *(Mt 5:6)*

COMMUNION ANTIPHON: You have not chosen me; I have chosen you. Go and bear fruit that will last. *(Jn 15:16)*

Thursday, December 30, 2010: Sixth Day in the Octave of Christmas / 203 [1 Jn 2:12–17/Lk 2:36–40]

ENTRANCE ANTIPHON: When peaceful silence lay over all, and night had run half of her swift course, your all-powerful word, O Lord, leaped down from heaven, from the royal throne. *(Wis 18:14–15)*

RESPONSE: Let the heavens be glad and the earth rejoice! *(Ps 96:11a)*

GOSPEL VERSE: R/. Alleluia. A holy day has dawned upon us. Come, you nations, and adore the Lord. Today a great light has come upon the earth. R/. Alleluia.

COMMUNION ANTIPHON: From his riches we have all received, grace for grace. *(Jn 1:16)*

Friday, December 31, 2010: Seventh Day in the Octave of Christmas / 204 [1 Jn 2:18–21/Jn 1:1–18]

ENTRANCE ANTIPHON: A child is born for us, a son given to us; dominion is laid on his shoulder, and he shall be called Wonderful-Counsellor. *(Is 9:6)*

RESPONSE: Let the heavens be glad and the earth rejoice! *(Ps 96:11a)*

GOSPEL VERSE: R/. Alleluia. The Word of God became flesh and dwelt among us. To those who accepted him he gave power to become the children of God. R/. Alleluia. *(Jn 1:14a, 12a)*

COMMUNION ANTIPHON: God's love for us was revealed when he sent his only Son into the world, so that we could have life through him. *(1 Jn 4:9)*

OR: ***Sylvester I***—*pope / 700 [Ez 34:11–16/Mt 16:13–19]*

ENTRANCE ANTIPHON: The Lord chose him to be his high priest; he opened his treasures and made him rich in all goodness.

RESPONSE: The Lord is my shepherd; there is nothing I shall want. *(Ps 23:1)*

GOSPEL VERSE: R/. Alleluia. Come after me, says the Lord, and I will make you fishers of men. R/. Alleluia. *(Mt 1:17)*

COMMUNION ANTIPHON: The good shepherd gives his life for his sheep. *(See Jn 10:11)*

Saturday, January 1, 2011: Octave Day of Christmas / Blessed Virgin Mary, Mother of God / 18 [Nm 6:22–27/Gal 4:4–7/Lk 2:16–21]

ENTRANCE ANTIPHON: A light will shine on us this day, the Lord is born for us: he shall be called Wonderful God, Prince of peace, Father of the world to cme; and his kingship will never end. *(See Is 9:2, 6; Lk 1:33)*

RESPONSE: May God bless us in his mercy. *(Ps 67:2a)*

GOSPEL VERSE: R/. Alleluia. In the past God spoke to our ancestors through the prophets; in these last days, he has spoken to us through his Son. R/. Alleluia. *(Heb 1:1–2)*

COMMUNION ANTIPHON: Jesus Christ is the same yesterday, today, and for ever. *(Heb 13:8)*

Monday, January 3, 2011: Christmas Weekday / 212 [1 Jn 3:22–4:6/Mt 4:12–17, 23–25]

ENTRANCE ANTIPHON: A holy day has dawned upon us. Come, you nations, and adore the Lord. Today a great light has come upon the earth.

RESPONSE: I will give you all the nations for an inheritance. *(Ps 2:8ab)*

GOSPEL VERSE: R/. Alleluia. Jesus proclaimed the Gospel of the Kingdom and cured every disease among the people. *(See Mt 4:23)*

COMMUNION ANTIPHON: We have seen his glory, the glory of the Father's only Son, full of grace and truth. *(Jn 1:14)*

OR: *Most Holy Name of Jesus* / *[Phil 2:1–11/Lk 2:21–24]*

ENTRANCE ANTIPHON: At the name of Jesus every knee must bend, in heaven, on earth, and under the earth; every tongue should proclaim to the glory of God the Father: Jesus Christ is Lord. *(Phil 2:10–11)*

RESPONSE: O Lord our God, how wonderful is your name in all the earth! *(Ps 8:2a)*

Or: Wake up and rise from death: Christ will shine upon you. *(Eph 5:14)*

GOSPEL VERSE: R/. Alleluia. She will bear a son and you are to name him Jesus, because he will save his people from their sins. R/. Alleluia. *(Mt 1:21)*

COMMUNION ANTIPHON: No other name under heaven has been given to men by which we can be saved. *(Acts 4:12)*

Tuesday, January 4, 2011: Elizabeth Ann Seton—religious / 510A, 737–742

ENTRANCE ANTIPHON: Praise to the holy woman whose home is built on faithful love and whose pathway leads to God. *(See Prv 14:1–2)*

RESPONSE: Blessed are those who fear the Lord. *(Ps 128:1)*

GOSPEL VERSE: R/. Alleluia. Blessed are the clean of heart, for they will see God. R/. Alleluia. *(Mt 5:8)*

COMMUNION ANTIPHON: I am the living bread from heaven, says the Lord. Whoever eats this bread will live forever; the bread I shall give is my flesh for the life of the world. *(Jn 6:51)*

OR: **Christmas Weekday** / 213 [1 Jn 4:7–10/Mk 6:34–44]

ENTRANCE ANTIPHON: Blessed is he who comes in the name of the Lord; the Lord God shines upon us. *(Ps 117:26–27)*

RESPONSE: Lord, every nation on earth will adore you. *(See Ps 72:11)*

GOSPEL VERSE: R/. Alleluia. The Lord has sent me to being glad tidings to the poor and to proclaim liberty to captives. R/. Alleluia. *(Lk 4:18)*

COMMUNION ANTIPHON: God loved us so much that he sent his own Son in the likeness of sinful flesh. *(Eph 2:4; Rom 8:3)*

Wednesday, January 5, 2011: John Neumann—bishop / 510B, 719–724

ENTRANCE ANTIPHON: O Lord, my alotted portion and my cup, you it is who hold fast my lot. For me the measuring lines have fallen on pleasant sites; fair to me indeed is my inheritance. *(Ps 16:5–6)*

RESPONSE: Proclaim God's marvelous deeds to all the nations. *(Ps 96:3)*

GOSPEL VERSE: R/. Alleluia. I am the good shepherd, says the Lord; I know my sheep, and mine know me. R/. Alleluia. *(Jn 10:14)*

COMMUNION ANTIPHON: Everyone who has given up home, brothers, or sisters, father or mother, wife or children or property for my sake will receive many times as much and inherit everlasting life. *(Mt 19:29)*

OR: **Christmas Weekday** / 214 [1 Jn 4:11–18/Mk 6:45–52]

ENTRANCE ANTIPHON: The people who walked in darkness have seen a great light; on those who lived in the shadow of death, light has shone. *(Is 9:2)*

RESPONSE: Lord, every nation on earth will adore you. *(See Ps 72:11)*

GOSPEL VERSE: R/. Alleluia. Glory to you, O Christ, proclaimed to the Gentiles. Glory to you, O Christ, believed in throughout the world. R/. Alleluia. *(See 1 Tm 3:16)*

COMMUNION ANTIPHON: The eternal life which was with the Father has been revealed to us. *(1 Jn 1:2)*

Thursday, January 6, 2011: Christmas Weekday / 215 [1 Jn 4:19–5:4/Lk 4:14–22]

ENTRANCE ANTIPHON: In the beginning, before all ages, the Word was God: that Word was born a man to save the world. *(See Jn 1:1)*

RESPONSE: Lord, every nation on earth will adore you. *(See Ps 72:11)*

GOSPEL VERSE: R/. Alleluia. The Lord has sent me to bring glad tidings to the poor and to proclaim liberty to captives. R/. Alleluia. *(Lk 4:18)*

COMMUNION ANTIPHON: God loved the world so much, he gave his only Son, that all who believe in him might not perish, but might have eternal life. *(Jn 3:16)*

*OR: **Blessed André Bessette**—religious / 510C, 737–742*

ENTRANCE ANTIPHON: The Lord is my inheritance and my cup; he alone will give me my reward. The measuring line has marked a lovely place for me; my inheritance is my great delight. *(Ps 15:5–6)*

RESPONSE: I will bless the Lord at all times. *(Ps 34:2)*

Or: Taste and see the goodness of the Lord. *(Ps 34:9)*

GOSPEL VERSE: R/. Alleluia. If you remain in my word, you will truly be my disciples, and you will know the truth, says the Lord. *(Jn 8:31b–32)*

COMMUNION ANTIPHON: I solemnly tell you: those who have left everything and followed me will be repaid a hundredfold and will gain eternal life. *(See Mt 19:27–29)*

Friday, January 7, 2011: Christmas Weekday / 216 [1 Jn 5:5–13/Lk 5:12–16]

ENTRANCE ANTIPHON: The Lord is a light in darkness to the upright; he is gracious, merciful, and just. *(Ps 111:4)*

RESPONSE: Praise the Lord, Jerusalem. *(Ps 147:12a)* *Or:* Alleluia.

GOSPEL VERSE: R/. Alleluia. Jesus proclaimed the Gospel of the Kingdom and cured every disease among the people. R/. Alleluia. *(See Mt 4:23)*

COMMUNION ANTIPHON: God's love for us was revealed when he sent his only Son into the world, so that we could have life through him. *(1 Jn 4:9)*

*OR: **Raymond of Peñafort**—priest / 511 [2 Cor 5:14–20/Lk 12:35–40]*

ENTRANCE ANTIPHON: I will give you shepherds after my own heart, and they shall feed you on knowledge and sound teaching. *(Jer 3:15)*

RESPONSE: O bless the Lord, my soul! *(Ps 103:1)*

GOSPEL VERSE: R/. Alleluia. Be vigilant at all times and pray that you may have the strength to stand before the Son of Man. R/. Alleluia. *(Lk 21:36)*

COMMUNION ANTIPHON: The Son of Man did not come to be served, but to serve, and to give his life as a ransom for many. *(Mt 20:28)*

Saturday, January 8, 2011: Christmas Weekday / 217 [1 Jn 5:14–21/Jn 3:22–30]

ENTRANCE ANTIPHON: God sent his own Son, born of a woman, so that we could be adopted as his sons. *(Gal 4:4–5)*

RESPONSE: The Lord takes delight in his people. *(See Ps 149:4a) Or:* Alleluia.

GOSPEL VERSE: R/. Alleluia. The people who sit in darkness have seen a great light, on those dwelling in a land overshadowed by death light has arisen. R/. Alleluia. *(See Mt 4:16)*

COMMUNION ANTIPHON: From his riches we have all received, grace for grace. *(Jn 1:16)*

Monday, January 10, 2011: First Week in Ordinary Time / 305 [Heb 1:1–6/Mk 1:14–20]

ENTRANCE ANTIPHON: I saw a man sitting on a high throne, being worshiped by a great number of angels who were singing together: This is he whose kingdom will last for ever.

RESPONSE: Let all his angels worship him. *(See Ps 97:7c)*

GOSPEL VERSE: R/. Alleluia. The Kingdom of God is at hand: repent and believe in the Gospel. R/. Alleluia. *(Mk 1:15)*

COMMUNION ANTIPHON: I came that men may have life, and have it to the full, says the Lord. *(Jn 10:10)*

Tuesday, January 11, 2011: First Week in Ordinary Time / 306 [Heb 2:5–12/Mk 1:21–28]

ENTRANCE ANTIPHON: I saw a man sitting on a high throne, being worshiped by a great number of angels who were singing together: This is he whose kingdom will last for ever.

RESPONSE: You have given your Son rule over the works of your hands. *(See Ps 8:7)*

GOSPEL VERSE: R/. Alleluia. Receive the word of God, not as the word of men, but as it truly is, the word of God. R/. Alleluia. *(See 1 Thes 2:13)*

COMMUNION ANTIPHON: I came that men may have life, and have it to the full, says the Lord. *(Jn 10:10)*

Wednesday, January 12, 2011: First Week in Ordinary Time / 307 [Heb 2:14-18/Mk 1:29-39]

ENTRANCE ANTIPHON: I saw a man sitting on a high throne, being worshiped by a great number of angels who were singing together: This is he whose kingdom will last for ever.

RESPONSE: The Lord remembers his covenant for ever. *(Ps 105:8a) Or: Alleluia.*

GOSPEL VERSE: R./. Alleluia. My sheep hear my voice, says the Lord. I know them, and they follow me. R/. Alleluia. *(Jn 10:27)*

COMMUNION ANTIPHON: I came that men may have life, and have it to the full, says the Lord. *(Jn 10:10)*

Thursday, January 13, 2011: First Week in Ordinary Time / 308 [Heb 3:7-14/Mk 1:40-45]

ENTRANCE ANTIPHON: I saw a man sitting on a high throne, being worshiped by a great number of angels who were singing together: This is he whose kingdom will last for ever.

RESPONSE: If today you hear his voice, harden not your hearts. *(Ps 95:8)*

GOSPEL VERSE: R/. Alleluia. Jesus preached the Gospel of the Kingdom and cured every disease among the people. R/. Alleluia *(See Mt 4:23)*

COMMUNION ANTIPHON: I came that men may have life, and have it to the full, says the Lord. *(Jn 10:10)*

OR: *Hilary—bishop, doctor of the Church / 512 [1 Jn 2:18-25/Mt 5:13-19]*

ENTRANCE ANTIPHON: I will look after my sheep, says the Lord, and I will raise up one shepherd who will pasture them. I, the Lord, will be their God. *(Ez 34:11, 23-24)*

RESPONSE: You are a priest for ever, in the line of Melchizedek. *(Ps 110:4b)*

GOSPEL VERSE: R/. Alleluia. Let your light shine before others, that they may see your good deeds and glorify your heavenly Father. R/. Alleluia. *(Mt 5:16)*

COMMUNION ANTIPHON: You have not chosen me; I have chosen you. Go and bear fruit that will last. *(Jn 15:16)*

Friday, January 14, 2011: First Week in Ordinary Time / 309 [Heb 4:1-5, 11/Mk 2:1-12]

ENTRANCE ANTIPHON: I saw a man sitting on a high throne, being worshiped by a great number of angels who were singing together: This is he whose kingdom will last for ever.

RESPONSE: Do not forget the works of the Lord! *(See Ps 78:7b)*

GOSPEL VERSE: R/. Alleluia. A great prophet has arisen in our midst and God has visited his people. R/. Alleluia. *(Lk 7:16)*

COMMUNION ANTIPHON: I came that men may have life, and have it to the full, says the Lord. *(Jn 10:10)*

Saturday, January 15, 2011: First Week in Ordinary Time / 310 [Heb 4:12-16/Mk 2:13-17]

ENTRANCE ANTIPHON: I saw a man sitting on a high throne, being worshiped by a great number of angels who were singing together: This is he whose kingdom will last for ever.

RESPONSE: Your words, Lord, are Spirit and life. *(See Jn 6:63c)*

GOSPEL VERSE: R/. Alleluia. The Lord sent me to bring glad tidings to the poor, and to proclaim liberty to captives. R/. Alleluia. *(Lk 4:18)*

COMMUNION ANTIPHON: I came that men may have life, and have it to the full, says the Lord. *(Jn 10:10)*

OR: *Blessed Virgin Mary / 707-712*

ENTRANCE ANTIPHON: You have been blessed, O Virgin Mary, above all other women on earth by the Lord the most high God; he has so exalted your name that your praises shall never fade from the mouths of men. *(See Jdt 13:23, 25)*

RESPONSE: Blessed be the name of the Lord for ever. *(Ps 113:2) Or: Alleluia.*

GOSPEL VERSE: R/. Alleluia. Hail, Mary, full of grace, the Lord is with you; blessed are you among women. R/. Alleluia. *(See Lk 1:28)*

COMMUNION ANTIPHON: All generations will call me blessed, because God has looked upon his lowly handmaid. *(See Lk 1:48)*

Monday, January 17, 2011:
Anthony—abbot / 513 [Eph 6:10–13, 18/Mt 19:16–26]

ENTRANCE ANTIPHON: The just man will flourish like the palm tree. Planted in the courts of God's house, he will grow great like the cedars of Lebanon. *(Ps 91:13–14)*

RESPONSE: You are my inheritance, O Lord. *(Ps 16:5)*

GOSPEL VERSE: R/. Alleluia. If you remain in my word, you will truly be my disciples, and you will know the truth, says the Lord. R/. Alleluia. *(Jn 8:31b–32)*

COMMUNION ANTIPHON: If you wish to be perfect, go, sell what you own, give it all to the poor, then come, follow me. *(Mt 19:21)*

OR: **Second Week in Ordinary Time** / 311 [Heb 5:1–10/Mk 2:18–22]

ENTRANCE ANTIPHON: May all the earth give you worship and praise, and break into song to your name, O God, Most High. *(Ps 65:4)*

RESPONSE: You are a priest for ever, in the line of Melchizedek. *(Ps 110:4b)*

GOSPEL VERSE: R/. Alleluia. The word of God is living and effective, able to discern reflections and thoughts of the heart. R/. Alleluia. *(Heb 4:12)*

COMMUNION ANTIPHON: We know and believe in God's love for us. *(1 Jn 4:16)*

Tuesday, January 18, 2011: Second
Week in Ordinary Time / 312 [Heb 6:10–20/Mk 2:23–28]

ENTRANCE ANTIPHON: May all the earth give you worship and praise, and break into song to your name, O God, Most High. *(Ps 65:4)*

RESPONSE: The Lord will remember his covenant for ever. *(Ps 111:5) Or:* Alleluia.

GOSPEL VERSE: R/. Alleluia. May the Father of our Lord Jesus Christ enlighten the eyes of our hearts, that we may know what is the hope that belongs to our call. R/. Alleluia. *(See Eph 1:17–18)*

COMMUNION ANTIPHON: We know and believe in God's love for us. *(1 Jn 4:16)*

Wednesday, January 19, 2011:
Second Week in Ordinary Time / 313 [Heb 7:1–3, 15–17/Mk 3:1–6]

ENTRANCE ANTIPHON: May all the earth give you worship and praise, and break into song to your name, O God, Most High. *(Ps 65:4)*

RESPONSE: You are a priest for ever, in the line of Mechizedek. *(Ps 110:4b)*

GOSPEL VERSE: R/. Alleluia. Jesus preached the Gospel of the Kingdom and cured every disease among the people. R/. Alleluia. *(See Mt 4:23)*

COMMUNION ANTIPHON: We know and believe in God's love for us. *(1 Jn 4:16)*

Thursday, January 20, 2011: Second
Week in Ordinary Time / 314 [Heb 7:25–8:6/Mk 3:7–12]

ENTRANCE ANTIPHON: May all the earth give you worship and praise, and break into song to your name, O God, Most High. *(Ps 65:4)*

RESPONSE: Here am I, Lord; I come to do your will. *(Ps 40:8a, 9a)*

GOSPEL VERSE: R/. Alleluia. Our Lord Jesus Christ has destroyed death and brought life to light through the Gospel. R/. Alleluia. *(See 2 Tm 1:10)*

COMMUNION ANTIPHON: We know and believe in God's love for us. *(1 Jn 4:16)*

OR: **Fabian**—*pope, martyr / 514 [1 Pt 5:1–4/Jn 21:15–17]*

ENTRANCE ANTIPHON: The Lord chose him to be his high priest; he opened his treasures and made him rich in all goodness.

RESPONSE: Here I am, Lord; I come to do your will. *(Ps 40:8a, 9a)*

GOSPEL VERSE: R/. Alleluia. I am the good shepherd, says the Lord; I know my sheep and mine know me. R/. Alleluia. *(Jn 10:14)*

COMMUNION ANTIPHON: The good shepherd gives his life for his sheep. *(See Jn 10:11)*

OR: **Sebastian**—*martyr / 515 [1 Pt 3:14–17/Mt 10:28–33]*

ENTRANCE ANTIPHON: Here is a true martyr who shed his blood for Christ; his judges could not shake him by their menaces, and so he won through to the kingdom of heaven.

RESPONSE: The Lord delivered me from all my fears. *(Ps 34:5)*

GOSPEL VERSE: R/. Alleluia. Blessed is the man who perseveres in temptation, for when he has been proved he will receive the crown of life. R/. Alleluia. *(Jn15:9b, 5b)*

COMMUNION ANTIPHON: I am the vine and you are the branches, says the Lord; he who lives in me, and I in him, will bear much fruit. *(Jn 15:5)*

Friday, January 21, 2011: Agnes— virgin, martyr / 516 [1 Cor 1:26– 31/Mt 13:44–46]

ENTRANCE ANTIPHON: Here is a true martyr who shed her blood for Christ; her judges could not shake her by their menaces, and so she won through to the kingdom of heaven.

RESPONSE: The Lord is my shepherd; there is nothing I shall want. *(Ps 23:1)*

GOSPEL VERSE: R/. Alleluia. Remain in my love, says the Lord; whoever remains in me and I in him will bear much fruit. R/. Alleluia. *(Jas 1:12)*

COMMUNION ANTIPHON: I am the vine and you are the branches, says the Lord; he who lives in me, and I in him, will bear much fruit. *(Jn 15:5)*

OR: **Second Week in Ordinary Time** / 315 [Heb 8:6–13/Mk 3:13–19]

ENTRANCE ANTIPHON: May all the earth give you worship and praise, and break into song to your name, O God, Most High. *(Ps 65:4)*

RESPONSE: Kindness and truth shall meet. *(Ps 85:11a)*

GOSPEL VERSE: R/. Alleluia. God was reconciling the world to himself in Christ, and entrusting to us the message of reconciliation. R/. Alleluia. *(2 Cor 5:19)*

COMMUNION ANTIPHON: We know and believe in God's love for us. *(1 Jn 4:16)*

Saturday, January 22, 2011: Second Week in Ordinary Time / 316 [Heb 9:2–3, 11–14/Mt 3:20–21]

ENTRANCE ANTIPHON: May all the earth give you worship and praise, and break into song to your name, O God, Most High. *(Ps 65:4)*

RESPONSE: God mounts his throne to shouts of joy: a blare of trumpets for the Lord. *(Ps 47:6)*

GOSPEL VERSE: R/. Alleluia. Open our hearts, O Lord, to listen to the words of your Son. R/. Alleluia. *(See Acts 16:14b)*

COMMUNION ANTIPHON: We know and believe in God's love for us. *(1 Jn 4:16)*

OR: **Vincent**—*deacon, martyr / 517 [2 Cor 4:7– 15/Mt 10:17–22]*

ENTRANCE ANTIPHON: This holy man fought to the death for the law of his God, never cowed by the threats of the wicked; his house was built on solid rock.

RESPONSE: The Lord delivered me from all my fears. *(Ps 34:5)*

GOSPEL VERSE: R/. Alleluia. Blessed are they who are persecuted for the sake of righteousness, for theirs is the Kingdom of heaven. *(Mt 5:10)*

COMMUNION ANTIPHON: If anyone wishes to come after me, he must renounce himself, take up his cross, and follow me, says the Lord. *(Mt 16:24)*

OR: **Blessed Virgin Mary** / 707–712

ENTRANCE ANTIPHON: Hail, holy Mother! The child to whom you gave birth is the King of heaven and earth for ever. *(Sedulius)*

RESPONSE: Listen to me, daughter; see and bend your ear. *(Ps 45:11)*

GOSPEL VERSE: R/. Alleluia. Hail, Mary, full of grace, the Lord is with you; blessed are you among women. R/. Alleluia. *(See Lk 1:28)*

COMMUNION ANTIPHON: Blessed is the womb of the Virgin Mary; she carried the Son of the eternal Father. *(See Lk 11:27)*

OR: **Mass for Peace and Justice (Day of Penance)** / 887–891

ENTRANCE ANTIPHON: Give peace, Lord, to those who wait for you; listen to the prayers fo your servants, and guide us in the way of justice. *(See Sir 36:18–19)*

RESPONSE: Justice shall flourish in his time, and fullness of peace for ever. *(See Ps 72:7)*

GOSPEL VERSE: Blessed are the peacemakers; they shall be called children of God. *(Mt 5:9)*

COMMUNION ANTIPHON: Peace I leave with you, my own peace I give you, says the Lord. *(Jn 14:27)*

Monday, January 24, 2011: Francis de Sales—bishop, doctor of the Church / 518 [Eph 3:8–12/Jn 15:9–17]

ENTRANCE ANTIPHON: The Lord opened his mouth in the assembly, and filled him with the spirit of wisdom and understanding, and clothed him in a robe of glory. *(Sir 15:5)*

RESPONSE: The mouth of the just murmurs wisdom. *(Ps 37:30a)*

GOSPEL VERSE: R/. Alleluia. I give you a new commandment: love one another as I have loved you. R/. Alleluia. *(Jn 13:34)*

COMMUNION ANTIPHON: The Lord has put his faithful servant in charge of his household, to give them their share of bread at the proper time. *(Lk 12:42)*

OR: **Third Week in Ordinary Time** / 317 [Heb 9:15, 24–28/Mk 3:22–30]

ENTRANCE ANTIPHON: Sing a new song to the Lord! Sing to the Lord, all the earth. Truth and beauty surround him, he lives in holiness and glory. *(Ps 95:1, 6)*

RESPONSE: Sing to the Lord a new song, for he has done marvelous deeds. *(Ps 98:1a)*

GOSPEL VERSE: R/. Alleluia. Our Savior Jesus Christ has destroyed death and brought life to light through the Gospel. R/. Alleluia *(See 2 Tm 1:10)*

COMMUNION ANTIPHON: Look up at the Lord with gladness and smile; your face will never be ashamed. *(Ps 33:6)*

Tuesday, January 25, 2011: Conversion of Paul—apostle / 519 [Acts 22:3–16 or Acts 9:1–22/Mk 16:15–18]

ENTRANCE ANTIPHON: I know whom I have believed. I am sure that he, the just judge, will guard my pledge until the day of judgment. *(2 Tm 1:12; 4:8)*

RESPONSE: Go out to all the world and tell the Good News. *(Mk 16:15) Or:* Alleluia, alleluia.

GOSPEL VERSE: R/. Alleluia. I chose you from the world, to go and bear fruit that will last, says the Lord.. R/. Alleluia. *(See Jn 15:16)*

COMMUNION ANTIPHON: I live by faith in the Son of God, who loved me and sacrificed himself for me. *(Gal 2:20)*

Wednesday, January 26, 2011: Timothy and Titus—bishops / 520 [2 Tm 1:1–8 or Ti 1:1–5/Lk 10:1–9]

ENTRANCE ANTIPHON: I will raise up for myself a faithful priest; he will do what is in my heart and in my mind, says the Lord. *(1 Sm 2:35)*

RESPONSE: Proclaim God's marvelous deeds to all the nations. *(Ps 96:3)*

GOSPEL VERSE: R/. Alleluia. The Lord sent me to bring glad tidings to the poor and to proclaim liberty to captives. R/. Alleluia. *(Lk 4:18)*

COMMUNION ANTIPHON: I came that men may have life, and have it to the full, says the Lord. *(Jn 10:10)*

OR: **Third Week in Ordinary Time** / 319 [2 Tm 1:1–8 or Ti 1:1–5/Mk 4:1–20]

ENTRANCE ANTIPHON: Sing a new song to the Lord! Sing to the Lord, all the earth. Truth and beauty surround him, he lives in holiness and glory. *(Ps 95:1, 6)*

RESPONSE: Proclaim God's marvelous deeds to all the nations. *(Ps 96:3)*

GOSPEL VERSE: R/. Alleluia. The seed is the word of God, Christ is the sower; all who come to him will live for ever. R/. Alleluia.

COMMUNION ANTIPHON: Look up at the Lord with gladness and smile; your face will never be ashamed. *(Ps 33:6)*

Thursday, January 27, 2011: Third Week in Ordinary Time / 320 [Heb 10:19–25/Mk 4:21–25]

ENTRANCE ANTIPHON: Sing a new song to the Lord! Sing to the Lord, all the earth. Truth and beauty surround him, he lives in holiness and glory. *(Ps 95:1, 6)*

RESPONSE: Lord, this is the people that longs to see your face. *(See Ps 24:6)*

GOSPEL VERSE: R/. Alleluia. A lamp to my feet is your word, a light to my path. R/. Alleluia. *(Ps 119:105)*

COMMUNION ANTIPHON: Look up at the Lord with gladness and smile; your face will never be ashamed. *(Ps 33:6)*

OR: **Angela Merici**—*virgin / 521 [1 Pt 4:7b–11/ Mk 9:34b–37]*

ENTRANCE ANTIPHON: Let the children come to me, and do not stop them, says the Lord; to such belongs the kingdom of God. (Mk 10:14)

RESPONSE: Young men and women, praise the name of the Lord. (See Ps 148:12a, 13a) Or: Alleluia.

GOSPEL VERSE: R/. Alleluia. Blessed are you, Father, Lord of heaven and earth; you have revealed to little ones the mysteries of the Kingdom. R/. Alleluia. (See Mt 11:25)

COMMUNION ANTIPHON: Unless you change, and become like little children, says the Lord, you shall not enter the kingdom of heaven. (Mt 18:3)

Friday, January 28, 2011: Thomas Aquinas—priest, doctor of the Church / 522 [Wis 7:7–10, 15–16/ Mt 23:8–12]

ENTRANCE ANTIPHON: The learned will shine like the brilliance of the firmament, and those who train many in the ways of justice will sparkle like the stars for all eternity. (Dn 12:3)

RESPONSE: Lord, teach me your statutes. (Ps 119:12)

GOSPEL VERSE: R/. Alleluia. You have but one Father in heaven; you have but one master, the Christ. R/. Alleluia (Mt 23:9b, 10b)

COMMUNION ANTIPHON: We preach a Christ who was crucified; he is the power and the wisdom of God. (1 Cor 1:23–24)

OR: Third Week in Ordinary Time / 321 [Heb 10:32–39/Mk 4:26–34]

ENTRANCE ANTIPHON: Sing a new song to the Lord! Sing to the Lord, all the earth. Truth and beauty surround him, he lives in holiness and glory. (Ps 95:1, 6)

RESPONSE: The salvation of the just comes from the Lord. (Ps 37:39a)

GOSPEL VERSE: R/. Alleluia. Blessed are you, Father, Lord of heaven and earth; you have revealed to little ones the mysteries of the Kingdom. R/. Alleluia. (See Mt 11:25)

COMMUNION ANTIPHON: Look up at the Lord with gladness and smile; your face will never be ashamed. (Ps 33:6)

Saturday, January 29, 2011: Third Week in Ordinary Time/ 322 [Heb 11:1–2, 8–19/Mk 4:35–41]

ENTRANCE ANTIPHON: Sing a new song to the Lord! Sing to the Lord, all the earth. Truth and beauty surround him, he lives in holiness and glory. (Ps 95:1, 6)

RESPONSE: Blessed be the Lord the God of Israel; he has come to his people. (See Lk 1:68)

GOSPEL VERSE: R/. Alleluia. God so loved the world that he gave his only-begotten Son, so that everyone who believes in him might have eternal life. R/. Alleluia. (Jn 3:16)

COMMUNION ANTIPHON: Look up at the Lord with gladness and smile; your face will never be ashamed. (Ps 33:6)

OR: *Blessed Virgin Mary* / 707–712

ENTRANCE ANTIPHON: Blessed are you, Virgin Mary, who carried the creator of all things in your womb; you gave birth to your maker, and remain for ever a virgin.

RESPONSE: Blessed be the name of the Lord for ever. (Ps 113:2) Or: Alleluia.

GOSPEL VERSE: R/. Alleluia. Blessed are you, O Virgin Mary, who believed that what was spoken to you by the Lord would be fulfilled. R/. Alleluia. (Lk 1:45)

COMMUNION ANTIPHON: The Almighty has done great things for me. Holy is his name. (Lk 1:49)

Monday, January 31, 2011: John Bosco—priest / 523 [Phil 4:4–9/Mt 18:1–5]

ENTRANCE ANTIPHON: The man that keeps these commandments and teaches them, he is the one who will be called great in the kingdom of heaven, says the Lord. (Mt 5:19)

RESPONSE: O bless the Lord, my soul! (Ps 103:1)

GOSPEL VERSE: R/. Alleluia. The greatest among you must be your servant. Whoever humbles himself will be exalted. R/. Alleluia. (Mt 23:11, 12b)

COMMUNION ANTIPHON: Unless you change, and become like little children, says the Lord, you shall not enter the kingdom of heaven. (Mt 18:3)

OR: Fourth Week in Ordinary Time / 323 [Heb 11:32–40/Mk 5:1–20]

ENTRANCE ANTIPHON: Save us, Lord our God, and gather us together from the nations, that we may proclaim your holy name and glory in your praise. *(Ps 105:47)*

RESPONSE: Let your hearts take comfort, all who hope in the Lord. *(Ps 31:25)*

GOSPEL VERSE: R/. Alleluia. A great prophet has arisen in our midst and God has visited his people. R/. Alleluia. *(Lk 7:16)*

COMMUNION ANTIPHON: Let your face shine on your servant, and save me by your love. Lord, keep me from shame, for I have called to you. *(Ps 30:17–18)*

Tuesday, February 1, 2011: Fourth Week in Ordinary Time / 324 [Heb 12:1–4/Mk 5:21–43]

ENTRANCE ANTIPHON: Save us, Lord our God, and gather us together from the nations, that we may proclaim your holy name and glory in your praise. *(Ps 105:47)*

RESPONSE: They will praise you, Lord, who long for you. *(Ps 22:27b)*

GOSPEL VERSE: R/. Alleluia. Christ took away our infirmities and bore our diseases. R/. Alleluia. *(Mt 8:17)*

COMMUNION ANTIPHON: Let your face shine on your servant, and save me by your love. Lord, keep me from shame, for I have called to you. *(Ps 30:17–18)*

Wednesday, February 2, 2011: Presentation of the Lord / 524 [Mal 3:1–4/Heb 2:14–18/Lk 2:22–40 or Lk 2:22–32

ANTIPHON I: The Lord will come with mighty power, and give light to the eyes of all who serve him, alleluia.

ANTIPHON II: Christ is the light of the nations and the glory of Israel his people.

ENTRANCE ANTIPHON: Within your temple, we ponder your loving kindness, O God. As your name, so also your praise reaches to the ends of the earth; your right hand is filled with justice. *(Ps 47:10–11)*

RESPONSE: Who is this king of glory? It is the Lord! *(Ps 24:8)*

GOSPEL VERSE: R/. Alleluia. A light of revelation to the Gentiles, and glory for your people Israel. R/. Alleluia *(Lk 2:32)*

COMMUNION ANTIPHON: With my own eyes I have seen the salvation which you have prepared in the sight of all the nations. *(Lk 2:30–31)*

Thursday, February 3, 2011: Fourth Week in Ordinary Time / 326 [Heb 12:18–19, 21–24/Mk 6:7–13]

ENTRANCE ANTIPHON: Save us, Lord our God, and gather us together from the nations, that we may proclaim your holy name and glory in your praise. *(Ps 105:47)*

RESPONSE: O God, we ponder your mercy within your temple. *(See Ps 48:10)*

GOSPEL VERSE: R/. Alleluia. The Kingdom of God is at hand; repent and believe in the Gospel. R/. Alleluia. *(Mk 1:15)*

COMMUNION ANTIPHON: Let your face shine on your servant, and save me by your love. Lord, keep me from shame, for I have called to you. *(Ps 30:17–18)*

*OR: **Blase**—bishop, martyr / 525 [Rom 5:1–5/Mk 16:15–20]*

ENTRANCE ANTIPHON: I will look after my sheep, says the Lord, and I will raise up one shepherd who will pasture them. I, the Lord, will be their God. *(Ez 34:11, 23–24)*

RESPONSE: Go out to all the world and tell the Good News. *(Mk 16:15) Or:* Alleluia.

GOSPEL VERSE: R/. Alleluia. Go and teach all nations, says the Lord; I am with you always, until the end of the world. R/. Alleluia. *(Mt 28:19a, 20b)*

COMMUNION ANTIPHON: You have not chosen me; I have chosen you. Go and bear fruit that will last. *(Jn 15:16)*

*OR: **Ansgar**—bishop / 526 [Is 52:7–10/Mk 1:14–20]*

ENTRANCE ANTIPHON: These are holy men who became God's friends and glorious heralds of his truth.

RESPONSE: Proclaim God's marvelous deeds to all the nations. *(Ps 96:3)*

GOSPEL VERSE: R/. Alleluia. Come after me, says the Lord, and I will make you fishers of men. R/. Alleluia. *(Mk 1:17)*

COMMUNION ANTIPHON: I will feed my sheep, says the Lord, and give them repose. *(Ez 34:15)*

Friday, February 4, 2011: Fourth Week in Ordinary Time / 327 [Heb 13:1–8/Mk 6:14–29]

ENTRANCE ANTIPHON: Save us, Lord our God, and gather us together from the nations, that we may proclaim your holy name and glory in your praise. *(Ps 105:47)*

RESPONSE: The Lord is my light and my salvation. *(Ps 27:1a)*

GOSPEL VERSE: R/. Alleluia. Blessed are they who have kept the word with a generous heart, and yield a harvest through perseverance. R/. Alleluia. *(See Lk 8:15)*

COMMUNION ANTIPHON: Let your face shine on your servant, and save me by your love. Lord, keep me from shame, for I have called to you. *(Ps 30:17–18)*

Saturday, February 5, 2011: Agatha—virgin, martyr / 527 [1 Cor 1:26–31/Lk 9:23–26]

ENTRANCE ANTIPHON: Come, bride of Christ, and receive the crown, which the Lord has prepared for you for ever.

RESPONSE: Into your hands, O Lord, I commend my spirit. *(Ps 31:6)*

GOSPEL VERSE: R/. Alleluia. If you are insulted for the name of Christ, blessed are you, for the Spirit of God rests upon you. R/. Alleluia. *(1 Pt 4:14)*

COMMUNION ANTIPHON: The wise virgin chose the better part for herself, and it shall not be taken away from her. *(See Lk 10:42)*

OR: **Fourth Week in Ordinary Time** / 328 [Heb 13:15–17, 20–21/Mk 6:30–34]

ENTRANCE ANTIPHON: Save us, Lord our God, and gather us together from the nations, that we may proclaim your holy name and glory in your praise. *(Ps 105:47)*

RESPONSE: The Lord is my shepherd; there is nothing I shall want. *(Ps 23:1)*

GOSPEL VERSE: R/. Alleluia. My sheep hear my voice, says the Lord; I know them, and they follow me. R/. Alleluia. *(Jn 10:27)*

COMMUNION ANTIPHON: Let your face shine on your servant, and save me by your love. Lord, keep me from shame, for I have called to you. *(Ps 30:17–18)*

Monday, February 7, 2011: Fifth Week in Ordinary Time / 329 [Gn 1:1–19/Mk 6:53–56]

ENTRANCE ANTIPHON: Come, let us worship the Lord. Let us bow down in the presence of our maker, for he is the Lord our God. *(Ps 94:6–7)*

RESPONSE: May the Lord be glad in his works. *(Ps 104:31b)*

GOSPEL VERSE: R/. Alleluia. Jesus preached the Gospel of the Kingdom and cured every disease among the people. R/. Alleluia. *(See Mt 4:23)*

COMMUNION ANTIPHON: Happy are the sorrowing; they shall be consoled. Happy those who hunger and thirst for what is right; they shall be satisfied. *(Mt 5:5–6)*

Tuesday, February 8, 2011: Fifth Week in Ordinary Time / 330 [Gn 1:20–2:4a/Mk 7:1–13]

ENTRANCE ANTIPHON: Come, let us worship the Lord. Let us bow down in the presence of our maker, for he is the Lord our God. *(Ps 94:6–7)*

RESPONSE: O Lord, our God, how wonderful your name in all the earth! *(Ps 8:2ab)*

GOSPEL VERSE: R/. Alleluia. Incline my heart, O God, to your decrees; and favor me with your law. R/. Alleluia. *(Ps 119:36, 29b)*

COMMUNION ANTIPHON: Happy are the sorrowing; they shall be consoled. Happy those who hunger and thirst for what is right; they shall be satisfied. *(Mt 5:5–6)*

OR: *Jerome Emiliani—priest* / 529 [Tb 12:6–13/Mk 10:17–30 or Mk 10:17–27]

ENTRANCE ANTIPHON: Let the children come to me, and do not stop them, says the Lord; to such belongs the kingdom of God. *(Mk 10:14)*

RESPONSE: I will bless the Lord at all times. *(Ps 34:2)*

Or: Taste and see the goodness of the Lord. *(Ps 34:9)*

GOSPEL VERSE: R/. Alleluia. Blessed are the poor in spirit; for theirs is the Kingdom of heaven. R/. Alleluia. *(Mt 5:3)*

COMMUNION ANTIPHON: Unless you change, and become like little children, says the Lord, you shall not enter the kingdom of heaven. *(Mt 18:3)*

OR: **Josephine Bakhita**—virgin / 731–736 *[1 Cor 7:23–35/Mt 25:1–13]*

ENTRANCE ANTIPHON: Come, bride of Christ, and receive the crown, which the Lord has prepared for you for ever.

RESPONSE: Listen to me, daughter; see and bend your ear. *(Ps 45:11)*

Or: The bridegroom is here; let us go out to meet Christ the Lord.

GOSPEL VERSE: R/. Alleluia. This is the wise virgin, whom the Lord found watching; she went into the wedding feast with him when he came. R/. Alleluia.

COMMUNION ANTIPHON: The wise virgin chose the better part for herself, and it shall not be taken away from her. *(See Lk 10:42)*

Wednesday, February 9, 2010: Fifth Week in Ordinary Time / 331 [Gn 2:4b–9, 15–17/Mk 7:14–23]

ENTRANCE ANTIPHON: Come, let us worship the Lord. Let us bow down in the presence of our maker, for he is the Lord our God. *(Ps 94:6–7)*

RESPONSE: O bless the Lord, my soul! *(Ps 104:1a)*

GOSPEL VERSE: R/. Alleluia. Your word, O Lord, is truth: consecrate us in the truth. R/. Alleluia. *(See Jn 17:17b, 17a)*

COMMUNION ANTIPHON: Happy are the sorrowing; they shall be consoled. Happy those who hunger and thirst for what is right; they shall be satisfied. *(Mt 5:5–6)*

Thursday, February 10, 2011: Scholastica—virgin / 530 [Sg 8:6–7/Lk 10:38–42]

ENTRANCE ANTIPHON: The Lord is my inheritance and my cup; he alone will give me my reward. The measuring line has marked a lovely place for me; my inheritance is my great delight. *(Ps 15:5–6)*

RESPONSE: Young men and women, praise the name of the Lord. *(See Ps 148:12a, 13a) Or:* Alleluia.

GOSPEL VERSE: R/. Alleluia. Whoever loves me will keep my word, and my Father will love him and we will come to him. R/. Alleluia. *(Jn 14:23)*

COMMUNION ANTIPHON: I solemnly tell you: those who have left everything and followed me will be repaid a hundredfold and will gain eternal life. *(See Mt 19:27–29)*

OR: **Fifth Week in Ordinary Time** / 332 [Gn 2:18–25/Mk 7:24–30]

ENTRANCE ANTIPHON: Come, let us worship the Lord. Let us bow down in the presence of our maker, for he is the Lord our God. *(Ps 94:6–7)*

RESPONSE: Blessed are those who fear the Lord. *(See Ps 128:1a)*

GOSPEL VERSE: R/. Alleluia. Humbly welcome the word that has been planted in you and is able to save your souls. R/. Alleluia. *(Jas 1:21bc)*

COMMUNION ANTIPHON: Happy are the sorrowing; they shall be consoled. Happy those who hunger and thirst for what is right; they shall be satisfied. *(Mt 5:5–6)*

Friday, February 11, 2011: Fifth Week in Ordinary Time / 333 [Gn 3:1–8/Mk 7:31–37]

ENTRANCE ANTIPHON: Come, let us worship the Lord. Let us bow down in the presence of our maker, for he is the Lord our God. *(Ps 94:6–7)*

RESPONSE: Blessed are those whose sins are forgiven. *(Ps 32:1a)*

GOSPEL VERSE: R/. Alleluia. Open our hearts, O Lord, to listen to the words of your Son. R/. Alleluia. *(See Acts 16:14b)*

COMMUNION ANTIPHON: Happy are the sorrowing; they shall be consoled. Happy those who hunger and thirst for what is right; they shall be satisfied. *(Mt 5:5–6)*

OR: **Our Lady of Lourdes** / 531 *[Is 66:10–14c/Jn 2:1–11]*

ENTRANCE ANTIPHON: Hail, holy Mother! The child to whom you gave birth is the King of heaven and earth for ever. *(Sedulius)*

RESPONSE: You are the highest honor of our race. *(Jud 15:9)*

GOSPEL VERSE: R/. Alleluia. Blessed are you, O Virgin Mary, who believed that what was spoken to you by the Lord would be fulfilled. R/. Alleluia. *(See Lk 1:45)*

COMMUNION ANTIPHON: Blessed is the womb of the Virgin Mary; she carried the Son of the eternal Father. *(See Lk 11:27)*

Saturday, February 12, 2011: Fifth Week in Ordinary Time / 334 [Gn 3:9–24/Mk 8:1–10]

ENTRANCE ANTIPHON: Come, let us worship the Lord. Let us bow down in the presence of our maker, for he is the Lord our God. (Ps 94:6–7)

RESPONSE: In every age, O Lord, you have been our refuge. (Ps 90:1)

GOSPEL VERSE: R/. Alleluia. One does not live on bread alone, but on every word that comes from the mouth of God. R/. Alleluia. (Mt 4:4b)

COMMUNION ANTIPHON: Happy are the sorrowing; they shall be consoled. Happy those who hunger and thirst for what is right; they shall be satisfied. (Mt 5:5–6)

OR: **Blessed Virgin Mary** / 707–712

ENTRANCE ANTIPHON: Blessed are you, Virgin Mary, who carried the creator of all things in your womb; you gave birth to your maker, and remain for ever a virgin.

RESPONSE: Blessed be the name of the Lord for ever. (Ps 113:2) Or: Alleluia

GOSPEL VERSE: R/. Alleluia. Blessed are you, O Virgin Mary, who believed that what was spoken to you by the Lord would be fulfilled. R/. Alleluia.(Lk 1:45)

COMMUNION ANTIPHON: The Almighty has done great things for me. Holy is his name. (Lk 1:49)

Monday, February 14, 2011: Cyril—monk; and Methodius—bishop / 532 [Acts13:46–49/Lk 10:1–9]

ENTRANCE ANTIPHON: The Lord chose these holy men for their unfeigned love, and gave them eternal glory. The church has light by their teaching.

RESPONSE: Go out to all the world and tell the Good News. (Mk 16:15) Or: Alleluia

GOSPEL VERSE: R/. Alleluia. The Lord sent me to bring glad tidings to the poor and to proclaim liberty to captives. R/. Alleluia. (Lk 4:18)

COMMUNION ANTIPHON: No longer shall I call you servants, for a servant knows not what his master does. Now I shall call you friends, for I have revealed to you all that I have heard from my Father. (Jn 15:15)

OR: **Sixth Week in Ordinary Time** / 335 [Gn 4:1–15, 25/Mk 8:11–13]

ENTRANCE ANTIPHON: Lord, be my rock of safety, the stronghold that saves me. For the honor of your name, lead me and guide me. (Ps 30:3–4)

RESPONSE: Offer to God a sacrifice of praise. (Ps 50:14a)

GOSPEL VERSE: R/. Alleluia. I am the way and the truth and the life, says the Lord; no one comes to the Father except through me. R/. Alleluia. (Jn 14:6)

COMMUNION ANTIPHON: They ate and were filled; the Lord gave them what they wanted: they were not deprived of their desire. (Ps 77:29–30)

Tuesday, February 15, 2011: Sixth Week in Ordinary Time / 336 [Gn 6:5–8; 7:1–5, 10/Mk 8:14–21]

ENTRANCE ANTIPHON: Lord, be my rock of safety, the stronghold that saves me. For the honor of your name, lead me and guide me. (Ps 30:3–4)

RESPONSE: The Lord will bless his people with peace. (Ps 29:11b)

GOSPEL VERSE: R/. Alleluia. Whoever loves me will keep my word, says the Lord; and my Father will love him and we will come to him. R/. Alleluia. (Jn 14:23)

COMMUNION ANTIPHON: They ate and were filled; the Lord gave them what they wanted: they were not deprived of their desire. (Ps 77:29–30)

Wednesday, February 16, 2011: Sixth Week in Ordinary Time / 337 [Gn 8:6–13, 20–22/Mk 8:22–26]

ENTRANCE ANTIPHON: Lord, be my rock of safety, the stronghold that saves me. For the honor of your name, lead me and guide me. (Ps 30:3–4)

RESPONSE: To you, Lord, I will offer a sacrifice of praise. (Ps 116:17a) Or: Alleluia

GOSPEL VERSE: R/. Alleluia. May the Father of our Lord Jesus Christ enlighten the eyes of our hearts, that we may know what is the hope that belongs to his call. R/. Alleluia. (See Eph 1:17–18)

COMMUNION ANTIPHON: They ate and were filled; the Lord gave them what they wanted: they were not deprived of their desire. (Ps 77:29–30)

Thursday, February 17, 2011: Sixth Week in Ordinary Time / 338 [Gn 9:1–13/Mk 8:27–33]

ENTRANCE ANTIPHON: Lord, be my rock of safety, the stronghold that saves me. For the honor of your name, lead me and guide me. *(Ps 30:3–4)*

RESPONSE: From heaven the Lord looks down on the earth. *(Ps 102:20b)*

GOSPEL VERSE: R/. Alleluia. Your words, Lord, are Spirit and life; you have the words of everlasting life. R/. Alleluia. *(See Jn 6:63c, 68c)*

COMMUNION ANTIPHON: They ate and were filled; the Lord gave them what they wanted: they were not deprived of their desire. *(Ps 77:29–30)*

*OR: **Seven Founders of the Order of Servites**—religious / 533 [Rom 8:26–30/Mt 19:27–29]*

ENTRANCE ANTIPHON: These are the saints who received blessings from the Lord, a prize from God their Savior. They are the people that long to see his face. *(See Ps 23:5–6)*

RESPONSE: I will bless the Lord at all times. *(Ps 34:2)*

Or: Taste and see the goodness of the Lord. *(Ps 34:9)*

GOSPEL VERSE: R/. Alleluia. Blessed are the poor in spirit; for theirs is the Kingdom of heaven. R/. Alleluia. *(Mt 5:3)*

COMMUNION ANTIPHON: Taste and see the goodness of the Lord: blessed is he who hopes in God. *(Ps 34:9)*

Friday, February 18, 2011: Sixth Week in Ordinary Time / 339 [Gn 11:1–9/Mk 8:34–9:1]

ENTRANCE ANTIPHON: Lord, be my rock of safety, the stronghold that saves me. For the honor of your name, lead me and guide me. *(Ps 30:3–4)*

RESPONSE: Blessed the people the Lord has chosen to be his own. *(Ps 33:12)*

GOSPEL VERSE: R/. Alleluia. I call you my friends, says the Lord, for I have made known to you all that the Father has told me. R/. Alleluia. *(Jn 15:15b)*

COMMUNION ANTIPHON: They ate and were filled; the Lord gave them what they wanted: they were not deprived of their desire. *(Ps 77:29–30)*

Saturday, February 19, 2011: Sixth Week in Ordinary Time / 340 [Heb 11:1–7/Mk 9:2–13]

ENTRANCE ANTIPHON: Lord, be my rock of safety, the stronghold that saves me. For the honor of your name, lead me and guide me. *(Ps 30:3–4)*

RESPONSE: I will praise your name for ever, Lord. *(See Ps 145:1)*

GOSPEL VERSE: R/. Alleluia. The heavens were opened and the voice of the Father thundered: This is my beloved Son. Listen to him. R/. Alleluia. *(See Mk 9:6)*

COMMUNION ANTIPHON: They ate and were filled; the Lord gave them what they wanted: they were not deprived of their desire. *(Ps 77:29–30)*

*OR: **Blessed Virgin Mary** / 707–712*

ENTRANCE ANTIPHON: Blessed are you, Virgin Mary, who carried the creator of all things in your womb; you gave birth to your maker, and remain for ever a virgin.

RESPONSE: Blessed be the name of the Lord for ever. *(Ps 113:2) Or:* Alleluia.

GOSPEL VERSE: R/. Alleluia. Blessed are you, O Virgin Mary, who believed that what was spoken to you by the Lord would be fulfilled. R/. Alleluia. *(See Lk 1:45)*

COMMUNION ANTIPHON: The Almighty has done great things for me. Holy is his name. *(Lk 1:49)*

Monday, February 21, 2011: Seventh Week in Ordinary Time / 341 [Sir 1:1–10/Mk 9:14–29]

ENTRANCE ANTIPHON: Lord, your mercy is my hope, my heart rejoices in your saving power. I will sing to the Lord for his goodness to me. *(Ps 12:6)*

RESPONSE: The Lord is king; he is robed in majesty. *(Ps 93:1a)*

GOSPEL VERSE: R/. Alleluia. Our Savior Jesus Christ has destroyed death and brought life to light through the Gospel. R/. Alleluia. *(2 Tm 1:10)*

COMMUNION ANTIPHON: Lord, I believe that you are the Christ, the Son of God, who was to come into this world. *(Jn 11:27)*

*OR: **Peter Damian**—bishop, doctor of the Church / 534 [2 Tm 4:1–5/Jn 15:1–8]*

ENTRANCE ANTIPHON: The mouth of the just man utters wisdom, and his tongue speaks what is right; the law of his God is in his heart. (*Ps 36:30–31*)

RESPONSE: You are my inheritance, O Lord. (*See Ps 16:5a*)

GOSPEL VERSE: R/. Alleluia. Remain in my love, says the Lord; whoever remains in me and I in him will bear much fruit. R/. Alleluia. (*Jn 15:9b, 5b*)

COMMUNION ANTIPHON: The Lord has put his faithful servant in charge of his household, to give them their share of bread at the proper time. (*Lk 12:42*)

Tuesday, February 22, 2011: The Chair of Peter—apostle / 535 [1 Pt 5:1–4/Mt 16:13–19]

ENTRANCE ANTIPHON: The Lord said to Simon Peter: I have prayed that your faith may not fail; and you in your turn must strengthen your brothers. (*Lk 22:32*)

RESPONSE: The Lord is my shepherd; there is nothing I shall want. (*Ps 23:1*)

GOSPEL VERSE: R/. Alleluia. You are Peter, and upon this rock I will build my Church; the gates of the netherworld shall not prevail against it.. R/. Alleluia. (*Mt 16:18*)

COMMUNION ANTIPHON: Peter said: You are the Christ, the Son of the living God. Jesus answered: You are Peter, the rock on which I will build my Church. (*Mt 16:16, 18*)

Wednesday, February 23, 2011: Polycarp—bishop, martyr / 536 [Rv 2:8–11/Jn 15:18–21]

ENTRANCE ANTIPHON: This holy man fought to the death for the law of his God, never cowed by the threats of the wicked; his house was built on solid rock.

RESPONSE: Into your hands, O Lord, I commend my spirit. (*Ps 31:6*)

GOSPEL VERSE: R/. Alleluia. We praise you, O God, we acclaim you as Lord; the white-robed army of martyrs praise you. R/. Alleluia. (*See Te Deum*)

COMMUNION ANTIPHON: If anyone wishes to come after me, he must renounce himself, take up his cross, and follow me, says the Lord. (*Mt 16:24*)

OR: **Seventh Week in Ordinary Time** / 343 [Sir 4:11–19/Mk 9:38–40]

ENTRANCE ANTIPHON: Lord, your mercy is my hope, my heart rejoices in your saving power. I will sing to the Lord for his goodness to me. (*Ps 12:6*)

RESPONSE: O Lord, great peace have they who love your law. (*Ps 119:165a*)

GOSPEL VERSE: R/. Alleluia. I am the way and the truth and the life, says the Lord; no one comes to the Father except through me. R/. Alleluia. (*Jn 14:6*)

COMMUNION ANTIPHON: Lord, I believe that you are the Christ, the Son of God, who was to come into this world. (*Jn 11:27*)

Thursday, February 24, 2011: Seventh Week in Ordinary Time / 344 [Sir 5:1–8/Mk 9:41–50]

ENTRANCE ANTIPHON: Lord, your mercy is my hope, my heart rejoices in your saving power. I will sing to the Lord for his goodness to me. (*Ps 12:6*)

RESPONSE: Blessed are they who hope in the Lord. (*Ps 40:5a*)

GOSPEL VERSE: R/. Alleluia. Receive the word of God, not as the word of men, but as it truly is, the word of God. R/. Alleluia. (*See 1 Thes 2:13*)

COMMUNION ANTIPHON: Lord, I believe that you are the Christ, the Son of God, who was to come into this world. (*Jn 11:27*)

Friday, February 25, 2011: Seventh Week in Ordinary Time / 345 [Sir 6:5–17/Mk 10:1–12]

ENTRANCE ANTIPHON: Lord, your mercy is my hope, my heart rejoices in your saving power. I will sing to the Lord for his goodness to me. (*Ps 12:6*)

RESPONSE: Guide me, Lord, in the way of your commands. (*Ps 119:35a*)

GOSPEL VERSE: R/. Alleluia. Your word, O Lord, is truth; consecrate us in the truth. R/. Alleluia. (*See Jn 17:17b, 17a*)

COMMUNION ANTIPHON: Lord, I believe that you are the Christ, the Son of God, who was to come into this world. (*Jn 11:27*)

Saturday, February 26, 2011: Seventh Week in Ordinary Time / 346 [Sir 17:1–15/Mk 10:13–16]

ENTRANCE ANTIPHON: Lord, your mercy is my hope, my heart rejoices in your saving power. I will sing to the Lord for his goodness to me. *(Ps 12:6)*

RESPONSE: The Lord's kindness is everlasting to those who fear him. *(See Ps 103:17)*

GOSPEL VERSE: R/. Alleluia. Blessed are you, Father, Lord of heaven and earth; you have revealed to little ones the mysteries of the Kingdom. R/. Alleluia. *(See Mt 11:25)*

COMMUNION ANTIPHON: Lord, I believe that you are the Christ, the Son of God, who was to come into this world. *(Jn 11:27)*

*OR: **Blessed Virgin Mary** / 707–712*

ENTRANCE ANTIPHON: Hail, holy Mother! The child to whom you gave birth is the King of heaven and earth for ever. *(Sedulius)*

RESPONSE: You are the highest honor of our race. *(Jdt 15:9d)*

GOSPEL VERSE: R/. Alleluia. Hail, Mary, full of grace, the Lord is with you; blessed are you among women. R/. Alleluia. *(See Lk 1:28)*

COMMUNION ANTIPHON: Blessed is the womb of the Virgin Mary; she carried the Son of the eternal Father. *(See Lk 11:27)*

Monday, February 28, 2011: Eighth Week in Ordinary Time / 347 [Sir 17:20–24/Mk 10:17–27]

ENTRANCE ANTIPHON: The Lord has been my strength; he has led me into freedom. He saved me because he loves me. *(Ps 17:19–20)*

RESPONSE: Let the just exult and rejoice in the Lord. *(Ps 32:11a)*

GOSPEL VERSE: R/. Alleluia. Jesus Christ became poor although he was rich, so that by his poverty you might become rich. R/. Alleluia. *(2 Cor 8:9)*

COMMUNION ANTIPHON: I, the Lord, am with you always, until the end of the world. *(Mt 28:20)*

Tuesday, March 1, 2011: Eighth Week in Ordinary Time / 348 [Sir 35:1–12/Mk 10:28–31]

ENTRANCE ANTIPHON: The Lord has been my strength; he has led me into freedom. He saved me because he loves me. *(Ps 17:19–20)*

RESPONSE: To the upright I will show the saving power of God. *(Ps 50:23b)*

GOSPEL VERSE: R/. Alleluia. Blessed are you, Father, Lord of heaven and earth; you have revealed to little ones the mysteries of the Kingdom. R/. Alleluia. *(See Mt 11:25)*

COMMUNION ANTIPHON: I, the Lord, am with you always, until the end of the world. *(Mt 28:20)*

Wednesday, March 2, 2011: Eighth Week in Ordinary Time / 349 [Sir 36:1, 4–5a, 10–17/Mk 10:32–45]

ENTRANCE ANTIPHON: The Lord has been my strength; he has led me into freedom. He saved me because he loves me. *(Ps 17:19–20)*

RESPONSE: Show us, O Lord, the light of your kindness. *(Sir 36:1b)*

GOSPEL VERSE: R/. Alleluia. The Son of Man came to serve, and to give his life as a ransom for many. R/. Alleluia. *(Mk 10:45)*

COMMUNION ANTIPHON: I, the Lord, am with you always, until the end of the world. *(Mt 28:20)*

Thursday, March 3, 2011: Eighth Week in Ordinary Time / 350 [Sir 42:15–25/Mk 10:46–52]

ENTRANCE ANTIPHON: The Lord has been my strength; he has led me into freedom. He saved me because he loves me. *(Ps 17:19–20)*

RESPONSE: By the word of the Lord the heavens were made. *(Ps 33:6a)*

GOSPEL VERSE: R/. Alleluia. I am the light of the world, says the Lord; whoever follows me will have the light of life. R/. Alleluia. *(Jn 8:12)*

COMMUNION ANTIPHON: I, the Lord, am with you always, until the end of the world. *(Mt 28:20)*

*OR: **Katharine Drexel**—virgin / 536A, 731–736*

ENTRANCE ANTIPHON: Here is a wise and faithful virgin who went with lighted lamp to meet her Lord.

RESPONSE: Listen to me, daughter; see and bend your ear. *(Ps 45:11)*

OR: The bridegroom is here; let us go out to meet Christ the Lord.

GOSPEL VERSE: : R/. Alleluia. This is the wise virgin, whom the Lord found waiting; at his coming, she went in with him to the wedding feast. : R/. Alleluia.

COMMUNION ANTIPHON: The bridegroom is here; let us go out to meet Christ the Lord. *(Mt 25:6)*

Friday, March 4, 2011: Eighth Week in Ordinary Time / 351 [Sir 44:1, 9–13/Mk 11:11–26]

ENTRANCE ANTIPHON: The Lord has been my strength; he has led me into freedom. He saved me because he loves me. *(Ps 17:19–20)*

RESPONSE: The Lord takes delight in his people. *(See Ps 149:4a) Or:* Alleluia.

GOSPEL VERSE: R/. Alleluia. I chose you from the world, to go and bear fruit that will last, says the Lord. R/. Alleluia. *(See Jn 15:16)*

COMMUNION ANTIPHON: I, the Lord, am with you always, until the end of the world. *(Mt 28:20)*

OR: *Casimir* / 537 *[Phil 3:8–14/Jn 15:9–17]*

ENTRANCE ANTIPHON: The just man will rejoice in the Lord and hope in him, and all the upright of heart will be praised. *(Ps 63:11)*

RESPONSE: The just one shall live on your holy mountain, O Lord. *(Ps 15:1)*

GOSPEL VERSE: R/. Alleluia. I give you a new commandment: love one another as I have loved you. R/. Alleluia. *(Jn 13:34)*

COMMUNION ANTIPHON: He who serves me, follows me, says the Lord; and where I am, my servant will also be. *(Jn 12:26)*

Saturday, March 5, 2011: Eighth Week in Ordinary Time / 352 [Sir 51:12cd–20/Mk 11:27–33]

ENTRANCE ANTIPHON: The Lord has been my strength; he has led me into freedom. He saved me because he loves me. *(Ps 17:19–20)*

RESPONSE: The precepts of the Lord give joy to the heart. *(Ps 19:9ab)*

GOSPEL VERSE: R/. Alleluia. Let the word of Christ dwell in you richly; giving thanks to God the Father through him. R/. Alleluia. *(See Col 3:16a, 17c)*

COMMUNION ANTIPHON: I, the Lord, am with you always, until the end of the world. *(Mt 28:20)*

OR: *Blessed Virgin Mary* / 707–712

ENTRANCE ANTIPHON: Blessed are you, Virgin Mary, who carried the creator of all things in your womb; you gave birth to your maker, and remain for ever a virgin.

RESPONSE: Blessed be the name of the Lord for ever. *(Ps 113:2) Or:* Alleluia.

GOSPEL VERSE: R/. Alleluia. Blessed are you, O Virgin Mary, who believed that what was spoken to you by the Lord would be fulfilled. R/. Alleluia. *(See Lk 1:45)*

COMMUNION ANTIPHON: The Almighty has done great things for me. Holy is his name. *(Lk 1:49)*

Monday, March 7, 2011: Ninth Week in Ordinary Time / 353 [Tb 1:3, 2:1a–8/Mk 12:1–12]

ENTRANCE ANTIPHON: O look at me and be merciful, for I am wretched and alone. See my hardship and my poverty, and pardon all my sins. *(Ps 24:16, 18)*

RESPONSE: Blessed the man who fears the Lord. *(Ps 112:1b) Or:* Alleluia.

GOSPEL VERSE: R/. Alleluia. Jesus Christ, you are the faithful witness, the firstborn of the dead; you have loved us and freed us from our sins by your Blood. R/. Alleluia. *(See Rv 1:5ab)*

COMMUNION ANTIPHON: I tell you solemnly, whatever you ask for in prayer, believe that you have received it, and it will be yours, says the Lord. *(Mk 11:23–24)*

OR: *Perpetua and Felicity—martyrs* / 538 *[Rom 8:31b–39/Mt 10:34–39]*

ENTRANCE ANTIPHON: The holy martyrs shed their blood on earth for Christ; therefore they have received an everlasting reward.

RESPONSE: Our soul has escaped like a bird from the fowler's snare. *(Ps 124:7)*

GOSPEL VERSE: R/. Alleluia. Blessed are they who are persecuted for the sake of righteousness, for theirs is the Kingdom of heaven. R/. Alleluia. *(Mt 5:10)*

COMMUNION ANTIPHON: Neither death nor life nor anything in creation can come between us and Christ's love for us. *(See Rom 8:38–39)*

Tuesday, March 8, 2011: Ninth Week in Ordinary Time / 354 [Tb 2:9–14/Mk 12:13–17]

ENTRANCE ANTIPHON: O look at me and be merciful, for I am wretched and alone. See my hardship and my poverty, and pardon all my sins. *(Ps 24:16, 18)*

RESPONSE: The heart of the just one is firm, trusting in the Lord. *(See Ps 112:7c) Or:* Alleluia.

GOSPEL VERSE: R/. Alleluia. May the Father of our Lord Jesus Christ enlighten the eyes of our hearts, that we may know what is the hope that belongs to his call. R/. Alleluia. *(See Eph 1:17–18)*

COMMUNION ANTIPHON: I tell you solemnly, whatever you ask for in prayer, believe that you have received it, and it will be yours, says the Lord. *(Mk 11:23–24)*

*OR: **John of God**—religious / 539 [1 Jn 3:14–18/ Mt 25:31–40]*

ENTRANCE ANTIPHON: Come, you whom my Father has blessed, says the Lord: I was ill and you comforted me. I tell you, anything you did for one of my brothers, you did for me. *(Mt 25:34, 36, 40)*

RESPONSE: Blessed the man who fears the Lord. *(Ps 112:1) Or:* Alleluia.

GOSPEL VERSE: R/. Alleluia. I give you a new commandment: love one another as I have loved you. R/. Alleluia. *(Jn 13:34)*

COMMUNION ANTIPHON: By the love you have for one another, says the Lord, everyone will know that you are my disciples. *(Jn 13:35)*

Wednesday, March 9, 2011: Ash Wednesday / 219 [Jl 2:12–18/2 Cor 5:20–6:2/Mt 6:1–6, 16–18]

(or see Sunday section for this date)

ENTRANCE ANTIPHON: Lord, you are merciful to all, and hate nothing you have created. You overlook the sins of men to bring them to repentance. You are the Lord our God. *(See Wis 11:24–25, 27)*

RESPONSE: Be merciful, O Lord, for we have sinned. *(See Ps 51:3a)*

GOSPEL VERSE: If today you hear his voice, harden not your hearts. *(See Ps 95:8)*

COMMUNION ANTIPHON: The man who meditates day and night on the law of the Lord will yield fruit in due season. *(Ps 1:2–3)*

Thursday, March 10, 2011: Lenten Weekday after Ash Wednesday / 220 [Dt 30:15–20/Lk 9:22–25]

ENTRANCE ANTIPHON: When I cry to the Lord, he hears my voice and saves me from the foes who threaten me. Unload your burden onto the Lord, and he will support you. *(See Ps 54:17–20, 23)*

RESPONSE: Blessed are they who hope in the Lord. *(Ps 40:5a)*

GOSPEL VERSE: Repent, says the Lord; the Kingdom of heaven is at hand. *(Mt 4:17)*

COMMUNION ANTIPHON: Create a clean heart in me, O God; give me a new and steadfast spirit. *(Ps 50:12)*

Friday, March 11, 2011: Lenten Weekday after Ash Wednesday / 221 [Is 58:1–9a/Mt 9:14–15]

ENTRANCE ANTIPHON: The Lord heard me and took pity on me. He came to my help. *(Ps 29:11)*

RESPONSE: A heart contrite and humbled, O God, you will not spurn. *(Ps 51:19b)*

GOSPEL VERSE: Seek good and not evil so that you may live, and the Lord will be with you. *(See Am 5:14)*

COMMUNION ANTIPHON: Teach us your ways, O Lord, and lead us in your paths. *(Ps 24:4)*

Saturday, March 12, 2011: Lenten Weekday after Ash Wednesday / 222 [Is 58:9b–14/Lk 5:27–32]

ENTRANCE ANTIPHON: Answer us, Lord, with your loving kindness, turn to us in your great mercy. *(Ps 68:17)*

RESPONSE: Teach me your way, O Lord, that I may walk in your truth. *(Ps 86:11ab)*

GOSPEL VERSE: I take no pleasure in the death of the wicked man, says the Lord, but rather in his conversion, that he may live. *(Ez 33:11)*

COMMUNION ANTIPHON: It is mercy that I want, and not sacrifice, says the Lord; I did not come to call the virtuous, but sinners. *(Mt 9:13)*

Monday, March 14, 2011: First Week of Lent / 224 [Lv 19:1–2, 11–18/Mt 25:31–46]

ENTRANCE ANTIPHON: As the eyes of servants are on the hands of their master, so our eyes are fixed on the Lord our God, pleading for his mercy. Have mercy on us, Lord, have mercy. *(Ps 122:2–3)*

RESPONSE: Your words, Lord, are Spirit and life. *(Jn 6:63b)*

GOSPEL VERSE: Behold, now is a very acceptable time; behold, now is the day of salvation. *(2 Cor 6:2b)*

COMMUNION ANTIPHON: I tell you, anything you did for the least of my brothers, you did for me, says the Lord. Come, you whom my Father has blessed; inherit the kingdom prepared for you since the foundation of the world. *(Mt 25:40, 34)*

Tuesday, March 15, 2011: First Week of Lent / 225 [Is 55:10–11/Mt 6:7–15]

ENTRANCE ANTIPHON: In every age, O Lord, you have been our refuge. From all eternity, you are God. *(Ps 89:1–2)*

RESPONSE: From all their distress, God rescues the just. *(Ps 34:18b)*

GOSPEL VERSE: One does not live on bread alone, but on every word that comes forth from the mouth of God. *(Mt 4:4b)*

COMMUNION ANTIPHON: My God of justice, you answer my cry; you come to my help when I am in trouble. Take pity on me, Lord, and hear my prayer. *(Ps 4:2)*

Wednesday, March 16, 2011: First Week of Lent / 226 [Jon 3:1–10/Lk 11:29–32]

ENTRANCE ANTIPHON: Remember your mercies, Lord, your tenderness from ages past. Do not let our enemies triumph over us; O God, deliver Israel from all her distress. *(Ps 24:6, 3, 22)*

RESPONSE: A heart contrite and humbled, O God, you will not spurn. *(Ps 51:19b)*

GOSPEL VERSE: Even now, says the LORD, return to me with your whole heart for I am gracious and merciful. *(Jl 2:12–13)*

COMMUNION ANTIPHON: Lord, give joy to all who trust in you; be their defender and make them happy for ever. *(Ps 5:12)*

Thursday, March 17, 2011: First Week of Lent / 227 [Est C:12, 14–16, 23–25/Mt 7:7–12]

ENTRANCE ANTIPHON: Let my words reach your ears, Lord; listen to my groaning, and hear the cry of my prayer, O my King, my God. *(Ps 5:2–3)*

RESPONSE: Lord, on the day I called for help, you answered me. *(Ps 138:3a)*

GOSPEL VERSE: A clean heart create for me, God; give me back the joy of your salvation. *(Ps 51:12a, 14a)*

COMMUNION ANTIPHON: Everyone who asks will receive; whoever seeks shall find, and to him who knocks it shall be opened. *(Mt 7:8)*

OR: *Patrick—bishop / 541 [1 Pt 4:7b–11/Lk 5: 1–11]*

ENTRANCE ANTIPHON: Proclaim his glory among the nations, his marvelous deeds to all the peoples; great is the Lord and worthy of all praise *(Ps 95:3–4)*

RESPONSE: Proclaim God's marvelous deeds to all the nations. *(Ps 96:3)*

GOSPEL VERSE: Come after me, says the Lord, and I will make you fishers of men. *(Mk 1:17)*

COMMUNION ANTIPHON: The Lord sent disciples to proclaim to all the towns: the kingdom of God is very near to you. *(See Lk 10:1, 9)*

Friday, March 18, 2011: First Week of Lent / 228 [Ez 18:21–28/Mt 5:20–26]

ENTRANCE ANTIPHON: Lord, deliver me from my distress. See my hardship and my poverty, and pardon all my sins. *(Ps 24:17–18)*

RESPONSE: If you, O Lord, mark iniquities, who can stand? *(Ps 130:3)*

GOSPEL VERSE: Cast away from you all the crimes you have committed, says the Lord, and make for yourselves a new heart and a new spirit. *(Ez 18:31)*

COMMUNION ANTIPHON: By my life, I do not wish the sinner to die, says the Lord, but to turn to me and live. *(Ez 33:11)*

OR: **Cyril of Jerusalem**—*bishop, doctor of the Church / 542 [1 Jn 5:1–5/Jn 15:1–8]*

ENTRANCE ANTIPHON: Let the peoples declare the wisdom of the saints and the Church proclaim their praises; their names shall live for ever. *(See Sir 44:15, 14)*

RESPONSE: The judgments of the Lord are true, and all of them are just. *(Ps 19:10)*

Or: Your words, Lord, are Spirit and life. *(Jn 6:63)*

GOSPEL VERSE: Remain in my love, says the Lord; whoever remains in me and I in him will bear much fruit. *(Jn 15:9b, 5b)*

COMMUNION ANTIPHON: We preach a Christ who was crucified; he is the power and the wisdom of God. *(1 Cor 1:23–24)*

Saturday, March 19, 2011: Joseph— husband of the Blessed Virgin Mary / 543 [2 Sm 7:4–5a, 12–14a, 16/ Rom 4:13, 16–18, 22/Mt 1:16, 18–21, 24a or Lk 2:41–51a]

ENTRANCE ANTIPHON: The Lord has put his faithful servant in charge of his household. *(Lk 12:42)*

RESPONSE: The son of David will live for ever. *(Ps 89:37)*

GOSPEL VERSE: Blessed are those who dwell in your house, O Lord; they never cease to praise you. *(Ps 84:5)*

COMMUNION ANTIPHON: Come, good and faithful servant! Share the joy of your Lord! *(Mt 25:21)*

Monday, March 21, 2011: Second Week of Lent / 230 [Dn 9:4b–10/Lk 6:36–38]

ENTRANCE ANTIPHON: Redeem me, Lord, and have mercy on me; my foot is set on the right path, I worship you in the great assembly. *(Ps 25:11–12)*

RESPONSE: Lord, do not deal with us according to our sins. *(See Ps 103:10a)*

GOSPEL VERSE: Your words, Lord, are Spirit and life; you have the words of everlasting life. *(See Jn 6:63c, 68c)*

COMMUNION ANTIPHON: Be merciful as your Father is merciful, says the Lord. *(Lk 6:36)*

Tuesday, March 22, 2011: Second Week of Lent / 231 [Is 1:10, 16–20/Mt 23:1–12]

ENTRANCE ANTIPHON: Give light to my eyes, Lord, lest I sleep in death, and my enemy say: I have overcome him. *(Ps 12:4–5)*

RESPONSE: To the upright I will show the saving power of God. *(Ps 50:23b)*

GOSPEL VERSE: Cast away from you all the crimes you have committed, says the Lord, and make for yourselves a new heart and a new spirit. *(Ez 18:31)*

COMMUNION ANTIPHON: I will tell all your marvelous works. I will rejoice and be glad in you, and sing to your name, Most High. *(Ps 9:2–3)*

Wednesday, March 23, 2011: Second Week of Lent / 232 [Jer 18:18–20/ Mt 20:17–28]

ENTRANCE ANTIPHON: Do not abandon me, Lord. My God, do not go away from me! Hurry to help me, Lord, my Savior. *(Ps 37:22–23)*

RESPONSE: Save me, O Lord, in your kindness. *(Ps 31:17b)*

GOSPEL VERSE: I am the light of the world, says the Lord; whoever follows me will have the light of life. *(Jn 8:12)*

COMMUNION ANTIPHON: The Son of Man did not come to be served, but to serve, and to give his life as a ransom for many. *(Mt 20:28)*

OR: **Toribio de Mogrovejo**—*bishop / 544 [2 Tm 1:13–14; 2:1–3/Mt 9:35–38]*

ENTRANCE ANTIPHON: I will raise up for myself a faithful priest; he will do what is in my heart and in my mind, says the Lord. *(1 Sm 2:35)*

RESPONSE: Proclaim God's marvelous deeds to all the nations. *(Ps 96:3)*

GOSPEL VERSE: I am the good shepherd, says the Lord; I know my sheep, and mine know me. *(Jn 10:14)*

COMMUNION ANTIPHON: I came that men may have life, and have it to the full, says the Lord. *(Jn 10:10)*

Thursday, March 24, 2011: Second Week of Lent / 233 [Jer 17:5–10/Lk 16:19–31]

ENTRANCE ANTIPHON: Test me, O God, and know my thoughts; see whether I step in the wrong path, and guide me along the everlasting way. *(Ps 138:23–24)*

RESPONSE: Blessed are they who hope in the Lord. *(Ps 40:5a)*

GOSPEL VERSE: Blessed are they who have kept the word with a generous heart and yield a harvest through perseverance. *(See Lk 8:15)*

COMMUNION ANTIPHON: Happy are those of blameless life, who follow the law of the Lord. *(Ps 118:1)*

Friday, March 25, 2011: The Annunciation of the Lord / 545 [Is 7:10–14; 8:10/Heb 10:4–10/Lk 1:26–38]

ENTRANCE ANTIPHON: As Christ came into the world, he said: Behold! I have come to do your will, O God. *(Heb 10:5, 7)*

RESPONSE: Here I am, Lord; I come to do your will. *(Ps 40:8a, 9a)*

GOSPEL VERSE: The Word of God became flesh and made his dwelling among us; and we saw his glory. *(Jn 1:14ab)*

COMMUNION ANTIPHON: The Virgin is with child and shall bear a son, and she will call him Emmanuel. *(Is 7:14)*

Saturday, March 26, 2011: Second Week of Lent / 235 [Mi 7:14–15, 18–20/Lk 15:1–3, 11–32]

ENTRANCE ANTIPHON: The Lord is loving and merciful, to anger slow, and full of love; the Lord is kind to all, and compassionate to all his creatures. *(Ps 144:8–9)*

RESPONSE: The Lord is kind and merciful. *(Ps 103:8a)*

GOSPEL VERSE: I will get up and go to my father and shall say to him, Father, I have sinned against heaven and against you. *(Lk 15:18)*

COMMUNION ANTIPHON: My son, you should rejoice, because your brother was dead and has come back to life; he was lost and is found. *(Lk 15:32)*

Monday, March 28, 2011: Third Week of Lent / 237 [2 Kgs 5:1–15ab/Lk 4:24–30]

ENTRANCE ANTIPHON: My soul is longing and pining for the courts of the Lord; my heart and my flesh sing for joy to the living God. *(Ps 83:3)*

RESPONSE: Athirst is my soul for the living God. When shall I go and behold the face of God? *(See Ps 42:3)*

GOSPEL VERSE: I hope in the Lord, I trust in his word; with him there is kindness and plenteous redemption. *(See Ps 130:5, 7)*

COMMUNION ANTIPHON: All you nations, praise the Lord, for steadfast is his kindly mercy to us. *(Ps 116:1–2)*

OR: Optional Mass for Use Any Day of the Third Week of Lent / 236 [Ex 17:1–7/Jn 4:5–42]

ENTRANCE ANTIPHON: I will prove my holiness through you. I will gather you from the ends of the earth; I will pour clean water on you and wash away all your sins. I will give you a new spirit within you, says the Lord. *(Ez 36:23–26)*

RESPONSE: If today you hear his voice, harden not your hearts. *(Ps 95:8)*

GOSPEL VERSE: Lord, you are truly the Savior of the world; give me living water, that I may never thirst again. *(See Jn 4:42, 15)*

COMMUNION ANTIPHON: Whoever drinks the water that I shall give him, says the Lord, will have a spring inside him, welling up for eternal life. *(Jn 4:13–14)*

Tuesday, March 29, 2011: Third Week of Lent / 238 [Dn 3:25, 34–43/Mt 18:21–35]

ENTRANCE ANTIPHON: I call upon you, God, for you will answer me; bend your ear and hear my prayer. Guard me as the pupil of your eye; hide me in the shade of your wings. *(Ps 16:6, 8)*

RESPONSE: Remember your mercies, O Lord. *(Ps 25:6a)*

GOSPEL VERSE: Even now, says the LORD, return to me with your whole heart; for I am gracious and merciful. *(Jl 2:12–13)*

COMMUNION ANTIPHON: Lord, who may stay in your dwelling place? Who shall live on your holy mountain? He who walks without blame and does what is right. *(Ps 14:1–2)*

Wednesday, March 30, 2011: Third Week of Lent / 239 [Dt 4:1, 5–9/Mt 5:17–19]

ENTRANCE ANTIPHON: Lord, direct my steps as you have promised, and let no evil hold me in its power. *(Ps 118:133)*

RESPONSE: Praise the Lord, Jerusalem. *(Ps 147:12a)*

GOSPEL VERSE: Your words, Lord, are Spirit and life; you have the words of everlasting life. *(See Jn 6:63c, 68c)*

COMMUNION ANTIPHON: Lord, you will show me the path of life and fill me with joy in your presence. *(Ps 15:11)*

Thursday, March 31, 2011: Third Week of Lent / 240 [Jer 7:23–28/Lk 11:14–23]

ENTRANCE ANTIPHON: I am the Savior of all people, says the Lord. Whatever their troubles, I will answer their cry, and I will always be their Lord.

RESPONSE: If today you hear his voice, harden not your hearts. *(Ps 95:8)*

GOSPEL VERSE: Even now, says the LORD, return to me with your whole heart, for I am gracious and merciful. *(Jl 2:12–13)*

COMMUNION ANTIPHON: You have laid down your precepts to be faithfully kept. May my footsteps be firm in keeping your commands. *(Ps 118:4–5)*

Friday, April 1, 2011: Third Week of Lent / 241 [Hos 14:2–10/Mk 12:28–34]

ENTRANCE ANTIPHON: Lord, there is no god to compare with you; you are great and do wonderful things, you are the only God. *(Ps 85:8, 10)*

RESPONSE: I am the Lord your God: hear my voice. *(See Ps 81:11, 9a)*

GOSPEL VERSE: Repent, says the Lord; the Kingdom of heaven is at hand. *(Mt 4:17)*

COMMUNION ANTIPHON: To love God with all your heart, and your neighbor as yourself, is a greater thing than all the temple sacrifices. *(See Mk 12:33)*

Saturday, April 2, 2011: Third Week of Lent / 242 [Hos 6:1–6/Lk 18:9–14]

ENTRANCE ANTIPHON: Bless the Lord, my soul, and remember all his kindnesses, for he pardons all my faults. *(Ps 102:2–3)*

RESPONSE: It is mercy I desire, and not sacrifice. *(See Hos 6:6)*

GOSPEL VERSE: If today you hear his voice, harden not your hearts. *(Ps 95:8)*

COMMUNION ANTIPHON: He stood at a distance and beat his breast, saying: O God, be merciful to me, a sinner. *(Lk 18:13)*

OR: *Francis of Paola—hermit / 546 [Phil 3:8–14/Lk 12:32–34]*

ENTRANCE ANTIPHON: The Lord is my inheritance and my cup; he alone will give me my reward. The measuring line has marked a lovely place for me; my inheritance is my great delight. *(Ps 15:5–6)*

RESPONSE: You are my inheritance, O Lord. *(See Ps 16:5a)*

GOSPEL VERSE: Blessed are the poor in spirit; for theirs is the Kingdom of God. *(Mt 5:3)*

COMMUNION ANTIPHON: I solemnly tell you: those who have left everything and followed me will be repaid a hundredfold and will gain eternal life. *(See Mt 19:27–29)*

Monday, April 4, 2011: Fourth Week of Lent / 244 [Is 65:17–21/Jn 4:43–54]

ENTRANCE ANTIPHON: Lord, I put my trust in you; I shall be glad and rejoice in your mercy, because you have seen my affliction. *(Ps 30:7–8)*

RESPONSE: I will praise you, Lord, for you have rescued me. *(Ps 30:2a)*

GOSPEL VERSE: Seek good and not evil so that you may live, and the LORD will be with you. *(Am 5:14)*

COMMUNION ANTIPHON: I shall put my spirit within you, says the Lord; you will obey my laws and keep my decrees. *(Ez 36:27)*

OR: **Optional Mass for Use Any Day of the Fourth Week of Lent / 243** [Mi 7:7–9/ Jn 9:1–41]

ENTRANCE ANTIPHON: Rejoice, Jerusalem! Be glad for her, you who love her; rejoice with her, you who mourned for her, and you will find contentment at her consoling breasts. *(See Is 66:10–11)*

RESPONSE: The Lord is my light and my salvation. (Ps 27:1a)

GOSPEL VERSE: I am the light of the world, says the Lord; he who follows me will have the light of life. (Jn 8:12)

COMMUNION ANTIPHON: The Lord rubbed my eyes: I went away and washed; then I could see, and I believed in God. (See Jn 9:11)

OR: *Isidore—bishop, doctor of the Church / 547* [2 Cor 4:1–2, 5–7/Lk 6:43–45]

ENTRANCE ANTIPHON: I will raise up for myself a faithful priest; he will do what is in my heart and in my mind, says the Lord. (1 Sm 2:35)

RESPONSE: The mouth of the just murmurs wisdom. (Ps 37:30a)

GOSPEL VERSE: I am the vine, you are the branches, says the Lord; whoever remains in me and I in him will bear much fruit. (Jn 15:5)

COMMUNION ANTIPHON: I came that men may have life, and have it to the full, says the Lord. (Jn 10:10)

Tuesday, April 5, 2011: Fourth Week of Lent / 245 [Ez 47:1–9, 12/Jn 5:1–16]

ENTRANCE ANTIPHON: Come to the waters, all who thirst; though you have no money, come and drink with joy. (See Is 55:1)

RESPONSE: The Lord of hosts is with us; our stronghold is the God of Jacob. (Ps 46:8)

GOSPEL VERSE: A clean heart create for me, O God; give me back the joy of your salvation. (Ps 51:12a, 14a)

COMMUNION ANTIPHON: The Lord is my shepherd; there is nothing I shall want. In green pastures he gives me rest, he leads me beside the waters of peace. (Ps 22:1–2)

OR: *Vincent Ferrer—priest / 548* [2 Tm 4:1–5/Lk 12:35–40]

ENTRANCE ANTIPHON: These are holy men who became God's friends and glorious heralds of his truth.

RESPONSE: Here I am, Lord; I come to do your will. (Ps 40:8a, 9a)

GOSPEL VERSE: Be vigilant at all times and pray that you may have the strength to stand before the Son of Man. (Lk 21:36)

COMMUNION ANTIPHON: I will feed my sheep, says the Lord, and give them repose. (Ez 34:15)

Wednesday, April 6, 2011: Fourth Week of Lent / 246 [Is 49:8–15/Jn 5:17–30]

ENTRANCE ANTIPHON: I pray to you, O God, for the time of your favor. Lord, in your great love, answer me. (Ps 68:14)

RESPONSE: The Lord is gracious and merciful. (Ps 145:8a)

GOSPEL VERSE: I am the resurrection and the life, says the Lord; whoever believes in me will never die. (Jn 11:25a, 26)

COMMUNION ANTIPHON: God sent his Son into the world, not to condemn it, but so that the world might be saved through him. (Jn 3:17)

Thursday, April 7, 2011: Fourth Week of Lent / 247 [Ex 32:7–14/Jn 5:31–47]

ENTRANCE ANTIPHON: Let hearts rejoice who search for the Lord. Seek the Lord and his strength, seek always the face of the Lord. (Ps 104:3–4)

RESPONSE: Remember us, O Lord, as you favor your people. (Ps 106:4a)

GOSPEL VERSE: God so loved the wold that he gave his only-begotten Son, so that everyone who believes in him might have eternal life. (Jn 3:16)

COMMUNION ANTIPHON: I will put my law within them, I will write in on their hearts; then I shall be their God, and they will be my people. (Jer 31:33)

OR: *John Baptist de la Salle—priest / 549* [2 Tm 1:13–14; 2:1–3/Mt 18:1–5]

ENTRANCE ANTIPHON: Let the children come to me, and do not stop them, says the Lord; to such belongs the kingdom of God. (Mk 10:14)

RESPONSE: Blessed are they who hope in the Lord. (Ps 40:5a)

Or: Blessed are they who delight in the law of the Lord. (Ps 1:2a)

Or: The just will flourish like the palm tree in the garden of the Lord. (Ps 92:13–14)

GOSPEL VERSE: The greatest among you must be your servant. Whoever humbles himself will be exalted. (Mt 23:11, 12b)

COMMUNION ANTIPHON: Unless you change, and become like little children, says the Lord, you shall not enter the kingdom of heaven. (Mt 18:3)

Friday, April 8, 2011: Fourth Week of Lent / 248 [Wis 2:1a, 12–22/Jn 7:1–2, 10, 25–30]

ENTRANCE ANTIPHON: Save me, O God, by your power, and grant me justice! God, hear my prayer; listen to my plea. *(Ps 53:3–4)*

RESPONSE: The Lord is close to the brokenhearted. *(Ps 34:19a)*

GOSPEL VERSE: One does not live on bread alone, but on every word that comes forth from the mouth of God. *(Mt 4:4b)*

COMMUNION ANTIPHON: In Christ, through the shedding of his blood, we have redemption and forgiveness of our sins by the abundance of his grace. *(Eph 1:7)*

Saturday, April 9, 2011: Fourth Week of Lent / 249 [Jer 11:18–20/Jn 7:40–53]

ENTRANCE ANTIPHON: The snares of death overtook me, the ropes of hell tightened around me; in my distress I called upon the Lord, and he heard my voice. *(Ps 17:5–7)*

RESPONSE: O Lord, my God, in you I take refuge. *(Ps 7:2a)*

GOSPEL VERSE: Blessed are they who have kept the word with a generous heart and yield a harvest through perseverance. *(See Lk 8:15)*

COMMUNION ANTIPHON: We have been ransomed with the precious blood of Christ, as with the blood of a lamb without blemish or spot. *(1 Pt 1:19)*

Monday, April 11, 2011: Fifth Week of Lent / 251 [Dn 13:1–9, 15–17, 19–30, 33–62 or 13:41c–62/Jn 8:1–11]

ENTRANCE ANTIPHON: God, take pity on me! My enemies are crushing me; all day long they wage war on me. *(Ps 55:2)*

RESPONSE: Even though I walk in the dark valley, I fear no evil; for you are at my side. *(Ps 23:4ab)*

GOSPEL VERSE: I take no pleasure in the death of the wicked man, says the Lord, but rather in his conversion, that he may live. *(Ez 33:11)*

COMMUNION ANTIPHON: I am the light of the world, says the Lord; the man who follows me will have the light of life. *(Jn 8:12)*

OR: **Optional Mass for Use Any Day of the Fifth Week of Lent** / 250 [2 Kgs 4:18b–21, 32–37/Jn 11:1–45]

ENTRANCE ANTIPHON: Give me justice, O God, and defend my cause against the wicked; rescue me from deceitful and unjust men. You, O God, are my refuge. *(Ps 42:1–2)*

RESPONSE: Lord, when your glory appears, my joy will be full. *(Ps 17:15b)*

GOSPEL VERSE: I am the resurrection and the life, says the Lord; whoever believes in me will never die. *(Jn 11:25a, 26)*

COMMUNION ANTIPHON: He who lives and believes in me will not die for ever, said the Lord. *(Jn 11:26)*

OR: **Stanislaus**—*bishop, martyr* / 550 [Rv 12:10–12a/Jn 17:11b–19]

ENTRANCE ANTIPHON: I will raise up for myself a faithful priest; he will do what is in my heart and in my mind, says the Lord. *(1 Sm 2:35)*

RESPONSE: The Lord delivered me from all my fears. *(Ps 34:5)*

GOSPEL VERSE: Blessed be the Father of compassion and God of all encouragement, who encourages us in our every affliction. *(2 Cor 1:3b–4)*

COMMUNION ANTIPHON: I came that men may have life, and have it to the full, says the Lord. *(Jn 10:10)*

Tuesday, April 12, 2011: Fifth Week of Lent / 252 [Nm 21:4–9/Jn 8:21–30]

ENTRANCE ANTIPHON: Put your hope in the Lord. Take courage and be strong. *(Ps 26:14)*

RESPONSE: O Lord, hear my prayer, and let my cry come to you. *(Ps 102:2)*

GOSPEL VERSE: The seed is the word of God, Christ is the sower; all who come to him will live for ever.

COMMUNION ANTIPHON: When I am lifted up from the earth, I will draw all men to myself, says the Lord. *(Jn 12:32)*

Wednesday, April 13, 2011: Fifth Week of Lent / 253 [Dn 3:14–20, 91–92, 95/Jn 8:31–42]

ENTRANCE ANTIPHON: Lord, you rescue me from raging enemies, you lift me up above my attackers, you deliver me from violent men. *(Ps 17:48–49)*

RESPONSE: Glory and praise for ever! *(Dn 3:52b)*

GOSPEL VERSE: Blessed are they who have kept the word with a generous heart and yield a harvest through perseverance. *(See Lk 8:15)*

COMMUNION ANTIPHON: God has transferred us into the kingdom of the Son he loves; in him we are redeemed, and find forgiveness of our sins. *(Col 1:13–14)*

OR: *Martin I—pope, martyr / 551 [2 Tm 2:8–13; 3:10–12/Jn 15:18–21]*

ENTRANCE ANTIPHON: This holy man fought to the death for the law of his God, never cowed by the threats of the wicked; his house was built on solid rock.

RESPONSE: Those who sow in tears, shall reap rejoicing. *(Ps 126:5)*

GOSPEL VERSE: We praise you, O God, we acclaim you as Lord; the white-robed army of martyrs praise you. *(See Te Deum)*

COMMUNION ANTIPHON: If anyone wishes to come after me, he must renounce himself, take up his cross, and follow me, says the Lord. *(Mt 16:24)*

Thursday, April 14, 2011: Fifth Week of Lent / 254 [Gn 17:3–9/Jn 8:51–59]

ENTRANCE ANTIPHON: Christ is the mediator of a new covenant so that since he has died, those who are called may receive the eternal inheritance promised to them. *(Heb 9:15)*

RESPONSE: The Lord remembers his covenant for ever. *(Ps 105:8a)*

GOSPEL VERSE: If today you hear his voice, harden not your hearts. *(Ps 95:8)*

COMMUNION ANTIPHON: God did not spare his own Son, but gave him up for us all: with Christ he will surely give us all things. *(Rom 8:32)*

Friday, April 15, 2011: Fifth Week of Lent / 255 [Jer 20:10–13/Jn 10:31–42]

ENTRANCE ANTIPHON: Have mercy on me, Lord, for I am in distress; rescue me from the hands of my enemies. Lord, keep me from shame, for I have called to you. *(Ps 30:10, 16, 18)*

RESPONSE: In my distress I called upon the Lord, and he heard my voice. *(See Ps 18:7)*

GOSPEL VERSE: Your words, Lord, are Spirit and life; you have the words of everlasting life. *(See Jn 6:63c, 68c)*

COMMUNION ANTIPHON: Jesus carried our sins in his own body on the cross so that we could die to sin and live in holiness; by his wounds we have been healed. *(1 Pt 2:24)*

Saturday, April 16, 2011: Fifth Week of Lent / 256 [Ez 37:21–28/Jn 11:45–56]

ENTRANCE ANTIPHON: Lord, do not stay away; come quickly to help me! I am a worm and no man: men scorn me, people despise me. *(Ps 21:20, 7)*

RESPONSE: The Lord will guard us, as a shepherd guards his flock. *(See Jer 31:10d)*

GOSPEL VERSE: Cast away from you all the crimes you have committed, says the Lord, and make for yourselves a new heart and a new spirit. *(Ez 18:31)*

COMMUNION ANTIPHON: Christ was sacrificed so that he could gather together the scattered children of God. *(Jn 11:52)*

Monday, April 18, 2011: Monday of Holy Week / 257 [Is 42:1–7/Jn 12:1–11]

ENTRANCE ANTIPHON: Defend me, Lord, from all my foes: take up your arms and come swiftly to my aid for you have the power to save me. *(Ps 34:1–2; 139:8)*

RESPONSE: The Lord is my light and my salvation. *(Ps 27:1a)*

GOSPEL VERSE: Hail to you, our King; you alone are compassionate with our faults.

COMMUNION ANTIPHON: When I am in trouble, Lord, do not hide your face from me; hear me when I call, and answer me quickly. *(Ps 101:3)*

Tuesday, April 19, 2011: Tuesday of Holy Week / 258 [Is 49:1–6/Jn 13:21–33, 36–38]

ENTRANCE ANTIPHON: False witnesses have stood up against me, and my enemies threaten violence; Lord, do not surrender me into their power! *(Ps 26:12)*

RESPONSE: I will sing of your salvation. *(See Ps 71:15ab)*

GOSPEL VERSE: Hail to you, our King, obedient to the Father; you were led to your crucifixion like a gentle lamb to the slaughter.

COMMUNION ANTIPHON: God did not spare his own Son, but gave him up for us all. *(Rom 8:32)*

Wednesday, April 20, 2011: Wednesday of Holy Week / 259 [Is 50:4–9a/Mt 26:14–25]

ENTRANCE ANTIPHON: At the name of Jesus every knee must bend, in heaven, on earth, and under the earth; Christ became obedient for us even to death, dying on the cross. Therefore, to the glory of God the Father: Jesus Christ is Lord. *(Phil 2:10, 8, 11)*

RESPONSE: Lord, in your great love, answer me. *(Ps 69:14c)*

GOSPEL VERSE: Hail to you, our King; you alone are compassionate with our errors.

Or: Hail to you, our King, obedient to the Father; you were led to your crucifixion like a gentle lamb to the slaughter.

COMMUNION ANTIPHON: The Son of Man did not come to be served, but to serve, and to give his life as a ransom for many. *(Mt 20:28)*

Thursday, April 21, 2011—Sunday, April 24, 2011: Easter Triduum

(See Sunday section)

Monday, April 25, 2011: Easter Monday / 261 [Acts 2:14, 22–33/ Mt 28:8–15]

ENTRANCE ANTIPHON: The Lord brought you to a land flowing with milk and honey, so that his law would always be given honor among you, alleluia. *(Ex 13:5, 9)*

RESPONSE: Keep me safe, O God; you are my hope. *(Ps 16:1) Or:* Alleluia.

GOSPEL VERSE: R/. Alleluia. This is the day the LORD has made; let us be glad and rejoice in it. R/. Alleluia. *(Ps 118:24)*

COMMUNION ANTIPHON: Christ now raised from the dead will never die again; death no longer has power over him, alleluia. *(Rom 6:9)*

Tuesday, April 26, 2011: Easter Tuesday / 262 [Acts 2:36–41/Jn 20:11–18]

ENTRANCE ANTIPHON: If men desire wisdom, she will give them the water of knowledge to drink. They will never waver from the truth; they will stand firm for ever, alleluia. *(Sir 15:3–4)*

RESPONSE: The earth is full of the goodness of the Lord. *(Ps 33:5b) Or:* Alleluia.

GOSPEL VERSE: R/. Alleluia. This is the day the LORD has made; let us be glad and rejoice in it. R/. Alleluia. *(Ps 118:24)*

COMMUNION ANTIPHON: If you have been raised with Christ, seek the things that are above, where Christ is seated at the right hand of God, alleluia. *(Col 3:1–2)*

Wednesday, April 27, 2011: Easter Wednesday / 263 [Acts 3:1–10/Lk 24:13–35]

ENTRANCE ANTIPHON: Come, you whom my Father has blessed; inherit the kingdom prepared for you since the foundation of the world, alleluia. *(Mt 25:34)*

RESPONSE: Rejoice, O hearts that seek the Lord. *(Ps 105:3b) Or:* Alleluia.

GOSPEL VERSE: R/. Alleluia. This is the day the LORD has made; let us be glad and rejoice in it. R/. Alleluia. *(Ps 118:24)*

COMMUNION ANTIPHON: The disciples recognized the Lord Jesus in the breaking of bread, alleluia. *(Lk 24:35)*

Thursday, April 28, 2011: Easter Thursday / 264 [Acts 3:11–26/Lk 24:35–48]

ENTRANCE ANTIPHON: Your people praised your great victory, O Lord. Wisdom opened the mouth that was dumb, and made the tongues of babies speak, alleluia. *(Wis 10:20–21)*

RESPONSE: O Lord, our God, how wonderful your name in all the earth! *(Ps 8:2ab) Or:* Alleluia.

GOSPEL VERSE: R/. Alleluia. This is the day the LORD has made; let us be glad and rejoice in it. R/. Alleluia. *(Ps 118:24)*

COMMUNION ANTIPHON: You are a people God claims as his own, to praise him who called you out of darkness into his marvelous light, alleluia. *(1 Pt 2:9)*

Friday, April 29, 2011: Easter Friday / 265 [Acts 4:1–12/Jn 21:1–14]

ENTRANCE ANTIPHON: The Lord led his people out of slavery. He drowned their enemies in the sea, alleluia. *(Ps 77:53)*

RESPONSE: The stone rejected by the builders has become the cornerstone. *(Ps 118:22) Or:* Alleluia.

GOSPEL VERSE: R/. Alleluia. This is the day the LORD has made; let us be glad and rejoice in it. R/. Alleluia. *(Ps 118:24)*

COMMUNION ANTIPHON: Jesus said to his disciples: Come and eat. And he took the bread, and gave it to them, alleluia. *(See Jn 21:12–13)*

Saturday, April 30, 2011: Easter Saturday / 266 [Acts 4:13–21/Mk 16:9–15]

ENTRANCE ANTIPHON: The Lord led his people to freedom and they shouted with joy and gladness, alleluia. *(Ps 104:43)*

RESPONSE: I will give thanks to you, for you have answered me. *(Ps 118:21a) Or:* Alleluia.

GOSPEL VERSE: R/. Alleluia. This is the day the LORD has made; let us be glad and rejoice in it. R/. Alleluia. *(Ps 118:24)*

COMMUNION ANTIPHON: All you who have been baptized have been clothed in Christ, alleluia. *(Gal 3:27)*

Monday, May 2, 2011: Athanasius— bishop, doctor of the Church / 560 [1 Jn 5:1–5/Mt 10:22–25]

ENTRANCE ANTIPHON: The Lord opened his mouth in the assembly, and filled him with the spirit of wisdom and understanding, and clothed him in a robe of glory, alleluia. *(Sir 15:5)*

RESPONSE: The mouth of the just murmurs wisdom. *(Ps 37:30a)*

GOSPEL VERSE: R/. Alleluia. Blessed are they who are persecuted for the sake of righteousness, for theirs is the Kingdom of heaven. R/. Alleluia. *(Mt 5:10)*

COMMUNION ANTIPHON: The Lord has put his faithful servant in charge of his household, to give them their share of bread at the proper time, alleluia. *(Lk 12:42)*

OR: **Second Week of Easter** / 267 [Acts 4:23–31/ Jn 3:1–8]

ENTRANCE ANTIPHON: Christ now raised from the dead will never die again; death no longer has power over him, alleluia. *(Rom 6:9)*

RESPONSE: Blessed are all who take refuge in the Lord. *(See Ps 2:11d) Or:* Alleluia.

GOSPEL VERSE: R/. Alleluia. If then you were raised with Christ, seek what is above, where Christ is seated at the right hand of God. R/. Alleluia. *(Col 3:1)*

COMMUNION ANTIPHON: Jesus came and stood among his disciples and said to them: Peace be with you, alleluia. *(Jn 20:19)*

Tuesday, May 3, 2011: Philip and James—apostles / 561 [1 Cor 15:1–8/Jn 14:6–14]

ENTRANCE ANTIPHON: The Lord chose these holy men for their unfeigned love, and gave them eternal glory, alleluia.

RESPONSE: Their message goes out through all the earth. *(Ps 19:5) Or:* Alleluia.

GOSPEL VERSE: R/. Alleluia. I am the way, the truth, and the life, says the Lord; Philip, whoever has seen me has seen the Father. R/. Alleluia. *(Jn 14:6b, 9c)*

COMMUNION ANTIPHON: Lord, let us see the Father, and we shall be content. And Jesus said: Philip, he who sees me, sees the Father, alleluia. *(Jn 14:8–9)*

Wednesday, May 4, 2011: Second Week of Easter / 269 [Acts 5:17–26/Jn 3:16–21]

ENTRANCE ANTIPHON: I will be a witness to you in the world, O Lord. I will spread the knowledge of your name among my brothers, alleluia. *(Ps 17:50; 21:23)*

RESPONSE: The Lord hears the cry of the poor. *(Ps 34:7a) Or:* Alleluia.

GOSPEL VERSE: R/. Alleluia. God so loved the world that he gave his only-begotten Son, so that everyone who believes in him might have eternal life. R/. Alleluia. *(Jn 3:16)*

COMMUNION ANTIPHON: The Lord says, I have chosen you from the world to go and bear fruit that will last, alleluia. *(See Jn 15:16, 19)*

Thursday, May 5, 2011: Second Week of Easter / 270 [Acts 5:27–33/Jn 3:31–36]

ENTRANCE ANTIPHON: When you walked at the head of your people, O God, and lived with them on their journey, the earth shook at your presence, and the skies poured forth their rain, alleluia. *(See Ps 67:8–9, 20)*

RESPONSE: The Lord hears the cry of the poor. *(Ps 34:7a) Or:* Alleluia.

GOSPEL VERSE: R/. Alleluia. You believe in me, Thomas, because you have seen me, says the Lord; blessed are those who have not seen, but still believe! R/. Alleluia. *(Jn 20:29)*

COMMUNION ANTIPHON: I, the Lord, am with you always, until the end of the world, alleluia. *(Mt 28:20)*

Friday, May 6, 2011: Second Week of Easter / 271 [Acts 5:34–42/Jn 6:1–15]

ENTRANCE ANTIPHON: By your blood, O Lord, you have redeemed us from every tribe and tongue, from every nation and people: you have made us into the kingdom of God, alleluia. *(Rv 5:9–10)*

RESPONSE: One thing I seek: to dwell in the house of the Lord. *(See Ps 27:4abc) Or:* Alleluia.

GOSPEL VERSE: R/. Alleluia. One does not live on bread alone, but on every word that comes forth from the mouth of God. R/. Alleluia. *(Mt 4:4b)*

COMMUNION ANTIPHON: Christ our Lord was put to death for our sins; and he rose again to make us worthy of life, alleluia. *(Romans 4:25)*

Saturday, May 7, 2011: Second Week of Easter / 272 [Acts 6:1–7/Jn 6:16–21]

ENTRANCE ANTIPHON: You are a people God claims as his own, to praise him who called you out of darkness into his marvelous light, alleluia. *(1 Pt 2:9)*

RESPONSE: Lord, let your mercy be on us as we place our trust in you. *(Ps 33:22) Or:* Alleluia.

GOSPEL VERSE: R/. Alleluia. Christ is risen, who made all things; he has shown mercy on all people. R/. Alleluia.

COMMUNION ANTIPHON: Father, I want the men you have given me to be with me where I am, so that they may see the glory you have given me, alleluia. *(Jn 17:24)*

Monday, May 9, 2011: Third Week of Easter / 273 [Acts 6:8–15/Jn 6:22–29]

ENTRANCE ANTIPHON: The Good Shepherd is risen! He who laid down his life for his sheep, who died for his flock, he is risen, alleluia.

RESPONSE: Blessed are they who follow the law of the Lord! *(Ps 119:1ab) Or:* Alleluia.

GOSPEL VERSE: R/. Alleluia. One does not live on bread alone but on every word that comes forth from the mouth of God. R/. Alleluia. *(Mt 4:4b)*

COMMUNION ANTIPHON: The Lord says, peace I leave with you, my own peace I give you; not as the world gives, do I give, alleluia. *(Jn 14:27)*

Tuesday, May 10, 2011: Third Week of Easter / 274 [Acts 7:51–8:1a/Jn 6:30–35]

ENTRANCE ANTIPHON: All you who fear God, both the great and the small, give praise to him! For his salvation and strength have come, the power of Christ, alleluia. *(Rv 19:5; 12:10)*

RESPONSE: Into your hands, O Lord, I commend my spirit. *(Ps 31:6a) Or:* Alleluia.

GOSPEL VERSE: R/. Alleluia. I am the bread of life, says the Lord; whoever comes to me will never hunger. R/. Alleluia. *(Jn 6:35ab)*

COMMUNION ANTIPHON: Because we have died with Christ, we believe that we shall also come to life with him, alleluia. *(Rom 6:8)*

OR: ***Damien Joseph de Veuster of Moloka'i—priest / 561A, 719–724 or 737–742***

ENTRANCE ANTIPHON: The Spirit of God is upon me; he has anointed me. He sent me to bring good news to the poor, and to heal the broken-hearted, alleluia. *(Lk 4:18)*

RESPONSE: Proclaim God's marvelous deeds to all the nations. *(Ps 96:3)*

GOSPEL VERSE: R/. Alleluia. The Lord sent me to bring glad tidings to the poor and to proclaim liberty to captives. R/. Alleluia. *(Lk 4:18)*

COMMUNION ANTIPHON: I, the Lord, am with you always, until the end of the world, alleluia. *(Mt 28:20)*

Wednesday, May 11, 2011: Third Week of Easter / 275 [Acts 8:1b–8/ Jn 6:35–40]

ENTRANCE ANTIPHON: Fill me with your praise and I will sing your glory; songs of joy will be on my lips, alleluia. *(Ps 70:8, 23)*

RESPONSE: Let all the earth cry out to God with joy. *(Ps 66:1) Or:* Alleluia.

GOSPEL VERSE: R/. Alleluia. Everyone who believes in the Son has eternal life, and I shall raise him on the last day, says the Lord. R/. Alleluia. *(See Jn 6:40)*

COMMUNION ANTIPHON: Christ has risen and shines upon us, whom he has redeemed by his blood, alleluia.

Thursday, May 12, 2011: Third Week of Easter / 276 [Acts 8:26–40/Jn 6:44–51]

ENTRANCE ANTIPHON: Let us sing to the Lord, he has covered himself in glory! The Lord is my strength, and I praise him: he is the Savior of my life, alleluia. *(Ex 15:1–2)*

RESPONSE: Let all the earth cry out to God with joy. *(Ps 66:1) Or:* Alleluia.

GOSPEL VERSE: R/. Alleluia. I am the living bread that came down from heaven, says the Lord; whoever eats this bread will live forever. R/. Alleluia. *(Jn 6:51)*

COMMUNION ANTIPHON: Christ died for all, so that living men should not live for themselves, but for Christ who died and was raised to life for them, alleluia. *(2 Cor 5:15)*

OR: Nereus and Achilleus—martyrs / 562 [Rv 7:9–17/Mt 10:17–22]

ENTRANCE ANTIPHON: Come, you whom my Father has blessed; inherit the kingdom prepared for you since the foundation of the world, alleluia. *(Mt 25:34)*

RESPONSE: Our soul has been rescued like a bird from the fowler's snare. *(Ps 124:7)*

GOSPEL VERSE: R/. Alleluia. Blessed are they who are persecuted for the sake of righteousness, for theirs is the Kingdom of heaven. R/. Alleluia. *(Mt 5:10)*

COMMUNION ANTIPHON: Those who are victorious I will feed from the tree of life, which grows in the paradise of my God, alleluia. *(Rv 2:7)*

OR: Pancras—martyr / 563 [Rv 19:1, 5–9a/Mt 11:25–30]

ENTRANCE ANTIPHON: Light for ever will shine on your saints, O Lord, alleluia. *(See 4 Ezr 2:35)*

RESPONSE: O bless the Lord, my soul! *(Ps 103:1)*

GOSPEL VERSE: R/. Alleluia. Blessed are you, Father, Lord of heaven and earth, you have revealed to little ones the mysteries of the Kingdom. R/. Alleluia. *(See Mt 11:25)*

COMMUNION ANTIPHON: I tell you solemnly: Unless a grain of wheat falls on the ground and dies, it remains a single grain; but if it dies, it yields a rich harvest, alleluia. *(Jn 12:24–25)*

Friday, May 13, 2011: Third Week of Easter / 277 [Acts 9:1–20/Jn 6:52–59]

ENTRANCE ANTIPHON: The Lamb who was slain is worthy to receive strength and divinity, wisdom and power and honor, alleluia. *(Rv 5:12)*

RESPONSE: Go out to all the world and tell the Good News. *(Mk 16:15) Or:* Alleluia.

GOSPEL VERSE: R/. Alleluia. Whoever eats my Flesh and drinks my Blood, remains in me and I in him, says the Lord. R/. Alleluia. *(Jn 6:56)*

COMMUNION ANTIPHON: The man who died on the cross has risen from the dead, and has won back our lives from death, alleluia.

OR: Our Lady of Fatima / 707–712 [Is 61:9–11/ Lk 11:27–28]

ENTRANCE ANTIPHON: Blessed are you, Virgin Mary, who carried the creator of all things in your womb; you gave birth to your maker, and remain for ever a virgin, alleluia.

RESPONSE: Listen to me, daughter; see and bend your ear. *(Ps 45:11)*

GOSPEL VERSE: R/. Alleluia. Blessed are you, holy Virgin Mary, and worthy of all praise. For the sun of justice, Christ our God, was born of you. R/. Alleluia.

COMMUNION ANTIPHON: The Almighty has done great things for me. Holy is his name, alleluia. *(Lk 1:49)*

COMMUNION ANTIPHON: Christ had to suffer and to rise from the dead, and so enter into his glory, alleluia. *(See Lk 24:46, 26)*

Saturday, May 14, 2011: Matthias—apostle / 564 [Acts 1:15–17, 20–26/Jn 15:9–17]

ENTRANCE ANTIPHON: You have not chosen me; I have chosen you. Go and bear fruit that will last, alleluia. *(Jn 15:16)*

RESPONSE: The Lord will give him a seat with the leaders of his people. *(Ps 113:8) Or:* Alleluia.

GOSPEL VERSE: R/. Alleluia. I chose you from the world, to go and bear fruit that will last, says the Lord. R/. Alleluia. *(See Jn 15:16)*

COMMUNION ANTIPHON: This is my commandment: love one another as I have loved you, alleluia. *(Jn 15:12)*

Monday, May 16, 2011: Fourth Week of Easter / 279 [Acts 11:1–18/Jn 10:11–18]

ENTRANCE ANTIPHON: Christ now raised from the dead will never die again; death no longer has power over him, alleluia. *(Rom 6:9)*

RESPONSE: Athirst is my soul for the living God. *(See Ps 42:3a) Or:* Alleluia.

GOSPEL VERSE: R/. Alleluia. I am the good shepherd, says the Lord; I know my sheep, and mine know me. R/. Alleluia. *(Jn 10:14)*

COMMUNION ANTIPHON: Jesus came and stood among his disciples and said to them: Peace be with you, alleluia. *(Jn 20:19)*

Tuesday, May 17, 2011: Fourth Week of Easter / 280 [Acts 11:19–26/Jn 10:22–30]

ENTRANCE ANTIPHON: Let us shout out our joy and happiness, and give glory to God, the Lord of all, because he is our King, alleluia. *(Rv 19:7, 6)*

RESPONSE: All you nations, praise the Lord. *(Ps 117:1a) Or:* Alleluia.

GOSPEL VERSE: R/. Alleluia. My sheep hear my voice, says the Lord; I know them, and they follow me. R/. Alleluia. *(Jn 10:27)*

Wednesday, May 18, 2011: Fourth Week of Easter / 281 [Acts 12:24–13:5a/Jn 12:44–50]

ENTRANCE ANTIPHON: I will be a witness to you in the world, O Lord. I will spread the knowledge of your name among my brothers, alleluia. *(Ps 17:50; 21:23)*

RESPONSE: O God, let all the nations praise you! *(Ps 67:4) Or:* Alleluia.

GOSPEL VERSE: R/. Alleluia. I am the light of the world, says the Lord; whoever follows me will have the light of life. R/. Alleluia. *(Jn 8:12)*

COMMUNION ANTIPHON: The Lord says, I have chosen you from the world to go and bear fruit that will last, alleluia. *(See Jn 15:16, 19)*

OR: *John I—pope, martyr / 565 [Rv 3:14b, 20–22/Lk 22:24–30]*

ENTRANCE ANTIPHON: The Lord chose him to be his high priest; he opened his treasures and made him rich in all goodness, alleluia.

RESPONSE: The Lord is my shepherd; there is nothing I shall want. *(Ps 23:1)*

GOSPEL VERSE: R/. Alleluia. I call you my friends, says the Lord, for I have made known to you all that the Father has told me. R/. Alleluia. *(Jn 15:15)*

COMMUNION ANTIPHON: The good shepherd gives his life for his sheep, alleluia. *(See Jn 10:11)*

Thursday, May 19, 2011: Fourth Week of Easter / 282 [Acts 13:13–25/Jn 13:16–20]

ENTRANCE ANTIPHON: When you walked at the head of your people, O God, and lived with them on their journey, the earth shook at your presence and the skies poured forth their rain, alleluia. *(See Ps 67:8–9, 20)*

RESPONSE: Forever I will sing the goodness of the Lord. *(Ps 89:2) Or:* Alleluia.

GOSPEL VERSE: R/. Alleluia. Jesus Christ, you are the faithful witness, the firstborn of the dead, you have loved us and freed us from our sins by your Blood. R/. Alleluia. *(See Rv 1:5ab)*

COMMUNION ANTIPHON: I, the Lord, am with you always, until the end of the world, alleluia. *(Mt 28:20)*

Friday, May 20, 2011: Fourth Week of Easter / 283 [Acts 13:26–33/Jn 14:1–6]

ENTRANCE ANTIPHON: By your blood, O Lord, you have redeemed us from every tribe and tongue, from every nation and people: you have made us into the kingdom of God, alleluia. *(Rv 5:9–10)*

RESPONSE: You are my Son; this day I have begotten you. *(Ps 2:7bc) Or:* Alleluia.

GOSPEL VERSE: R/. Alleluia. I am the way and the truth and the life, says the Lord; no one comes to the Father except through me. R/. Alleluia. *(Jn 14:6)*

COMMUNION ANTIPHON: Christ our Lord was put to death for our sins; and he rose again to make us worthy of life, alleluia. *(Rom 4:25)*

OR: Bernardine of Siena—priest / 566 [Acts 4:8–12/Lk 9:57–62]

ENTRANCE ANTIPHON: These are holy men who became God's friends and glorious heralds of his truth.

RESPONSE: Here am I, Lord; I come to do your will. *(Ps 40:8a, 9a) Or:* Alleluia.

GOSPEL VERSE: R/. Alleluia. I am the light of the world, says the Lord; whoever follows me will have the light of life. R/. Alleluia. *(Jn 8:12)*

COMMUNION ANTIPHON: I will feed my sheep, says the Lord, and give them repose. *(Ez 34:15)*

Saturday, May 21, 2011: Fourth Week of Easter / 284 [Acts 13:44–52/Jn 14:7–14]

ENTRANCE ANTIPHON: You are a people God claims as his own, to praise him who called you out of darkness into his marvelous light, alleluia. *(1 Pt 2:9)*

RESPONSE: All the ends of the earth have seen the saving power of God. *(Ps 98:3cd) Or:* Alleluia.

GOSPEL VERSE: R/. Alleluia. If you remain in my word, you will truly be my disciples, and you will know the truth, says the Lord. R/. Alleluia. *(Jn 8:31b–32)*

COMMUNION ANTIPHON: Father, I want the men you have given me to be with me where I am, so that they may see the glory you have given me, alleluia. *(Jn 17:24)*

OR: Christopher Magallanes—priest, martyr; and his companions—martyrs / [Rv 7:9–17/ Jn 12:24–26]

ENTRANCE ANTIPHON: These are the saints who were victorious in the blood of the Lamb, and in the face of death they did not cling to life; therefore they are reigning with Christ for ever, alleluia. *(Rv 12:11)*

RESPONSE: The Lord delivered me from all my fears. *(Ps 34:5)*

GOSPEL VERSE: R/. Alleluia. Blessed are they who are persecuted for the sake of righteousness, for theirs is the Kingdom of heaven. R/. Alleluia. *(Mt 5:10)*

COMMUNION ANTIPHON: If we die with Christ, we shall live with him, and if we are faithful to the end, we shall reign with him, alleluia. *(2 Tm 2:11–12)*

Monday, May 23, 2011: Fifth Week of Easter / 285 [Acts 14:5–18/Jn 14:21–26]

ENTRANCE ANTIPHON: The Good Shepherd is risen! He who laid down his life for his sheep, who died for his flock, he is risen, alleluia.

RESPONSE: Not to us, O Lord, but to your name give the glory. *(Ps 115:1ab) Or:* Alleluia.

GOSPEL VERSE: R/. Alleluia. The Holy Spirit will teach you everything and remind you of all I told you. R/. Alleluia. *(Jn 14:26)*

COMMUNION ANTIPHON: The Lord says, peace I leave with you, my own peace I give you; not as the world gives, do I give, alleluia. *(Jn 14:27)*

Tuesday, May 24, 2011: Fifth Week of Easter / 286 [Acts 14:19–28/Jn 14:27–31a]

ENTRANCE ANTIPHON: All you who fear God, both the great and the small, give praise to him! For his salvation and strength have come, the power of Christ, alleluia. *(Rv 19:5; 12:10)*

RESPONSE: Your friends make known, O Lord, the glorious splendor of your kingdom. *(See Ps 145:12) Or:* Alleluia.

GOSPEL VERSE: R/. Alleluia. Christ had to suffer and to rise from the dead, and so enter into his glory. R/. Alleluia. *(See Lk 24:46, 26)*

COMMUNION ANTIPHON: Because we have died with Christ, we believe that we shall also come to life with him, alleluia. *(Rom 6:8)*

Wednesday, May 25, 2011: Fifth Week of Easter / 287 [Acts 15:1–6/ Jn 15:1–8]

ENTRANCE ANTIPHON: Fill me with your praise and I will sing your glory; songs of joy will be on my lips, alleluia. *(Ps 70:8, 23)*

RESPONSE: Let us go rejoicing to the house of the Lord. *(See Ps 122:1) Or:* Alleluia.

GOSPEL VERSE: R/. Alleluia. Remain in me, as I remain in you, says the Lord; whoever remains in me will bear much fruit. R/. Alleluia. *(Jn 15:4a, 5b)*

COMMUNION ANTIPHON: Christ has risen and shines upon us, whom he has redeemed by his blood, alleluia.

OR: Bede the Venerable—priest, doctor of the Church / 567 [1 Cor 2:10b–16/Mt 7:21–29]

ENTRANCE ANTIPHON: The learned will shine like the brilliance of the firmament, and those who train many in the ways of justice will sparkle like the stars for all eternity, alleluia. *(Dn 12:13)*

RESPONSE: Lord, teach me your statutes. *(Ps 119:12)*

GOSPEL VERSE: R/. Alleluia. Your words, Lord, are Spirit and life; you have the words of everlasting life. R/. Alleluia. *(See Jn 6:63, 68c)*

COMMUNION ANTIPHON: We preach a Christ who was crucified; he is the power and the widsom of God, alleluia. *(1 Cor 1:23–24)*

OR: Gregory VII—pope / 568 [Acts 20:17–18a, 28–32, 36/Mt 16:13–19]

ENTRANCE ANTIPHON: The Lord sealed a covenant of peace with him, and made him a prince, bestowing the priestly dignity upon him for ever, alleluia. *(See Sir 45:30)*

RESPONSE: You are a priest for ever, in the line of Melchizedek *(Ps 110:4b)*

GOSPEL VERSE: R/. Alleluia. Come after me, says the Lord, and I will make you fishers of men. R/. Alleluia. *(Mk 1:17)*

COMMUNION ANTIPHON: Lord, you know all things: you know that I love you, alleluia. *(Jn 21:17)*

OR: Mary Magdalene de' Pazzi—virgin / 569 [1 Cor 7:25–35/ Mk 3:31–35]

ENTRANCE ANTIPHON: Come, bride of Christ, and receive the crown, which the Lord has prepared for you for ever, alleluia.

RESPONSE: Young men and women, praise the name of the Lord. *(Ps 148:12a, 13a) Or:* Alleluia.

GOSPEL VERSE: R/. Alleluia. If you remain in my word, you will truly be my disciples, and you will know the truth, says the Lord. R/. Alleluia. *(Jn 8:31b–32)*

COMMUNION ANTIPHON: The wise virgin chose the better part for herself, and it shall not be taken away from her, alleluia. *(See Lk 10:42)*

Thursday, May 26, 2011: Philip Neri—priest / 570 [Phil 4:4–9/Jn 17:20–26]

ENTRANCE ANTIPHON: The Lord is my inheritance and my cup; he alone will give me my reward. The measuring line has marked a lovely place for me; my inheritance is my great delight, alleluia. *(Ps 15:5–6)*

RESPONSE: I will bless the Lord at all times. *(Ps 34:2)*

Or: Taste and see the goodness of the Lord. *(Ps 34:9)*

GOSPEL VERSE: R/. Alleluia. Remain in my love, says the Lord; whoever remains in me and I in him will bear much fruit. R/. Alleluia. *(Jn 15:9b, 5b)*

COMMUNION ANTIPHON: I solemnly tell you: those who have left everything and followed me will be repaid a hundredfold and will gain eternal life, alleluia. *(See Mt 19:27–29)*

OR: Fifth Week of Easter / 288 [Acts 15:7–21/Jn 15:9–11]

ENTRANCE ANTIPHON: Let us sing to the Lord, he has covered himself in glory! The Lord is my strength, and I praise him: he is the Savior of my life, alleluia. *(Ex 15:1–20)*

RESPONSE: Proclaim God's marvelous deeds to all the nations. *(Ps 96:3) Or:* Alleluia.

GOSPEL VERSE: R/. Alleluia. My sheep hear my voice, says the Lord; I know them, and they follow me. R/. Alleluia. *(Jn 10:27)*

COMMUNION ANTIPHON: Christ died for all, so that living men should not live for themselves, but for Christ who died and was raised to life for them, alleluia. *(2 Cor 5:15)*

Friday, May 27, 2011: Fifth Week of Easter / 289 [Acts 15:22–31/Jn 15:12–17]

ENTRANCE ANTIPHON: The Lamb who was slain is worthy to receive strength and divinity, wisdom and power and honor, alleluia. *(Rv 5:12)*

RESPONSE: I will give you thanks among the peoples, O Lord. *(Ps 57:10a) Or:* Alleluia.

GOSPEL VERSE: R/. Alleluia. I call you my friends, says the Lord, for I have made known to you all that the Father has told me. R/. Alleluia. *(Jn 15:15b)*

COMMUNION ANTIPHON: The man who died on the cross has risen from the dead, and has won back our lives from death, alleluia.

OR: Augustine of Canterbury—bishop / 571 [1 Thes 2:2b–8/Mt 9:35–38]

ENTRANCE ANTIPHON: These are holy men who became God's friends and glorious heralds of his truth.

RESPONSE: Proclaim God's marvelous deeds to all the nations. *(Ps 96:3)*

GOSPEL VERSE: R/. Alleluia. I am the good shepherd, says the Lord; I know my sheep, and mine know me. R/. Alleluia. *(Jn 10:14)*

COMMUNION ANTIPHON: I will feed my sheep, says the Lord, and give them repose. *(Ez 34:15)*

Saturday, May 28, 2011: Fifth Week of Easter / 290 [Acts 16:1–10/Jn 15:18–21]

ENTRANCE ANTIPHON: In baptism we have died with Christ, and we have risen to new life in him, because we believed in the power of God who raised him from the dead, alleluia. *(Col 2:12)*

RESPONSE: Let all the earth cry out to God with joy. *(Ps 100:2a) Or:* Alleluia.

GOSPEL VERSE: R/. Alleluia. If then you were raised with Christ, seek what is above, where Christ is seated at the right hand of God. R/. Alleluia. *(Col 3:1)*

COMMUNION ANTIPHON: Father, I pray for them: may they be one in us, so that the world may believe it was you who sent me, alleluia. *(Jn 17: 20–21)*

Monday, May 30, 2011: Sixth Week of Easter / 291 [Acts 16:11–15/Jn 15:26–16:4a]

ENTRANCE ANTIPHON: Christ now raised from the dead will never die again; death no longer has power over him, alleluia. *(Rom 6:9)*

RESPONSE: The Lord takes delight in his people. *(See Ps 149:4a) Or:* Alleluia.

GOSPEL VERSE: R/. Alleluia. The Spirit of truth will testify to me, says the Lord, and you also will testify. R/. Alleluia. *(Jn 15:26b, 27a)*

COMMUNION ANTIPHON: Jesus came and stood among his disciples and said to them: Peace be with you, alleluia. *(Jn 20:19)*

Tuesday, May 31, 2011: Visitation of the Blessed Virgin Mary / 572 [Zep 3:14–18a or Rom 12:9–16b/Lk 1:39–56]

ENTRANCE ANTIPHON: Come, all you who fear God, and hear the great things the Lord has done for me, alleluia. *(Ps 65:16)*

RESPONSE: Among you is the great and holy one of Israel. *(Is 12:6)*

GOSPEL VERSE: R/. Alleluia. Blessed are you, O Virgin Mary, who believed that what was spoken to you by the Lord would be fulfilled. R/. Alleluia. *(See Lk 1:45)*

COMMUNION ANTIPHON: All generations will call me blessed, for the Almighty has done great things for me. Holy is his name, alleluia. *(Lk 1:48–49)*

Wednesday, June 1, 2011: Justin—martyr / 574 [1 Cor 1:18–25/Mt 5:13–19]

ENTRANCE ANTIPHON: The wicked tempted me with their fables against your law, but I proclaimed your decrees before kings without fear or shame, alleluia. *(See Ps 118:85, 46)*

RESPONSE: The Lord delivered me from all my fears. *(Ps 34:5)*

GOSPEL VERSE: R/. Alleluia. Let your light shine before others, that they may see your good deeds and glorify your heavenly Father. R/. Alleluia. *(Mt 5:16)*

COMMUNION ANTIPHON: I resolved that while I was with you I would think of nothing but Jesus Christ and him crucified, alleluia. *(1 Cor 2:2)*

OR: **Sixth Week of Easter** / 293 [Acts 17:15, 22–18:1/Jn 16:12–15]

ENTRANCE ANTIPHON: I will be a witness to you in the world, O Lord. I will spread the knowledge of your name among my brothers, alleluia. *(Ps 17:50; 21:23)*

RESPONSE: Heaven and earth are full of your glory. *Or:* Alleluia.

GOSPEL VERSE: R/. Alleluia. I will ask the Father and he will give you another Advocate to be with you always. R/. Alleluia. *(Jn 14:16)*

COMMUNION ANTIPHON: The Lord says, I have chosen you from the world to go and bear fruit that will last, alleluia. *(See Jn 15:16, 19)*

Thursday, June 2, 2011: Sixth Week of Easter / 294 [Acts 18:1–8/Jn 16:16–20]

(The following texts are used in locales where the celebration of the Ascension is transferred to the Seventh Sunday of Easter. For Ascension texts, see the Sunday section.)

ENTRANCE ANTIPHON: When you walked at the head of your people, O God, and lived with them on their journey, the earth shook at your presence, and the skies poured forth their rain, alleluia. *(See Ps 67:8–9, 20)*

RESPONSE: The Lord has revealed to the nations his saving power. *(See Ps 98:2b) Or:* Alleluia.

GOSPEL VERSE: R/. Alleluia. I will not leave you orphans, says the Lord; I will come back to you, and your hearts will rejoice. R/. Alleluia. *(See Jn 14:18)*

COMMUNION ANTIPHON: I, the Lord, am with you always, until the end of the world, alleluia. *(Mt 28:20)*

OR: ***Marcellinus and Peter**—martyrs / 595 [2 Cor 6:4–10/Jn17:11b–19]*

ENTRANCE ANTIPHON: The salvation of the just comes from the Lord. He is their strength in time of need. *(Ps 36:39)*

RESPONSE: Our soul has been rescued like a bird from the fowler's snare. *(Psa 124:7)*

GOSPEL VERSE: R/. Alleluia. Blessed be the Father of compassion and the God of all encouragement, who encourages us in every affliction. R/. Alleluia. *(2 Cor 1:3b–4a)*

COMMUNION ANTIPHON: Whoever loses his life for my sake and the gospel, says the Lord, will save it. *(Mk 8:35)*

Friday, June 3, 2011: Charles Lwanga and his companions—martyrs / 576 [2 Mc 7:1–2, 9–14/Mt 5:1–12a]

ENTRANCE ANTIPHON: Come, you whom my Father has blessed; inherit the kingdom prepared for you since the foundation of the world, alleluia. *(Mt 25:34)*

RESPONSE: Our soul has been rescued like a bird from the fowler's snare. *(Ps 124:7)*

GOSPEL VERSE: R/. Alleluia. Blessed are the poor in spirit; for theirs is the Kingdom of heaven. R/. Alleluia. *(Mt 5:3)*

COMMUNION ANTIPHON: Those who are victorious I will feed from the tree of life, which grows in the paradise of my God, alleluia. *(Rv 2:7)*

OR: **Sixth Week of Easter** / 295 [Acts 18:9–18/Jn 16:20–23]

ENTRANCE ANTIPHON: By your blood, O Lord, you have redeemed us from every tribe and tongue, from every nation and people: you have made us into the kingdom of God, alleluia. *(See Rv 5:9–10)*

RESPONSE: God is king of all the earth. *(Ps 47:8a) Or:* Alelluia.

GOSPEL VERSE: R/. Alleluia. Christ had to suffer and to rise from the dead, and so enter into his glory. R/. Alleluia. *(See Lk 24:46, 26)*

COMMUNION ANTIPHON: Christ our Lord was put to death for our sins; and he rose again to make us worthy of life, alleluia. *(Rom 4:25)*

Saturday, June 4, 2011: Sixth Week of Easter / 296 [Acts 18:23–28/Jn 16:23b–28]

ENTRANCE ANTIPHON: You are a people God claims as his own, to praise him who called you out of darkness into his marvelous light, alleluia. *(1 Pt 2:9)*

RESPONSE: God is king of all the earth. *(Ps 47:8a) Or:* Alleluia.

GOSPEL VERSE: R/. Alleluia. I came from the Father and have come into the world; now I am leaving the world and going back to the Father. R/. Alleluia. *(Jn 16:28)*

COMMUNION ANTIPHON: Father, I want the men you have given me to be with me where I am, so that they may see the glory you have given me, alleluia. *(Jn 17:24)*

Monday, June 6, 2011: Seventh Week of Easter / 297 [Acts 19:1–8/Jn 16:29–33]

ENTRANCE ANTIPHON: You will receive power when the Holy Spirit comes upon you. You will be my witnesses to all the world, alleluia. *(Acts 1:8)*

RESPONSE: Sing to God, O kingdoms of the earth. *(Ps 68:33a) Or:* Alleluia.

GOSPEL VERSE: R/. Alleluia. If then you were raised with Christ, seek what is above, where Christ is seated at the right hand of God. R/. Alleluia. *(Col 3:1)*

COMMUNION ANTIPHON: The Lord said: I will not leave you orphans. I will come back to you, and your hearts will rejoice, alleluia. *(Jn 14:18; 16:22)*

OR: Norbert—bishop / 578 [Ez 34:11–16/Lk 14:25–33]

ENTRANCE ANTIPHON: The Lord is my inheritance and my cup; he alone will give me my reward. The measuring line has marked a lovely place for me; my inheritance is my great delight, alleluia. *(Ps 15:5–6)*

RESPONSE: The Lord is my shepherd; there is nothing I shall want *(Ps 23:1)*

GOSPEL VERSE: R/. Alleluia. Blessed are the poor in spirit; for theirs is the Kingdom of heaven. R/. Alleluia. *(Mt 5:3)*

COMMUNION ANTIPHON: I solemnly tell you: those who have left everything and followed me will be repaid a hundredfold and will gain eternal life, alleluia. *(See Mt 19:27–29)*

Tuesday, June 7, 2011: Seventh Week of Easter / 298 [Acts 20:17–27/Jn 17:1–11a]

ENTRANCE ANTIPHON: I am the beginning and the end of all things. I have met death, but I am alive, and I shall live for eternity, alleluia. *(Rv 1:17–18)*

RESPONSE: Sing to God, O kingdoms of the earth. *(Ps 68:33a) Or:* Alleluia.

GOSPEL VERSE: R/. Alleluia. I will ask the Father and he will give you another Advocate to be with you always. R/. Alleluia. *(Jn 14:16)*

COMMUNION ANTIPHON: The Lord says, the Holy Spirit whom the Father will send in my name will teach you all things, and remind you of all I have said to you, alleluia. *(Jn 14:26)*

Wednesday, June 8, 2011: Seventh Week of Easter / 299 [Acts 20:28–38/Jn 17:11b–19]

ENTRANCE ANTIPHON: All nations, clap your hands. Shout with a voice of joy to God, alleluia. *(Ps 46:2)*

RESPONSE: Sing to God, O kingdoms of the earth. *(Ps 68:33a) Or:* Alleluia.

GOSPEL VERSE: R/. Alleluia. Your word, O Lord, is truth; consecrate us in the truth. R/. Alleluia. *(See Jn 17:17b, 17a)*

COMMUNION ANTIPHON: The Lord says: When the Holy Spirit comes to you, the Spirit whom I shall send, the Spirit of truth who proceeds from the Father, he will bear witness to me, and you also will be my witnesses, alleluia. *(Jn 15:26–27)*

Thursday, June 9, 2011: Seventh Week of Easter / 300 [Acts 22:30, 23:6–11/Jn 17:20–26]

ENTRANCE ANTIPHON: Let us come to God's presence with confidence, because we will find mercy, and strength when we need it, alleluia. *(Heb 4:16)*

RESPONSE: Keep me safe, O God; you are my hope. *(Ps 16:1) Or:* Alleluia.

GOSPEL VERSE: R/. Alleluia. May they all be one as you, Father, are in me and I in you, that the world may believe that you sent me, says the Lord. R/. Alleluia. *(See Jn 17:21)*

COMMUNION ANTIPHON: This is the word of Jesus: It is best for me to leave you; because if I do not go, the Spirit will not come to you, alleluia. *(Jn 16:7)*

OR: Ephrem—deacon, doctor of the Church / 579 [Col 3:12–17/Lk 6:43–45]

ENTRANCE ANTIPHON: The learned will shine like the brilliance of the firmament, and those who train many in the ways of justice will sparkle like the stars for all eternity, alleluia. *(Dn 12:3)*

RESPONSE: The mouth of the just murmurs wisdom. *(Ps 37:30a)*

GOSPEL VERSE: R/. Alleluia. I am the vine, you are the branches, says the Lord: whoever remains in me and I in him will bear much fruit. R/. Alleluia. *(Jn 15:5)*

COMMUNION ANTIPHON: We preach a Christ who was crucified; he is the power and the wisdom of God, alleluia. *(1 Cor 1:23–24)*

Friday, June 10, 2011: Seventh Week of Easter / 301 [Acts 25:13b–21/Jn 21:15–19]

ENTRANCE ANTIPHON: Christ loved us and has washed away our sins with his blood, and has made us a kingdom of priests to serve his God and Father, alleluia. *(Rv 1:5–6)*

RESPONSE: The Lord has established his throne in heaven. *(Ps 103:19a) Or:* Alleluia.

GOSPEL VERSE: R/. Alleluia. The Holy Spirit will teach you everything and remind you of all I told you. R/. Alleluia. *(Jn 14:26)*

COMMUNION ANTIPHON: When the Spirit of truth comes, says the Lord, he will lead you to the whole truth, alleluia. *(Jn 16:13)*

Saturday, June 11, 2011: Barnabas— apostle / 580 [Acts 11:21b–26, 13:1–3/Mt 10:7–13]

(Morning Mass)

ENTRANCE ANTIPHON: Blessed are you, St. Barnabas: you were a man of faith filled with the Holy Spirit and counted among the apostles, alleluia. *(See Acts 11:24)*

RESPONSE: The Lord has revealed to the nations his saving power. *(See Ps 98:2b)*

GOSPEL VERSE: R/. Alleluia. Go and teach all nations, says the Lord; I am with you always, until the end of the world. R/. Alleluia. *(Mt 28:19a, 20b)*

COMMUNION ANTIPHON: No longer shall I call you servants, for a servant knows not what his master does. Now I call you friends, for I have revealed to you all that I have heard from my Father, alleluia. *(Jn 15:15)*

OR: **Seventh Week of Easter / 302** [Acts 11:21b–26, 13:1–3/Jn 21:20–25]

ENTRANCE ANTIPHON: The disciples were constantly at prayer together, with Mary the mother of Jesus, the other women, and the brothers of Jesus, alleluia. *(Acts 1:14)*

RESPONSE: The Lord has revealed to the nations his saving power. *(See Ps 98:2b)*

GOSPEL VERSE: R/. Alleluia. I will send you the Spirit of truth, says the Lord; he will guide you to all truth. R/. Alleluia. *(Jn 16:7,13)*

COMMUNION ANTIPHON: The Lord says: The Holy Spirit will give glory to me, because he takes my words from me and will hand them on to you, alleluia. *(Jn 16:14)*

Monday, June 13, 2011: Anthony of Padua—priest, doctor of the Church / 581 [Is 61:1–3d/Lk 10:1–9]

ENTRANCE ANTIPHON: I will give you shepherds after my own heart, and they shall feed you on knowledge and sound teaching. *(Jer 3:15)*

RESPONSE: For ever I will sing the goodness of the Lord. *(Ps 89:2)*

GOSPEL VERSE: R/. Alleluia. The Lord sent me to bring glad tidings to the poor and to proclaim liberty to captives. R/. Alleluia. *(Lk 4:18)*

COMMUNION ANTIPHON: The Son of Man did not come to be served, but to serve, and to give his life as a ransom for many. *(Mt 20:28)*

OR: **Eleventh Week in Ordinary Time / 365** [2 Cor 6:1–10/Mt 5:38–42]

ENTRANCE ANTIPHON: Lord, hear my voice when I call to you. You are my help; do not cast me off, do not desert me, my Savior God. *(Ps 26:7, 9)*

RESPONSE: The Lord has made known his salvation. *(Ps 98:2a)*

GOSPEL VERSE: R/. Alleluia. A lamp to my feet is your word, a light to my path. R/. Alleluia. *(Ps 119:105)*

COMMUNION ANTIPHON: One thing I seek: to dwell in the house of the Lord all the days of my life. *(Ps 26:4)*

Tuesday, June 14, 2011: Eleventh Week in Ordinary Time / 366 [2 Cor 8:1–9/Mt 5:43–48]

ENTRANCE ANTIPHON: Lord, hear my voice when I call to you. You are my help; do not cast me off, do not desert me, my Savior God. *(Ps 26:7, 9)*

RESPONSE: Praise the Lord, my soul! *(Ps 146:1b) Or:* Alleluia.

GOSPEL VERSE: R/. Alleluia. I give you a new commandment: love one another as I have loved you. R/. Alleluia. *(Jn 13:34)*

COMMUNION ANTIPHON: One thing I seek: to dwell in the house of the Lord all the days of my life. *(Ps 26:4)*

Wednesday, June 15, 2011: Eleventh Week in Ordinary Time / 367 [2 Cor 9:6–11/Mt 6:1–6, 16–18]

ENTRANCE ANTIPHON: Lord, hear my voice when I call to you. You are my help; do not cast me off, do not desert me, my Savior God. *(Ps 26:7, 9)*

RESPONSE: Blessed the man who fears the Lord. *(Ps 112:1b) Or:* Alleluia.

GOSPEL VERSE: R/. Alleluia. Whoever loves me will keep my word, and my Father will love him and we will come to him. R/. Alleluia. *(Jn 14:23)*

COMMUNION ANTIPHON: One thing I seek: to dwell in the house of the Lord all the days of my life. *(Ps 26:4)*

Thursday, June 16, 2011: Eleventh Week in Ordinary Time / 368 [2 Cor 11:1–11/Mt 6:7–15]

ENTRANCE ANTIPHON: Lord, hear my voice when I call to you. You are my help; do not cast me off, do not desert me, my Savior God. *(Ps 26:7, 9)*

RESPONSE: Your works, O Lord, are justice and truth. *(Ps 111:7a) Or:* Alleluia.

GOSPEL VERSE: R/. Alleluia. You have received a spirit of adoption as sons through which we cry: Abba! Father! R/. Alleluia. *(Rom 8:15bc)*

COMMUNION ANTIPHON: One thing I seek: to dwell in the house of the Lord all the days of my life. *(Ps 26:4)*

Friday, June 17, 2011: Eleventh Week in Ordinary Time / 369 [2 Cor 11:18, 21–30/Mt 6:19–23]

ENTRANCE ANTIPHON: Lord, hear my voice when I call to you. You are my help; do not cast me off, do not desert me, my Savior God. *(Ps 26:7, 9)*

RESPONSE: From all their distress God rescues the just. *(See Ps 34:18b*

GOSPEL VERSE: R/. Alleluia. Blessed are the poor in spirit; for theirs is the Kingdom of heaven. R/. Alleluia. *(Mt 5:3)*

COMMUNION ANTIPHON: One thing I seek: to dwell in the house of the Lord all the days of my life. *(Ps 26:4)*

Saturday, June 18, 2011: Eleventh Week in Ordinary Time / 370 [2 Cor 12:1–10/Mt 6:24–34]

ENTRANCE ANTIPHON: Lord, hear my voice when I call to you. You are my help; do not cast me off, do not desert me, my Savior God. *(Ps 26:7, 9)*

RESPONSE: Taste and see the goodness of the Lord. *(Ps 34:9a)*

GOSPEL VERSE: R/. Alleluia. Jesus Christ became poor although he was rich, so that by his poverty you might become rich. R/. Alleluia. *(2 Cor 8:9)*

COMMUNION ANTIPHON: One thing I seek: to dwell in the house of the Lord all the days of my life. *(Ps 26:4)*

OR: *Blessed Virgin Mary* / 707–712

ENTRANCE ANTIPHON: You have been blessed, O Virgin Mary, above all other women on earth by the Lord the most high God; he has so exalted your name that your praises shall never fade from the mouths of men. *(See Jdt 13:23, 25)*

RESPONSE: My heart exults in the Lord, my Savior. *(See 1 Sm 2:1b)*

GOSPEL VERSE: R/. Alleluia. Blessed are you, holy Virgin Mary, deserving of all praise; from you rose the sun of justice, Christ our God. R/. Alleluia.

COMMUNION ANTIPHON: All generations will call me blessed, because God has looked upon his lowly handmaid. *(See Lk 1:48)*

Monday, June 20, 2011: Twelfth Week in Ordinary Time / 371 [Gn 12:1–9/Mt 7:1–5]

ENTRANCE ANTIPHON: God is the strength of his people. In him, we his chosen live in safety. Save us, Lord, who share in your life, and give us your blessing; be our shepherd for ever. *(Ps 27:8–9)*

RESPONSE: Blessed the people the Lord has chosen to be his own. *(Ps 33:12)*

GOSPEL VERSE: R/. Alleluia. The word of God is living and effective, able to discern reflections and thoughts of the heart. R/. Alleluia. *(Heb 4:12)*

COMMUNION ANTIPHON: The eyes of all look to you, O Lord, and you give them food in due season. *(Ps 144:15)*

Tuesday, June 21, 2011: Aloysius Gonzaga—religious / 583 [1 Jn 5:1–5/Mt 22:34–40]

ENTRANCE ANTIPHON: Who shall climb the mountain of the Lord and stand in his holy place? The innocent man, the pure of heart! *(See Ps 23:4, 3)*

RESPONSE: You are my inheritance, O Lord. *(See Ps 16:5a)*

GOSPEL VERSE: R/. Alleluia. I give you a new commandment: love one another as I have loved you. R/. Alleluia. *(Jn 13:34)*

COMMUNION ANTIPHON: God gave them bread from heaven; men ate the bread of angels. *(Ps 77:24–25)*

OR: **Twelfth Week in Ordinary Time** / 372 [Gn 13:2, 5–18/Mt 7:6, 12–14]

ENTRANCE ANTIPHON: God is the strength of his people. In him, we his chosen live in safety. Save us, Lord, who share in your life, and give us your blessing; be our shepherd for ever. *(Ps 27:8–9)*

RESPONSE: He who does justice will live in the presence of the Lord. *(Ps 15:1b)*

GOSPEL VERSE: R/. Alleluia. I am the light of the world, says the Lord; whoever follows me will have the light of life. R/. Alleluia. *(Jn 8:12)*

COMMUNION ANTIPHON: The eyes of all look to you, O Lord, and you give them food in due season. *(Ps 144:15)*

Wednesday, June 22, 2011: Twelfth Week in Ordinary Time / 373 [Gn 15:1–12, 17–18/Mt 7:15–20]

ENTRANCE ANTIPHON: God is the strength of his people. In him, we his chosen live in safety. Save us, Lord, who share in your life, and give us your blessing; be our shepherd for ever. *(Ps 27:8–9)*

RESPONSE: The Lord remembers his covenant for ever. *(Ps 105:8a) Or:* Alleluia.

GOSPEL VERSE: R/. Alleluia. Remain in me as I remain in you, says the Lord; whoever remains in me will bear much fruit. R/. Alleluia. *(Jn 15:4a, 5b)*

COMMUNION ANTIPHON: The eyes of all look to you, O Lord, and you give them food in due season. *(Ps 144:15)*

OR: **Paulinus of Nola**—bishop / 584 [2 Cor 8:9–15/Lk 12:32–34]

ENTRANCE ANTIPHON: I will raise up for myself a faithful priest; he will do what is in my heart and in my mind, says the Lord. *(1 Sm 2:35)*

RESPONSE: Here I am, Lord; I come to do your will. *(Ps 40:8a, 9a)*

GOSPEL VERSE: R/. Alleluia. Blessed are the poor in spirit; the Kingdom of heaven is theirs! R/. Alleluia. *(Mt 5:3)*

COMMUNION ANTIPHON: I came that men may have life, and have it to the full, says the Lord. *(Jn 10:10)*

OR: **John Fisher**—bishop, martyr; and Thomas More—martyr / 585 [1 Pt 4:12–19/Mt 10:34–39]

ENTRANCE ANTIPHON: The salvation of the just comes from the Lord. He is their strength in time of need. *(Ps 36:39)*

RESPONSE: Those who sow in tears shall reap rejoicing. *(Ps 126:5)*

GOSPEL VERSE: R/. Alleluia. Blessed are they who are persecuted for the sake of righteousness, for theirs is the Kingdom of heaven. R/. Alleluia. *(Mt 5:10)*

COMMUNION ANTIPHON: Whoever loses his life for my sake and the gospel, says the Lord, will save it. *(Mk 8:35)*

Thursday, June 23, 2011: Twelfth Week in Ordinary Time / 374 [Gn 16:1–12, 15–16 or Gn 16:6b–12, 15–16/Mt 7:21–29]

(Morning Mass)

ENTRANCE ANTIPHON: God is the strength of his people. In him, we his chosen live in safety. Save us, Lord, who share in your life, and give us your blessing; be our shepherd for ever. *(Ps 27:8–9)*

RESPONSE: Give thanks to the Lord for he is good. *(Ps 106:1b) Or:* Alleluia.

GOSPEL VERSE: R/. Alleluia. Whoever loves me will keep my word, and my Father will love him and we will come to him. R/. Alleluia. *(Jn 14:23)*

COMMUNION ANTIPHON: The eyes of all look to you, O Lord, and you give them food in due season. *(Ps 144:15)*

Nativity of Saint John the Baptist—
Vigil / 586 [Jer 1:4–10/1 Pt 1:8–12/Lk 1:5–17]

(Evening Mass)

ENTRANCE ANTIPHON: From his mother's womb, he will be filled with the Holy Spirit, he will be great in the sight of the Lord, and many will rejoice at his birth. *(Lk 1:15, 14)*

RESPONSE: Since my mother's womb, you have been my strength. *(Ps 71:6)*

GOSPEL VERSE: R/. Alleluia. He came to testify to the light, to prepare a people fit for the Lord. R/. Alleluia. *(See Jn 1:7; Lk 1:17)*

COMMUNION ANTIPHON: Blessed be the Lord God of Israel, for he has visited and redeemed his people. *(Lk 1:68)*

Friday, June 24, 2011: Nativity of Saint John the Baptist / 587 [Is 49:1–6/Acts 13:22–26/Lk 1:57–66, 80]

ENTRANCE ANTIPHON: There was a man sent from God whose name was John. He came to bear witness to the light, to prepare an upright people for the Lord. *(Jn 1:6–7; Lk 1:17)*

RESPONSE: I praise you, for I am wonderfully made. *(Ps 139:14)*

GOSPEL VERSE: R/. Alleluia. You, child, will be called the prophet of the Most High, for you will go before the Lord to prepare his way. R/. Alleluia. *(See Lk 1:76)*

COMMUNION ANTIPHON: Through the tender compassion of our God, the dawn from on high shall break upon us. *(Lk 1:78)*

Saturday, June 25, 2011: Twelfth Week in Ordinary Time / 376 [Gn 18:1–15/Mt 8:5–17]

ENTRANCE ANTIPHON: God is the strength of his people. In him, we his chosen live in safety. Save us, Lord, who share in your life, and give us your blessing; be our shepherd for ever. *(Ps 27:8–9)*

RESPONSE: The Lord has remembered his mercy *(See Lk 1:54b)*

GOSPEL VERSE: R/. Alleluia. Christ took away our infirmities and bore our diseases. R/. Alleluia. *(Mt 8:17)*

COMMUNION ANTIPHON: The eyes of all look to you, O Lord, and you give them food in due season. *(Ps 144:15)*

OR: ***Blessed Virgin Mary*** */ 707–712*

ENTRANCE ANTIPHON: You have been blessed, O Virgin Mary, above all other women on earth by the Lord the most high God; he has so exalted your name that your praises shall never fade from the mouths of men. *(See Jdt 13:23, 25)*

RESPONSE: You are the highest honor of our race. *(Jdt 15:9d)*

GOSPEL VERSE: R/. Alleluia. Blessed are you, holy Virgin Mary, deserving of all praise; from you rose the sun of justice, Christ our God. R/. Alleluia.

COMMUNION ANTIPHON: All generations will call me blessed, because God has looked upon his lowly handmaid. *(See Lk 1:48)*

Monday, June 27, 2011: Thirteenth Week in Ordinary Time / 377 [Gn 18:16–33/Mt 8:18–22]

ENTRANCE ANTIPHON: All nations, clap your hands. Shout with a voice of joy to God. *(Ps 46:2)*

RESPONSE: The Lord is kind and merciful. *(Ps 103:8a)*

GOSPEL VERSE: R/. Alleluia. If today you hear his voice, harden not your hearts. R/. Alleluia. *(Ps 95:8)*

COMMUNION ANTIPHON: O, bless the Lord, my soul, and all that is within me bless his holy name. *(Ps 102:1)*

OR: ***Cyril of Alexandria****—bishop, doctor of the Church / 588 [2 Tm 4:1–5/Mt 5:13–19]*

ENTRANCE ANTIPHON: The Lord opened his mouth in the assembly, and filled him with the spirit of wisdom and understanding, and clothed him in a robe of glory. *(Sir 15:5)*

RESPONSE: For ever I will sing the goodness of the Lord. *(Ps 89:2)*

GOSPEL VERSE: R/. Alleluia. Let your light shine before others that they may see your good deeds and glorify your heavenly Father. R/. Alleluia. *(Mt 5:16)*

COMMUNION ANTIPHON: The Lord has put his faithful servant in charge of his household, to give them their share of bread at the proper time. *(Lk 12:42)*

Tuesday, June 28, 2011: Irenaeus—bishop, martyr / 589 [2 Tm 2:22b–26/Jn 17:20–26]

(Morning Mass)

ENTRANCE ANTIPHON: I will raise up for myself a faithful priest; he will do what is in my heart and in my mind, says the Lord. *(1 Sm 2:35)*

RESPONSE: The mouth of the just murmurs wisdom. *(Ps 37:30a)*

GOSPEL VERSE: R/. Alleluia. Remain in my love, says the Lord; whoever remains in me and I in him will bear much fruit. R/. Alleluia. *(Jn 15:19b, 5b)*

COMMUNION ANTIPHON: I came that men may have life, and have it to the full, says the Lord. *(Jn 10:10)*

OR: **Thirteenth Week in Ordinary Time** / 378 [Gn 19:15–29/Mt 8:23–27]

ENTRANCE ANTIPHON: All nations, clap your hands. Shout with a voice of joy to God. *(Ps 46:2)*

RESPONSE: O Lord, your mercy is before my eyes. *(Ps 26:3a)*

GOSPEL VERSE: R/. Alleluia. I trust in the LORD; my soul trusts in his word. R/. Alleluia. *(Ps 130:5)*

COMMUNION ANTIPHON: O, bless the Lord, my soul, and all that is within me bless his holy name. *(Ps 102:1)*

Peter and Paul—apostles; Vigil / 590 [Acts 3:1–10/Gal 1:11–20/Jn 21: 15–19]

(Evening Mass)

ENTRANCE ANTIPHON: Peter the apostle and Paul the teacher of the Gentiles have brought us to know the law of the Lord.

RESPONSE: Their message goes out through all the earth. *(Ps 19:5)*

GOSPEL VERSE: R/. Alleluia. Lord, you know everything: you know that I love you. R/. Alleluia. *(Jn 21:17)*

COMMUNION ANTIPHON: Simon, son of John, do you love me more than these? Lord, you know all things; you know that I love you. *(Jn 21:15, 17)*

Wednesday, June 29, 2011: Peter and Paul—apostles / 591 [Acts 12:1–11/2 Tm 4:6–8, 17–18/Mt 16:13–19]

ENTRANCE ANTIPHON: These men, conquering all human frailty, shed their blood and helped the Church to grow. By sharing the cup of the Lord's suffering, they became the friends of God.

RESPONSE: The angel of the Lord will rescue those who fear him. *(Ps 34:5)*

GOSPEL VERSE: R/. Alleluia. You are Peter, and upon this rock I will build my Church, and the gates of the netherworld shall not prevail against it. R/. Alleluia. *(Mt 16:18)*

COMMUNION ANTIPHON: Peter said: You are the Christ, the Son of the living God. Jesus answered: You are Peter, the rock on which I will build my Church. *(Mt 16:16, 18)*

Thursday, June 30, 2011: Thirteenth Week in Ordinary Time / 380 [Gn 22:1b–19/Mt 9:1–8

ENTRANCE ANTIPHON: All nations, clap your hands. Shout with a voice of joy to God. *(Ps 46:2)*

RESPONSE: I will walk in the presence of the Lord, in the land of the living. *(Ps 115:9) Or:* Alleluia.

GOSPEL VERSE: R/. Alleluia. God was reconciling the world to himself in Christ and entrusting to us the message of reconciliation. R/. Alleluia.*(2 Cor 5:19)*

COMMUNION ANTIPHON: O, bless the Lord, my soul, and all that is within me bless his holy name. *(Ps 102:1)*

*OR: **First Holy Martyrs of the Holy Roman Church** / 592 [Rom 8:31b–39/Mt 24:4–13]*

ENTRANCE ANTIPHON: The holy martyrs shed their blood on earth for Christ; therefore they have received an everlasting reward.

RESPONSE: Our soul has been rescued like a bird from the fowler's snare. *(Ps 124:7)*

GOSPEL VERSE: R/. Alleluia. Blessed are they who are persecuted for the sake of righteousness, for theirs is the Kingdom of heaven. R/. Alleluia. *(Mt 5:10)*

COMMUNION ANTIPHON: Neither death nor life nor anything in all creation can come between us and Christ's love for us. *(See Rom 8:38–39)*

Friday, July 1, 2011: Most Sacred Heart of Jesus / 170 [Dt 7:6–11/1 Jn 4:7–16/Mt 11:25–30]

ENTRANCE ANTIPHON: The thoughts of his heart last through every generation, that he will rescue them from death and feed them in time of famine. *(Ps 32:11, 19)*

RESPONSE: The Lord's kindness is everlasting to those who fear him. *(See Ps 103:17)*

GOSPEL VERSE: R/. Alleluia. Take my yoke upon you, says the Lord; and learn from me, for I am meek and humble of heart. R/. Alleluia. *(Mt 11:29ab)*

COMMUNION ANTIPHON: One of the soldiers pierced Jesus' side with a lance, and at once there flowed out blood and water. *(Jn 19:34)*

Saturday, July 2, 2011: The Immaculate Heart of Mary / 573 [Is 61:9–11/Lk 2:41–51]

ENTRANCE ANTIPHON: My heart rejoices in your saving power. I will sing to the Lord for his goodness to me. *(Ps 12:6)*

RESPONSE: My heart exults in the Lord, my Savior. *(See 1 Sm 2:1)*

GOSPEL VERSE: R/. Alleluia. Blessed is the Virgin Mary who kept the word of God, and pondered it in her heart. R/. Alleluia. *(See Lk 2:19)*

COMMUNION ANTIPHON: Mary treasured all these words and pondered them in her heart. *(Lk 2:19)*

OR: **Thirteenth Week of Ordinary Time** / 382 [Gn 27:1–5, 15–29/Lk 2:41–51]

ENTRANCE ANTIPHON: All nations, clap your hands. Shout with a voice of joy to God. *(Ps 46:2)*

RESPONSE: Praise the Lord for the Lord is good! *(Ps 135:3a) Or:* Alleluia.

GOSPEL VERSE: R/. Alleluia. Blessed is the Virgin Mary who kept the word of God, and pondered it in her heart. R/. Alleluia. *(See Lk 2:19)*

COMMUNION ANTIPHON: O, bless the Lord, my soul, and all that is within me bless his holy name. *(Ps 102:1)*

Monday, July 4, 2011: Fourteenth Week of Ordinary Time / 383 [Gn 28:10–22a/Mt 9:18–26]

ENTRANCE ANTIPHON: Within your temple, we ponder your loving kindness, O God. As your name, so also your praise reaches to the ends of the earth; your right hand is filled with justice. *(Ps 47:10–11)*

RESPONSE: In you, my God, I place my trust. *(See Ps 91:2b)*

GOSPEL VERSE: R/. Alleluia. Our Savior Jesus Christ has destroyed death, and brought life to light through the gospel. R/. Alleluia. *(See 2 Tm 1:10)*

COMMUNION ANTIPHON: Taste and see the goodness of the Lord; blessed is he who hopes in God. *(Ps 34:9)*

OR: **Elizabeth of Portugal** / 594 [1 Jn 3:14–18/ Mt 25:31–46 or Mt 25:31–40]

ENTRANCE ANTIPHON: Come, you whom my Father has blessed, says the Lord: I was ill and you comforted me. I tell you, anything you did for one of my brothers, you did for me. *(Mt 25:34, 36, 40)*

RESPONSE: Blessed the man who fears the Lord. *(Ps 112:1) Or:* Alleluia.

GOSPEL VERSE: R/. Alleluia. I give you a new commandment: love one another as I have loved you. R/. Alleluia. *(Jn 13:34)*

COMMUNION ANTIPHON: By the love you have for one another, says the Lord, everyone will know that you are my disciples. *(Jn 13:35)*

OR: **Independence Day** / 594A, 882–886, 887–891

ENTRANCE ANTIPHON: Give peace, Lord, to those who wait for you; listen to the prayers of your servants, and guide us in the way of justice. *(See Sir 36:18–19)*

RESPONSE: Justice shall flourish in his time, and fullness of peace for ever. *(Ps 72:7)*

GOSPEL VERSE: R/. Alleluia. Peace I leave with you, says the Lord, my own peace I give you. R/. Alleluia. *(Jn 14:27)*

COMMUNION ANTIPHON: Lord, you are the source of life, and in the light of glory we find happiness.. *(Ps 36:10)*

Tuesday, July 5, 2011: Fourteenth Week of Ordinary Time / 384 [Gn 32:23–33/Mt 9:32–38]

ENTRANCE ANTIPHON: Within your temple, we ponder your loving kindness, O God. As your name, so also your praise reaches to the ends of the earth; your right hand is filled with justice. *(Ps 47:10–11)*

RESPONSE: In justice, I shall behold your face, O Lord. *(Ps 17:15a)*

GOSPEL VERSE: R/. Alleluia. I am the good shepherd, says the Lord; I know my sheep, and mine know me. R/. Alleluia. *(Jn 10:14)*

COMMUNION ANTIPHON: Taste and see the goodness of the Lord; blessed is he who hopes in God. *(Ps 34:9)*

OR: ***Anthony Mary Zaccaria***—*priest / 595 [2 Tm 1:13–14, 2:1–3/Mk 10:13–16]*

ENTRANCE ANTIPHON: Let the children come to me, and do not stop them, says the Lord; to such belongs the kingdom of God. *(Mk 10:14)*

RESPONSE: Blessed are they who hope in the Lord. *(Ps 40:5a)*

Or: Blessed are they who delight in the law of the Lord. *(Ps 1:2a)*

Or: The just will flourish like the palm tree in the garden of the Lord. *(Ps 92:13–14)*

GOSPEL VERSE: R/. Alleluia. Blessed are you, Father, Lord of heaven and earth; you have revealed to little ones the mysteries of the Kingdom. R/. Alleluia. *(See Mt 11:25)*

COMMUNION ANTIPHON: Unless you change and become like little children, says the Lord, you shall not enter the kingdom of heaven. *(Mt 18:3)*

Wednesday, July 6, 2011: Fourteenth Week of Ordinary Time / 385 [Gn 41:55–57; 42:5–7a, 17–24a/Mt 10:1–7]

ENTRANCE ANTIPHON: Within your temple, we ponder your loving kindness, O God. As your name, so also your praise reaches to the ends of the earth; your right hand is filled with justice. *(Ps 47:10–11)*

RESPONSE: Lord, let your mercy be on us, as we place our trust in you. *(Ps 33:22)*

GOSPEL VERSE: R/. Alleluia. The Kingdom of God is at hand; repent and believe in the Gospel. R/. Alleluia. *(Mk 1:15)*

COMMUNION ANTIPHON: Taste and see the goodness of the Lord; blessed is he who hopes in God. *(Ps 34:9)*

OR: ***Maria Goretti***—*virgin, martyr / 596 [1 Cor 6:13c–15a, 17–20/Jn 12:24–26]*

ENTRANCE ANTIPHON: Here is a wise and faithful virgin who went with lighted lamp to meet her Lord.

RESPONSE: Into your hands, O Lord, I commend my spirit. *(Ps 31:6)*

GOSPEL VERSE: R/. Alleluia. Blessed is the man who perseveres in temptation, for when he has been proved he will receive the crown of life. R/. Alleluia. *(Jas 1:12)*

COMMUNION ANTIPHON: The bridegroom is here; let us go out to meet Christ the Lord. *(Mt 25:6)*

Thursday, July 7, 2011: Fourteenth Week in Ordinary Time / 386 [Gn 44:18–21, 23b–29; 45:1–5/Mt 10:7–15]

ENTRANCE ANTIPHON: Within your temple, we ponder your loving kindness, O God. As your name, so also your praise reaches to the ends of the earth; your right hand is filled with justice. *(Ps 47:10–11)*

RESPONSE: Remember the marvels the Lord has done. *(Ps 105:5a) Or:* Alleluia.

GOSPEL VERSE: R/. Alleluia. The Kingdom of God is at hand: repent and believe in the Gospel. R/. Alleluia. *(Mk 1:15)*

COMMUNION ANTIPHON: Taste and see the goodness of the Lord; blessed is he who hopes in God. *(Ps 34:9)*

Friday, July 8, 2011: Fourteenth Week in Ordinary Time / 387 [Gn 46:1–7, 28–30/Mt 10:16–23]

ENTRANCE ANTIPHON: Within your temple, we ponder your loving kindness, O God. As your name, so also your praise reaches to the ends of the earth; your right hand is filled with justice. *(Ps 47:10–11)*

RESPONSE: The salvation of the just comes from the Lord. *(Ps 37:39a)*

GOSPEL VERSE: R/. Alleluia. When the Spirit of truth comes, he will guide you to all truth and remind you of all I told you. R/. Alleluia. *(Jn 16:13a; 14:26d)*

189

COMMUNION ANTIPHON: Taste and see the goodness of the Lord; blessed is he who hopes in God. *(Ps 34:9)*

Saturday, July 9, 2011: Fourteenth Week in Ordinary Time / 388 [Gn 49:29–32, 50:15–26a/Mt 10:24–33]

ENTRANCE ANTIPHON: Within your temple, we ponder your loving kindness, O God. As your name, so also your praise reaches to the ends of the earth; your right hand is filled with justice. *(Ps 47:10–11)*

RESPONSE: Be glad, you lowly ones; may your hearts be glad! *(See Ps 69:33)*

GOSPEL VERSE: R/. Alleluia. If you are insulted for the name of Christ, blessed are you, for the Spirit of God rests upon you. R/. Alleluia. *(1 Pt 4:14)*

COMMUNION ANTIPHON: Taste and see the goodness of the Lord; blessed is he who hopes in God. *(Ps 34:9)*

OR: ***Augustine Zhao Rong—priest, martyr; and his companions—martyrs / 713–718***

ENTRANCE ANTIPHON: Many are the sufferings of the just, and from them all the Lord has delivered them; the Lord preserves all their bones, not one of them shall be broken. *(Ps 33:20–21)*

RESPONSE: The Lord delivered me from all my fears. *(Ps 34:5)*

GOSPEL VERSE: R/. Alleluia. Blessed be the Father of compassion and God of all encouragement, who encourages us in our affliction. R/. Alleluia. *(2 Cor 1:3b–4a)*

COMMUNION ANTIPHON: No one has greater love, says the Lord, than the man who lays down his life for his friends. *(Jn 15:13)*

OR: ***Blessed Virgin Mary / 707–712***

ENTRANCE ANTIPHON: Hail, holy Mother! The child to whom you gave birth is the King of heaven and earth for ever. *(Sedulius)*

RESPONSE: My heart exults in the Lord, my Savior. *(See 1 Sm 2:1b)*

GOSPEL VERSE: R/. Alleluia. Hail, Mary, full of grace, the Lord is with you; blessed are you among women. R/. Alleluia. *(See Lk 1:28)*

COMMUNION ANTIPHON: Blessed is the womb of the Virgin Mary; she carried the Son of the eternal Father. *(See Lk 11:27)*

Monday, July 11, 2011: Benedict— abbot, religious founder / 597 [Prv 2:1–9/Mt 19:27–29]

ENTRANCE ANTIPHON: The Lord is my inheritance and my cup; he alone will give me my reward. The measuring line has marked a lovely place for me; my inheritance is my great delight. *(Ps 15:5–6)*

RESPONSE: I will bless the Lord at all times *(Ps 34:2)*

Or: Taste and see the goodness of the Lord. *(Ps 34:9)*

GOSPEL VERSE: R/. Alleluia. Blessed are the poor in spirit; the Kingdom of heaven is theirs! R/. Alleluia. *(Mt 5:3)*

COMMUNION ANTIPHON: I solemnly tell you: those who have left everything and followed me will be repaid a hundredfold and will gain eternal life. *(See Mt 19:27–29)*

OR: **Fifteenth Week in Ordinary Time** / 389 [Ex 1:8–14, 22/Mt 10:34–11:1]

ENTRANCE ANTIPHON: In my justice I shall see your face, O Lord; when your glory appears, my joy will be full. *(Ps 16:15)*

RESPONSE: Our help is in the name of the Lord. *(Ps 124:8a)*

GOSPEL VERSE: R/. Alleluia. Blessed are they who are persecuted for the sake of righteousness, for theirs is the Kingdom of heaven. R/. Alleluia. *(Mt 5:10)*

COMMUNION ANTIPHON: The sparrow even finds a home, the swallow finds a nest wherein to place her young, near to your altars, Lord of hosts, my King, my God! How happy they who dwell in your house! For ever they are praising you. *(Ps 83:4–5)*

Tuesday, July 12, 2011: Fifteenth Week in Ordinary Time / 390 [Ex 2:1–15a/Mt 11:20–24]

ENTRANCE ANTIPHON: In my justice I shall see your face, O Lord; when your glory appears, my joy will be full. *(Ps 16:15)*

RESPONSE: Turn to the Lord in you need, and you will live. *(See Ps 69:33)*

GOSPEL VERSE: R/. Alleluia. If today you hear his voice, harden not your hearts. R/. Alleluia. *(Ps 95:8)*

COMMUNION ANTIPHON: The sparrow even finds a home, the swallow finds a nest wherein to place her young, near to your altars, Lord of hosts, my King, my God! How happy they who dwell in your house! For ever they are praising you. *(Ps 83:4–5)*

Wednesday, July 13, 2011: Fifteenth Week in Ordinary Time / 391 [Ex 3:1–6, 9–12/Mt 11:25–27]

ENTRANCE ANTIPHON: In my justice I shall see your face, O Lord; when your glory appears, my joy will be full. *(Ps 16:15)*

RESPONSE: The Lord is kind and merciful. *(Ps 103:8a)*

GOSPEL VERSE: R/. Alleluia. Blessed are you, Father, Lord of heaven and earth, you have revealed to little ones the mysteries of the Kingdom. R/. Alleluia. *(Mt 11:25)*

COMMUNION ANTIPHON: The sparrow even finds a home, the swallow finds a nest wherein to place her young, near to your altars, Lord of hosts, my King, my God! How happy they who dwell in your house! For ever they are praising you. *(Ps 83:4–5)*

*OR: **Henry** / 598 [Mi 6:6–8/Mt 7:21–27]*

ENTRANCE ANTIPHON: The just man will rejoice in the Lord and hope in him, and all the upright of heart will be praised. *(Ps 63:11)*

RESPONSE: Blessed are they who hope in the Lord. *(Ps 40:5a)*

Or: Blessed are they who delight in the law of the Lord. *(Ps 1:2a)*

Or: The just will flourish like the palm tree in the garden of the Lord. *(Ps 92:13–14)*

GOSPEL VERSE: R/. Alleluia. Whoever loves me will keep my word and my Father will love him and we will come to him. R/. Alleluia. *(Jn 14:23)*

COMMUNION ANTIPHON: He who serves me, follows me, says the Lord; and where I am, my servant will also be. *(Jn 12:26)*

Thursday, July 14, 2011: Blessed Kateri Tekakwitha—virgin /599A, 732–736

ENTRANCE ANTIPHON: Here is a wise and faithful virgin who went with lighted lamp to meet her Lord.

RESPONSE: Listen to me, daughter; see and bend your ear. *(Ps 45:11)*

Or: The bridegroom is here; let us go out to meet Christ the Lord.

GOSPEL VERSE: R/. Alleluia. This is the wise virgin, whom the Lord found waiting; at his coming, she went in with him to the wedding feast. R/. Alleluia.

COMMUNION ANTIPHON: The bridegroom is here; let us go out to meet Christ the Lord. *(Mt 25:6)*

OR: **Fifteenth Week in Ordinary Time** / 392 [Ex 3:13–20/Mt 11:28–30]

ENTRANCE ANTIPHON: In my justice I shall see your face, O Lord; when your glory appears, my joy will be full. *(Ps 16:15)*

RESPONSE: The Lord remembers his covenant for ever. *(Ps 105:8a) Or:* Alleluia.

GOSPEL VERSE: R/. Alleluia. Come to me, all you who labor and are burdened, and I will give you rest, says the Lord. R/. Alleluia. *(Mt 11:28)*

COMMUNION ANTIPHON: The sparrow even finds a home, the swallow finds a nest wherein to place her young, near to your altars, Lord of hosts, my King, my God! How happy they who dwell in your house! For ever they are praising you. *(Ps 83:4–5)*

Friday, July 15, 2010: Bonaventure— bishop, doctor of the Church / 600 [Eph 3:14–19/Mt 23:8–12]

ENTRANCE ANTIPHON: The mouth of the just man utters wisdom, and his tongue speaks what is right; the law of his God is in his heart. *(Ps 36:30–31)*

RESPONSE: Lord, teach me your statutes. *(Ps 119:12)*

GOSPEL VERSE: R/. Alleluia. You have but one Father in heaven; you have one master, the Christ. R/. Alleluia. *(Mt 23:9b, 10b)*

COMMUNION ANTIPHON: The Lord has put his faithful servant in charge of his household, to give them their share of bread at the proper time. *(Lk 12:42)*

OR: **Fifteenth Week in Ordinary Time** / 393 [Ex 11:10–12:14/Mt 12:1–8]

ENTRANCE ANTIPHON: In my justice I shall see your face, O Lord; when your glory appears, my joy will be full. *(Ps 16:15)*

RESPONSE: I will take the cup of salvation, and call upon the name of the Lord. *(Ps 116:13)*

GOSPEL VERSE: R/. My sheep hear my voice, says the Lord; I know them, and they follow me. R/. Alleluia. *(Jn 10:27)*

COMMUNION ANTIPHON: The sparrow even finds a home, the swallow finds a nest wherein to place her young, near to your altars, Lord of hosts, my King, my God! How happy they who dwell in your house! For ever they are praising you. *(Ps 83:4–5)*

Saturday, July 16, 2011: Fifteenth Week in Ordinary Time / 394 [Ex 12:37–42/Mt 12:14–21]

ENTRANCE ANTIPHON: In my justice I shall see your face, O Lord; when your glory appears, my joy will be full. *(Ps 16:15)*

RESPONSE: His mercy endures forever. *Or:* Alleluia.

GOSPEL VERSE: R/. Alleluia. God was reconciling the world to himself in Christ, and entrusting to us the message of reconciliation. R/. Alleluia. *(2 Cor 5:19)*

COMMUNION ANTIPHON: The sparrow even finds a home, the swallow finds a nest wherein to place her young, near to your altars, Lord of hosts, my King, my God! How happy they who dwell in your house! For ever they are praising you. *(Ps 83:4–5)*

OR: *Our Lady of Mount Carmel* / 601 [Zec 2:14–17/Mt 12:46–50]

ENTRANCE ANTIPHON: Hail, holy Mother! The child to whom you gave birth is the King of heaven and earth for ever. *(Sedulius)*

RESPONSE: The Almighty has done great things for me, and holy is his name. *(Lk 1:49)*

Or: Blessed Virgin Mary, you carried the Son of the eternal Father.

GOSPEL VERSE: R/. Alleluia. Blessed are those who hear the word of God and observe it. R/. Alleluia. *(Lk 11:28)*

COMMUNION ANTIPHON: Blessed is the womb of the Virgin Mary; she carried the Son of the eternal Father. *(See Lk 11:27)*

OR: *Blessed Virgin Mary* / 707–712

ENTRANCE ANTIPHON: Blessed are you, Virgin Mary, who carried the creator of all things in your womb; you gave birth to your maker, and remain for ever a virgin.

RESPONSE: My heart exults in the Lord, my Savior. *(1 Sm 2:1b)*

GOSPEL VERSE: R/. Alleluia. Blessed is the Virgin Mary who kept the word of God, and pondered it in her heart. R/. Alleluia. *(See Lk 2:19)*

COMMUNION ANTIPHON: The Almighty has done great things for me. Holy is his name. *(Lk 1:49)*

Monday, July 18, 2011: Sixteenth Week in Ordinary Time / 395 [Ex 14:5–18/Mt 12:38–42]

ENTRANCE ANTIPHON: God himself is my help. The Lord upholds my life. I will offer you a willing sacrifice; I will praise your name, O Lord, for its goodness. *(Ps 53:6, 8)*

RESPONSE: Let us sing to the Lord; he has covered himself in glory. *(Ex 15:1b)*

GOSPEL VERSE: R/. Alleluia. If today you hear his voice, harden not your hearts. R/. Alleluia. *(Ps 95:8)*

COMMUNION ANTIPHON: The Lord keeps in our minds the wonderful things he has done. He is compassion and love; he always provides for his faithful. *(Ps 110:4–5)*

OR: *Camillus de Lellis—priest* / 601A [1 Jn 3:14–18/Jn 15:9–17]

ENTRANCE ANTIPHON: Come, you whom my Father has blessed, says the Lord: I was ill and you comforted me. I tell you, anything you did for one of my brothers, you did for me. *(Mt 25:34, 36, 40)*

RESPONSE: Blessed the man who fears the Lord. *(Ps 112:1) Or:* Alleluia.

GOSPEL VERSE: R/. Alleluia. I give you a new commandment: love one another as I have loved you. R/. Alleluia. *(Jn 13:34)*

COMMUNION ANTIPHON: No one has greater love, says the Lord, than the man who lays down his life for his friends. *(Jn 15:13)*

Tuesday, July 19, 2011: Sixteenth Week in Ordinary Time / 396 [Ex 14:21–15:1/Mt 12:46–50]

ENTRANCE ANTIPHON: God himself is my help. The Lord upholds my life. I will offer you a willing sacrifice; I will praise your name, O Lord, for its goodness. *(Ps 53:6, 8)*

RESPONSE: Let us sing to the Lord; he has covered himself in glory. *(Ex 15:1b)*

GOSPEL VERSE: R/. Alleluia. Whoever loves me will keep my word, and my Father will love him and we will come to him. R/. Alleluia. *(Jn 14:23)*

COMMUNION ANTIPHON: The Lord keeps in our minds the wonderful things he has done. He is compassion and love; he always provides for his faithful. *(Ps 110:4–5)*

Wednesday, July 20, 2011: Sixteenth Week in Ordinary Time / 397 [Ex 16:1–5, 9–15/Mt 13:1–9]

ENTRANCE ANTIPHON: God himself is my help. The Lord upholds my life. I will offer you a willing sacrifice; I will praise your name, O Lord, for its goodness. *(Ps 53:6, 8)*

RESPONSE: The Lord gave them bread from heaven. *(Ps 78:24b)*

GOSPEL VERSE: R/. Alleluia. The seed is the word of God, Christ is the sower; all who come to him will live for ever. R/. Alleluia.

COMMUNION ANTIPHON: The Lord keeps in our minds the wonderful things he has done. He is compassion and love; he always provides for his faithful. *(Ps 110:4–5)*

OR: *Apollinaris—bishop, martyr / [Ez 34:11–16/ Jn 10:11–18]*

ENTRANCE ANTIPHON: I will look after my sheep, says the Lord, and I will raise up one shepherd who will pasture them. I, the Lord, will be their God. *(Ez 34:11, 23–24)*

RESPONSE: The Lord is my shepherd; there is nothing I shall want. *(Ps 23:1)*

GOSPEL VERSE: R/. Alleluia. I am the good shepherd. A good shepherd lays down his life for the sheep. R/. Alleluia. *(Jn 10:16)*

COMMUNION ANTIPHON: You have not chosen me; I have chosen you. Go and bear fruit that will last. *(Jn 15:16)*

Thursday, July 21, 2011: Sixteenth Week in Ordinary Time / 398 [Ex 19:1–2, 9–11, 16–20b/Mt 13:10–17]

ENTRANCE ANTIPHON: God himself is my help. The Lord upholds my life. I will offer you a willing sacrifice; I will praise your name, O Lord, for its goodness. *(Ps 53:6, 8)*

RESPONSE: Glory and praise for ever! *(Dn 3:52b)*

GOSPEL VERSE: R/. Alleluia. Blessed are you, Father, Lord of heaven and earth; you have revealed to little ones the mysteries of the Kingdom. R/. Alleluia. *(See Mt 11:25)*

COMMUNION ANTIPHON: The Lord keeps in our minds the wonderful things he has done. He is compassion and love; he always provides for his faithful. *(Ps 110:4–5)*

OR: *Lawrence of Brindisi—priest, doctor of the Church / 602 [2 Cor 4:1–2, 5–7/Mk 4:1–10, 13–20 or Mk 4:1–9]*

ENTRANCE ANTIPHON: I will give you shepherds after my own heart, and they shall feed you on knowledge and sound teaching. *(Jer 3:15)*

RESPONSE: Here I am, Lord; I come to do your will. *(Ps 40:8a, 9a)*

GOSPEL VERSE: R/. Alleluia. The seed is the word of God, Christ the sower; all who come to him will live for ever. R/. Alleluia.

COMMUNION ANTIPHON: The Son of Man did not come to be served, but to serve, and to give his life as a ransom for many. *(Mt 20:28)*

Friday, July 22, 2011: Mary Magdalene / 603 [Sg 3:1–4b or 2 Cor 5:14–17/Jn 20:1–2, 11–18]

ENTRANCE ANTIPHON: The Lord said to Mary Magdalene: Go and tell my brothers that I shall ascend to my Father and your Father; to my God and to your God. *(Jn 20:17)*

RESPONSE: My soul is thirsting for you, O Lord my God. *(Ps 63:2)*

GOSPEL VERSE: R/. Alleluia. Tell us, Mary, what did you see on the way? I saw the glory of the risen Christ, I saw his empty tomb. R/. Alleluia.

COMMUNION ANTIPHON: The love of Christ compels us to live not for ourselves but for him who died and rose for us. *(2 Cor 5:14–15)*

OR: Sixteenth Week in Ordinary Time / 399 [Ex 20:1–17/Jn 20:1–2, 11–18]

ENTRANCE ANTIPHON: God himself is my help. The Lord upholds my life. I will offer you a willing sacrifice; I will praise your name, O Lord, for its goodness. *(Ps 53:6, 8)*

RESPONSE: Lord, you have the words of everlasting life. *(Jn 6:68c)*

GOSPEL VERSE: R/. Alleluia. Tell us, Mary, what did you see on the way? I saw the glory of the risen Christ, I saw his empty tomb. R/. Alleluia.

COMMUNION ANTIPHON: The Lord keeps in our minds the wonderful things he has done. He is compassion and love; he always provides for his faithful. *(Ps 110:4–5)*

Saturday, July 23, 2011: Sixteenth Week in Ordinary Time/ 400 [Ex 24:3–8/Mt 13:24–30]

ENTRANCE ANTIPHON: God himself is my help. The Lord upholds my life. I will offer you a willing sacrifice; I will praise your name, O Lord, for its goodness. *(Ps 53:6, 8)*

RESPONSE: Offer to God a sacrifice of praise. *(Ps 50:14a)*

GOSPEL VERSE: R/. Alleluia. Humbly welcome the word that has been planted in you and is able to save your souls. R/. Alleluia. *(Jas 1:21bc)*

COMMUNION ANTIPHON: The Lord keeps in our minds the wonderful things he has done. He is compassion and love; he always provides for his faithful. *(Ps 110:4–5)*

OR: **Bridget of Sweden**—religious / [Gal 2:19–20/Jn 15:1–8]

ENTRANCE ANTIPHON: Honor the woman who fears the Lord. Her sons will bless her and her husband praise her. *(See Prv 31:30, 28)*

RESPONSE: I will bless the Lord at all times. *(Ps 34:2)*

Or: Taste and see the goodness of the Lord. *(Ps 34:9)*

GOSPEL VERSE: R/. Alleluia. Remain in my love, says the Lord; whoever remains in me and I in him will bear much fruit. R/. Alleluia. *(Jn 15:9b, 5b)*

COMMUNION ANTIPHON: The kingdom of heaven is like a merchant in search of fine pearls; on finding one rare pearl he sells everything he has and buys it. *(Mt 13:45–46)*

OR: **Blessed Virgin Mary** / 707–712

ENTRANCE ANTIPHON: You have been blessed, O Virgin Mary, above all other women on earth by the Lord the most high God; he has so exalted your name that your praises shall never fade from the mouths of men. *(See Judith 13:23, 25)*

RESPONSE: Blessed be the name of the Lord for ever. *(Ps 113:2) Or:* Alleluia.

GOSPEL VERSE: R/. Alleluia. Hail, Mary, full of grace, the Lord is with you; blessed are you among women. R/. Alleluia. *(Lk 1:28)*

COMMUNION ANTIPHON: All generations will call me blessed, because God has looked upon his lowly handmaid. *(See Lk 1:48)*

Monday, July 25, 2011: James— apostle / 605 [2 Cor 4:7–15/Mt 20:20–28]

ENTRANCE ANTIPHON: Walking by the Sea of Galilee, Jesus saw James and John, the sons of Zebedee, mending their nets, and he called them to follow him. *(See Mt 4:18, 21)*

RESPONSE: Those who sow in tears shall reap rejoicing. *(Ps 126:5)*

GOSPEL VERSE: R/. Alleluia. I chose you from the world, to go and bear fruit that will last, says the Lord. R/. Alleluia. *(See Jn 15:16)*

COMMUNION ANTIPHON: By sharing the cup of the Lord's suffering, they became the friends of God. *(See Mt 20:22–23)*

Tuesday, July 26, 2011: Joachim and Anne—parents of the Blessed Virgin Mary / 606 [Sir 44:1, 10–15/Mt 13:16–17]

ENTRANCE ANTIPHON: Praised be Joachim and Anne for the child they bore. The Lord gave them the blessing of all the nations.

RESPONSE: God will give him the throne of David, his father. *(Lk 1:32)*

GOSPEL VERSE: R/. Alleluia. They yearned for the comforting of Israel, and the Holy Spirit rested upon them. R/. Alleluia. *(See Lk 2:25c)*

COMMUNION ANTIPHON: They received a blessing from the Lord, and kindness from God their Savior. *(See Ps 23:5)*

OR: **Seventeenth Week in Ordinary Time** / 402 [Ex 33:7–11; 34:5b–9, 28/Mt 13:36–43]

ENTRANCE ANTIPHON: God is in his holy dwelling; he will give a home to the lonely, he gives power and strength to his people. *(Ps 67:6–7, 36)*

RESPONSE: The Lord is kind and merciful. *(Ps 103:8a)*

GOSPEL VERSE: R/. Alleluia. The seed is the word of God, Christ is the sower; all who come to him will live for ever. R/. Alleluia.

COMMUNION ANTIPHON: O bless the Lord, my soul, and remember all his kindness. *(Ps 102:2)*

Wednesday, July 27, 2011: Seventeenth Week in Ordinary Time / 403 [Ex 34:29–35/Mt 13:44–46]]

ENTRANCE ANTIPHON: God is in his holy dwelling; he will give a home to the lonely, he gives power and strength to his people. *(Ps 67:6–7, 36)*

RESPONSE: Holy is the Lord our God. *(See Ps 99:9c)*

GOSPEL VERSE: R/. Alleluia. I call you my friends, says the Lord, for I have made known to you all that the Father has told me. R/. Alleluia. *(Jn 15:15b)*

COMMUNION ANTIPHON: O bless the Lord, my soul, and remember all his kindness. *(Ps 102:2)*

Thursday, July 28, 2011: Seventeenth Week in Ordinary Time / 404 [Ex 40:16–21, 34–38/Mt 13:47–53]

ENTRANCE ANTIPHON: God is in his holy dwelling; he will give a home to the lonely, he gives power and strength to his people. *(Ps 67:6–7, 36)*

RESPONSE: How lovely is your dwelling place, O Lord, mighty God! *(Ps 84:2)*

GOSPEL VERSE: R/. Alleluia. Open our hearts, O Lord, to listen to the words of your Son. R/. Alleluia. *(See Acts 16:14b)*

COMMUNION ANTIPHON: O bless the Lord, my soul, and remember all his kindness. *(Ps 102:2)*

Friday, July 29, 2011: Martha / 607 [1 Jn 4:7–16/Jn 11:19–27 or Lk 10:38–42]

ENTRANCE ANTIPHON: As Jesus entered a certain village a woman called Martha welcomed him into her house. *(Lk 10:38)*

RESPONSE: I will bless the Lord at all times. *(Ps 34:2)*

Or: Taste and see the goodness of the Lord. *(Ps 34:9)*

GOSPEL VERSE: R/. Alleluia. I am the light of the world, says the Lord; whoever follows me will have the light of life. R/. Alleluia. *(Jn 8:12)*

COMMUNION ANTIPHON: Matha said to Jesus: You are the Christ, the Son of God, who was to come into this world. *(Jn 11:27)*

OR: **Seventeenth Week in Ordinary Time** / 405 [Lv 23:1, 4–11, 15–16, 27, 34b–37/Jn 11:19–27 or Lk 10:38–42]

ENTRANCE ANTIPHON: God is in his holy dwelling; he will give a home to the lonely, he gives power and strength to his people. *(Ps 67:6–7, 36)*

RESPONSE: Sing with joy to God our help. *(Ps 81:2a)*

GOSPEL VERSE: R/. Alleluia. I am the light of the world, says the Lord; whoever follows me will have the light of life. R/. Alleluia. *(Jn 8:12)*

COMMUNION ANTIPHON: O bless the Lord, my soul, and remember all his kindness. *(Ps 102:2)*

Saturday, July 30, 2011: Seventeenth Week in Ordinary Time / 406 [Lv 25:1, 8–17/Mt 14:1–12]

ENTRANCE ANTIPHON: God is in his holy dwelling; he will give a home to the lonely, he gives power and strength to his people. *(Ps 67:6–7, 36)*

RESPONSE: O God, let all the nations praise you! *(Ps 67:4)*

GOSPEL VERSE: R/. Alleluia. Blessed are they who are persecuted for the sake of righteousness for theirs is the Kingdom of heaven. R/. Alleluia. *(Mt 5:10)*

COMMUNION ANTIPHON: O bless the Lord, my soul, and remember all his kindness. *(Ps 102:2)*

OR: **Peter Chrysologus**—*bishop, doctor of the Church / 608 [Eph 3:8–12/Lk 6:43–45]*

ENTRANCE ANTIPHON: Let the peoples declare the wisdom of the saints and the Church proclaim their praises; their names shall live for ever. *(See Sir 44:15, 14)*

RESPONSE: Lord, teach me your statutes. *(Ps 119:12)*

GOSPEL VERSE: R/. Alleluia. I am the vine, you are the branches, says the Lord; whoever remains in me, and I in him, will bear much fruit. R/. Alleluia. *(Jn 15:5)*

COMMUNION ANTIPHON: We preach a Christ who was crucified; he is the power and the wisdom of God. *(1 Cor 1:23–24)*

OR: **Blessed Virgin Mary** / 707–712

ENTRANCE ANTIPHON: Blessed are you, Virgin Mary, who carried the creator of all things in your womb; you gave birth to your maker, and remain for ever a virgin.

RESPONSE: My heart exults in the Lord, my Savior. *(See 1 Sm 2:1b)*

GOSPEL VERSE: R/. Alleluia. Blessed is the Virgin Mary who kept the word of God and pondered it in her heart. R/. Alleluia. *(See Lk 2:19)*

COMMUNION ANTIPHON: The Almighty has done great things for me. Holy is his name. *(Lk 1:49)*

Monday, August 1, 2011: Alphonsus Liguori—priest, doctor of the Church / 610 [Rom 8:1–4/Mt 5:13–19]

ENTRANCE ANTIPHON: The Lord opened his mouth in the assembly, and filled him with the spirit of wisdom and understanding, and clothed him in a robe of glory. *(Sir 15:5)*

RESPONSE: Lord, teach me your statutes. *(Ps 119:12)*

GOSPEL VERSE: R/. Alleluia. Let your light shine before others, that they may see your good deeds and glorify your heavenly Father. R/. Alleluia. *(Mt 5:16)*

COMMUNION ANTIPHON: The Lord has put his faithful servant in charge of his household, to give them their share of bread at the proper time. *(Lk 12:42)*

OR: **Eighteenth Week in Ordinary Time** / 407 [Nm 11:4b–15/Mt 14:22–36]

ENTRANCE ANTIPHON: God, come to my help. Lord, quickly give me assistance. You are the one who helps me and sets me free: Lord, do not be long in coming. *(Ps 69:2, 6)*

RESPONSE: Sing with joy to God our help. *(Ps 81:2a)*

GOSPEL VERSE: R/. Alleluia. One does not live on bread alone, but on every word that comes forth from the mouth of God. R/. Alleluia. *(Mt 4:4)*

COMMUNION ANTIPHON: You gave us bread from heaven, Lord: a sweet-tasting bread that was very good to eat. *(Wis 16:20)*

Tuesday, August 2, 2011: Eighteenth Week in Ordinary Time / 408 [Nm 12:1–13/Mt 14:22–36 or Mt 15:1–2, 10–14]

ENTRANCE ANTIPHON: God, come to my help. Lord, quickly give me assistance. You are the one who helps me and sets me free: Lord, do not be long in coming. *(Ps 69:2, 6)*

RESPONSE: Be merciful, O Lord, for we have sinned. *(See Ps 51:3a)*

GOSPEL VERSE: R/. Alleluia. Rabbi, you are the Son of God; you are the King of Israel. R/. Alleluia. *(Jn 1:49b)*

COMMUNION ANTIPHON: You gave us bread from heaven, Lord: a sweet-tasting bread that was very good to eat. *(Wis 16:20)*

OR: **Eusebius of Vercelli—bishop** / 611 [1 Jn 5:1–5/Mt 5:1–12a]

ENTRANCE ANTIPHON: I will look after my sheep, says the Lord, and I will raise up one shepherd who will pasture them. I, the Lord, will be their God. *(Ez 34:11, 23–24)*

RESPONSE: For ever I will sing the goodness of the Lord. *(Ps 89:2)*

GOSPEL VERSE: R/. Alleluia. Blessed are the poor in spirit, for theirs is the Kingdom of heaven. R/. Alleluia. *(Mt 5:3)*

COMMUNION ANTIPHON: You have not chosen me; I have chosen you. Go and bear fruit that will last. *(Jn 15:16)*

OR: **Peter Julian Eymard—priest** / 611A [Acts 4:32–35/Jn 15:1–8]

ENTRANCE ANTIPHON: I will look after my sheep, says the Lord, and I will raise up one shepherd who will pasture them. I, the Lord, will be their God. *(Ez 34:11, 23–24)*

RESPONSE: Taste and see the goodness of the Lord. *(Ps 34:9)*

GOSPEL VERSE: R/. Alleluia. Remain in me as I remain in you, says the Lord; whoever remains in me will bear much fruit. R/. Alleluia. *(Jn 15:4a, 5b)*

COMMUNION ANTIPHON: You have not chosen me; I have chosen you. Go and bear fruit that will last. *(Jn 15:16)*

Wednesday, August 3, 2011: Eighteenth Week in Ordinary Time / 409 [Nm 13:1–2, 25–14:1, 26–29a, 34–35/Mt 15:21–28]

ENTRANCE ANTIPHON: God, come to my help. Lord, quickly give me assistance. You are the one who helps me and sets me free: Lord, do not be long in coming. *(Ps 69:2, 6)*

RESPONSE: Remember us, O Lord, as you favor your people. *(Ps 106:4a)*

GOSPEL VERSE: R/. Alleluia. A great prophet has arisen in our midst and God has visited his people. R/. Alleluia. *(Lk 7:16)*

COMMUNION ANTIPHON: You gave us bread from heaven, Lord: a sweet-tasting bread that was very good to eat. *(Wis 16:20)*

Thursday, August 4, 2011: John Mary Vianney—priest / 612 [Ez 3:17–21/Mt 9:35–10:1]

ENTRANCE ANTIPHON: The Spirit of God is upon me; he has anointed me. He sent me to bring good news to the poor, and to heal the broken-hearted. *(Lk 4:18)*

RESPONSE: Go out to all the world and tell the Good News. *(Mk 16:15)*

GOSPEL VERSE: R/. Alleluia. The Lord sent me to bring glad tidings to the poor and to proclaim liberty to captives. R/. Alleluia. *(Lk 4:18)*

COMMUNION ANTIPHON: I, the Lord, am with you always, until the end of the world. *(Mt 28:20)*

OR: **Eighteenth Week in Ordinary Time** / 410 [Nm 20:1–13/Mt 16:13–23]

ENTRANCE ANTIPHON: God, come to my help. Lord, quickly give me assistance. You are the one who helps me and sets me free: Lord, do not be long in coming. *(Ps 69:2, 6)*

RESPONSE: If today you hear his voice, harden not your hearts. *(Ps 95:8)*

GOSPEL VERSE: R/. Alleluia. You are Peter, and upon this rock I will build my Church, and the gates of the netherworld shall not prevail against it. R/. Alleluia. *(Mt 16:18)*

COMMUNION ANTIPHON: You gave us bread from heaven, Lord: a sweet-tasting bread that was very good to eat. *(Wis 16:20)*

Friday, August 5, 2011: Eighteenth Week in Ordinary Time / 411 [Dt 4:32–40/Mt 16:24–28]

ENTRANCE ANTIPHON: God, come to my help. Lord, quickly give me assistance. You are the one who helps me and sets me free: Lord, do not be long in coming. *(Ps 69:2, 6)*

RESPONSE: I remember the deeds of the LORD. *(Ps 77:12a)*

GOSPEL VERSE: R/. Alleluia. Blessed are they who are persecuted for the sake of righteousness; for theirs is the Kingdom of heaven. R/. Alleluia. *(Mt 5:10)*

COMMUNION ANTIPHON: You gave us bread from heaven, Lord: a sweet-tasting bread that was very good to eat. *(Wis 16:20)*

OR: Dedication of the Basilica of Saint Mary Major in Rome / 613 [Rv 21:1–5a/Lk 11:27–28]

ENTRANCE ANTIPHON: Hail, holy Mother! The child to whom you gave birth is the King of heaven and earth for ever. *(Sedulius)*

RESPONSE: You are the highest honor of our race. *(Jud 15:9)*

GOSPEL VERSE: R/. Alleluia. Blessed are those who hear the word of God and observe it. R/. Alleluia. *(Lk 11:28)*

COMMUNION ANTIPHON: Blessed is the womb of the Virgin Mary; she carried the Son of the eternal Father. *(See Lk 11:27)*

Saturday, August 6, 2011: The Transfiguration of the Lord / 614 [Dn 7:9–10, 13–14/2 Pt 1:16–19/Mt 17:1–9]

ENTRANCE ANTIPHON: In the shining cloud the Spirit is seen; from it the voice of the Father is heard: This is my Son, my beloved, in whom is all my delight. Listen to him. *(See Mt 17:5)*

RESPONSE: The Lord is king, the Most High over all the earth. *(Ps 97:1a, 9a)*

GOSPEL VERSE: R/. Alleluia. This is my beloved Son, with whom I am well pleased; listen to him. R/. Alleluia. *(Mt 17:5c)*

COMMUNION ANTIPHON: When Christ is revealed we shall be like him, for we shall see him as he is. *(1 Jn 3:2)*

Monday, August 8, 2011: Dominic—priest / 617 [1 Cor 2:1–10a/Lk 9:57–62]

ENTRANCE ANTIPHON: The Lord is my inheritance and my cup; he alone will give me my reward. The measuring line has marked a lovely place for me; my inheritance is my great delight. *(Ps 15:5–6)*

RESPONSE: Proclaim God's marvelous deeds to all the nations. *(Ps 96:3)*

GOSPEL VERSE: R/. Alleluia. I am the light of the world, says the Lord; whoever follows me will have the light of life. R/. Alleluia. *(Jn 8:12)*

COMMUNION ANTIPHON: I solemnly tell you: those who have left everything and followed me will be repaid a hundredfold and will gain eternal life. *(See Mt 19:27–29)*

OR: **Nineteenth Week in Ordinary Time** / 413 [Dt 10:12–22/Mt 17:22–27]

ENTRANCE ANTIPHON: Lord, be true to your covenant, forget not the life of your poor ones for ever. Rise up, O God, and defend your cause; do not ignore the shouts of your enemies. (Ps 73:20, 19, 22, 23)

RESPONSE: Praise the Lord, Jerusalem. (Ps 147:12a)

GOSPEL VERSE: R/. Alleluia. God has called you through the Gospel to possess the glory of our Lord Jesus Christ. R/. Alleluia. (See 2 Thes 2:14)

COMMUNION ANTIPHON: Praise the Lord, Jerusalem; he feeds you with the finest wheat. (Ps 147:12, 14)

Tuesday, August 9, 2011: Nineteenth Week in Ordinary Time / 414 [Dt 31:1–8/Mt 18:1–5, 10, 12–14]

ENTRANCE ANTIPHON: Lord, be true to your covenant, forget not the life of your poor ones for ever. Rise up, O God, and defend your cause; do not ignore the shouts of your enemies. (Ps 73:20, 19, 22, 23)

RESPONSE: The portion of the Lord is his people. (Dt 32:9a)

GOSPEL VERSE: R/. Alleluia. Take my yoke upon you and learn from me, for I am meek and humble of heart. R/. Alleluia. (Mt 11:29ab)

COMMUNION ANTIPHON: Praise the Lord, Jerusalem; he feeds you with the finest wheat. (Ps 147:12, 14)

OR: *Teresa Benedicta of the Cross—virgin, martyr / 713–718, 731–736*

ENTRANCE ANTIPHON: Here is a wise and faithful virgin who went with lighted lamp to meet her Lord.

RESPONSE: Listen to me, daughter; see and bend your ear. (Ps 45:11)

Or: The bridegroom is here; let us go out to meet Christ the Lord.

GOSPEL VERSE: R/. Alleluia. Come, bride of Christ, and receive the crown, which the Lord has prepared for you for ever. R/. Alleluia.

COMMUNION ANTIPHON: The bridegroom is here; let us go out to meet Christ the Lord. (Mt 25:6)

Wednesday, August 10, 2011: Lawrence—deacon, martyr / 618 [2 Cor 9:6–10/Jn 12:24–26]

ENTRANCE ANTIPHON: Today let us honor St. Lawrence, who spent himself for the poor of the Church. Thus he merited to suffer martyrdom and to ascend in joy to Jesus Christ the Lord.

RESPONSE: Blessed the man who is gracious and lends to those in need. (Ps 112:5)

GOSPEL VERSE: R/. Alleluia. Whoever follows me will not walk in darkness but will have the light of life, says the Lord. R/. Alleluia. (Jn 8:12bc)

COMMUNION ANTIPHON: He who serves me, follows me, says the Lord; and where I am, my servant will also be. (Jn 12:26)

Thursday, August 11, 2011: Clare—virgin / 619 [Phil 3:8–14/Mt 19:27–29]

ENTRANCE ANTIPHON: The Lord is my inheritance and my cup; he alone will give me my reward. The measuring line has marked a lovely place for me; my inheritance is my great delight. (Ps 15:5–6)

RESPONSE: You are my inheritance, O Lord. (See Ps 16:5a)

GOSPEL VERSE: R/. Alleluia. Blessed are the poor in spirit; the Kingdom of heaven is theirs! R/. Alleluia. (Mt 5:3)

COMMUNION ANTIPHON: I solemnly tell you: those who have left everything and followed me will be repaid a hundredfold and will gain eternal life. (See Mt 19:27–29)

OR: **Nineteenth Week in Ordinary Time / 416** (Jos 3:7–10a, 11, 13–17/Mt 18:21–19:1)

ENTRANCE ANTIPHON: Lord, be true to your covenant, forget not the life of your poor ones for ever. Rise up, O God, and defend your cause; do not ignore the shouts of your enemies. (Ps 73:20, 19, 22, 23)

RESPONSE: Alleluia!

GOSPEL VERSE: R/. Alleluia. Let your countenance shine upon your servant and teach me your statutes. R/. Alleluia. (Ps 119:135)

COMMUNION ANTIPHON: Praise the Lord, Jerusalem; he feeds you with the finest wheat. (Ps 147:12, 14)

Friday, August 12, 2011: Nineteenth Week in Ordinary Time / 417 [Jos 24:1-13/Mt 19:3-12]

ENTRANCE ANTIPHON: Lord, be true to your covenant, forget not the life of your poor ones for ever. Rise up, O God, and defend your cause; do not ignore the shouts of your enemies. *(Ps 73:20, 19, 22, 23)*

RESPONSE: His mercy endures for ever.

GOSPEL VERSE: R/. Alleluia. Receive the word of God, not as the word of men, but, as it truly is, the word of God. R/. Alleluia. *(See 1 Thes 2:13)*

COMMUNION ANTIPHON: Praise the Lord, Jerusalem; he feeds you with the finest wheat. *(Ps 147:12, 14)*

OR: *Jane Frances de Chantal—religious / 619A [Prv 31:10-13, 19-20, 30-31/Mk 3:31-35]*

ENTRANCE ANTIPHON: These are the saints who received blessings from the Lord, a prize from God their Savior. They are the people that long to see his face. *(See Ps 23:5-6)*

RESPONSE: In you, Lord, I have found my peace.

GOSPEL VERSE: R/. Alleluia. If you remain in my word, you will truly be my diciples, and you will know the truth, says the Lord. R/. Alleluia. *(Jn 8:31b-32)*

COMMUNION ANTIPHON: Taste and see the goodness of the Lord; blessed is he who hopes in God. *(Ps 34:9)*

Saturday, August 13, 2011: Nineteenth Week in Ordinary Time / 418 [Jos 24:14-29/Mt 19:13-15]

ENTRANCE ANTIPHON: Lord, be true to your covenant, forget not the life of your poor ones for ever. Rise up, O God, and defend your cause; do not ignore the shouts of your enemies. *(Ps 73:20, 19, 22, 23)*

RESPONSE: You are my inheritance, O Lord. *(See Ps 16:5a)*

GOSPEL VERSE: R/. Alleluia. Blessed are you, Father, Lord of heaven and earth; you have revealed to little ones the mysteries of the Kingdom. R/. Alleluia. *(See Mt 11:25)*

COMMUNION ANTIPHON: Praise the Lord, Jerusalem; he feeds you with the finest wheat. *(Ps 147:12, 14)*

OR: *Pontian—pope, martyr; and Hippolytus— priest, martyr / 620 [1 Pt 4:12-19/Jn 15:18-21]*

ENTRANCE ANTIPHON: The saints are happy in heaven because they followed Christ. They rejoice with him for ever because they shed their blood for love of him.

RESPONSE: Our soul has been rescued like a bird from the fowler's snare. *(Ps 124:7)*

GOSPEL VERSE: R/. Alleluia. We praise you, O God, we acclaim you as Lord; the white-robed army of martyrs praise you. R/. Alleluia. *(See Te Deum)*

COMMUNION ANTIPHON: You are the men who have stood by me faithfully in my trials, and now I confer a kingdom on you, says the Lord. You will eat and drink at my table in my kingdom. *(Lk 22:28-30)*

OR: *Blessed Virgin Mary / 707-712*

ENTRANCE ANTIPHON: You have been blessed, O Virgin Mary, above all other women on earth by the Lord the most high God; he has so exalted your name that your praises shall never fade from the mouths of men. *(See Jdt 13:23, 25)*

RESPONSE: You are the highest honor of our race. *(Jdt 15:9d)*

GOSPEL VERSE: R/. Alleluia. Blessed are you, holy Virgin Mary, deserving of all praise; from you rose the sun of justice, Christ our God. R/. Alleluia.

COMMUNION ANTIPHON: All generations will call me blessed, because God has looked upon his lowly handmaid. *(See Lk 1:48)*

Sunday, August 14, 2011: Assumption of the Blessed Virgin Mary—Vigil / 621 [1 Chr 15:3-4, 15-16; 16:1-2/1 Cor 15:54b-57/Lk 11:27-28]

[Evening Mass]

ENTRANCE ANTIPHON: All honor to you, Mary! Today you were raised above the choirs of angels to lasting glory with Christ.

RESPONSE: Lord, go up to the place of your rest, you and the ark of your holiness. *(Ps 132:8)*

GOSPEL VERSE: R/. Alleluia. Blessed are they who hear the word of God and observe it. R/. Alleluia. *(Lk 11:28)*

COMMUNION ANTIPHON: Blessed is the womb of the Virgin Mary; she carried the Son of the eternal Father. *(See Lk 11:27)*

Monday, August 15, 2011: Assumption of the Blessed Virgin Mary / 622 [Rv 11:19a; 12:1–6a, 10ab/1 Cor 15:20–27/Lk 1:39–56]

ENTRANCE ANTIPHON: A great sign appeared in heaven: a woman clothed with the sun, the moon beneath her feet, and a crown of twelve stars on her head. *(Rv 12:1)*

RESPONSE: The queen stands at your right hand, arrayed in gold. *(Ps 45:10bc)*

GOSPEL VERSE: R/. Alleluia. Mary is taken up to heaven; a chorus of angels exults. R/. Alleluia.

COMMUNION ANTIPHON: All generations will call me blessed, for the Almighty has done great things for me. *(Lk 1:48–49)*

Tuesday, August 16, 2011: Twentieth Week in Ordinary Time / 420 [Jgs 6:11–24a/Mt 19:23–30]

ENTRANCE ANTIPHON: God, our protector, keep us in mind; always give strength to your people. For if we can be with you even one day, it is better than a thousand without you. *(Ps 83:10–11)*

RESPONSE: The Lord speaks of peace to his people. *(See Ps 85:9b)*

GOSPEL VERSE: R/. Alleluia. Jesus Christ became poor although he was rich so that by his poverty you might become rich. R/. Alleluia. *(2 Cor 8:9)*

COMMUNION ANTIPHON: With the Lord there is mercy, and fullness of redemption. *(Ps 129:7)*

OR: *Stephen of Hungary / 623 [Dt 6:3–9/Mt 25:14–30 or Mt 25:14–23]*

ENTRANCE ANTIPHON: The just man will rejoice in the Lord and hope in him, and all the upright of heart will be praised. *(Ps 63:11)*

RESPONSE: Blessed the man who fears the Lord. *(Ps 112:1)*

GOSPEL VERSE: R/. Alleluia. Whoever loves me will keep my word, and my Father will love him, and we will come to him. R/. Alleluia. *(Jn 14:23)*

COMMUNION ANTIPHON: He who serves me, follows me, says the Lord; and where I am, my servant will also be. *(Jn 12:26)*

Wednesday, August 17, 2011: Twentieth Week in Ordinary Time / 421 [Jgs 9:6–15/Mt 20:1–16]

ENTRANCE ANTIPHON: God, our protector, keep us in mind; always give strength to your people. For if we can be with you even one day, it is better than a thousand without you. *(Ps 83:10–11)*

RESPONSE: Lord, in your strength the king is glad. *(Ps 21:2a)*

GOSPEL VERSE: R/. Alleluia. The word of God is living and effective, able to discren the reflections and thoughts of the heart. R/. Alleluia. *(Heb 4:12)*

COMMUNION ANTIPHON: With the Lord there is mercy, and fullness of redemption. *(Ps 129:7)*

Thursday, August 18, 2011: Twentieth Week in Ordinary Time / 422 [Jgs 11:29–39a/Mt 22:1–14]

ENTRANCE ANTIPHON: God, our protector, keep us in mind; always give strength to your people. For if we can be with you even one day, it is better than a thousand without you. *(Ps 83:10–11)*

RESPONSE: Here I am, Lord; I come to do your will. *(Ps 40:8a, 9a)*

GOSPEL VERSE: R/. Alleluia. If today you hear his voice, harden not your hearts. R/. Alleluia. *(Ps 95:8)*

COMMUNION ANTIPHON: With the Lord there is mercy, and fullness of redemption. *(Ps 129:7)*

Friday, August 19, 2011: Twentieth Week in Ordinary Time / 423 [Ru 1:1, 3–6, 14b–16, 22/Mt 22:34–40]

ENTRANCE ANTIPHON: God, our protector, keep us in mind; always give strength to your people. For if we can be with you even one day, it is better than a thousand without you. *(Ps 83:10–11)*

RESPONSE: Praise the Lord, my soul! *(Ps 146:1b)*

GOSPEL VERSE: R/. Alleluia. Teach me your paths, my God, guide me in your truth. R/. Alleluia. *(Ps 25:4b, 5a)*

COMMUNION ANTIPHON: With the Lord there is mercy, and fullness of redemption. *(Ps 129:7)*

OR: *John Eudes—priest / 624 [Eph 3:14–19/Mt 11:25–30]*

ENTRANCE ANTIPHON: These are the saints who received blessings from the Lord, a prize from God their Savior. They are the people that long to see his face. *(See Ps 23:5–6)*

RESPONSE: In you, Lord, I have found my peace.

GOSPEL VERSE: R/. Alleluia. Blessed are you, Father, Lord of heaven and earth; you have revealed to little ones the mysteries of the Kingdom. R/. Alleluia. *(See Mt 11:25)*

COMMUNION ANTIPHON: Taste and see the goodness of the Lord; blessed is he who hopes in God. *(Ps 34:9)*

Saturday, August 20, 2011: Bernard— abbot, doctor of the Church / 625 [Sir 15:1–6/Jn 17:20–26]

ENTRANCE ANTIPHON: The Lord is my inheritance and my cup; he alone will give me my reward. The measuring line has marked a lovely place for me; my inheritance is my great delight. *(Ps 15:5–6)*

RESPONSE: Lord, teach me your statutes. *(Ps 119:12)*

GOSPEL VERSE: R/. Alleluia. Remain in my love, says the Lord; whoever lives in me and I in him will bear much fruit. R/. Alleluia. *(Jn 15:9b, 5b)*

COMMUNION ANTIPHON: I solemnly tell you: those who have left everything and followed me will be repaid a hundredfold and will gain eternal life. *(See Mt 19:27–29)*

OR: **Twentieth Week in Ordinary Time** / 424 [Ru 2:1–3, 8–11; 4:13–17/Mt 23:1–12]

ENTRANCE ANTIPHON: God, our protector, keep us in mind; always give strength to your people. For if we can be with you even one day, it is better than a thousand without you. *(Ps 83:10–11)*

RESPONSE: See how the Lord blesses those who fear him. *(Ps 128:4)*

GOSPEL VERSE: R/. Alleluia. You have but one Father in heaven; you have but one master, the Christ. R/. Alleluia. *(Mt 23:9b, 10b)*

COMMUNION ANTIPHON: With the Lord there is mercy, and fullness of redemption. *(Ps 129:7)*

Monday, August 22, 2011: The Queenship of the Blessed Virgin Mary / 627 [Is 9:1–6/Lk 1:26–38]

ENTRANCE ANTIPHON: The queen stands at your right hand arrayed in cloth of gold. *(Ps 44:10)*

RESPONSE: Blessed be the name of the Lord for ever. *(Ps 113:2) Or:* Alleluia.

GOSPEL VERSE: R/. Alleluia. Hail, Mary, full of grace, the Lord is with you; blessed are you among women. R/. Alleluia. *(See Lk 1:28)*

COMMUNION ANTIPHON: Blessed are you for your firm believing, that the promises of the Lord would be fulfilled. *(Lk 1:45)*

OR: **Twenty-First Week in Ordinary Time** / 425 [1 Thes 1:1–5, 8b–10/Mt 23:13–22]

ENTRANCE ANTIPHON: Listen, Lord, and answer me. Save your servant who trusts in you. I call to you all day long, have mercy on me, O Lord. *(Ps 85:1–3)*

RESPONSE: The Lord takes delight in his people. *(See Ps 149:4a) Or:* Alleluia.

GOSPEL VERSE: R/. Alleluia. My sheep hear my voice, says the Lord; I know them, and they follow me. R/. Alleluia. *(Jn 10:27)*

COMMUNION ANTIPHON: Lord, the earth is filled with your gift from heaven; man grows bread from earth, and wine to cheer his heart. *(Ps 103:13–15)*

Tuesday, August 23, 2011: Twenty-first week in Ordinary Time / 426 [1 Thes 2:1–8/Mt 23:23–26]

ENTRANCE ANTIPHON: Listen, Lord, and answer me. Save your servant who trusts in you. I call to you all day long, have mercy on me, O Lord. *(Ps 85:1–3)*

RESPONSE: You have searched me and you know me, Lord. *(Ps 139:1)*

GOSPEL VERSE: R/. Alleluia. The word of God is living and effective, able to discern reflections and thoughts of the heart. R/. Alleluia. *(Heb 4:12)*

COMMUNION ANTIPHON: Lord, the earth is filled with your gift from heaven; man grows bread from earth, and wine to cheer his heart. *(Ps 103:13–15)*

OR: ***Rose of Lima***—virgin / 628 [2 Cor 10:17–11:2/Mt 13:44–46]

ENTRANCE ANTIPHON: Here is a wise and faithful virgin who went with lighted lamp to meet her Lord.

RESPONSE: Young men and women, praise the name of the Lord. *(See Ps 148:12a, 13a) Or:* Alleluia.

GOSPEL VERSE: R/. Alleluia. Remain in my love, says the Lord; whoever remains in me and I in him will bear much fruit. R/. Alleluia. *(Jn 15:9b, 5b)*

COMMUNION ANTIPHON: The bridegroom is here; let us go out to meet Christ the Lord. *(Mt 25:6)*

Wednesday, August 24, 2011: Bartholomew—apostle / 629 [Rv 21:9b–14/Jn 1:45–51]

ENTRANCE ANTIPHON: Day after day proclaim the salvation of the Lord. Proclaim his glory to all nations. *(Ps 95:2–3)*

RESPONSE: Your friends make known, O Lord, the glorious splendor of your Kingdom. *(Ps 145:12)*

GOSPEL VERSE: R/. Alleluia. Rabbi, you are the Son of God; you are the King of Israel. R/. Alleluia. *(Jn 1:49b)*

COMMUNION ANTIPHON: I will give you the kingdom that my Father gave to me, and in that kingdom you will eat and drink at my table. *(Lk 22:29–30)*

Thursday, August 25, 2011: Twenty-first Week in Ordinary Time / 428 [1 Thes 3:7–13/Mt 24:42–51]

ENTRANCE ANTIPHON: Listen, Lord, and answer me. Save your servant who trusts in you. I call to you all day long, have mercy on me, O Lord. *(Ps 85:1–3)*

RESPONSE: Fill us with your love, O Lord, and we will sing for joy! *(Ps 90:14)*

GOSPEL VERSE: R/. Alleluia. Stay awake! For you do not know when the Son of Man will come. R/. Alleluia. *(Mt 24:42a, 44)*

COMMUNION ANTIPHON: Lord, the earth is filled with your gift from heaven; man grows bread from earth, and wine to cheer his heart. *(Ps 103:13–15)*

OR: *Louis of France* / 630 *[Is 58:6–11/Mt 22:34–40]*

ENTRANCE ANTIPHON: May all your works praise you, Lord, and your saints bless you; they will tell of the glory of your kingdom and proclaim you power. *(Ps 144:10–11)*

RESPONSE: Blessed the man who fears the Lord. *(Ps 112:1) Or:* Alleluia.

GOSPEL VERSE: R/. Alleluia. I give you a new commandment: love one another, as I have loved you. R/. Alleluia. *(Jn 13:34)*

COMMUNION ANTIPHON: May the just rejoice as they feast in God's presence, and delight in gladness of heart. *(Ps 67:4)*

OR: *Joseph Calasanz—priest* / 631 *[1 Cor 12:31–13:13 or 1 Cor 13:4–13/Mt 18:1–5]*

ENTRANCE ANTIPHON: Let the children come to me, and do not stop them, says the Lord; to such belongs the kingdom of God. *(Mk 10:14)*

RESPONSE: I will bless the Lord at all times. *(Ps 34:2)*

Or: Taste and see the goodness of the Lord. *(Ps 34:9)*

GOSPEL VERSE: R/. Alleluia. Remain in my love, says the Lord; whoever remains in me and I in him will bear much fruit. R/. Alleluia. *(Jn 15:9b, 5b)*

COMMUNION ANTIPHON: Unless you change, and become like little children, says the Lord, you shall not enter the kingdom of heaven. *(Mt 18:3)*

Friday, August 26, 2011: Twenty-first Week in Ordinary Time / 429 [1 Thes 4:1–8/Mt 25:1–13]

ENTRANCE ANTIPHON: Listen, Lord, and answer me. Save your servant who trusts in you. I call to you all day long, have mercy on me, O Lord. *(Ps 85:1–3)*

RESPONSE: Rejoice in the Lord, you just! *(Ps 97:12a)*

GOSPEL VERSE: R/. Alleluia. Be vigilant at all times and pray, that you may have the strength to stand before the Son of Man. R/. Alleluia. *(Lk 21:36)*

COMMUNION ANTIPHON: Lord, the earth is filled with your gift from heaven; man grows bread from earth, and wine to cheer his heart. *(Ps 103:13–15)*

Saturday, August 27, 2011: Monica / 632 [Sir 26:1–4, 13–16/Lk 7:11–17]

ENTRANCE ANTIPHON: Praise to the holy woman whose home is built on faithful love and whose pathway leads to God. *(See Prv 14:1–2)*

RESPONSE: In you, Lord, I have found my peace.

GOSPEL VERSE: R/. Alleluia. I am the light of the world, says the Lord; whoever follows me will have the light of life. R/. Alleluia. *(Jn 8:12)*

COMMUNION ANTIPHON: Whoever does the will of my Father in heaven is my brother and sister and mother, says the Lord. *(Mt 12:50)*

OR: **Twenty-first Week in Ordinary Time** / 430 [1 Thes 4:9–11/Mt 25:14–30]

ENTRANCE ANTIPHON: Listen, Lord, and answer me. Save your servant who trusts in you. I call to you all day long, have mercy on me, O Lord. *(Ps 85:1–3)*

RESPONSE: The Lord comes to rule the earth with justice. *(Ps 98:9)*

GOSPEL VERSE: R/. Alleluia. I give you a new commandment: love one another as I have loved you. R/. Alleluia. *(Jn 13:34)*

COMMUNION ANTIPHON: Lord, the earth is filled with your gift from heaven; man grows bread from earth, and wine to cheer his heart. *(Ps 103:13–15)*

Monday, August 29, 2011: The Martyrdom of John the Baptist / 634 [Jer 1:17–19/Mk 6:17–29]

ENTRANCE ANTIPHON: Lord, I shall expound your law before kings and not fear disgrace; I shall ponder your decrees, which I have always loved. *(Ps 118:46–47)*

RESPONSE: I will sing your salvation. *(See Ps 71: 15ab)*

GOSPEL VERSE: R/. Alleluia. Blessed are those who are persecuted for the sake of righteousness, for theirs is the Kingdom of heaven. R/. Alleluia. *(Mt 5:10)*

COMMUNION ANTIPHON: John's answer was: He must grow greater and I must grow less. *(Jn 3:27, 30)*

OR: **Twenty-second Week in Ordinary Time /** 431 [1 Thes 4:13–18/Mk 6:17–29]

ENTRANCE ANTIPHON: I call to you all day long, have mercy on me, O Lord. You are good and forgiving, full of love for all who call to you. *(Ps 85:3, 5)*

RESPONSE: The Lord comes to judge the earth. *(Ps 96:13b)*

GOSPEL VERSE: R/. Alleluia. Blessed are those who are persecuted for the sake of righteousness, for theirs is the Kingdom of heaven. R/. Alleluia. *(Mt 5:10)*

COMMUNION ANTIPHON: O Lord, how great is the depth of the kindness which you have shown to those who love you. *(Ps 30:20)*

Tuesday, August 30, 2011: Twenty-second Week in Ordinary Time / 432 [1 Thes 5:1–6, 9–11/Lk 4:31–37]

ENTRANCE ANTIPHON: I call to you all day long, have mercy on me, O Lord. You are good and forgiving, full of love for all who call to you. *(Ps 85:3, 5)*

RESPONSE: I believe that I shall see the good things of the Lord in the land of the living. *(Ps 27:13)*

GOSPEL VERSE: R/. Alleluia. A great prophet has arisen in our midst and God has visited his people. R/. Alleluia.*(Lk 7:16)*

COMMUNION ANTIPHON: O Lord, how great is the depth of the kindness which you have shown to those who love you. *(Ps 30:20)*

Wednesday, August 31, 2011: Twenty-second Week in Ordinary Time / 433 [Col 1:1–8/Lk 4:38–44]

ENTRANCE ANTIPHON: I call to you all day long, have mercy on me, O Lord. You are good and forgiving, full of love for all who call to you. *(Ps 85:3, 5)*

RESPONSE: I trust in the mercy of God for ever. *(Ps 52:10)*

GOSPEL VERSE: R/. Alleluia. The Lord sent me to bring glad tidings to the poor and to proclaim liberty to captives. R/. Alleluia.*(Lk 4:18)*

COMMUNION ANTIPHON: O Lord, how great is the depth of the kindness which you have shown to those who love you. *(Ps 30:20)*

Thursday, September 1, 2011: Twenty-second Week in Ordinary Time / 433 [Col 1:9–14/Lk 5:1–11]

ENTRANCE ANTIPHON: I call to you all day long, have mercy on me, O Lord. You are good and forgiving, full of love for all who call to you. *(Ps 85:3, 5)*

RESPONSE: The Lord has made known his salvation. *(Ps 98:2)*

GOSPEL VERSE: R/. Alleluia. Come after me, says the Lord, and I will make you fishers of men. R/. Alleluia. *(Mt 4:19)*

COMMUNION ANTIPHON: O Lord, how great is the depth of the kindness which you have shown to those who love you. *(Ps 30:20)*

Friday, September 2, 2011: Twenty-second Week in Ordinary Time / 435 [Col 1:15–20/Lk 5:33–39]

ENTRANCE ANTIPHON: I call to you all day long, have mercy on me, O Lord. You are good and forgiving, full of love for all who call to you. *(Ps 85:3, 5)*

RESPONSE: Come with joy into the presence of the Lord. *(Ps 100:2b)*

GOSPEL VERSE: R/. Alleluia. I am the light of the world, says the Lord; whoever follows me will have the light of life. R/. Alleluia. *(Jn 8:12)*

COMMUNION ANTIPHON: O Lord, how great is the depth of the kindness which you have shown to those who love you. *(Ps 30:20)*

Saturday, September 3, 2011: Gregory the Great̶ pope, doctor of the Church / 635 [2 Cor 4:1–2, 5–7/Lk 22:24–30]

ENTRANCE ANTIPHON: The learned will shine like the brilliance of the firmament, and those who train many in the ways of justice will sparkle like the stars for all eternity. *(Dn 12:3)*

RESPONSE: Proclaim God's marvelous deeds to all the nations. *(Ps 96:3)*

GOSPEL VERSE: R/. Alleluia. I call you my friends, says the Lord, for I have made known to you all that the Father has told me. R/. Alleluia. *(Jn 15:15b)*

COMMUNION ANTIPHON: We preach a Christ who was crucified; he is the power and the wisdom of God. *(1 Cor 1:23–24)*

OR: **Twenty-second Week in Ordinary Time /** 436 [Col 1:21–23/Lk 6:1–5]

ENTRANCE ANTIPHON: I call to you all day long, have mercy on me, O Lord. You are good and forgiving, full of love for all who call to you. *(Ps 85:3, 5)*

RESPONSE: God himself is my help. *(Ps 54:6)*

GOSPEL VERSE: R/. Alleluia. I am the way and the truth and the life, says the Lord; no one comes to the Father except through me. R/. Alleluia. *(Jn 14:6)*

COMMUNION ANTIPHON: O Lord, how great is the depth of the kindness which you have shown to those who love you. *(Ps 30:20)*

Monday, September 5, 2011: Twenty-third Week in Ordinary Time / 437 [Col 1:24–2:3/Lk 6:6–11]

ENTRANCE ANTIPHON: Lord, you are just, and the judgments you make are right. Show mercy when you judge me, your servant. *(Ps 118:137, 124)*

RESPONSE: In God is my safety and my glory. *(Ps 62:8)*

GOSPEL VERSE: R/. Alleluia. My sheep hear my voice, says the Lord; I know them, and they follow me. R/. Alleluia. *(2 Thes 2:14)*

COMMUNION ANTIPHON: Like a deer that longs for running streams, my soul longs for you, my God. My soul is thirsting for the living God. *(Ps 41:2–3)*

*OR: **Labor Day** / 907–911*

ENTRANCE ANTIPHON: May the goodness of the Lord be upon us, and give success to the work of our hands. *(Ps 89:17)*

RESPONSE: The Lord will build a house for us and guard our city. *(See Ps 127:1)*

GOSPEL VERSE: R/. Alleluia. Blessed be the Lord day after day, God, our salvation, who bears our burdens. R/. Alleluia. *(Ps 68:20)*

COMMUNION ANTIPHON: Let everything you do or say be in the name of the Lord with thanksgiving to God. *(Col 3:17)*

Tuesday, September 6, 2011: Twenty-third Week in Ordinary Time / 438 [Col 2:6–15/Lk 6:12–19]

ENTRANCE ANTIPHON: Lord, you are just, and the judgments you make are right. Show mercy when you judge me, your servant. *(Ps 118:137, 124)*

RESPONSE: The Lord is compassionate toward all his works. *(Ps 145:9)*

GOSPEL VERSE: R/. Alleluia. I chose you from the world, that you may go and bear fruit that will last, says the Lord. R/. Alleluia. *(See Jn 15:16)*

COMMUNION ANTIPHON: Like a deer that longs for running streams, my soul longs for you, my God. My soul is thirsting for the living God. *(Ps 41:2–3)*

Wednesday, September 7, 2011: Twenty-third Week in Ordinary Time / 439 [Col 3:1–11/Lk 6:20–26]

ENTRANCE ANTIPHON: Lord, you are just, and the judgments you make are right. Show mercy when you judge me, your servant. (Ps 118:137, 124)

RESPONSE: The Lord is compassionate toward all his works. (Ps 145:9)

GOSPEL VERSE: R/. Alleluia. Rejoice and leap for joy! Your reward will be great in heaven. R/. Alleluia. (Lk 6:23ab)

COMMUNION ANTIPHON: Like a deer that longs for running streams, my soul longs for you, my God. My soul is thirsting for the living God. (Ps 41:2–3)

Thursday, September 8, 2011: Nativity of the Blessed Virgin Mary / 636 [Mi 5:1–4a or Rom 8:28–30/Mt 1:1–16, 18–23 or Mt 1:18–23]

ENTRANCE ANTIPHON: Let us celebrate with joyful hearts the birth of the Virgin Mary, of whom was born the sun of justice, Christ our Lord.

RESPONSE: With delight I rejoice in the Lord. (Is 61:10)

GOSPEL VERSE: R/. Alleluia. Blessed are you, holy Virgin Mary, deserving of all praise; from you rose the sun of justice, Christ our God. R/. Alleluia.

COMMUNION ANTIPHON: The Virgin shall bear a son, who will save his people from their sins. (Is 7:14; Mt 1:21)

Friday, September 9, 2011: Peter Claver—priest / 636A, 719–724

ENTRANCE ANTIPHON: These are holy men who became God's friends and glorious heralds of his truth.

RESPONSE: The Lord is my shepherd; there is nothing I shall want. (Ps 23:1)

GOSPEL VERSE: R/. Alleluia. Come after me, says the Lord, and I will make you fishers of men. R/. Alleluia. (Mk 1:17)

COMMUNION ANTIPHON: I will feed my sheep, says the Lord, and give them repose (Ez 34:15)

OR: Twenty-third Week in Ordinary Time / 441 [1 Tm 1:1–2, 12–14/Lk 6:39–42]

ENTRANCE ANTIPHON: Lord, you are just, and the judgments you make are right. Show mercy when you judge me, your servant. (Ps 118:137, 124)

RESPONSE: You are my inheritance, O Lord. (See Ps 16:5)

GOSPEL VERSE: R/. Alleluia. Your word, O Lord, is truth; consecrate us in the truth. R/. Alleluia. (Lk 6:39–42)

COMMUNION ANTIPHON: Like a deer that longs for running streams, my soul longs for you, my God. My soul is thirsting for the living God. (Ps 41:2–3)

Saturday, September 10, 2011: Twenty-third Week in Ordinary Time / 442 [1 Tm 1:15–17/Lk 6:43–49]

ENTRANCE ANTIPHON: Lord, you are just, and the judgments you make are right. Show mercy when you judge me, your servant. (Ps 118:137, 124)

RESPONSE: Blessed be the name of the Lord for ever. (Ps 113:2)

GOSPEL VERSE: R/. Alleluia. Whoever loves me will keep my word, and my Father will love him and we will come to him. R/. Alleluia. (Jn 14:23)

COMMUNION ANTIPHON: Like a deer that longs for running streams, my soul longs for you, my God. My soul is thirsting for the living God. (Ps 41:2–3)

OR: *Blessed Virgin Mary* / 707–712

ENTRANCE ANTIPHON: Hail, holy Mother! The child to whom you gave birth is the King of heaven and earth for ever. (Sedulius)

RESPONSE: The Almighty has done great things for me, and holy is his Name. (Lk 1:49)

Or: O Blessed Virgin Mary, you carried the Son of the eternal Father.

GOSPEL VERSE: R/. Alleluia. Blessed are you, O Virgin Mary, who believed that what was spoken to you by the Lord would be fulfilled. R/. Alleluia. (See Lk 1:45)

COMMUNION ANTIPHON: Blessed is the womb of the Virgin Mary; she carried the Son of the eternal Father. (See Lk 11:27)

Monday, September 12, 2011: Twenty-fourth Week in Ordinary Time / 443 [1 Tm 2:1–8/Lk 7:1–10]

ENTRANCE ANTIPHON: Give peace, Lord, to those who wait for you and your prophets will proclaim you as you deserve. Hear the prayers of your servant and of your people Israel. *(See Sir 36:18)*

RESPONSE: Blessed be the Lord, for he has heard my prayer. *(Ps 28:6)*

GOSPEL VERSE: R/. Alleluia. God so loved the world that he gave his only-begotten Son, so that everyone who believes in him might have eternal life. R/. Alleluia. *(Jn 3:16)*

COMMUNION ANTIPHON: The cup that we bless is a communion with the blood of Christ; and the bread that we break is a communion with the body of the Lord. *(See 1 Cor 10:16)*

OR: *Most Holy Name of the Blessed Virgin Mary / [Gal 4:4–7 or Eph 1:3–6, 11–12/Lk 1:39–47]*

ENTRANCE ANTIPHON: You have been blessed, O Virgin Mary, above all other women on earth by the Lord the most high God; he has so exulted your name that your praises shall never fade from the mouths of men *(See Jdt 13:23, 25)*

RESPONSE: Blessed is the Virgin Mary, who has brought forth the Son of the eternal Father.

GOSPEL VERSE: R/. Alleluia. Blessed are you, O Virgin Mary, who believed that what was spoken to you by the Lord would be fulfilled. R/. Alleluia. *(See Lk 1:45)*

COMMUNION ANTIPHON: All generations will call me blessed, because God has looked upon his lowly handmaid. *(See Lk 1:48)*

Tuesday, September 13, 2011: John Chrysostom—bishop, doctor of the Church / 637 [Eph 4:1–7, 11–13/ Mk 4:1–10, 13–20 or Mk 4:1–9]

ENTRANCE ANTIPHON: The Lord opened his mouth in the assembly and filled him with the spirit of wisdom and understanding, and clothed him in a robe of glory. *(Sir 15:5)*

RESPONSE: Here I am, Lord; I come to do your will. *(Ps 40:8a, 9a)*

GOSPEL VERSE: R/. Alleluia. The seed is the word of God; Christ is the sower; all who come to him will live for ever. R/. Alleluia.

COMMUNION ANTIPHON: The Lord has put his faithful servant in charge of his household, to give them their share of bread at the proper time. *(Lk 12:42)*

OR: *Twenty-fourth Week in Ordinary Time / 444* [1 Tm 3:1–13/Lk 7:11–17]

ENTRANCE ANTIPHON: Give peace, Lord, to those who wait for you and your prophets will proclaim you as you deserve. Hear the prayers of your servant and of your people Israel. *(See Sir 36:18)*

RESPONSE: I will walk with blameless heart. *(Ps 101:2)*

GOSPEL VERSE: R/. Alleluia. A great prophet has arisen in our midst and God has visited his people. R/. Alleluia. *(Lk 7:16)*

COMMUNION ANTIPHON: The cup that we bless is a communion with the blood of Christ; and the bread that we break is a communion with the body of the Lord. *(See 1 Cor 10:16)*

Wednesday, September 14, 2011: Exaltation of the Holy Cross / 638 [Nm 21:4b–9/Phil 2:6–11/Jn 3:13–17]

ENTRANCE ANTIPHON: We should glory in the cross of our Lord Jesus Christ, for he is our salvation, our life and our resurrection; through him we are saved and made free. *(See Gal 6:14)*

RESPONSE: Do not forget the works of the Lord! *(Ps 78:7b)*

GOSPEL VERSE: R/. Alleluia. We adore you, O Christ, and we bless you, because by your Cross you have redeemed the world. R/. Alleluia.

COMMUNION ANTIPHON: When I am lifted up from the earth, I will draw all men to myself, says the Lord. *(Jn 12:32)*

Thursday, September 15, 2011: Our Lady of Sorrows / 639 [Heb 5:7–9/ Jn 19:25–27 or Lk 2:33–35]

ENTRANCE ANTIPHON: Simeon said to Mary: This child is destined to be a sign which men will reject; he is set for the fall and the rising of many in Israel; and your own soul a sword shall pierce. *(Lk 2:34–35)*

RESPONSE: Save me, O Lord, in your kindness. *(Ps 31:17)*

GOSPEL VERSE: R/. Alleluia. Blessed are you, O Virgin Mary; without dying you won the martyr's crown beside the Cross of the Lord. R/. Alleluia.

COMMUNION ANTIPHON: Be glad to share in the sufferings of Christ! When he comes in glory, you will be filled with joy. *(1 Pt 4:13)*

OR: **Twenty-fourth Week in Ordinary Time** / 446 [1 Tm 4:12–16/Jn 19:25–27 or Lk 2:33–35]

ENTRANCE ANTIPHON: Give peace, Lord, to those who wait for you and your prophets will proclaim you as you deserve. Hear the prayers of your servant and of your people Israel. *(See Sir 36:18)*

RESPONSE: How great are the works of the Lord! *(Ps 111:2)*

GOSPEL VERSE: R/. Alleluia. Blessed are you, O Virgin Mary; without dying you won the martyr's crown beside the Cross of the Lord. R/. Alleluia.

COMMUNION ANTIPHON: The cup that we bless is a communion with the blood of Christ; and the bread that we break is a communion with the body of the Lord. *(See 1 Cor 10:16)*

Friday, September 16, 2011: Cornelius—pope, martyr; **and Cyprian**—bishop, martyr / 640 [2 Cor 4:7–15/Jn 17:11b–19]

ENTRANCE ANTIPHON: The Lord chose him to be his high priest; he opened his treasures and made him rich in all goodness.

RESPONSE: Those who sow in tears shall reap rejoicing. *(Ps 126:5)*

GOSPEL VERSE: R/. Alleluia. Blessed be the Father of compassion and God of all encouragement, who encourages us in our every affliction. R/. Alleluia. *(2 Cor 1:3b–4)*

COMMUNION ANTIPHON: The good shepherd gives his life for his sheep. *(See Jn 10:11)*

OR: **Twenty-fourth Week in Ordinary Time** / 447 [1 Tm 6:2c–12/Lk 8:1–3]

ENTRANCE ANTIPHON: Give peace, Lord, to those who wait for you and your prophets will proclaim you as you deserve. Hear the prayers of your servant and of your people Israel. *(See Sir 36:18)*

RESPONSE: Blessed the poor in spirit; the Kingdom of heaven is theirs!

GOSPEL VERSE: R/. Alleluia. Blessed are you, Father, Lord of heaven and earth; you have revealed to little ones the mysteries of the Kingdom. R/. Alleluia. *(See Mt 11:25)*

COMMUNION ANTIPHON: The cup that we bless is a communion with the blood of Christ; and the bread that we break is a communion with the body of the Lord. *(See 1 Cor 10:16)*

Saturday, September 17, 2011: Twenty-fourth Week in Ordinary Time / 448 [1 Tm 6:13–16/Lk 8:4–15]

ENTRANCE ANTIPHON: Give peace, Lord, to those who wait for you and your prophets will proclaim you as you deserve. Hear the prayers of your servant and of your people Israel. *(See Sir 36:18)*

RESPONSE: Come with joy into the presence of the Lord. *(Ps 100:2)*

GOSPEL VERSE: R/. Alleluia. Blessed are they who have kept the word with a generous heart and yield a harvest through perseverance. R/. Alleluia. *(See Lk 8:15)*

COMMUNION ANTIPHON: The cup that we bless is a communion with the blood of Christ; and the bread that we break is a communion with the body of the Lord. *(See 1 Cor 10:16)*

OR: **Robert Bellarmine**—*bishop, doctor of the Church* / 641 [Wis 7:7–10, 15–16/Mt 7:21–29]

ENTRANCE ANTIPHON: The learned will shine like the brilliance of the firmament, and those who train many in the ways of justice will sparkle like the stars for all eternity. *(Dn 12:3)*

RESPONSE: The judgments of the Lord are true, and all of them are just. *(Ps 19:10)*

Or: Your words, Lord, are Spirit and life. *(Jn 6:63)*

GOSPEL VERSE: R/. Alleluia. Your words, Lord, ae Spirit and life; you have the words of everlasting life. R/. Alleluia. *(See Jn 6:63c, 68c)*

COMMUNION ANTIPHON: We preach a Christ who was crucified; he is the power and the wisdom of God. *(1 Cor 1:23–24)*

OR: **Blessed Virgin Mary** / 707–712

ENTRANCE ANTIPHON: You have been blessed, O Virgin Mary, above all other women on earth by the Lord the most high God; he has so exalted your name that your praises shall never fade from the mouths of men. *(See Jdt 13:23, 25)*

RESPONSE: Blessed be the name of the Lord for ever. *(Ps 113:2)* Or: Alleluia.

GOSPEL VERSE: R/. Alleluia. Hail, Mary, full of grace, the Lord is with you; blessed are you among women. R/. Alleluia. *(See Lk 1:28)*

COMMUNION ANTIPHON: All generations will call me blessed, because God has looked upon his lowly handmaid. *(See Lk 1:48)*

Monday, September 19, 2011: Twenty-fifth Week in Ordinary Time / 449 [Ezr 1:1–6/Lk 8:16–18]

ENTRANCE ANTIPHON: I am the Savior of all people, says the Lord. Whatever their troubles, I will answer their cry, and I will always be their Lord.

RESPONSE: The Lord has done marvels for us. *(Ps 126:3)*

GOSPEL VERSE: R/. Alleluia. Let your light shine before others, that they may see you good deeds and glorify your heavenly Father. R/. Alleluia. *(Mt 5:16)*

COMMUNION ANTIPHON: You have laid down your precepts to be faithfully kept. May my footsteps be firm in keeping your commands. *(Ps 118:4–5)*

OR: Januarius—bishop, martyr / 642 [Heb 10: 32–36/Jn 12:24–26]

ENTRANCE ANTIPHON: This holy man fought to the death for the law of his God, never cowed by the threats of the wicked; his house was built on solid rock.

RESPONSE: Those who sow in tears shall reap rejoicing. *(Ps 126:5)*

GOSPEL VERSE: R/. Alleluia. Blessed is the man who perseveres in temptation, for when he has been proved he will receive the crown of life. R/. Alleluia. *(Jas 1:12)*

COMMUNION ANTIPHON: If anyone wishes to come after me, he must renounce himself, take up his cross, and follow me, says the Lord. *(Mt 16:24)*

Tuesday, September 20, 2011: Andrew Kim Taegŏn—priest, martyr; Paul Chŏng Hasang—martyr; and their companions—martyrs / 642A [Wis 3:1–9 or Rom 8:31b–39/Lk 9:23–26]

ENTRANCE ANTIPHON: Let us all rejoice in the Lord, and keep a festival in honor of Andrew and Paul and their companios. Let us join with the angels in joyful praise to the Son of God.

RESPONSE: Those who sow in tears shall reap rejoicing. *(Ps 126:5)*

GOSPEL VERSE: R/. Alleluia. If you are insulted for the name of Christ, blessed are you, for the Spirit of Christ rests upon you. R/. Alleluia. *(1 Pt 4:14)*

COMMUNION ANTIPHON: Whoever acknowledges me before the world, I will acknowledge before my Father in heaven. *(Mt 10:32)*

OR: Twenty-fifth Week in Ordinary Time / 450 [Ezr 6:7–8, 12b, 14–20/Lk 8:19–21]

ENTRANCE ANTIPHON: I am the Savior of all people, says the Lord. Whatever their troubles, I will answer their cry, and I will always be their Lord.

RESPONSE: Let us go rejoicing to the house of the Lord. *(Ps 122:1)*

GOSPEL VERSE: R/. Alleluia. Blessed are those who hear the word of God and observe it. R/. Alleluia. *(Lk 11:28)*

COMMUNION ANTIPHON: You have laid down your precepts to be faithfully kept. May my footsteps be firm in keeping your commands. *(Ps 118:4–5)*

Wednesday, September 21, 2011: Matthew—apostle, evangelist / 643 [Eph 4:1–7, 11–13/Mt 9:9–13]

ENTRANCE ANTIPHON: Go and preach to all nations: baptize them and teach them to observe all that I have commanded you, says the Lord. *(Mt 28:19–20)*

RESPONSE: Their message goes out through all the earth. *(Ps 19:5)*

GOSPEL VERSE: R/. Alleluia. We praise you, O God, we acclaim you as Lord; the glorious company of Apostles praise you. R/. Alleluia. *(See Te Deum)*

COMMUNION ANTIPHON: I did not come to call the virtuous, but sinners, says the Lord. *(Mt 9:13)*

Thursday, September 22, 2011: Twenty-fifth Week in Ordinary Time / 452 [Hg 1:1–8/Lk 9:7–9]

ENTRANCE ANTIPHON: I am the Savior of all people, says the Lord. Whatever their troubles, I will answer their cry, and I will always be their Lord.

RESPONSE: The Lord takes delight in his people. *(See Ps 149:4a)*

GOSPEL VERSE: R/. Alleluia. I am the way and the truth and the life, says the Lord; no one comes to the Father except through me. R/. Alleluia. *(Jn 14:6)*

COMMUNION ANTIPHON: You have laid down your precepts to be faithfully kept. May my footsteps be firm in keeping your commands. *(Ps 118:4–5)*

Friday, September 23, 2011: Pio of Pietrelcina—priest / 719–724 [Dt 10:8–9/Mt 23:8–12]

ENTRANCE ANTIPHON: Priests of God, bless the Lord; praise God, all you that are holy and humble of heart. *(Dn 3:84, 87)*

RESPONSE: The Lord is my shepherd; there is nothing I shall want. *(Ps 23:1)*

GOSPEL VERSE: R/. Alleluia. God was reconciling the world to himself in Christ, and entrusting to us the message of reconciliation. R/. Alleluia. *(2 Cor 5:19)*

COMMUNION ANTIPHON: The Son of Man did not come to be served, but to serve, and to give his life as a ransom for many. *(Mt 20:28)*

OR: **Twenty-fifth Week in Ordinary Time** / 453 [Hg 2:1–9/Lk 9:18–22]

ENTRANCE ANTIPHON: I am the Savior of all people, says the Lord. Whatever their troubles, I will answer their cry, and I will always be their Lord.

RESPONSE: Hope in God; I will praise him, my savior and my God. *(Ps 43:5)*

GOSPEL VERSE: R/. Alleluia. The Son of Man came to serve and to give his life as a ransom for many. R/. Alleluia. *(Mk 10:45)*

COMMUNION ANTIPHON: You have laid down your precepts to be faithfully kept. May my footsteps be firm in keeping your commands. *(Ps 118:4–5)*

Saturday, September 24, 2011: Twenty-fifth Week in Ordinary Time / 454 [Zec 2:5–9, 14–15a/Lk 9:43b–45]

ENTRANCE ANTIPHON: I am the Savior of all people, says the Lord. Whatever their troubles, I will answer their cry, and I will always be their Lord.

RESPONSE: The Lord will guard us as a shepherd guards his flock. *(See Jer 31:10d)*

GOSPEL VERSE: R/. Alleluia. Our Savior Christ Jesus destroyed death and brought life to light through the Gospel. R/. Alleluia. *(See 2 Tm 1:10)*

COMMUNION ANTIPHON: You have laid down your precepts to be faithfully kept. May my footsteps be firm in keeping your commands. *(Ps 118:4–5)*

*OR: **Blessed Virgin Mary** / 707–712*

ENTRANCE ANTIPHON: You have been blessed, O Virgin Mary, above all other women on earth by the Lord the most high God; he has so exalted your name that your praises shall never fade from the mouths of men. *(See Jdt 13:23, 25)*

RESPONSE: The Almighty has done great things for me, and holy is his Name. *(Lk 1:49)*

Or: O Blessed Virgin Mary, you carried the Son of the eternal Father.

GOSPEL VERSE: R/. Alleluia. Blessed is the Virgin Mary who kept the word of God and pondered it in her heart. R/. Alleluia. *(See Lk 2:19)*

COMMUNION ANTIPHON: All generations will call me blessed, because God has looked upon his lowly handmaid. *(See Lk 1:48)*

Monday, September 26, 2011: Twenty-sixth Week in Ordinary Time / 455 [Zec 8:1–8/Lk 9:46–50]

ENTRANCE ANTIPHON: O Lord, you had just cause to judge men as you did: because we sinned against you and disobeyed your will. But now show us your greatness of heart, and treat us with your unbounded kindness. *(Dn 3:31, 29, 30, 43, 42)*

RESPONSE: The Lord will build up Zion again, and appear in all his glory. *(Ps 102:17)*

GOSPEL VERSE: R/. Alleluia. The Son of Man came to serve and to give his life as a ransom for many. R/. Alleluia. *(See Mk 10:45)*

COMMUNION ANTIPHON: O Lord, remember the words you spoke to me, your servant, which made me live in hope and consoled me when I was downcast. *(Ps 118:49–50)*

*OR: **Cosmas and Damian**—martyrs / 644 [Wis 3:1–9/Mt 10:28–33]*

ENTRANCE ANTIPHON: The holy martyrs shed their blood on earth for Christ; therefore they have received an everlasting reward.

RESPONSE: Those who sow in tears shall reap rejoicing. *(Ps 126:5)*

GOSPEL VERSE: R/. Alleluia. Blessed is the man who perseveres in temptation, for when he has been proved he will receive the crown of life. R/. Alleluia. *(Jas 1:12)*

COMMUNION ANTIPHON: Neither death nor life nor anything in all creation can come between us and Christ's love for us. *(See Rom 8:38–39)*

Tuesday, September 27, 2011: Vincent de Paul—priest / 645 [1 Cor 1:26–31/Mt 9:35–38]

ENTRANCE ANTIPHON: The Spirit of God is upon me; he has anointed me. He sent me to bring good news to the poor, and to heal the broken-hearted. *(Lk 4:18)*

RESPONSE: Blessed the man who fears the Lord. *(Ps 112:1) Or:* Alleluia.

GOSPEL VERSE: R/. Alleluia. I am the good shepherd, says the Lord; I know my sheep, and mine know me. R/. Alleluia. *(Jn 10:14)*

COMMUNION ANTIPHON: Give praise to the Lord for his kindness, for his wonderful deeds toward men. He has filled the hungry with good things, he has satisfied the thirsty. *(Ps 106:8–9)*

OR: **Twenty-sixth Week in Ordinary Time** / 456 [Zec 8:20–23/Lk 9:51–56]

ENTRANCE ANTIPHON: O Lord, you had just cause to judge men as you did: because we sinned against you and disobeyed your will. But now show us your greatness of heart, and treat us with your unbounded kindness. *(Dn 3:31, 29, 30, 43, 42)*

RESPONSE: God is with us. *(Zec 8:23)*

GOSPEL VERSE: R/. Alleluia. The Son of Man came to serve and to give his life as a ransom for many. R/. Alleluia. *(Mk 10:45)*

COMMUNION ANTIPHON: O Lord, remember the words you spoke to me, your servant, which made me live in hope and consoled me when I was downcast. *(Ps 118:49–50)*

Wednesday, September 28, 2011: Twenty-sixth Week in Ordinary Time / 457 [Neh 2:1–8/Lk 9:57–62]

ENTRANCE ANTIPHON: O Lord, you had just cause to judge men as you did: because we sinned against you and disobeyed your will. But now show us your greatness of heart, and treat us with your unbounded kindness. *(Dn 3:31, 29, 30, 43, 42)*

RESPONSE: Let my tongue be silenced, if I ever forget you! *(Ps 137:6ab)*

GOSPEL VERSE: R/. Alleluia. I consider all things so much rubbish that I may gain Christ and be found in him. R/. Alleluia. *(Phil 3:8–9)*

COMMUNION ANTIPHON: O Lord, remember the words you spoke to me, your servant, which made me live in hope and consoled me when I was downcast. *(Ps 118:49–50)*

OR: **Lawrence Ruiz—martyr; and his companions—martyrs** / 645A, 713–718

ENTRANCE ANTIPHON: The holy martyrs shed their blood on earth for Christ; therefore they have received an everlasting reward.

RESPONSE: The Lord delivered me from all my fears. *(Ps 34:5)*

GOSPEL VERSE: R/. Alleluia. I consecrate myself for them, so that they also may be consecrated in the truth. R/. Alleluia. *(Jn 17:19)*

COMMUNION ANTIPHON: Neither death nor life nor anything in all creation can come between us and Christ's love for us. *(See Rom 8:38–39)*

OR: **Wenceslaus—martyr** / 646 [1 Pt 3:14–17/Mt 10:34–39]

ENTRANCE ANTIPHON: Here is a true martyr who shed his blood for Christ; his judges could not shake him by their menaces, and so he won through to the kingdom of heaven.

RESPONSE: Those who sow in tears shall reap rejoicing. *(Ps 126:5)*

GOSPEL VERSE: R/. Alleluia. Blessed are they who are persecuted for the sake of righteousness, for theirs is the Kingdom of heaven. R/. Alleluia. *(Mt 5:10)*

COMMUNION ANTIPHON: I am the vine and you are the branches, says the Lord; he who lives in me, and I in him, will bear much fruit. *(Jn 15:5)*

Thursday, September 29, 2011: Michael, Gabriel, and Raphael—archangels / 647 [Dn 7:9–10, 13–14 or Rv 12:7–12ab/Jn 1:47–51]

ENTRANCE ANTIPHON: Bless the Lord, all you his angels, mighty in power, you obey his word and heed the sound of his voice. *(Ps 102:20)*

RESPONSE: In the sight of the angels I will sing your praises, Lord. *(Ps 138:1)*

GOSPEL VERSE: R/. Alleluia. Bless the LORD, all you his angels, you ministers, who do his will. R/. Alleluia. *(Ps 103:21)*

COMMUNION ANTIPHON: In the sight of the angels I will sing your praises, my God. *(Ps 138:1)*

Friday, September 30, 2011: Jerome—priest, doctor of the Church / 648 [2 Tm 3:14–17/Mt 13:47–52]

ENTRANCE ANTIPHON: The book of the law must be ever on your lips; reflect on it night and day. Observe and do all that it commands: then you will direct your life with understanding. *(Jos 1:8)*

RESPONSE: Lord, teach me your statutes. *(Ps 119:12)*

GOSPEL VERSE: R/. Alleluia. Open our hearts, O Lord, to listen to the words of your Son. R/. Alleluia. *(See Acts 16:14b)*

COMMUNION ANTIPHON: When I discovered your teaching, I devoured it. Your words brought me joy and gladness; you have called me your own, O Lord my God. *(Jer 15:16)*

OR: **Twenty-sixth Week in Ordinary Time** / 459 [Bar 1:15–22/Lk 10:13–16]

ENTRANCE ANTIPHON: O Lord, you had just cause to judge men as you did: because we sinned against you and disobeyed your will. But now show us your greatness of heart, and treat us with your unbounded kindness. *(Dn 3:31, 29, 30, 43, 42)*

RESPONSE: For the glory of your name, O Lord, deliver us. *(Ps 79:9)*

GOSPEL VERSE: R/. Alleluia. If today you hear his voice, harden not your hearts. R/. Alleluia. *(Ps 95:8)*

COMMUNION ANTIPHON: O Lord, remember the words you spoke to me, your servant, which made me live in hope and consoled me when I was downcast. *(Ps 118:49–50)*

Saturday, October 1, 2011: Thérèse of the Child Jesus—virgin, doctor of the Church / 649 [Is 66:10–14c/Mt 18:1–4]

ENTRANCE ANTIPHON: The Lord nurtured and taught her; he guarded her as the apple of his eye. As the eagle spreads its wings to carry its young, he bore her on his shoulders. The Lord alone was her leader. *(See Dt 32:10–12)*

RESPONSE: In you, Lord, I have found my peace.

GOSPEL VERSE: R/. Alleluia. Blessed are you, Father, Lord of heaven and earth; you have revealed to little ones the mysteries of the Kingdom. R/. Alleluia. *(See Mt 11:25)*

COMMUNION ANTIPHON: Unless you change and become like little children, says the Lord, you shall not enter the kingdom of heaven. *(Mt 18:3)*

OR: **Twenty-sixth Week in Ordinary Time** / 460 [Bar 4:5–12, 27–29/Lk 10:17–24]

ENTRANCE ANTIPHON: O Lord, you had just cause to judge men as you did: because we sinned against you and disobeyed your will. But now show us your greatness of heart, and treat us with your unbounded kindness. *(Dn 3:31, 29, 30, 43, 42)*

RESPONSE: The Lord listens to the poor. *(Ps 69:34)*

GOSPEL VERSE: R/. Alleluia. Blessed are you, Father, Lord of heaven and earth; you have revealed to little ones the mysteries of the Kingdom. R/. Alleluia. *(See Mt 11:25)*

COMMUNION ANTIPHON: O Lord, remember the words you spoke to me, your servant, which made me live in hope and consoled me when I was downcast. *(Ps 118:49–50)*

Monday, October 3, 2011: Twenty-seventh Week in Ordinary Time / 461 [Jon 1:1–2:2, 11/Lk 10:25–37]

ENTRANCE ANTIPHON: O Lord, you have given everything its place in the world, and no one can make it otherwise. For it is your creation, the heavens and the earth and the stars: you are the Lord of all. *(Est 13:9, 10–11)*

RESPONSE: You will rescue my life from the pit, O Lord. *(Jon 2:7)*

GOSPEL VERSE: R/. Alleluia. I give you a new commandment: love one another as I have loved you. R/. Alleluia. *(Jn 13:34)*

COMMUNION ANTIPHON: The Lord is good to those who hope in him, to those who are searching for his love. *(Lam 3:25)*

Tuesday, October 4, 2011: Francis of Assisi—religious/ 651 [Gal 6:14–18/Mt 11:25–30]

ENTRANCE ANTIPHON: Francis, a man of God, left his home and gave away his wealth to become poor and in need. But the Lord cared for him.

RESPONSE: You are my inheritance, O Lord. *(See Ps 16:5a)*

GOSPEL VERSE: R/. Alleluia. Blessed are you, Father, Lord of heaven and earth; you have revealed to little ones the mysteries of the Kingdom. R/. Alleluia. *(See Mt 11:25)*

COMMUNION ANTIPHON: Blessed are the poor in spirit; the kingdom of heaven is theirs! *(Mt 5:3)*

OR: **Twenty-seventh Week in Ordinary Time** / 462 [Jon 3:1–10/Lk 10:38–42]

ENTRANCE ANTIPHON: O Lord, you have given everything its place in the world, and no one can make it otherwise. For it is your creation, the heavens and the earth and the stars: you are the Lord of all. *(Est 13:9, 10–11)*

RESPONSE: If you, O Lord, mark iniquities, who can stand? *(Ps 130:3)*

GOSPEL VERSE: R/. Alleluia. Blessed are those who hear the word of God and observe it. R/. Alleluia. *(Lk 11:28)*

COMMUNION ANTIPHON: The Lord is good to those who hope in him, to those who are searching for his love. *(Lam 3:25)*

Wednesday, October 5, 2011: Twenty-seventh Week in Ordinary Time / 463 [Jon 4:1–11/Lk 11:1–4]

ENTRANCE ANTIPHON: O Lord, you have given everything its place in the world, and no one can make it otherwise. For it is your creation, the heavens and the earth and the stars: you are the Lord of all. *(Est 13:9, 10–11)*

RESPONSE: Lord, you are merciful and gracious. *(Ps 86:15)*

GOSPEL VERSE: R/. Alleluia. You have received a spirit of adoption as sons through which we cry: Abba! Father! R/. Alleluia. *(Rom 8:15bc)*

COMMUNION ANTIPHON: The Lord is good to those who hope in him, to those who are searching for his love. *(Lam 3:25)*

Thursday, October 6, 2011: Twenty-seventh Week in Ordinary Time / 464 [Mal 3:13–20b/Lk 11:5–13]

ENTRANCE ANTIPHON: O Lord, you have given everything its place in the world, and no one can make it otherwise. For it is your creation, the heavens and the earth and the stars: you are the Lord of all. *(Est 13:9, 10–11)*

RESPONSE: Blessed are they who hope in the Lord. *(Ps 40:5a)*

GOSPEL VERSE: R/. Alleluia. Open our hearts, O Lord, to listen to the words of your Son. R/. Alleluia. *(See Acts 16:14b)*

COMMUNION ANTIPHON: The Lord is good to those who hope in him, to those who are searching for his love. *(Lam 3:25)*

OR: *Bruno—priest* / 652 [Phil 3:8–14/Lk 9:57–62]

ENTRANCE ANTIPHON: Lord, may your priests be clothed in justice, and your holy ones leap for joy. *(Ps 131:9)*

RESPONSE: Blessed are they who hope in the Lord. *(Ps 40:5a)*

Or: Blessed are they who delight in the law of the Lord. *(Ps 1:2a)*

Or: The just will flourish like the palm tree in the garden of the Lord. *(Ps 92:13–14)*

GOSPEL VERSE: R/. Alleluia. I am the light of the world, says the Lord; whoever follows me will have the light of life. R/. Alleluia. *(Jn 8:12)*

COMMUNION ANTIPHON: Blessed is the servant whom the Lord finds watching when he comes; truly I tell you, he will set him over all his possessions. *(Mt 24:46–47)*

OR: *Blessed Marie-Rose Durocher—virgin* / 652A, 731–736, 737–742

ENTRANCE ANTIPHON: Here is a wise and faithful virgin who went with lighted lamp to meet her Lord.

RESPONSE: Listen to me, daughter; see and bend your ear. *(Ps 45:11)*

Or: The bridegroom is here; let us go out to meet Christ the Lord.

GOSPEL VERSE: R/. Alleluia. This is the wise virgin, whom the Lord found waiting; at his coming, she went in with him to the wedding feast. R/. Alleluia.

COMMUNION ANTIPHON: The bridegroom is here; let us go out to meet Christ the Lord. *(Mt 25:6)*

Friday, October 7, 2011: Our Lady of the Rosary / 653 [Acts 1:12–14/Lk 1:26–38]

ENTRANCE ANTIPHON: Hail Mary, full of grace, the Lord is with you; blessed are you among women and blessed is the fruit of your womb. *(Lk 1:28, 42)*

RESPONSE: The Almighty has done great things for me, and holy is his name. *(Lk 1:49)*

Or: O Blessed Virgin Mary, you carried the Son of the eternal Father.

GOSPEL VERSE: R/. Alleluia. Hail Mary, full of grace, the Lord is with you; blessed are you among women. R/. Alleluia. *(See Lk 1:28)*

COMMUNION ANTIPHON: You shall conceive and bear a Son, and you shall call his name Jesus. (*Lk 1:31*)

OR: **Twenty-seventh Week in Ordinary Time /** 465 [Jl 1:13–15; 2:1–2/Lk 11:15–26]

ENTRANCE ANTIPHON: O Lord, you have given everything its place in the world, and no one can make it otherwise. For it is your creation, the heavens and the earth and the stars: you are the Lord of all. (*Est 13:9, 10–11*)

RESPONSE: The Lord will judge the world with justice. (*Ps 9:9*)

GOSPEL VERSE: R/. Alleluia. The prince of this world will now be cast out, and when I am lifted up from the earth I will draw all to myself, says the Lord. R/. Alleluia. (*Jn 12:31b–32*)

COMMUNION ANTIPHON: The Lord is good to those who hope in him, to those who are searching for his love. (*Lam 3:25*)

Saturday, October 8, 2011: Twenty-seventh Week in Ordinary Time / 466 [Jl 4:12–21/Lk 11:27–28]

ENTRANCE ANTIPHON: O Lord, you have given everything its place in the world, and no one can make it otherwise. For it is your creation, the heavens and the earth and the stars: you are the Lord of all. (*Est 13:9, 10–11*)

RESPONSE: Rejoice in the Lord, you just! (*Ps 97:12a*)

GOSPEL VERSE: R/. Alleluia. Blessed are those who hear the word of God and observe it. R/. Alleluia. (*Lk 11:28*)

COMMUNION ANTIPHON: The Lord is good to those who hope in him, to those who are searching for his love. (*Lam 3:25*)

*OR: **Blessed Virgin Mary** / 707–712*

ENTRANCE ANTIPHON: Blessed are you, Virgin Mary, who carried the creator of all things in your womb; you gave birth to your maker, and remain for ever a virgin.

RESPONSE: Blessed by the name of the Lord for ever. (*Ps 113:2*) *Or:* Alleluia.

GOSPEL VERSE: R/. Alleluia. Blessed are you, holy Virgin Mary, deserving of all praise; from you rose the sun of justice, Christ our God. R/. Alleluia.

COMMUNION ANTIPHON: The Almighty has done great things for me. Holy is his name. (*Lk 1:49*)

Monday, October 10, 2011: Twenty-eighth Week in Ordinary Time / 467 [Rom 1:1–7/Lk 11:29–32]

ENTRANCE ANTIPHON: If you, O Lord, laid bare our guilt, who could endure it? But you are forgiving, God of Israel. (*Ps 129:3–4*)

RESPONSE: The Lord has made known his salvation. (*Ps 98:2a*)

GOSPEL VERSE: R/. Alleluia. If today you hear his voice, harden not your hearts. R/. Alleluia. (*Ps 95:8*)

COMMUNION ANTIPHON: The rich suffer want and go hungry, but nothing shall be lacking to those who fear the Lord. (*Ps 33:11*)

Tuesday, October 11, 2011: Twenty-eighth Week in Ordinary Time / 468 [Rom 1:16–25/Lk 11:37–41]

ENTRANCE ANTIPHON: If you, O Lord, laid bare our guilt, who could endure it? But you are forgiving, God of Israel. (*Ps 129:3–4*)

RESPONSE: The heavens proclaim the glory of God. (*Ps 19:2a*)

GOSPEL VERSE: R/. Alleluia. The word of God is living and effective, able to discern reflections and thoughts of the heart. R/. Alleluia. (*Heb 4:12*)

COMMUNION ANTIPHON: The rich suffer want and go hungry, but nothing shall be lacking to those who fear the Lord. (*Ps 33:11*)

Wednesday, October 12, 2011: Twenty-eighth Week in Ordinary Time / 469 [Rom 2:1–11/Lk 11:42–46]

ENTRANCE ANTIPHON: If you, O Lord, laid bare our guilt, who could endure it? But you are forgiving, God of Israel. (*Ps 129:3–4*)

RESPONSE: Lord, you give back to everyone according to his works. (*Ps 62:13b*)

GOSPEL VERSE: R/. Alleluia. My sheep hear my voice, says the Lord; I know them, and they follow me. R/. Alleluia. (*Jn 10:27*)

COMMUNION ANTIPHON: The rich suffer want and go hungry, but nothing shall be lacking to those who fear the Lord. (*Ps 33:11*)

Thursday, October 13, 2011: Twenty-eighth Week in Ordinary Time / 470 [Rom 3:21–30/Lk 11:47–54]

ENTRANCE ANTIPHON: If you, O Lord, laid bare our guilt, who could endure it? But you are forgiving, God of Israel. *(Ps 129:3–4)*

RESPONSE: With the Lord there is mercy, and fullness of redemption. *(Ps 130:7)*

GOSPEL VERSE: R/. Alleluia. I am the way and the truth and the life, says the Lord; no one comes to the Father except through me. R/. Alleluia. *(Jn 14:6)*

COMMUNION ANTIPHON: The rich suffer want and go hungry, but nothing shall be lacking to those who fear the Lord. *(Ps 33:11)*

Friday, October 14, 2011: Twenty-eighth Week in Ordinary Time / 471 [Rom 4:1–8/Lk 12:1–7]

ENTRANCE ANTIPHON: If you, O Lord, laid bare our guilt, who could endure it? But you are forgiving, God of Israel. *(Ps 129:3–4)*

RESPONSE: I turn to you, Lord, in time of trouble, and you fill me with the joy of salvation. *(See Ps 32:7)*

GOSPEL VERSE: R/. Alleluia. May your kindness, O LORD, be upon us; who have put our hope in you. R/. Alleluia. *(Ps 33:22)*

COMMUNION ANTIPHON: The rich suffer want and go hungry, but nothing shall be lacking to those who fear the Lord. *(Ps 33:11)*

OR: *Callistus I—pope, martyr / 656 [1 Pt 5:1–4/Lk 22:24–30]*

ENTRANCE ANTIPHON: Here is a true martyr who shed his blood for Christ; his judges could not shake him by their menaces, and so he won through to the kingdom of heaven.

RESPONSE: Here I am, Lord; I come to do your will. *(Ps 40:8a, 9a)*

GOSPEL VERSE: R/. Alleluia. I call you my friends, says the Lord, for I have made known to you all that the Father has told me. R/. Alleluia. *(Jn 15:15b)*

COMMUNION ANTIPHON: I am the vine and you are the branches, says the Lord; he who lives in me, and I in him, will bear much fruit. *(Jn 15:5)*

Saturday, October 15, 2011: Teresa of Jesus—virgin, doctor of the Church / 657 [Rom 8:22–27/Jn 15:1–8]

ENTRANCE ANTIPHON: Like a deer that longs for running streams, my soul longs for you, my God. My soul is thirsting for the living God. *(Ps 41:2–3)*

RESPONSE: The judgments of the Lord are true, and all of them are just. *(Ps 19:10)*

Or: Your words, Lord, are Spirit and life. *(Jn 6:63)*

GOSPEL VERSE: R/. Alleluia. Remain in my love, says the Lord; whoever remains in me and I in him will bear much fruit. R/. Alleluia. *(Jn 15:9b, 5b)*

COMMUNION ANTIPHON: For ever I will sing the goodness of the Lord; I will proclaim your faithfulness to all generations. *(Ps 88:2)*

OR: **Twenty-eighth Week in Ordinary Time** / 472 [Rom 4:13, 16–18/Lk 12:8–12]

ENTRANCE ANTIPHON: If you, O Lord, laid bare our guilt, who could endure it? But you are forgiving, God of Israel. *(Ps 129:3–4)*

RESPONSE: The Lord remembers his covenent for ever. *(Ps 105:8a)*

GOSPEL VERSE: R/. Alleluia. The Spirit of truth will testify to me, says the Lord, and you also will testify. R/. Alleluia. *(Jn 15:26b, 27a)*

COMMUNION ANTIPHON: The rich suffer want and go hungry, but nothing shall be lacking to those who fear the Lord. *(Ps 33:11)*

Monday, October 17, 2011: Ignatius of Antioch—bishop, martyr / 660 [Phil 3:17–4:1/Jn 12:24–26]

ENTRANCE ANTIPHON: With Christ I am nailed to the cross. I live now not with my own life, but Christ lives within me. I live by faith in the Son of God, who loved me and sacrificed himself for me. *(Gal 2:19–20)*

RESPONSE: The Lord delivered me from all my fears. *(Ps 34:5)*

GOSPEL VERSE: R/. Alleluia. Blessed is the man who perseveres in temptation, for when he has been proved, he will receive the crown of life. R/. Alleluia. *(Jas 1:12)*

COMMUNION ANTIPHON: I am the wheat of Christ, ground by the teeth of beasts to become pure bread.

OR: **Twenty-ninth Week in Ordinary Time** / 473
[Rom 4:20–25/Lk 12:13–21]

ENTRANCE ANTIPHON: I call upon you, God, for you will answer me; bend your ear and hear my prayer. Guard me as the pupil of your eye; hide me in the shade of your wings. *(Ps 16:6, 8)*

RESPONSE: Blessed be the Lord, the God of Israel; he has come to his people. *(See Lk 1:68)*

GOSPEL VERSE: R/. Alleluia. Blessed are the poor in spirit; for theirs is the Kingdom of heaven. R/. Alleluia. *(Mt 5:3)*

COMMUNION ANTIPHON: See how the eyes of the Lord are on those who fear him, on those who hope in his love, that he may rescue them from death and feed them in time of famine. *(Ps 33:18–19)*

Tuesday, October 18, 2011: Luke—evangelist / 661 [2 Tm 4:10–17b/Lk 10:1–9]

ENTRANCE ANTIPHON: How beautiful on the mountains are the feet of the man who brings tidings of peace, joy and salvation. *(Is 52:7)*

RESPONSE: Your friends make known, O Lord, the glorious splendor of your Kingdom. *(Ps 145:12)*

GOSPEL VERSE: R/. Alleluia. I chose you from the world, to go and bear fruit that will last, says the Lord. R/. Alleluia. *(See Jn 15:16)*

COMMUNION ANTIPHON: The Lord sent disciples to proclaim to all the towns: the kingdom of God is very near to you. *(See Lk 10:1, 9)*

Wednesday, October 19, 2011: Isaac Jogues and John de Brébeuf—priests, martyrs, and their companions—martyrs / 662 [2 Cor 4:7–15/ Mt 28:16–20]

ENTRANCE ANTIPHON: The Lord will hear the just when they cry out, from all their afflictions he will deliver them. *(Ps 33:18)*

RESPONSE: Those who sow in tears, shall reap rejoicing. *(Ps 126:5)*

GOSPEL VERSE: R/. Alleluia. Go and teach all nations, says the Lord; I am with you always, until the end of the world. R/. Alleluia. *(Mt 28:19a, 20b)*

COMMUNION ANTIPHON: We are given over to death for Jesus, that the life of Jesus may be revealed in our dying flesh. *(2 Cor 4:11)*

OR: **Twenty-ninth Week in Ordinary Time** / 475
[Rom 6:12–18/Lk 12:39–48]

ENTRANCE ANTIPHON: I call upon you, God, for you will answer me; bend your ear and hear my prayer. Guard me as the pupil of your eye; hide me in the shade of your wings. *(Ps 16:6, 8)*

RESPONSE: Our help is in the name of the Lord. *(Ps 124:8a)*

GOSPEL VERSE: R/. Alleluia. Stay awake! For you do not know when the Son of Man will come. R/. Alleluia. *(Mt 24:42a, 44)*

COMMUNION ANTIPHON: See how the eyes of the Lord are on those who fear him, on those who hope in his love, that he may rescue them from death and feed them in time of famine. *(Ps 33:18–19)*

Thursday, October 20, 2011: Twenty-ninth Week in Ordinary Time / 476 [Rom 6:19–23/Lk 12:49–53]

ENTRANCE ANTIPHON: I call upon you, God, for you will answer me; bend your ear and hear my prayer. Guard me as the pupil of your eye; hide me in the shade of your wings. *(Ps 16:6, 8)*

RESPONSE: Blessed are they who hope in the Lord. *(Ps 40:5)*

GOSPEL VERSE: R/. Alleluia. I consider all things so much rubbish that I may gain Christ and be found in him. R/. Alleluia. *(Phil 3:8–9)*

COMMUNION ANTIPHON: See how the eyes of the Lord are on those who fear him, on those who hope in his love, that he may rescue them from death and feed them in time of famine. *(Ps 33:18–19)*

OR: **Paul of the Cross**—priest / 663 [1 Cor 1:18–25/Mt 16:24–27]

ENTRANCE ANTIPHON: I resolved that while I was with you I would think of nothing but Jesus Christ and him crucified. *(1 Cor 2:2)*

RESPONSE: Go out to all the world and tell the Good News. *(Mk 16:15)*

GOSPEL VERSE: R/. Alleluia. Blessed are those who hunger and thirst for righteousness; for they will be satisfied. R/. Alleluia. *(Mt 5:6)*

COMMUNION ANTIPHON: We preach a Christ who was crucified; he is the power and the wisdom of God. *(1 Cor 1:23–24)*

Friday, October 21, 2011: Twenty-ninth Week in Ordinary Time / 477 [Rom 7:18–25a/Lk 12:54–59]

ENTRANCE ANTIPHON: I call upon you, God, for you will answer me; bend your ear and hear my prayer. Guard me as the pupil of your eye; hide me in the shadow of your wings. *(Ps 16:6, 8)*

RESPONSE: Lord, teach me your statutes, *(Ps 119:68b)*

GOSPEL VERSE: R/. Alleluia. Blessed are you, Father, Lord of heaven and earth; you have revealed to little ones the mysteries of the Kingdom. R/. Alleluia. *(Mt 11:25)*

COMMUNION ANTIPHON: See how the eyes of the Lord are on those who fear him, on those who hope in his love, that he may rescue them from death and feed them in time of famine. *(Ps 32:18–19)*

Saturday, October 22, 2011: Twenty-ninth Week in Ordinary Time / 478 [Rom 8:1–11/Lk 13:1–9]

ENTRANCE ANTIPHON: I call upon you, God, for you will answer me; bend your ear and hear my prayer. Guard me as the pupil of your eye; hide me in the shade of your wings. *(Ps 16:6, 8)*

RESPONSE: Lord, this is the people that longs to see your face. *(See Ps 24:6)*

GOSPEL VERSE: R/. Alleluia. I take no pleasure in the death of the wicked man, says the Lord, but rather in his conversion that he may live. R/. Alleluia. *(Ez 33:11)*

COMMUNION ANTIPHON: See how the eyes of the Lord are on those who fear him, on those who hope in his love, that he may rescue them from death and feed them in time of famine. *(Ps 33:18–19)*

OR: *Blessed Virgin Mary / 707–712*

ENTRANCE ANTIPHON: Blessed are you, Virgin Mary, who carried the creator of all things in your womb; you gave birth to your maker, and remain for ever a virgin.

RESPONSE: O Blessed Virgin Mary, you carried the Son of the eternal Father.

Or: The Almighty has done great things for me, and holy is his Name. *(Lk 1:49)*

GOSPEL VERSE: R/. Alleluia. Blessed are you, holy Virgin Mary, deserving of all praise; from you rose the sun of justice, Christ our God. R/. Alleluia.

COMMUNION ANTIPHON: The Almighty has done great things for me. Holy is his name. *(Lk 1:49)*

Monday, October 24, 2011: Thirtieth Week in Ordinary Time / 479 [Rom 8:12–17/Lk 13:10–17]

ENTRANCE ANTIPHON: Let hearts rejoice who search for the Lord. Seek the Lord and his strength, seek always the face of the Lord. *(Ps 104:3–4)*

RESPONSE: Our God is the God of salvation. *(Ps 68:21a)*

GOSPEL VERSE: R/. Alleluia. Your word, O Lord, is truth; consecrate us in the truth. R/. Alleluia. *(Jn 17:17b, 17a)*

COMMUNION ANTIPHON: We will rejoice at the victory of God and make our boast in his great name. *(Ps 19:6)*

OR: *Anthony Mary Claret—bishop / 665 [Is 52:7–10/Mk 1:14–20]*

ENTRANCE ANTIPHON: I will look after my sheep, says the Lord, and I will raise up one shepherd who will pasture them. I, the Lord, will be their God. *(Ez 34:11, 23–24)*

RESPONSE: Proclaim God's marvelous deeds to all the nations. *(Ps 96:3)*

GOSPEL VERSE: R/. Alleluia. Come after me, says the Lord, and I will make you fishers of men. R/. Alleluia. *(Mk 1:17)*

COMMUNION ANTIPHON: You have not chosen me; I have chosen you. Go and bear fruit that will last. *(Jn 15:16)*

Tuesday, October 25, 2011: Thirtieth Week in Ordinary Time / 480 [Rom 8:18–25/Lk 13:18–21]

ENTRANCE ANTIPHON: Let hearts rejoice who search for the Lord. Seek the Lord and his strength, seek always the face of the Lord. *(Ps 104:3–4)*

RESPONSE: The Lord has done marvels for us. *(Ps 126:3a)*

GOSPEL VERSE: R/. Alleluia. Blessed are you, Father, Lord of heaven and earth; you have revealed to little ones the mysteries of the Kingdom. R/. Alleluia. *(See Mt 11:25)*

COMMUNION ANTIPHON: We will rejoice at the victory of God and make our boast in his great name. *(Ps 19:6)*

Wednesday, October 26, 2011: Thirtieth Week in Ordinary Time / 481 [Rom 8:26–30/Lk 13:22–30]

ENTRANCE ANTIPHON: Let hearts rejoice who search for the Lord. Seek the Lord and his strength, seek always the face of the Lord. *(Ps 104:3–4)*

RESPONSE: My hope, O Lord, is in your mercy. *(Ps 13:6a)*

GOSPEL VERSE: R/. Alleluia. God has called us through the Gospel to possess the glory of our Lord Jesus Christ. R/. Alleluia. *(See 2 Thes 2:14)*

COMMUNION ANTIPHON: We will rejoice at the victory of God and make our boast in his great name. *(Ps 19:6)*

Thursday, October 27, 2011: Thirtieth Week in Ordinary Time / 482 [Rom 8:31b–39/Lk 13:31–35]

ENTRANCE ANTIPHON: Let hearts rejoice who search for the Lord. Seek the Lord and his strength, seek always the face of the Lord. *(Ps 104:3–4)*

RESPONSE: Save me, O Lord, in your mercy. *(Ps 109:26b)*

GOSPEL VERSE: R/. Alleluia. Blessed is the king who comes in the name of the Lord. Glory to God in the highest and on earth peace to those on whom his favor rests. R/. Alleluia. *(See Lk 19:38; 2:14)*

COMMUNION ANTIPHON: We will rejoice at the victory of God and make our boast in his great name. *(Ps 19:6)*

Friday, October 28, 2011: Simon and Jude—apostles / 666 [Eph 2:19–22/Lk 6:12–16]

ENTRANCE ANTIPHON: The Lord chose these holy men for their unfeigned love, and gave them eternal glory.

RESPONSE: Their message goes out through all the earth. *(Ps 19:5a)*

GOSPEL VERSE: R/. Alleluia. We praise you, O God, we acclaim you as Lord; the glorious company of Apostles praise you. R/. Alleluia. *(See Te Deum)*

COMMUNION ANTIPHON: If anyone loves me, he will hold to my words, and my Father will love him, and we will come to him, and make our home with him. *(Jn 14:23)*

Saturday, October 29, 2011: Thirtieth Week in Ordinary Time / 484 [Rom 11:1–2a, 11–12, 25–29/Lk 14:1, 7–11]

ENTRANCE ANTIPHON: Let hearts rejoice who search for the Lord. Seek the Lord and his strength, seek always the face of the Lord. *(Ps 104:3–4)*

RESPONSE: The Lord will not abandon his people. *(Ps 94:14a)*

GOSPEL VERSE: R/. Alleluia. Take my yoke upon you and learn from me, for I am meek and humble of heart. R/. Alleluia. *(Mt 11:29ab)*

COMMUNION ANTIPHON: We will rejoice at the victory of God and make our boast in his great name. *(Ps 19:6)*

OR: *Blessed Virgin Mary / 707–712*

ENTRANCE ANTIPHON: Blessed are you, Virgin Mary, who carried the creator of all things in your womb; you gave birth to your maker, and remain for ever a virgin.

RESPONSE: My heart exults in the Lord, my Savior. *(See 1 Sm 2:1b)*

GOSPEL VERSE: R/. Alleluia. Blessed is the Virgin Mary who kept the word of God and pondered it in her heart. R/. Alleluia. *(See Lk 2:19)*

COMMUNION ANTIPHON: The Almighty has done great things for me. Holy is his name. *(Lk 1:49)*

Monday, October 31, 2011: Thirty-first Week in Ordinary Time / 485 [Rom 11:29–36/Lk 14:12–14]

ENTRANCE ANTIPHON: Do not abandon me, Lord. My God, do not go away from me! Hurry to help me, Lord, my Savior. *(Ps 37:22–23)*

RESPONSE: Lord, in your great love, answer me. *(Ps 69:14c)*

GOSPEL VERSE: R/. Alleluia. If you remain in my word, you will truly be my disciples, and you will know the truth, says the Lord. R/. Alleluia. *(Jn 8:31b–32)*

COMMUNION ANTIPHON: Lord, you will show me the path of life and fill me with joy in your presence. *(Ps 15:11)*

Tuesday, November 1, 2011: All Saints

(See Sunday section)

Wednesday, November 2, 2011: Commemoration of All the Faithful Departed (All Souls) / 668, 1011–1016 [Wis 3:1–9/Rom 5:5–11 or 6:3–9/Jn 6:37–40]

(or see Sunday section for this date)

ENTRANCE ANTIPHON I: Just as Jesus died and rose again, so will the Father bring with him those who have died in Jesus. Just as in Adam all men die, so in Christ all will be made alive. *(1 Thes 4:14; 1 Cor 15:22)*

II: Give them eternal rest, O Lord, and may your light shine on them for ever. *(See 4 Ezr 2:34–35)*

III: God, who raised Jesus from the dead, will give new life to our own mortal bodies through his Spirit living in us. *(Rom 8:11)*

RESPONSE: The Lord is my shepherd; there is nothing I shall want. *(Ps 23:1)*

Or: Though I walk in the valley of darkness, I fear no evil, for you are with me.

GOSPEL VERSE: R/. Alleluia. Come, you who are blessed by my Father; inherit the kingdom prepared for you from the foundation of the world. R/. Alleluia. *(Mt 25:34)*

COMMUNION ANTIPHON: I am the resurrection and the life, says the Lord. If anyone believes in me, even though he dies, he will live. Anyone who lives and believes in me, will not die. *(Jn 11:25–26)*

II: May eternal light shine on them, O Lord, with all your saints for ever, for you are rich in mercy. Give them eternal rest, O Lord, and may perpetual light shine on them for ever, for you are rich in mercy. *(See 4 Ezr 2:35, 34)*

III: We are waiting for our Savior, the Lord Jesus Christ; he will transfigure our lowly bodies into copies of his own glorious body. *(Phil 3:20–21)*

Thursday, November 3, 2011: Thirty-first Week in Ordinary Time / 488 [Rom 14:7–12/Lk 15:1–10]

ENTRANCE ANTIPHON: Do not abandon me, Lord. My God, do not go away from me! Hurry to help me, Lord, my Savior. *(Ps 37:22–23)*

RESPONSE: I believe that I shall see the good things of the Lord in the land of the living. *(Ps 27:13)*

GOSPEL VERSE: R/. Alleluia. Come to me, all you who labor and are burdened, and I will give you rest, says the Lord. R/. Alleluia. *(Mt 11:28)*

COMMUNION ANTIPHON: Lord, you will show me the path of life and fill me with joy in your presence. *(Ps 15:11)*

*OR: **Martin de Porres**—religious / 669 [Phil 4:4–9/Mt 22:34–40]*

ENTRANCE ANTIPHON: These are the saints who received blessings from the Lord, a prize from God their Savior. They are the people that long to see his face. *(See Ps 23:5–6)*

RESPONSE: In you, Lord, I have found my peace.

GOSPEL VERSE: R/. Alleluia. I give you a new commandment: love one another as I have loved you. R/. Alleluia. *(Jn 13:34)*

COMMUNION ANTIPHON: Taste and see the goodness of the Lord; blessed is he who hopes in God. *(Ps 34:9)*

Friday, November 4, 2011: Charles Borromeo—bishop / 670 [Rom 12:3–13/Jn 10:11–16]

ENTRANCE ANTIPHON: I will look after my sheep, says the Lord, and I will raise up one shepherd who will pasture them. I, the Lord, will be their God. *(Ez 34:11, 23–24)*

RESPONSE: Forever I will sing the goodness of the Lord. *(See Ps 89:2a)*

GOSPEL VERSE: R/. Alleluia. I am the good shepherd, says the Lord; I know my sheep, and mine know me. R/. Alleluia. *(Jn 10:14)*

COMMUNION ANTIPHON: You have not chosen me; I have chosen you. Go and bear fruit that will last. *(Jn 15:16)*

*OR: **Thirty-first Week in Ordinary Time** / 489 [Rom 15:14–21/Lk 16:1–8]*

ENTRANCE ANTIPHON: Do not abandon me, Lord. My God, do not go away from me! Hurry to help me, Lord, my Savior. *(Ps 37:22–23)*

RESPONSE: The Lord has revealed to the nations his saving power. *(See Ps 98:2b)*

GOSPEL VERSE: R/. Alleluia. Whoever keeps the word of Christ, the love of God is truly perfected in him. R/. Alleluia. *(1 Jn 2:5)*

COMMUNION ANTIPHON: Lord, you will show me the path of life and fill me with joy in your presence. *(Ps 15:11)*

Saturday, November 5, 2011: Thirty-first Week in Ordinary Time / 490 [Rom 16:3–9, 16, 22–27/Lk 16:9–15]

ENTRANCE ANTIPHON: Do not abandon me, Lord. My God, do not go away from me! Hurry to help me, Lord, my Savior. *(Ps 37:22–23)*

RESPONSE: I will praise your name for ever, Lord. *(Ps 145:1b)*

GOSPEL VERSE: R/. Alleluia. Jesus Christ became poor although he was rich, so that by his poverty you might become rich. R/. Alleluia. *(2 Cor 8:9)*

COMMUNION ANTIPHON: Lord, you will show me the path of life and fill me with joy in your presence. *(Ps 15:11)*

OR: *Blessed Virgin Mary* / 707–712

ENTRANCE ANTIPHON: Hail, holy Mother! The child to whom you gave birth is the King of heaven and earth for ever. *(Sedulius)*

RESPONSE: My heart exults in the Lord, my Savior. *(See 1 Sm 2:1b)*

GOSPEL VERSE: R/. Alleluia. Hail, Mary, full of grace, the Lord is with you; blessed are you among women. R/. Alleluia. *(See Lk 1:28)*

COMMUNION ANTIPHON: Blessed is the womb of the Virgin Mary; she carried the Son of the eternal Father. *(See Lk 11:27)*

Monday, November 7, 2011: Thirty-second Week in Ordinary Time / 491 [Wis 1:1–7/Lk 17:1–6]

ENTRANCE ANTIPHON: Let my prayer come before you, Lord; listen, and answer me. *(Ps 87:3)*

RESPONSE: Guide me, Lord, along the everlasting way. *(Ps 139:24b)*

GOSPEL VERSE: R/. Alleluia. Shine like lights in the world, as you hold on to the word of life. R/. Alleluia. *(Phil 2:15d, 16a)*

COMMUNION ANTIPHON: The disciples recognized the Lord Jesus in the breaking of bread. *(Lk 24:35)*

Tuesday, November 8, 2011: Thirty-second Week in Ordinary Time / 492 [Wis 2:23–3:9/Lk 17:7–10]

ENTRANCE ANTIPHON: Let my prayer come before you, Lord; listen, and answer me. *(Ps 87:3)*

RESPONSE: I will bless the Lord at all times. *(Ps 34:2a)*

GOSPEL VERSE: R/. Alleluia. Whoever loves me will keep my word, and my Father will love him, and we will come to him. R/. Alleluia. *(Jn 14:23)*

COMMUNION ANTIPHON: The disciples recognized the Lord Jesus in the breaking of bread. *(Lk 24:35)*

Wednesday, November 9, 2011: Dedication of the Lateran Basilica in Rome / 671 [Ez 47:1–2, 8–9, 12/1 Cor 3:9c–11, 16–17/Jn 2:13–22]

ENTRANCE ANTIPHON: I saw the holy city, new Jerusalem, coming down from God out of heaven, like a bride adorned in readiness for her husband. *(Rv 21:2)*

RESPONSE: The waters of the river gladden the city of God, the holy dwelling of the Most High! *(Ps 46:5)*

GOSPEL VERSE: R/. Alleluia. I have chosen and consecrated this house, says the Lord, that my name may be there forever. R/. Alleluia. *(2 Chr 7:16)*

COMMUNION ANTIPHON: Like living stones let yourselves be guilt on Christ as a siriual house, a holy priesthood. *(1 Pt 2:5)*

Thursday, November 10, 2011: Leo the Great—pope, doctor of the Church / 672 [Sir 39:6–10/Mt 16:13–19]

ENTRANCE ANTIPHON: The Lord sealed a covenant of peace with him, and made him a prince, bestowing the priestly dignity upon him for ever. *(See Sir 45:30)*

RESPONSE: The mouth of the just murmurs wisdom. *(Ps 37:30a)*

GOSPEL VERSE: R/. Alleluia. Come after me, says the Lord, and I will make you fishers of men. R/. Alleluia. *(Mk 1:17)*

COMMUNION ANTIPHON: Lord, you know all things; you know that I love you. *(Jn 21:17)*

OR: **Thirty-second Week in Ordinary Time / 494**
[Wis 7:22b–8:1/Lk 17:20–25]

ENTRANCE ANTIPHON: Let my prayer come before you, Lord; listen, and answer me. *(Ps 87:3)*

RESPONSE: Your word is for ever, O Lord. *(Ps 119: 89a)*

GOSPEL VERSE: R/. Alleluia. I am the vine, you are the branches, says the Lord; whoever remains in me and I in him will bear much fruit. R/. Alleluia. *(Jn 15:5)*

COMMUNION ANTIPHON: The disciples recognized the Lord Jesus in the breaking of bread. *(Lk 24:35)*

Friday November 11, 2011: Martin of Tours—bishop / 673 [Is 61:1–3abcd/Mt 25:31–40]

ENTRANCE ANTIPHON: I will raise up for myself a faithful priest; he will do what is in my heart and in my mind, says the Lord. *(1 Sm 2:35)*

RESPONSE: Forever I will sing the goodness of the Lord. *(See Ps 89:2a)*

GOSPEL VERSE: R/. Alleluia. I give you a new commandment: love one another as I have loved you. R/. Alleluia. *(Jn 13:34)*

COMMUNION ANTIPHON: I tell you, anything you did for the least of my brothers, you did for me, says the Lord. *(Mt 25:40)*

OR: **Thirty-second Week in Ordinary Time / 495**
[Wis 13:1–9/Lk 17:26–37]

ENTRANCE ANTIPHON: Let my prayer come before you, Lord; listen, and answer me. *(Ps 87:3)*

RESPONSE: The heavens proclaim the glory of God. *(Ps 19:2a)*

GOSPEL VERSE: R/. Alleluia. Stand erect and raise your heads because your redemption is at hand. R/. Alleluia. *(Lk 21:28)*

COMMUNION ANTIPHON: The disciples recognized the Lord Jesus in the breaking of bread. *(Lk 24:35)*

Saturday, November 12, 2011: Josaphat—bishop, martyr / 674 [Eph 4:1–7, 11–13/Jn 17:20–26]

ENTRANCE ANTIPHON: I will look after my sheep, says the Lord, and I will raise up one shepherd who will pasture them. I, the Lord, will be their God. *(Ez 34:11, 23–24)*

RESPONSE: Blessed are they who hope in the Lord. *(Ps 40:5a)*

Or: Blessed are they who delight in the law of the Lord. *(Ps 1:2a)*

Or: The just will flourish like the palm tree in the garden of the Lord. *(Ps 92:13–14)*

GOSPEL VERSE: R/. Alleluia. Remain in my love, says the Lord; whoever lives in me and I in him will bear much fruit. R/. Alleluia. *(Jn 15:9b, 5b)*

COMMUNION ANTIPHON: You have not chosen me; I have chosen you. Go and bear fruit that will last. *(Jn 15:16)*

OR: **Thirty-second Week in Ordinary Time / 496**
[Wis 18:14–16; 19:6–9/Lk 18:1–8]

ENTRANCE ANTIPHON: Let my prayer come before you, Lord; listen, and answer me. *(Ps 87:3)*

RESPONSE: Remember the marvels the Lord has done! *(Ps 105:5a) Or:* Alleluia.

GOSPEL VERSE: R/. Alleluia. God has called us through the Gospel, to possess the glory of our Lord Jesus Christ. R/. Alleluia. *(2 Thes 2:14)*

COMMUNION ANTIPHON: The disciples recognized the Lord Jesus in the breaking of bread. *(Lk 24:35)*

Monday, November 14, 2011: Thirty-third Week in Ordinary Time / 497 [1 Mc 1:10–15, 41–43, 54–57, 62–63/Lk 18:35–43]

ENTRANCE ANTIPHON: The Lord says: my plans for you are peace and not disaster; when you call to me, I will listen to you, and I will bring you back to the place from which I exiled you. *(Jer 29:11, 12, 14)*

RESPONSE: Give me life, O Lord, and I will do your commands. *(Ps 119:88)*

GOSPEL VERSE: R/. Alleluia. I am the light of the world, says the Lord; whoever follows me will have the light of life. R/. Alleluia. *(Jn 8:12)*

COMMUNION ANTIPHON: I tell you solemnly, whatever you ask for in prayer, believe that you have received it, and it will be yours, says the Lord. *(Mk 11:23, 24)*

Tuesday, November 15, 2011: Thirty-third Week in Ordinary Time / 498 [2 Mc 6:18–31/Lk 19:1–10]

ENTRANCE ANTIPHON: The Lord says: my plans for you are peace and not disaster; when you call to me, I will listen to you, and I will bring you back to the place from which I exiled you. *(Jer 29:11, 12, 14)*

RESPONSE: The Lord upholds me. *(Ps 3:6b)*

GOSPEL VERSE: R/. Alleluia. God loved us, and sent his Son as expiation for our sins. R/. Alleluia. *(1 Jn 4:10b)*

COMMUNION ANTIPHON: I tell you solemnly, whatever you ask for in prayer, believe that you have received it, and it will be yours, says the Lord. *(Mk 11:23, 24)*

OR: *Albert the Great—bishop, doctor of the Church / 675 [Sir 15:1–6/Mt 13:47–52]*

ENTRANCE ANTIPHON: The mouth of the just man utters wisdom, and his tongue speaks what is right; the law of his God is in his heart. *(Ps 36:30–31)*

RESPONSE: Lord, teach me your statutes. *(Ps 119:12)*

GOSPEL VERSE: R/. Alleluia. Open our hearts, O Lord, to listen to the words of your Son. R/. Alleluia. *(See Acts 16:14b)*

COMMUNION ANTIPHON: The Lord has put his faithful servant in charge of his household, to give them their share of bread at the proper time. *(Lk 12:42)*

Wednesday, November 16, 2011: Thirty-third Week in Ordinary Time/ 499 [2 Mc 7:1, 20–31/Lk 19:11–28]

ENTRANCE ANTIPHON: The Lord says: my plans for you are peace and not disaster; when you call to me, I will listen to you, and I will bring you back to the place from which I exiled you. *(Jer 29:11, 12, 14)*

RESPONSE: Lord, when your glory appears, my joy will be full. *(Ps 17:15b)*

GOSPEL VERSE: R/. Alleluia. I chose you from the world, to go and bear fruit that will last, says the Lord. R/. Alleluia. *(See Jn 15:16)*

COMMUNION ANTIPHON: I tell you solemnly, whatever you ask for in prayer, believe that you have received it, and it will be yours, says the Lord. *(Mk 11:23, 24)*

OR: *Margaret of Scotland / 676 [Is 58:6–11/Jn 15:9–17]*

ENTRANCE ANTIPHON: Come, you whom my Father has blessed, says the Lord: I was ill and you comforted me. I tell you, anything you did for one of my brothers, you did for me. *(Mt 25:34, 36, 40)*

RESPONSE: Blessed the man who fears the Lord. *(Ps 112:1) Or:* Alleluia.

GOSPEL VERSE: R/. Alleluia. I give you a new commandment: love one another as I have loved you. R/. Alleluia. *(Jn 13:34)*

COMMUNION ANTIPHON: By the love you have for one another, says the Lord, everyone will know that you are my disciples. *(Jn 13:35)*

OR: *Gertrude—virgin / 677 [Eph 3:14–19/Jn 15:1–8]*

ENTRANCE ANTIPHON: The Lord is my inheritance and my cup; he alone will give me my reward. The measuring line has marked a lovely place for me; my inheritance is my great delight. *(Ps 15:5–6)*

RESPONSE: The Lord is my shepherd; there is nothing I shall want. *(Ps 23:1)*

GOSPEL VERSE: R/. Alleluia. Remain in my love, says the Lord; whoever remains in me and I in him will bear much fruit. R/. Alleluia. *(Jn 15:9b, 5b)*

COMMUNION ANTIPHON: I solemnly tell you: those who have left everything and followed me will be repaid a hundredfold and will gain eternal life. *(See Mt 19:27–29)*

Thursday, November 17, 2011: Elizabeth of Hungary—religious / 678 [1 Jn 3:14–18/Lk 6:27–38]

ENTRANCE ANTIPHON: Come, you whom my Father has blessed, says the Lord: I was ill and you comforted me. I tell you, anything you did for one of my brothers, you did for me. *(Mt 25:34, 36, 40)*

RESPONSE: I will bless the Lord at all times *(Ps 34:2)*

Or: Taste and see the goodness of the Lord. *(Ps 34:9)*

GOSPEL VERSE: R/. Alleluia. I give you a new commandment: love one another as I have loved you. R/. Alleluia. *(Jn 13:34)*

COMMUNION ANTIPHON: By the love you have for one another, says the Lord, everyone will know that you are my disciples. *(Jn 13:35)*

OR: **Thirty-third Week in Ordinary Time** / 500 [1 Mc 2:15–29/Lk 19:41–44]

ENTRANCE ANTIPHON: The Lord says: my plans for you are peace and not disaster; when you call to me, I will listen to you, and I will bring you back to the place from which I exiled you. *(Jer 29:11, 12, 14)*

RESPONSE: To the upright I will show the saving power of God. *(Ps 50:23b)*

GOSPEL VERSE: R/. Alleluia. If today you hear his voice, harden not your hearts. R/. Alleluia. *(Ps 95:8)*

COMMUNION ANTIPHON: I tell you solemnly, whatever you ask for in prayer, believe that you have received it, and it will be yours, says the Lord. *(Mk 11:23, 24)*

Friday, November 18, 2011: Thirty-third Week in Ordinary Time / 501 [1 Mc 4:36–37, 52–59/Lk 19:45–48]

ENTRANCE ANTIPHON: The Lord says: my plans for you are peace and not disaster; when you call to me, I will listen to you, and I will bring you back to the place from which I exiled you. *(Jer 29:11, 12, 14)*

RESPONSE: We praise your glorious name, O mighty God. *(1 Chr 29:13b)*

GOSPEL VERSE: R/. Alleluia. My sheep hear my voice, says the Lord; I know them and they follow me. R/. Alleluia. *(Jn 10:27)*

COMMUNION ANTIPHON: I tell you solemnly, whatever you ask for in prayer, believe that you have received it, and it will be yours, says the Lord. *(Mk 11:23, 24)*

OR: **The Dedication of the Basilicas of Saint Peter and Saint Paul** / 679 *[Acts 28:11–16, 30–31/Mt 14:22–33]*

ENTRANCE ANTIPHON: You have made them princes over all the earth; they declared your fame to all generations; for ever will the nations declare your praise. *(Ps 44:17–18)*

RESPONSE: The Lord has revealed to the nations his saving power. *(See Ps 96:2b)*

GOSPEL VERSE: R/. Alleluia. We praise you, O God, we acclaim you as Lord; the glorious company of Apostles praise you. R/. Alleluia. *(See Te Deum)*

COMMUNION ANTIPHON: Lord, you have the words of everlasting life, and we believe that you are God's Holy One. *(Jn 6:69–70)*

OR: **Rose Philippine Duschesne**—*virgin* / 679A, 731–736, 737–742

ENTRANCE ANTIPHON: Come, bride of Christ, and receive the crown, which the Lord has prepared for you for ever.

RESPONSE: Listen to me, daughter; see and bend your ear. *(Ps 45:11)*

Or: The bridegroom is here; let us go out to meet Christ the Lord.

GOSPEL VERSE: R/. Alleluia. This is the wise virgin, whom the Lord found waiting; at his coming she went in with him to the wedding feast. R/. Alleluia.

COMMUNION ANTIPHON: The wise virgin chose the better part for herself, and it shall not be taken away from her. *(See Lk 10:42)*

Saturday, November 19, 2011: Thirty-third Week in Ordinary Time / 502 [1 Mc 6:1–13/Lk 20:27–40]

ENTRANCE ANTIPHON: The Lord says: my plans for you are peace and not disaster; when you call to me, I will listen to you, and I will bring you back to the place from which I exiled you. *(Jer 29:11, 12, 14)*

RESPONSE: I will rejoice in your salvation, O Lord. *(Ps 9:16a)*

GOSPEL VERSE: R/. Alleluia. Our Savior Jesus Christ has destroyed death and brought life to light through the Gospel R/. Alleluia. *(See 2 Tm 1:10)*

COMMUNION ANTIPHON: I tell you solemnly, whatever you ask for in prayer, believe that you have received it, and it will be yours, says the Lord. *(Mk 11:23, 24)*

OR: **Blessed Virgin Mary** / 707–712

ENTRANCE ANTIPHON: You have been blessed, O Virgin Mary, above all other women on earth by the Lord the most high God; he has so exalted your name that your praises shall never fade from the mouths of men. *(See Jdt 13:23, 25)*

RESPONSE: You are the highest honor of our race. *(Jdt 15:9d)*

GOSPEL VERSE: R/. Alleluia. Blessed are you, holy Virgin Mary, deserving of all praise; from you rose the sun of justice, Christ our God. R/. Alleluia.

COMMUNION ANTIPHON: All generations will call me blessed, because God has looked upon his lowly handmaid. *(See Lk 1:48)*

Monday, November 21, 2011: Presentation of the Virgin Mary / 680 [Zec 2:14–17/Mt 12:46–50]

ENTRANCE ANTIPHON: You have been blessed, O Virgin Mary, above all other women on earth by the Lord the most high God; he has so exalted your name that your praises shall never fade from the mouths of men. *(See Jdt 13:23, 25)*

RESPONSE: The Almighty has done great things for me, and holy is his name. *(Lk 1:49)*

Or: O Blessed Virgin Mary, you carried the Son of the eternal Father.

GOSPEL VERSE: R/. Alleluia. Blessed are those who hear the word of God and observe it. R/. Alleluia. *(Lk 11:28)*

COMMUNION ANTIPHON: All generations will call me blessed, because God has looked upon his lowly handmaid. *(See Lk 1:48)*

OR: **Thirty-fourth Week in Ordinary Time** / 503 [Dn 1:1–6, 8–20/Lk 21:1–4]

ENTRANCE ANTIPHON: The Lord speaks of peace to his holy people, to those who turn to him with all their heart. *(Ps 84:9)*

RESPONSE: Glory and praise for ever! *(Dn 3:52b)*

GOSPEL VERSE: R/. Alleluia. Stay awake! For you do not know when the Son of Man will come. R/. Alleluia. *(Mt 24:42a, 44)*

COMMUNION ANTIPHON: All you nations, praise the Lord, for steadfast is his kindly mercy to us. *(Ps 116:1–2)*

Tuesday, November 22, 2011: Cecilia—virgin, martyr / 681 [Hos 2:16bc, 17cd, 21–22/Mt 25:1–13]

ENTRANCE ANTIPHON: Here is a wise and faithful virgin who went with lighted lamp to meet her Lord.

RESPONSE: Listen to me, daughter; see and bend your ear. *(Ps 45:11)*

Or: The bridegroom is here; let us go out to meet Christ the Lord.

GOSPEL VERSE: R/. Alleluia. This is the wise bridesmaid, whom the Lord found waiting; at his coming, she went in with him to the wedding feast. R/. Alleluia.

COMMUNION ANTIPHON: The bridegroom is here; let us go out to meet Christ the Lord. *(Mt 25:6)*

OR: **Thirty-fourth Week in Ordinary Time** / 504 [Dn 2:31–45/Lk 21:5–11]

ENTRANCE ANTIPHON: The Lord speaks of peace to his holy people, to those who turn to him with all their heart. *(Ps 84:9)*

RESPONSE: Give glory and eternal praise to him. *(Dn 3:59b)*

GOSPEL VERSE: R/. Alleluia. Remain faithful until death, and I will give you the crown of life. R/. Alleluia. *(Rv 2:10c)*

COMMUNION ANTIPHON: All you nations, praise the Lord, for steadfast is his kindly mercy to us. *(Ps 116:1–2)*

Wednesday, November 23, 2011: Thirty-fourth Week in Ordinary Time / 505 [Dn 5:1–6, 13–14, 16–17, 23–28/Lk 21:12–19]

ENTRANCE ANTIPHON: The Lord speaks of peace to his holy people, to those who turn to him with all their heart. *(Ps 84:9)*

RESPONSE: Give glory and eternal praise to him. *(Dn 3:59b)*

GOSPEL VERSE: R/. Alleluia. Remain faithful until death, and I will give you the crown of life. R/. Alleluia. *(Rv 2:10c)*

COMMUNION ANTIPHON: All you nations, praise the Lord, for steadfast is his kindly mercy to us. *(Ps 116:1–2)*

OR: **Clement I—pope, martyr / 682 [1 Pt 5:1–4/ Mt 16:13–19]**

ENTRANCE ANTIPHON: The Lord chose him to be his high priest; he opened his treasures and made him rich in all goodness.

RESPONSE: For ever I will sing the goodness of the Lord.

GOSPEL VERSE: R/. Alleluia. Come after me, says the Lord, and I will make you fishers of men. R/. Alleluia. *(Mk 1:17)*

COMMUNION ANTIPHON: The good shepherd gives his life for his sheep. *(See Jn 10:11)*

*OR: **Columban**—abbot / 683 [Is 52:7–10/Lk 9:57–62]*

ENTRANCE ANTIPHON: How beautiful on the mountains are the feet of the man who brings tidings of peace, joy and salvation. *(Is 52:7)*

RESPONSE: Proclaim God's marvelous deeds to all the nations. *(Ps 96:3)*

GOSPEL VERSE: R/. Alleluia. I am the light of the world, says the Lord; whoever follows me will have the light of life. R/. Alleluia. *(Jn 8:12)*

COMMUNION ANTIPHON: Go out to all the world, and tell the good news: I am with you always, says the Lord. *(Mk 16:15; Mt 28:20)*

*OR: **Blessed Miguel Agustin Pro**—priest, martyr / 683A, 713–718, 719–724*

ENTRANCE ANTIPHON: The Spirit of God is upon me; he has anointed me. He sent me to bring good news to the poor, and to heal the broken-hearted. *(Lk 4:18)*

RESPONSE: You are a priest for ever, in the line of Melchizedek. *(Ps 110:4b)*

GOSPEL VERSE: R/. Alleluia. I call you my friends, says the Lord, for I have made known to you all that the Father has told me. R/. Alleluia. *(Jn 15:15b)*

COMMUNION ANTIPHON: I, the Lord, am with you always, until the end of the world. *(Mt 28:20)*

Thursday, November 24, 2011: Andrew Dũng-Lac—priest, martyr; and his companions—martyrs / 683B, 713–718

ENTRANCE ANTIPHON: The salvation of the just comes from the Lord. He is their strength in time of need. *(Ps 36:39)*

RESPONSE: Our soul has been rescued like a bird from the fowler's snare. *(Ps 124:7)*

GOSPEL VERSE: R/. Alleluia. Blessed be the Father of compassion and God of all encouragement, who encourages us in our every affliction. R/. Alleluia. *(2 Cor 1:3b–4a)*

COMMUNION ANTIPHON: Whoever loses his life for my sake and the gospel, says the Lord, will save it. *(Mk 8:35)*

*OR: **Thirty-fourth Week in Ordinary Time** / 506 [Dn 6:12–28/Lk 21:20–28]*

ENTRANCE ANTIPHON: The Lord speaks of peace to his holy people, to those who turn to him with all their heart. *(Ps 84:9)*

RESPONSE: Give glory and eternal praise to him. *(Dn 3:59b)*

GOSPEL VERSE: R/. Alleluia. Stand erect and raise your heads because your redemption is at hand. R/. Alleluia. *(Lk 21:28)*

COMMUNION ANTIPHON: All you nations, praise the Lord, for steadfast is his kindly mercy to us. *(Ps 116:1–2)*

*OR: **Thanksgiving Day** / 648A, 943–947*

(or see Sunday section for this date)

ENTRANCE ANTIPHON: Sing and play music in your hearts to the Lord, always giving thanks for everything to God the Father in the name of our Lord Jesus Christ. *(Eph 5:19–20)*

RESPONSE: I will praise your name for ever, Lord. *(See Ps 145:1)*

GOSPEL VERSE: R/. Alleluia. We praise you, O God, we acclaim you the Lord; throughout the world the holy Church acclaims you. R/. Alleluia. *(See Te Deum)*

COMMUNION ANTIPHON: What return can I make to the Lord for all that he gives to me? I will take the cup of salvation, and call on the name of the Lord. *(Ps 115:12–13)*

Friday, November 25, 2011: Thirty-fourth Week in Ordinary Time / 507 [Dn 7:2–14/Lk 21:29–33]

ENTRANCE ANTIPHON: The Lord speaks of peace to his holy people, to those who turn to him with all their heart. *(Ps 84:9)*

RESPONSE: Give glory and eternal praise to him. *(Dn 3:59b)*

GOSPEL VERSE: R/. Alleluia. Stand erect and raise your heads because your redemption is at hand. R/. Alleluia. *(Lk 21:28)*

COMMUNION ANTIPHON: All you nations, praise the Lord, for steadfast is his kindly mercy to us. *(Ps 116:1–2)*

*OR: **Catherine of Alexandria**—virgin, martyr / 731–736, 713–738 [Rv 21:5–7/Mt 10:28–38]*

ENTRANCE ANTIPHON: Here is a true martyr who shed her blood for Christ; her judges could not shake her by their manaces, so she won through to the kingdom of heaven.

RESPONSE: Our soul has been rescued like a bird from the fowler's snare. *(Ps 124:7)*

GOSPEL VERSE: R/. Alleluia. We praise you, O God, we acclaim you as Lord; the white-robed army of martyrs praise you. R/. Alleluia. *(See Te Deum)*

COMMUNION ANTIPHON: I am the vine and you are the branches, says the Lord; he who believes in me, and I in him, will bear much fruit. *(Jn 15:5)*

Saturday, November 26, 2011: Thirty-fourth Week in Ordinary Time / 508 [Dn 7:15–27/Lk 21:34–36]

ENTRANCE ANTIPHON: The Lord speaks of peace to his holy people, to those who turn to him with all their heart. *(Ps 84:9)*

RESPONSE: Give glory and eternal praise to him. *(Dn 3:59b)*

GOSPEL VERSE: R/. Alleluia. Be vigilant at all times and pray that you may have the strength to stand before the Son of Man. R/. Alleluia. *(Lk 21:36)*

COMMUNION ANTIPHON: All you nations, praise the Lord, for steadfast is his kindly mercy to us. *(Ps 116:1–2)*

OR: Blessed Virgin Mary / 707–712

ENTRANCE ANTIPHON: Blessed are you, Virgin Mary, who carried the creator of all things in your womb; you gave birth to your maker, and remain for ever a virgin.

RESPONSE: Blessed be the name of the Lord for ever. *(Ps 113:2) Or:* Alleluia.

GOSPEL VERSE: R/. Alleluia. Blessed are you, O Virgin Mary, who believed that what was spoken to you by the Lord would be fulfilled. R/. Alleluia.*(See Lk 1:45)*

COMMUNION ANTIPHON: The Almighty has done great things for me. Holy is his name. *(Lk 1:49)*

Prayers of the Individual and Household

MORNING PRAYERS

ANCIENT PRAYERS FOR MORNING

The first of these is the beginning of the "Hear, O Israel" prayer; this is the cornerstone of Jewish prayer and would have been the daily prayer of Jesus, his family and his disciples. The blessings which follow accompany some of the actions of early morning. The final text is from Psalm 95, long used at morning prayer.

Hear, O Israel: the Lord is our God, the Lord is One!
Blessed is his glorious kingdom for ever and ever!

Blessed are you, Lord our God, ruler of the universe,
opening the eyes of the blind.

Blessed are you, Lord our God, ruler of the universe,
clothing the naked.

Blessed are you, Lord our God, ruler of the universe,
setting captives free.

Blessed are you, Lord our God, ruler of the universe,
guiding our footsteps.

Blessed are you, Lord our God, ruler of the universe,
taking the sleep from my eyes and the slumber from my eyelids.

Come, let us sing to the Lord;
    and shout with joy to the Rock who saves us.
Let us approach him with praise and thanksgiving
    and sing joyful songs to the Lord.

The Lord is God, the almighty God,
    the great king over all the gods.
He holds in his hands the depths of the earth
    and the highest mountains as well.
He made the sea; it belongs to him,
    the dry land, too, for it was formed by his hands.

Come, then, let us bow down and worship,
    bending the knee before the Lord, our maker.
For he is our God and we are his people,
    the flock he shepherds.

Today, listen to the voice of the Lord:
    Do not grow stubborn, as your father did in the wilderness,

When at Meriba and Massah
they challenged me and provoked me,
Although they had seen all of my works.

Forty years I endured that generation.
I said, "They are a people whose hearts go astray
and they do not know my ways."
So I swore in my anger,
"They shall not enter into my rest."

Glory to the Father, and to the Son, and to the Holy Spirit:
as it was in the beginning, is now, and will be for ever.
Amen.

MORNING PSALMS

In addition to Psalm 95, above, the psalms of morning are the psalms of praise, especially Psalms 148, 149 and 150. Other morning prayers are Psalm 51 and Psalm 63.

THE BENEDICTUS

The Benedictus or Song of Zachary from Luke 1:68-69 is a morning prayer for the day when God's compassion like "the dawn from on high shall break upon us, to shine on those who dwell in darkness and the shadow of death, and to guide our feet into the way of peace."

MORNING PRAYER OF ST. PATRICK

The Lorica or "Breastplate" is an ancient Celtic prayer attributed to St. Patrick.

I arise today
through the strength of heaven,
light of the sun,
radiance of the moon,
splendor of fire,
speed of lightning,
swiftness of the wind,
depth of the sea,
stability of the earth,
firmness of the rock.

I arise today
through God's strength to pilot me,
God's might to uphold me,
God's wisdom to guide me,
God's eye to look before me,
God's ear to hear me,
God's word to speak for me,
God's hand to guard me,

God's way to lie before me,
God's shield to protect me,
God's hosts to save me
from the snares of the devil,
from everyone who desires me ill,
afar and near,
alone or in a multitude.
Christ with me, Christ before me, Christ behind me,
Christ in me, Christ beneath me, Christ above me,
Christ on my right, Christ on my left,
Christ when I lie down, Christ when I sit down, Christ when I arise,
Christ in the heart of everyone who thinks of me,
Christ in the mouth of everyone who speaks of me,
Christ in the eye that sees me,
Christ in the ear that hears me.

DAYTIME PRAYERS

THE JESUS PRAYER
This is one of the most widely used of those prayers which are meant to be repeated over and over again so that the one praying becomes completely caught up in prayer. Often prayers like this one are intended to be in rhythm with one's breathing.

Lord Jesus Christ,
Son of the living God,
have mercy on me, a sinner.

THE ROSARY
The rosary is another prayer which in its repetition draws us into contemplation of the mysteries of our salvation. The rosary begins with the Apostle's Creed and consists of groups of ten Hail Marys, each group preceded by the Lord's Prayer and followed by the Glory to the Father. Each decade has traditionally been given to pondering one aspect of the paschal mystery:

The Joyful Mysteries
　　1. The Annunciation (Luke 1:30–33)
　　2. The Visitation (Luke 1:50–53)
　　3. The Nativity (Luke 2:10–11)
　　4. The Presentation (Luke 2:29–32)
　　5. The Finding of Jesus in the Temple (Luke 2:48–52)

The Luminous Mysteries
　　1. The Baptism of the Lord (Matthew 3:13–17)
　　2. The Wedding at Cana (John 2:1–11)
　　3. The Proclamation of the Kingdom (Mark 1:15)
　　4. The Transfiguration (Luke 9:28-36)
　　5. The Institution of the Eucharist (Matthew 26:26–30)

The Sorrowful Mysteries
1. The Agony in the Garden (Matthew 26:38–39)
2. The Scourging (John 19:1)
3. The Crowning with Thorns (Mark 15:16–17)
4. Jesus Carries His Cross (John 19:17)
5. The Crucifixion (John 19:28–30)

The Glorious Mysteries
1. The Resurrection (Mark 16:6–8)
2. The Ascension (Acts 1:10–11)
3. The Coming of the Holy Spirit (Acts 2:1–4)
4. The Assumption (Song of Songs 2:3–6)
5. The Coronation of Mary (Luke 1:51–54)

The prayer which makes up the rosary is the Hail Mary. Its words are drawn from the scriptures and the intercession of the church.

Hail Mary, full of grace,
the Lord is with you!
Blessed are you among women
and blessed is the fruit of your womb, Jesus.
Holy Mary, mother of God,
pray for us sinners,
now and at the hour of our death. Amen.

THE ANGELUS
This is the prayer prayed in early morning, at noon, and at the end of the work day. Through this constant presence in the midst of everyday, the Christian proclaims that all of our time and all of our human space is transformed by the incarnation, the presence of God with us.

V. The angel spoke God's message to Mary
R. and she conceived of the Holy Spirit.
Hail Mary...

V. "I am the lowly servant of the Lord:
R. let it be done to me according to your word."
Hail Mary...

V. And the Word became flesh
R. and lived among us.
Hail Mary...

V. Pray for us, holy Mother of God,
R. that we may become worthy of the promises of Christ.

Let us pray.

Lord,
fill our hearts with your grace:
once, through the message of an angel
you revealed to us the incarnation of your Son:
now, through his suffering and death
lead us to the glory of his resurrection.

We ask this through Christ our Lord.
Amen.

DIVINE PRAISES
These prayers may be used together, or each short line can be repeated over and over (as with the Jesus Prayer).

Blessed be God.
Blessed be his holy name.
Blessed be Jesus Christ, true God and true man.
Blessed be the name of Jesus.
Blessed be his most sacred heart.
Blessed be his most precious blood.
Blessed be Jesus in the most holy sacrament of the altar.
Blessed be the Holy Spirit, the Paraclete.
Blessed be the great mother of God, Mary most holy.
Blessed be her holy and immaculate conception.
Blessed be her glorious assumption.
Blessed be the name of Mary, virgin and mother.
Blessed be Joseph, her most chaste spouse.
Blessed be God in his angels and in his saints.

EVENING PRAYERS

PRAISE OF GOD FOR CHRIST, OUR LIGHT
The prayer as day ends has often begun with a verse or hymn in praise of God who has given us in Christ our true light. The ancient hymn Phos Hilaron, "O Radiant Light," is a beautiful expression of this. This praise is also contained in the simple invocation:

Jesus Christ is the light of the world,
a light no darkness can overpower.

EVENING PSALMS
Psalm 141 prays:

Let my prayer arise before you like incense,
the raising of my hands like an evening oblation.

This is the primary psalm of evening prayer as it prays for God's protection. Other appropriate psalms of the evening are Psalm 23, Psalm 121 and Psalm 123.

THE MAGNIFICAT
The Song of Mary from Luke 1:46-55 has long been a part of evening prayer for Christians. It is strong in its praise and in its vision of justice brought by God.

NIGHT PRAYERS

CONFESSION
Before sleep, the Christian recalls with sorrow the failures of the day and gives thanks to God for the love which surrounds us.

I confess to almighty God,
and to you, my brothers and sisters,
that I have sinned through my own fault
in my thoughts and in my words,
in what I have done,
and in what I have failed to do;
and I ask blessed Mary, ever virgin,
all the angels and saints,
and you, my brothers and sisters,
to pray for me to the Lord our God.

SHORT PRAYERS
May the almighty Lord give us a restful night
and a peaceful death.

Keep us, Lord, as the apple of your eye
and shelter us in the shadow of your wing.

Protect us, Lord, as we stay awake;
watch over us as we sleep,
that awake, we may keep watch with Christ,
and asleep, rest in his peace.

Into your hands, Lord, I commend my spirit.
O Lord our God, make us lie down in peace
and raise us up to life.

Visit this house,
we beg you, Lord,
and banish from it
the deadly power of the evil one.

May your holy angels dwell here
to keep us in peace,
and may your blessing be always upon us.

Hear us, Lord,
and send your angel from heaven
to visit and protect,
to comfort and defend
all who live in this house.

NIGHT PSALMS
The traditional psalms of night are Psalm 4, Psalm 91 and Psalm 134.

CANTICLE OF SIMEON
The words spoken by Simeon in the Temple (Luke 2:29-32) are often used as a night prayer for the church.

ANTHEMS OF MARY
The last prayer of night is addressed to our mother. The Salve Regina *is used throughout the year; during Eastertime it is replaced by the* Regina Caeli. *Another appropriate prayer is the* Memorare.

Remember, most loving virgin Mary,
never was it heard
that anyone who turned to you for help
was left unaided.
Inspired by this confidence,
though burdened by my sins,
I run to your protection
for you are my mother.
Mother of the Word of God,
do not despise my words of pleading
but be merciful and hear my prayer.

MEAL PRAYERS
At table we learn to give God thanks and praise for all the fruit of the earth and work of human hands.

BEFORE MEALS
Bless us, O Lord, and these thy gifts
which we are about to receive
from thy bounty;
through Christ our Lord. Amen.

Or:

The eyes of all hope in you, Lord,
and you give them food in due season.
You open your hand,
and every creature is filled with your blessing.

Or:

Blessed are you, Lord our God, ruler of the universe,
for you bring forth bread from the earth.

AFTER MEALS
We give you thanks
for all your gifts,
almighty God,
living and reigning
now and for ever.

Or:

Blessed be the Lord
of whose bounty we have received
and by whose goodness we live.

SUNDAY PRAYER

ANIMA CHRISTI
Soul of Christ, sanctify me.
Body of Christ, heal me.
Blood of Christ, drench me.
Water from the side of Christ, wash me.
Passion of Christ, strengthen me.
Good Jesus, hear me.
In your wounds shelter me.
From turning away keep me.
From the evil one protect me.
At the hour of my death call me.
Into your presence lead me,
to praise you with all your saints
for ever and ever. Amen.

TIMES OF NEED
*There are many scriptures, hymns and psalms in this book which give voice
to our prayers for our own needs, for the needs of others and of the world. A
familiarity with the psalms especially will lead the Christian to many prayers in
troubled times.*

IN TIMES OF SICKNESS

All-powerful and ever-living God,
the lasting health of all who believe in you,
hear us as we ask your loving help for the sick;
restore their health,
that they may again offer joyful thanks in your Church.

Or:

God of love,
ever caring,
ever strong,
stand by us in our time of need.
Watch over your child who is sick,
Look after him/her in every danger,
and grant him/her your healing and peace.

IN TIME OF SUFFERING

Lord Jesus Christ, by your patience in suffering you hallowed earthly pain
and gave us the example of obedience to your Father's will:
Be near me in my time of weakness and pain;
sustain me by your grace, that my strength and courage may not fail;
heal me, if it be your will;
and help me always to believe that what happens to me here
is of little account if you hold me in eternal life,
my Lord and my God.

WHEN DEATH IS NEAR

Go forth, Christian soul, from this world
in the name of God the almighty Father, who created you,
in the name of Jesus Christ, Son of the living God, who suffered for you,
in the name of the Holy Spirit, who has poured out upon you,
go forth, faithful Christian.
May you live in peace this day,
may your home be with God in Zion,
with Mary, the virgin mother of God,
with Joseph, and all the angels and saints.

Or:

Saints of God, come to his/her aid!
Come to meet him/her, angels of the Lord!

WHEN SOMEONE HAS DIED

Eternal rest grant to him/her/them, O Lord,
and let perpetual light shine upon him/her/them.

Or:

Loving and merciful God,
we entrust our brother/sister to your mercy.
You loved him/her greatly in this life:
now that he/she is freed from all its cares,
give him/her happiness and peace for ever.
The old order has passed away;
welcome him/her now into paradise
where there will be no more sorrow,
no more weeping or pain,
but only peace and joy
with Jesus, your Son,
and the Holy Spirit
for ever and ever. Amen.

PSALMS IN TIME OF NEED
Among the psalms which are prayed in times of sickness and sorrow are the following: Psalm 6, Psalm 25, Psalm 42, Psalm 63, and Psalm 103.

PRAYER TO MARY
We turn to you for protection,
holy Mother of God.
Listen to our prayers
and help us in our needs.
Save us from every danger,
glorious and blessed Virgin.

PRAYER FOR PEACE
Lord, make me an instrument of your peace:
    where there is hatred, let me sow love;
    where there is injury, pardon;
    where there is doubt, faith;
    where there is despair, hope;
    where there is darkness, light;
    where there is sadness, joy.
O divine Master, grant that I may not so much seek
    to be consoled as to console,
    to be understood as to understand,
    to be loved as to love.
For it is in giving that we receive,
    it is in pardoning that we are pardoned,
    it is in dying that we are born to eternal life.

PENANCE AND RECONCILIATION

ACTS OF CONTRITION
My God,
I am sorry for my sins with all my heart.
In choosing to do wrong
and failing to do good,
I have sinned against you
whom I should love above all things.
I firmly intend, with your help,
to do penance,
to sin no more,
and to avoid whatever leads me to sin.

Or:

Lord,
turn to us in mercy,
and forgive all our sins
that we may serve you in true freedom.

VARIOUS PRAYERS OF PENANCE AND RECONCILIATION
Father of mercies
and God of consolation,
you do not wish the sinner to die
but to be converted and live.
Come to the aid of your people,
that they may turn from their sins
and live for you alone.
May we be attentive to your word,
confess our sins, receive your forgiveness,
and be always grateful for your loving kindness.
Help us to live the truth in love
and grow into the fullness of Christ, your Son,
who lives and reigns for ever and ever. Amen.

Or:

God and Father of us all,
you have forgiven our sins
and sent us your peace.
Help us to forgive each other
and to work together to establish peace in the world.

PSALMS OF PENANCE AND RECONCILIATION
Among the psalms which speak of sin, of sorrow and of forgiveness are the following: Psalm 51, Psalm 90, Psalm 123, Psalm 130 and Psalm 139.